Contents

Foreword by Walker Royce

Over the last several decades, the software industry has advanced at a breakneck pace. Few of us have stopped to reflect on all the foundations, breakthroughs, and know-how that have made software the world's most dominant product.

Our world now depends on software. It is everywhere, in almost every man-made thing, and used by almost everybody. All that invisible stuff in our phones, cars, gadgets, banks, and hospitals was once considered to be magical. Now it is taken for granted as just another necessary part, service, or feature. Don't you wonder how it all evolved? And where it came from? And why it was built? If you are curious about the evolution of all this magical technology, this book provides an authoritative chronology of software's evolution. Moreover, if your profession depends on software—and there are very few that don't— you will find this book to be a valuable and educational history lesson. It is loaded with quantified benchmarks of performance that you won't find anywhere else in the literature.

As a young engineer, I was introduced to Capers Jones through his books and papers on software measurement. He was one of the go-to thought leaders on software economics, and he was bold enough to publish facts and figures that helped quantify the challenges and opportunities. He has written more than a dozen books since then. When I wrote my first book in the 1990s, Capers was one of my top choices for peer review. To some degree back then, we were competitors, and his review of my manuscript was . . . well . . . let's just say that it was brutal. However, his review was, by far, the most valuable, insightful, and constructive. He knows how to write. His strong convictions are credible because he compiles extensive data and statistics on software quality and productivity across diverse industries. The big lesson he taught me was this: *In the software world dominated by uncertainty, the person with the best data will be the most persuasive.* His critique was effective for steering me in a better direction, and we have maintained a great professional relationship ever since by frequently exchanging ideas, presentations, and provocative positions.

The measurements and forecasts of progress, quality, and business trends in most software organizations sound like the sleight-of-hand statistics quoted by politicians rather than the matter-of-fact measurements expressed by engineers and scientists. Is this statement too harsh? No. Politicians have a well-deserved reputation and a track record similar to the software industry for under-delivering on committed forecasts and productivity improvements. The software marketplace is full of cynical customers because their experience with software productivity improvement—internally from their own people as well as externally from vendors—is plagued by hyperbole and spin. Software delivery endeavors have a high degree of uncertainty and complexity.

Reducing uncertainty through better measurement can increase trust among consumers, suppliers, and developers. Through his decades of work on measurement, Capers Jones has contributed immensely to the trust we put in today's software industry. Capers is a great writer and an authority on software history. He was a firsthand participant in the evolution of software from its infancy. This book synthesizes his research, knowledge, and quantified insights into a history lesson that every software professional will find useful and every software user will find enlightening. His writing is fluid, engaging, and crisp. Enjoy this measured story of software advances and learn from it.

—Walker Royce
Chief Software Economist, IBM

Foreword by Tony Salvaggio

When we founded Computer Aid, Inc., (CAI) in the early 1980s, we stated that our business mission would be to strive toward thought leadership in the areas of software engineering, software development productivity, and application support productivity. The founders of CAI had a strong belief that doing things the right way, repeatedly, would unlock tremendous business value for our future clients. Although our startup team had deep experience in software engineering, as well as large-project design and development, we knew that such experience alone would not be sufficient to qualify us as "thought leaders."

There is a great quote from Isaac Newton about how scientists "stand on the shoulders of giants." Newton meant that all scientific discovery and progress—in particular, his own historic breakthroughs—were built upon the hard work and insight of previous individuals. At CAI, our team members and associates have all stood solidly on the shoulders of Capers Jones. Over the course of CAI's 30-year history, Capers has been the most learned, most knowledgeable, and most prolific discoverer in the software engineering industry, perhaps even in the entire history of computing. He has written more than eighteen books across the entire spectrum of IT management, and each one has unlocked and revealed new insights, both for engineers and managers. I have personally given countless executive-level presentations on productivity and process improvement while waving a copy of Capers's original thick "yellow book" in one hand.

Capers has accumulated, without doubt, the most comprehensive data on every aspect of software engineering, and he has performed the most scientific analysis on this data. To say that he has forgotten more than the average top software professional ever learns would be an understatement. In his new book, Capers performs yet another invaluable service to our industry, and for each current and future IT professional, by documenting, for the first time, the long and fascinating history of information technology.

This profession, which was unheard of in the 1960s and '70s, has evolved through so many dramatic changes in the course of my lifetime. I have seen the software industry lead the business reengineering revolution and watched how this, in turn, has revolutionized life on our planet for billions of people. History will repeat itself, whether we study it or not, and in this sense, Capers's new book is a must-read for every software engineering student and IT professional. In spite of our revolutionary successes, there has been a consistent record within the IT industry of not diligently putting to work the lessons of the past, the lessons first documented so well in Capers's original "yellow book."

Over these past three decades, Capers has become a treasured friend of mine who often starts my day with early morning emails in which we discuss quality management, removing early defects, and avoiding project failures. His words ring in my ear with their clarity and insight and for thirty years have helped me guide our business here at CAI. I highly recommend Capers's new book, as well as many of his earlier works. The messages are timeless in their value.

—Tony Salvaggio
CEO and President, Computer Aid, Inc. (CAI)

Preface

I was born prior to World War II and therefore just before the dawn of the computer era. From growing up, I have personal recollections of the announcement of the transistor being invented and of reading about integrated circuits. I also remember the arrival of television and later of color television.

When I attended the University of Florida, there were no on-campus computers, no computer science programs, and no software engineering programs. In fact, engineering students still used slide rules, and there was an active debate about whether new electronic calculators could be used for exams.

There were no personal computers, no personal music players, no social networks other than fraternities and sororities, and certainly no smartphones. There were no embedded software applications and no embedded medical devices such as cochlear implants; all of these things would come later.

Older readers have lived through the entire history of the computing and software industries from the very beginning. So many inventions have occurred so rapidly, and so many companies have sprung up, that they tend to blur together. We are living in remarkable times with technical advances occurring almost every month.

This is the fifteenth book I have written. Although I had been a professional programmer in the 1960s, my first eleven books, which included *Programming Productivity*; *Assessment and Control of Software Risks*; *Applied Software Measurement*; and *Estimating Software Costs*, were all about software management issues. I became interested in management topics while working at IBM when I was commissioned to develop IBM's first software estimating tool in 1973 with a colleague, Dr. Charles Turk.

My first book was published while I was at IBM. Later, I moved to ITT and then founded my own software company when ITT sold its telecommunications businesses. In general, I have written a book every two years.

As a lifelong reader of *Scientific American*, I like to stay current on scientific topics. (One of the highlights of my publication career was publishing an article about sizing software in *Scientific American* in December 1998. This article featured function point metrics.)

Having sold my first software company in 1998, my wife and I moved to Rhode Island, a state where I had never lived before but where my wife was born and had many relatives. Soon after we arrived, the history of the state attracted my interest.

The economic history of Rhode Island was almost a microcosm of the U.S. economy, having started with ship building and commerce, then manufacturing, then moving toward services as labor costs drove out manufacturing. In 2006, I published *The History and Future of Narragansett Bay*, which was my first non-software-related book as well as my first history book.

The "future" part of the Rhode Island book dealt with modern problems that are also becoming endemic: rising taxes; unsustainable government pensions; pollution of the Bay and fresh-water aquifers; political corruption; new exotic diseases such as West Nile virus and Lyme disease; the dwindling numbers of professionals such as physicians and dentists; and an ever-expanding bureaucracy that primarily supports special interests rather than the general population. These are national problems as well as state and local problems.

In any case, having written a history of Rhode Island, it seemed useful to consider a history of the software engineering field, but at the time I had other book projects in mind. Two of these other books were *Software Engineering Best Practices* and *The Economics of Software Quality*. I was also busy starting a new software company, Namcook Analytics LLC, with my business partner, Ted Maroney.

The specific event that led to this book was a casual visit to a used book store adjacent to the University of Rhode Island. At the store, I happened to pick up a book with an interesting title: Paul Starr's book *The Social Transformation of American Medicine*. This book won a Pulitzer Prize in 1984 and is highly recommended for software professionals. It shows the transformation of medicine from a craft with barely adequate training to the top tier of respected professions with perhaps the best training of any profession.

Starr's book was the inspiration for this book. Software "engineering" is still also a craft and only approaching the status of being a true profession. For example, licensing is just getting started for software; formal specialization and board certifications are still in the future. Malpractice monitoring is in the future. Starr's book contains a good road map for what software engineering needs to accomplish.

I had always had an interest in medical topics since my first programming job was in the Office of the Surgeon General at the U.S. Public Health Service in Washington, D.C. We were working on software for the National Institutes of Health.

In fact, one of my earlier books from 1994 was titled *Assessment and Control of Software Risks*. This book used the exact structure and format of a medical textbook titled *Control of Communicable Diseases in Man*. The medical format has worked very well for discussing software problems.

There have been so many inventions and so many companies springing up in the computer and software domains that this new book needed a workable structure. What I decided was to look at software innovations, inventions, and companies decade by decade starting in 1930 and running through 2012 and beyond. Social and professional organizations such as the Institute of Electrical and Electronics Engineers, the Association for Computing Machinery, the Society for Information Management, SHARE, and so on would also be discussed.

The final chapter begins in 2010 and includes projections of potential future progress through 2019. This is reminiscent of the "future" chapter of my Rhode Island history, which also projected ten years from the completion of the book.

However, starting in 1930 was a bit too abrupt. Therefore, I decided to add a prelude chapter that would summarize the human drive toward faster computation from ancient times though the modern era. The overall structure of the book includes 12 chapters:

- Chapter 1 is a prelude on computing from ancient times to the current era. It deals with several interlinked topics, including the evolution of mathematics; the drive to speed up mathematical calculations using mechanical devices; methods for communicating mathematical results from person to person; and methods for storing or archiving mathematical results for historical purposes, including famous libraries from the ancient world.

- Chapter 2 deals with the 1930s and discusses the foundations of digital computing and software. The seminal works of Alan Turing, Konrad Zuse, and other pioneers are covered. The Great Depression was in force during this decade, and many companies failed. IBM came close to failing, but the arrival of social security in 1935 revived IBM earnings and led toward future growth for forty-five years in a row. Without social security, IBM might not have survived the decade, and computer and software history would be very different than it is today.

- Chapter 3 deals with the 1940s. This chapter covers computers and software among the belligerent countries during World War II and also the postwar era. The famous British code-breaking devices at Bletchley Park are discussed, as are Konrad Zuse's computers in Germany. However, during World War II, analog computers were the real workhorses, so the book also discusses ship-board gun controls, torpedo-aiming computers, bombsights, and other analog computing devices. The end of the chapter deals with the early electronic digital computers and the dawn of programming as we know it today.

- Chapter 4 deals with the 1950s. This decade witnessed computers and software moving from military and scientific purposes to business purposes. Two huge efforts bracketed this decade: The SAGE air-defense system at the beginning of the decade and the SABRE airline reservation system at the end were the two largest systems built up until that time. Many enabling inventions occurred, such as transistors and integrated circuits. High-level programming languages, like COBOL, began to appear.

- Chapter 5 deals with the 1960s. This decade saw computers and software becoming business tools for hundreds of corporations. Physical sizes of computers shrank as transistors and integrated circuits replaced tubes and discrete wiring. This decade also saw IBM growing rapidly due to computers such as the IBM 1401 and later the System 360. Minicomputers and special computers also emerged. Software expanded as operating systems and database applications made computers easier to use. Some universities began offering computer science and software engineering degree programs. Software jobs were exploding in numbers.

- Chapter 6 deals with the 1970s. This decade witnessed the birth of Apple and Microsoft and a push toward commercial packages. Several companies began to use computers to create new business models such as Southwest Airlines and Federal Express, with its unique hub-and-spoke arrangement to optimize shipping logistics. Software engineering became a common academic subject. Programming jobs expanded rapidly. Structured development emerged to control software chaos as applications got larger and harder to manage. Several companies founded in this decade would later grow and create wealth beyond imagination and become global powerhouses: Apple and Microsoft are two. Embedded medical devices, such as cochlear implants, appeared.

- Chapter 7 deals with the 1980s. This decade is clearly dominated by the IBM personal computer and the advent of the DOS and Windows operating systems. Hundreds of specialized software companies sprang up like mushrooms. Programming jobs continued to grow rapidly in numbers. Object-oriented development and object-oriented languages began to appear. Programming languages expanded from dozens to hundreds for reasons that are hard to understand. Personal computers began to move toward portability, although the first of these weighed more than twenty-five pounds. The Software Engineering Institute (SEI) was founded to assist the military sector in achieving better and more reliable software.

- Chapter 8 deals with the 1990s. The big news during this decade was the development and rapid expansion of the internet and the World Wide Web. Toward the end of this decade, the famous dot-com bubble began to inflate as hundreds of companies tried to market products and services via the web. This bubble burst early within the next decade. Cybercrime began to expand as the internet made remote hacking of data centers fairly easy to accomplish. Outsourcing, in particular international outsourcing, expanded rapidly as companies decided that building their own software programs was not cost-effective.

- Chapter 9 deals with the 2000s. The start of this decade saw the bursting of the dot-com bubble. However, dot-coms that survived, such as Amazon, would grow to become giants. Social networks appeared, as did new search engines and new web browsers. The Agile development method began to expand in popularity, but so did others, such as the team software process (TSP) and the rational unified process (RUP). The number of programming languages topped 2,500 by the end of the decade and continues to grow, with new languages appearing almost every month. All of these programming languages and the aging of software make maintenance very expensive. During this decade, maintenance and support of legacy software applications moved past new software development as the dominant work of the industry. A new subindustry of "patent trolls" appeared, and patent litigation became endemic among computer, software, and telecommunication companies as they each tried to use patents to damage competitors and push ahead.

- Chapter 10 deals with the 2010s, with speculation about possible future inventions. Current trends that will expand include clouds, crowds, big data, and predictive analytics. Some possible future inventions may be wearable computers, virtual education, and significant advances in embedded medical devices. Quantum computing may occur, with another increase in speed and another reduction in physical size. Intelligent agents will become increasingly powerful in extracting useful information from heterogeneous, big data sources. Cybercrime will certainly increase and cyberwarfare is already happening. The nations of the world now have formal cyberwarfare units, and attacks on industrial, financial, and military sectors are becoming common.

- Chapter 11 deals with topics that are difficult to pin down to a specific decade. This chapter revisits famous software failures and explains what happened and how they might have been avoided. It seemed better to show these in one place than to separate them by decade.

- Chapter 12 outlines the nature and forms of various cybercrime and cyberwarfare issues, which are becoming increasingly severe and increasingly common. Here, too, there are so many kinds of cyberattacks that it was best to put them in one chapter in order to emphasize their magnitude and seriousness.

History books are enjoyable for authors to write. Hopefully, this book will be enjoyable to read. It quickly became obvious while writing it that if the book attempted to include every company and every invention that appeared during this timeframe, it might top 1,000 pages, which no publisher would want and probably no reader would want either.

Therefore, quite a few companies are omitted in the interest of space. When a number of companies occupy a similar niche, only one or two are cited to explain the niche. There is no need, for example, to name fifty static analysis companies, fifty computer game companies, twenty-five webinar tool companies, or twenty-five antivirus companies.

Note

It is an interesting social characteristic of the software industry that as soon as a niche becomes hot, dozens of similar companies and products rush into it. It is sometimes hard for a new invention to get venture funding, but it is much easier for the next dozen companies within the same space.

When stringing together dates and timelines, some of the source information is inconsistent. One source might say a company was founded in 1982, while another might cite 1983 for the same company. Hopefully, this book is generally correct in timelines and dates, but it is easy to be off by a year in either direction.

The purpose of this book is to show the overall sweep of progress and the bubbles of inventions that keep occurring. The software engineering field has been one of the most innovative and exciting fields in human history, and I hope younger readers will enjoy learning about older inventions that might have occurred before they were born. I hope older readers will enjoy reading about the many new inventions such as social networks and (soon) wearable computers.

Acknowledgments

As always, thanks to my wife, Eileen, for her support through fifteen books over a thirty-year period. Thanks also to my business partner, Ted Maroney, for his interest and support of my various patents and inventions.

Thanks to Bernard Goodwin, acquisitions editor at Addison-Wesley Professional, for his support of this book and several of my past books, too. Thanks to the capable editorial and production staff as well.

Many thanks to the reviewers of the drafts of this book and also of my older books, because often the same reviewers have seen more than one. Thanks to Rex Black, Gary Gack, Peter Hill, Leon Kappelman, Alex Pettit, Walker Royce, and Joe Schofield. Some unofficial reviewers, such as Tom DePetrillo, Pontus Johnson, Tony Salvaggio, Paul Strassmann, and Jerry Weinberg, also deserve thanks.

Thanks also to the editors of web journals who have published excerpts from this book and some of my older books: Andrew Binstock of *Dr. Dobb's Journal*; Greg Hutchins of the Certified Enterprise Risk Management Academy; Ben Linders of InfoQ; and Michael Milutis of the Information Technology Metrics and Productivity Institute.

All of us in the software field owe thanks to the pioneers and inventors who make this field so interesting: Al Albrecht, Barry Boehm, Fred Brooks, Ward Cunningham, Esther Dyson, Bill Gates, Grace Hopper, Watts Humphrey, Steve Jobs, Steve Kan, Mitch Kapor, Ken Olson, Alan Turing, An Wang, Jerry Weinberg, Stephen Wolfram, and hundreds more.

Over the years, I've had the good fortune of meeting several senior executives who understood the value of software to the world and to their companies. These executives funded research centers chartered to improve software methods and practices, and I was fortunate to work in some of them.

Among these top corporate executives have been Thomas J. Watson, Jr., of IBM, Harold Geneen and Rand Araskog of ITT, Mort Myerson of Electronic Data Systems, and Dr. Hishahi Tomino of Kozo Keikaku Engineering. Dr. Tomino's company has translated most of my older books into Japanese, and the translation teams did an excellent job. Hopefully, this new book will also find its way into Japanese and other languages.

Software and computers have changed human communications in profound ways. Today, many people have more virtual friends than real friends. Some young people spend more time texting and using social networks than speaking face to face. The internet and World Wide Web have opened up vast new collections of information, larger than the sum of every library in the world. Almost every complex device is now controlled by embedded software, including automobiles, aircraft, and even smart appliances. Computers and software have changed the world, and more changes are still in store for us.

About the Author

 **Capers Jones** is a cofounder, vice president, and chief technology officer of Namcook Analytics LLC. Namcook Analytics builds patent-pending advanced risk, quality, and cost-estimation tools. The website is www.namcook.com. Capers Jones's blog is http://namcookanalytics.com.

Until cofounding Namcook Analytics LLC in 2011, he was the president of Capers Jones & Associates LLC from 2000 through 2011.

He is also the founder and former chairman of Software Productivity Research LLC (SPR). Capers Jones founded SPR in 1984.

Before founding SPR, Capers was assistant director of Programming Technology for the ITT Corporation at the Programming Technology Center in Stratford, Connecticut. He created the first software measurement program at ITT.

Capers Jones was also a manager and software researcher at IBM in California, where he designed IBM's first software cost-estimating tools in 1973 and 1974.

In total, Capers Jones has designed seven proprietary software estimation tools and four commercial software estimation tools.

Capers Jones is a well-known author and international public speaker. Some of his books have been translated into five languages. His four most recent books are *The Economics of Software Quality* (Addison-Wesley, 2011); *Software Engineering Best Practices* (McGraw-Hill, 2010); *Applied Software Measurement, Third Edition* (McGraw-Hill, 2008); and *Estimating Software Costs, Second Edition* (McGraw-Hill, 2007).

The Technical and Social History of Software Engineering is his second history book. This book was inspired by Paul Starr's book *The Social Transformation of American Medicine*, which won a Pulitzer Prize in 1984.

Among Capers's older book titles are *Patterns of Software Systems Failure and Success* (Prentice Hall, 1994); *Software Quality: Analysis and Guidelines for Success* (International Thomson, 1997); and *Software Assessments, Benchmarks, and Best Practices* (Addison-Wesley Longman, 2000).

Chapter 1

Prelude: Computing from Ancient Times to the Modern Era

The human need to compute probably originated in prehistory when humans began to accumulate physical possessions. It soon became desirable to keep track of how many specific possessions (e.g., cattle) were owned by a family or tribe. Once simple addition and subtraction became possible, a related need was to record the information so it could be kept for long time periods and could be shared with others. Early recording devices were pebbles or physical objects, but it was eventually found that these could be replaced with symbols.

As humans evolved and began to settle in communities, other calculating needs arose, such as measuring the dimensions of bricks or marking off fields. With leisure came curiosity and a need for more complex calculations of time, distance, and the positions of the stars.

Fairly soon, the labor involved with calculations was seen as burdensome and tedious, so mechanical devices that could speed up calculations (the abacus being among the first) were developed.

Tools for assisting with logical decisions were the last to be developed. The needs for rapid calculations, long-range data storage, and complex decision making were the critical factors that eventually came together to inspire the design of computers and software.

The Human Need to Compute

A book on the history of software engineering and computers should not just start abruptly at a specific date such as 1930. It is true that digital computers and the beginnings of software were first articulated between 1930 and 1939, but many prior inventions over thousands of years had set the stage.

From ancient times through today, there was a human need for various kinds of calculations. There has also been a human need to keep the results of those calculations in some kind of a permanent format.

Another human need that is harder to articulate is the need for logical analysis of alternative choices. An example of such a choice is whether to take a long flat road or a short hilly road when moving products to a marketplace. Another choice is what kind of crop is most suited to a particular piece of land.

More important alternatives are whether or not a community should go to war with another community. In today's world, some choices have life and death importance, such as what is the best therapy to treat a serious medical condition like antibiotic-resistant tuberculosis.

Other choices have economic importance. The Republicans and Democrats are examples of totally opposite views of what choices are best for the U.S. economy.

For choices with diametrically opposing alternatives, it is not possible for both sides to be right, but it is easily possible for both sides to be wrong. (It is also possible that some other choice and neither of the alternatives is the best.)

From analysis of what passes for arguments between the Democrats and Republicans, both sides seem to be wrong and the end results will probably damage the U.S. economy, no matter which path is taken.

From the point of view of someone who works with computers and software on a daily basis, it would not be extremely difficult to create mathematical models of the comparative impacts on the economy of raising taxes (the Democratic goal), reducing spending (the Republican goal), or some combination of both.

But instead of rational discussions augmented by realistic financial models, both sides have merely poured out rhetoric with hardly any factual information or proof of either side's argument. It is astonishing to listen to the speeches of Republicans and Democrats. They both rail against each other, but neither side presents anything that looks like solid data.

The same kinds of problems occur at state and municipal levels. For example, before the 2012 elections, the General Assembly of Rhode Island passed unwise legislation that doubled the number of voters per voting station, which effectively reduced the places available for citizens to vote by half.

The inevitable results of this foolish decision were huge lines of annoyed voters, waits of up to four hours to vote, and having to keep some voting stations open almost until midnight to accommodate the voters waiting in line.

This was not a very complicated issue. The numbers of voters passing through voting stations per hour have been known for years. But the Rhode Island Assembly failed to perform even rudimentary calculations about what halving the number of voting stations would do to voter wait times.

As a result, in the 2012 elections, many Rhode Island citizens who could not afford to wait four hours or more simply left without voting. They were disfranchised by the folly of a foolish law passed by an inept general assembly. This law by the Rhode Island Assembly was incompetent and should never have been passed without mathematical modeling of the results of reducing polling places on voting wait times.

The point of carping about governments passing unwise laws and issuing foolish regulations is because in today's world, computers and software could easily provide impact assessments and perhaps even eliminate thoughts of passing such foolish laws and regulations.

The fact that humans have used mathematics, made logical choices, and kept records from prehistory through today brings up questions that are relevant to the history of software and computers:

- What kinds of calculations do we use?

- What kinds of information or data do we need to save?

- What are the best storage methods for long-range retention of information?

- What methods of analysis can help in making complicated choices or decisions?

- What are the best methods of communicating data and knowledge?

It is interesting to consider these five questions from ancient times through the modern era and see how computers and software gradually emerged to help in dealing with them.

Early Sequence of Numerical Knowledge

Probably soon after humans could speak they could also count, at least up to ten, by using their fingers. It is possible that Neanderthals or Cro-Magnons could count as early as 35,000 years ago, based on parallel incised scratches on both a wolf bone in Czechoslovakia from about 33,000 years ago and a baboon bone in Africa from about 35,000 years ago.

Whether the scratches recorded the passage of days, numbers of objects, or were just scratched as a way to pass time is not known. The wolf bone is the most interesting due to having 55 scratches grouped into sets of five. This raises the probability that the scratches were used to count either objects or time.

An even older mastodon tusk from about 50,000 years ago had 16 holes drilled into it, of unknown purpose. Because Neanderthals and Cro-Magnons overlapped from about 43,000 BCE to 30,000 BCE, these artifacts could have come from either group or from other contemporaneous groups that are now extinct.

It is interesting that the cranial capacity and brain sizes of both Neanderthals and Cro-Magnons appear to be slightly larger than modern homo sapiens, although modern frontal lobes are larger. Brain size does not translate directly into intelligence, but it does indicate that some form of abstract reasoning might have occurred very early. Cave paintings date back more than 40,000 years, so at least some form of abstraction did exist.

In addition to counting objects and possessions, it was also important to be able to keep at least approximate track of the passage of time. Probably the length of a year was known at least subjectively more than 10,000 years ago. With the arrival of agriculture, also about 10,000 years ago, knowing when to plant certain crops and when to harvest them would have aided in food production.

One of the first known settlements was Catal Huyuk in Turkey, dating from around 7,000 BCE. This village, constructed of mud bricks, probably held several hundred people. Archaeological findings indicate agriculture of wheat, barley, and peas. Meat came from cattle and wild animals.

Findings of arrowheads, mace heads, pottery, copper, and lead indicate that probably some forms of trading took place at Catul Huyuk. Trading is not easily accomplished without some method of keeping track of objects. There were also many images painted on walls and this may indicate artistic interests.

The probable early sequence of humans acquiring numerical knowledge may have started with several key topics:

- Prehistoric numeric and mathematical knowledge:
  - Counting objects to record ownership
  - Understanding the two basic operations of addition and subtraction
  - Measuring angles, such as due east or west, to keep from getting lost

- Counting the passage of time during a year to aid agriculture
- Counting the passage of daily time to coordinate group actions
- Numeric and mathematical knowledge from early civilizations:
  - Counting physical length, width, and height in order to build structures
  - Measuring weights and volumes for trade purposes
  - Measuring long distances such as those between cities
  - Measuring the heights of mountains and the position of the sun above the horizon
  - Understanding the mathematical operations of multiplication and division
- Numeric and mathematical knowledge probably derived from priests or shamans:
  - Counting astronomical time such as eclipses and positions of stars
  - Measuring the speed or velocity of moving objects
  - Measuring curves, circles, and irregular shapes
  - Measuring rates of change such as acceleration
  - Measuring invisible phenomena such as the speed of sound and light
- Numeric and mathematical knowledge developed by mathematicians:
  - Analyzing probabilities for games and gambling
  - Understanding abstract topics such as zero and negative numbers
  - Understanding complex topics such as compound interest
  - Understanding very complex topics such as infinity and uncertainty
  - Understanding abstract topics such as irrational numbers and quantum uncertainty

Prehistoric numeric and mathematical knowledge probably could have been handled with careful observation assisted by nothing more than tokens such as stones or scratches, plus sticks for measuring length. Addition and subtraction are clearly demonstrated by just adding or removing stones from a pile.

Numeric and mathematical knowledge from early civilizations would have needed a combination of abstract reasoning aided by physical devices. Obviously, some kind of balance scale is needed to measure weight. Some kind of angle calculator is needed to measure the heights of mountains. Some kind of recording method is needed to keep track of events, such as star positions over long time periods.

Numeric and mathematical knowledge probably derived from priests or shamans would need a combination of abstract reasoning; accurate time keeping; accurate physical measures; and awareness that mathematics could represent intangible topics that cannot be seen, touched, or measured directly. This probably required time devoted to intellectual studies rather than to farming or hunting.

Numeric and mathematical knowledge developed by mathematicians is perhaps among the main incentives leading to calculating devices and eventually to computers and software. This required sophisticated knowledge of the previous topics, combined with fairly accurate measurements and intellectual curiosity in minds that have a bent for mathematical reasoning. These probably originated with people who had been educated in mathematical concepts and were inventive enough to extend earlier mathematical concepts in new directions.

One of the earliest cities, Mohenjo-Daro, which was built in Northern India about 3,700 years ago, shows signs of sophisticated mathematics. In fact, balance scales and weights have been excavated from Mohenjo-Daro.

This city may have held a population of 35,000 at its peak. The streets are laid out in a careful grid pattern; bricks and construction showed signs of standard dimensions and reusable pieces. These things require measurements.

Both Mohenjo-Daro and another city in Northern India, Harappa, show signs of some kind of central authority because they are built in similar styles. Both cities produced large numbers of clay seals incised both with images of animals and with symbols thought to be writing, although these remain undeciphered. Some of these clay seals date as far back as 3,300 BCE.

Other ancient civilizations also developed counting, arithmetic, measures of length, and weights and scales. Egypt and Babylonia had arithmetic from before 2,000 BCE.

As cities became settled and larger, increased leisure time permitted occupations to begin that were not concerned with physical labor or hunting. These occupations did not depend on physical effort and no doubt included priests and shamans. With time freed from survival and food gathering, additional forms of mathematical understanding began to appear.

Keeping track of the positions of the stars over long periods, measuring longer distances such as property boundaries and distances between villages, and measuring the headings and distances traveled by boats required more complex forms of mathematics and also precise measurements of angles and time periods. The advent of boat building also required an increase in mathematical knowledge. Boat hulls are of necessity curved, so straight dimensional measurements were not enough.

Rowing or sailing a boat in fresh water or within sight of land can be done with little or no mathematical knowledge. But once boats began to venture onto the oceans, it became necessary to understand the positions of the stars to keep from getting lost.

Australia is remote from all other continents and was not connected by a land bridge to any other location since the continents broke up. Yet it was settled about 40,000 years ago, apparently by means of a long ocean voyage from one (or more) of the continents. The islands of Polynesia and Easter Island are also far from any mainland and yet were settled thousands of years ago. These things indicate early knowledge of star positions and some kind of math as well.

Many early civilizations in Egypt, Mesopotamia, China, India, and South America soon accumulated surprisingly sophisticated mathematical knowledge. This mathematical knowledge was often associated with specialists who received substantial training.

Many ancient civilizations, such as the ancient Chinese, Sumerians, Babylonians, Egyptians, and Greeks, invested substantial time and energy into providing training for children. Not so well known in the West are the similar efforts for training in India and among the people of Central and South America, such as the Olmecs, Mayans, Incans, and later the Aztecs.

Japan also had formal training. For the upper classes, Japanese training included both physical skills in weapons and also intellectual topics such as reading, writing, and mathematics. All of these ancient civilizations developed formal training for children and also methods of recording information.

The University of Nalanda in Northern India was founded circa 472 BC and lasted until about the 12th century, with a peak enrollment during around 500 AD. It was one of the largest in the ancient world, with more than 10,000 students from throughout Asia and more than 2,000 professors. It was among the first universities to provide training in mathematics, physics, medicine, astronomy, and foreign languages.

The University of Nalanda had an active group of translators who translated Sanskrit and Prakrit into a variety of other languages. In fact, much of the information about the University of Nalanda comes from Chinese translations preserved in China since the University of Nalanda library was destroyed during the Moslem invasion of India in the 12th century. It was reported to be so large that it burned for almost six weeks.

Indian scholars were quite advanced even when compared to Greece and Rome. Concepts such as zero and the awareness of numerous star systems were known in India prior to being known in Europe. (The Olmecs of Central America also used zero prior to the Greeks.)

In ancient times, out of a population of perhaps 1,000 people in a Neolithic village, probably more than 950 were illiterate or could only do basic counting of objects and handle simple dimensional measures. But at least a few people were able to learn more complex calculations, including those associated with astronomy, construction of buildings and bridges, navigation, and boat building.

Inventions for Improved Mathematics

From the earliest knowledge of counting and numerical concepts, those who used numerical information were troubled by the needs for greater speed in calculating and for greater reliability of results than the unaided human mind could provide. In order to explain the later importance of computers and software, it is useful to begin with some of the earliest attempts to improve mathematical performance.

It is also useful to think about what computers and software really do and why they are valuable. The services that are provided to the human mind by various calculating devices include, but are not limited to, the following:

- Basic arithmetic operations of addition, subtraction, multiplication, and division

- Scientific mathematics, including powers, sines, cosines, and others

- Financial mathematics, including simple and compound interest and rates of return

- Logical calculations, such as routing and choices between alternatives

- Calculations of time, distance, height, and speed

- Deriving useful inductive knowledge from large collections of disparate information

- Deductive logic, such as drawing conclusions from rules

In doing research for this chapter, a great many interesting and useful sources were found during my web searches. For example, IBM has a graphical history of mathematics that can even be downloaded onto iPhones. Wikipedia and other web sources have dozens of histories of computer hardware and some histories of software development, too. More than a dozen computer museums were noted in a number of countries, such as the London Science Museum, which has a working version of the Babbage analytical engine on display.

For this book, it seemed useful to combine six kinds of inventions that are all synergistic and ultimately related to each other as well as to modern software.

Mathematics is the first of these six forms of invention. Calculating devices, computers, and software were all first invented to speed up mathematical calculations. Mathematics probably started with addition and subtraction and were then followed later by multiplication and division. After that, many other and more abstract forms appeared: geometry, trigonometry, algebra, and calculus, for example.

The second form of invention is the *recording of ideas and information* so they can be shared and transmitted and also to keep the ideas available over long time periods. The inventions in this category include writing systems and physical storage of writing. Physical storage of writing includes stone tablets, clay tablets, papyrus, animal skins, paper, and eventually magnetic and optical storage. Storage also includes manuscripts, books, libraries, and eventually databases and cloud storage.

The third form of invention is that of physical *calculating devices* that could assist human scholars in faster and more accurate calculations than would be possible using only the human mind and the human body. Tables of useful values were perhaps the first method used to speed up calculations. Physical devices include the abacus, protractors, astrolabes, measuring devices, mechanical calculating devices, slide rules, analog computers, and eventually electronic digital computers.

A fourth form of invention involves the available *channels for distributing information* to many people. The first channel was no doubt word of mouth and passing information along to be memorized by students or apprentices. But soon information transmission started to include markings on stones and bones; markings on clay; and eventually pictographs, ideographs, and finally alphabets.

The fifth form of invention is that of *software* itself. This is the most recent form of invention; essentially all software used in 2013 is less than 55 years old, probably more than 50% of the software is less than 20 years old.

A sixth form of invention is indirect. These are *enabling inventions* that are not directly connected to computers and software but that helped in their development. One such enabling invention is the patent system. A second and very important enabling invention was plastic.

Mathematics and Calculating

Table 1.1 shows the approximate evolution of mathematics, calculating devices, and software from prehistory through the modern era. It is intended to show the overall sweep of inventions and is not a precise timeline. The table focuses on the inventions themselves rather than providing the names of the inventors, such as Newton, Leibnitz, Turing, Mauchly, von Neumann, Hopper, and many others. The topics in Table 1.1 that eventually had an impact on computers and software are shown in italic.

Table 1.1   *Evolution of Mathematics, Calculating Devices, and Software*

Mathematics, Calculating Devices, and Software	Approximate Number of Years Prior to 2013
Counting objects	35,000
Addition and subtraction	30,000
Measuring angles	25,000
Counting the annual passage of time	20,000
Pebbles used for calculation	*20,000*
Counting the daily passage of time	19,000
Quantifying physical length, width, and height	18,000
Measuring weights and volumes	15,000
Measuring long distances between towns	10,000
Measuring astronomical time	7,000
Geometry	5,500
Sundials	5,500
Measuring the height of the sun and mountains	5,000

Table 1.1 *(Continued)*

Mathematics, Calculating Devices, and Software	Approximate Number of Years Prior to 2013
Multiplication and division	4,500
Measuring the speed of moving objects	4,000
Analog computing devices	*4,000*
Algebra	4,000
Trigonometry	4,000
Fractions	4,000
Multiplication tables	3,900
Clocks: water	3,300
Decimal numbers	3,100
Abacus and mechanical calculations	*3,000*
Clocks: mechanical	3,000
Binary numbers	2,700
Zero	2,600
Measuring curves, circles, and irregular objects	2,500
Measuring temperature	2,500
Antikythera mechanism	*2,200*
Astrolabe	*2,100*
Abstract topics such as zero and negative numbers	2,000
Hourglasses	1,500
Complex topics such as compound interest	1,400
Measuring probabilities for games of chance	1,000
Accounting	900
Graphs	800
Slide rules	*575*
Measuring rates of change and acceleration	500
Mechanical calculators for addition and subtraction	*425*
Measuring power	400
Calculating trajectories	*400*
Mechanical calculators for multiplication and division	*375*

(Continued)

Table 1.1   *(Continued)*

Mathematics, Calculating Devices, and Software	Approximate Number of Years Prior to 2013
Measuring invisible phenomena such as sound	350
Abstract topics such as irrational numbers and uncertainty	350
Punch-card calculating devices	*350*
Calculus	350
Counting short passages of time (<1 second)	300
Large-scale statistical studies with millions of samples	250
Very complex topics such as infinity and uncertainty	250
Mathematical weather prediction	250
Measuring electrical and magnetic phenomena	200
Mechanical tabulating machines	*200*
Boolean algebra	*175*
Set theory	*150*
Fuzzy sets	*145*
Relativity	105
Measuring the strong and weak forces and gravity	100
Digital computers	*70*
Operations research	*65*
Programming languages	*65*
Sorting algorithms	*55*
Databases	*55*
Pocket calculators	*50*
Mathematical software applications	*50*
Scientific software applications	*50*
Financial software applications	*45*
Statistical software applications	*40*
Accounting software applications	*40*
Architectural and engineering applications	*40*
Graphics rendering engines for games	*35*

Table 1.1 illustrates the fact that the human use of mathematics is ancient and can be traced almost as far back as speech. The reason for this is that mathematical knowledge became a critical factor when human beings started to live in villages and trade with others.

Those who hunt and gather wild plants have little need for math and only rudimentary needs for sophisticated communications of any kind. But the advent of agriculture, living in communities, and trade with other communities brought the needs for weights, measures, awareness of seasonal changes, and at least basic arithmetic such as addition and subtraction.

Table 1.2   *Evolution of Recording Methods and Media*

Recording Methods and Media	Approximate Number of Years Prior to 2013
On stone or bones	50,000
On clay	6,000
With pictographs such as hieroglyphics	4,500
On papyrus	4,000
With ideographs such as Chinese characters	4,000
Using encryption	2,500
With alphabetic information	2,500
On vellum	2,000
On paper	2,000
In full color	700
Graphically	400
On punched cards	*350*
Using tactile symbols such as Braille	250
On paper tape	*250*
Using cameras and film	*160*
Recording sounds	*130*
Magnetically on tape	*125*
On vinyl	125
Dynamically in full motion	100
On microfilm	80

(Continued)

Table 1.2   *(Continued)*

Recording Methods and Media	Approximate Number of Years Prior to 2013
Recording in three dimensions	75
Magnetically on disks	55
Optically on disks	50
On solid-state devices	35
Using multimedia	30
Using digital cameras	25
On e-books	25
On smartphones	10
Using quantum bits	5
Heterogeneous databases (big data)	5

Recording Information

Once calculations have been performed, there is also a need to keep the information in a permanent or at least long-lasting format so that the information can be shared with others or used later on as needed. Table 1.2 considers all of the various methods used from ancient times through the modern era for recording information in a permanent form.

As can be seen from Table 1.2, the recording of information is an ancient activity that dates back about as far as the invention of writing and numerals. Without a method of recording the information, calculations or ownership of articles could not be shared with others or used later to verify transactions.

A modern problem that will be discussed in later chapters is the fact that storage methods are not permanent and there is uncertainty about how long either paper records or computerized records might last.

Paper is flammable and also affected by insects, moisture, and other forms of destruction. Magnetic memory is long lasting but not permanent. What's worse is that any kind of stray magnetic field can damage or destroy magnetic records.

Optical records stored on plastic disks might last 100 years or more, but the plastic itself has an unknown life expectancy and the recording surfaces are easily damaged by abrasion, soot, fire, or mechanical stress.

The bottom line is that the earliest known forms of records, such as carvings on stone or clay, probably have the longest life expectancies of any form of recording yet invented.

Communicating Information

Table 1.3 lists the inventions for how information can be transmitted or shared with other human beings once calculations have been performed and the results stored in some fashion. It is obvious that almost all information will be needed by more than one person, so communication and information sharing are almost as old as mathematics.

Table 1.3 *Evolution of Communication Channels*

Communication Channels	Approximate Number of Years Prior to 2013
Word of mouth	50,000
Couriers	6,000
Flashing lights	5,000
Smoke signals	5,000
Music notation	4,500
Carrier pigeons	3,500
Codes and ciphers	2,500
Handwritten books	2,500
Mirrors or polished surfaces	2,000
Sign languages	1,750
Knotted strings	1,500
Printed books	1,000
Graphs for mathematical values	800
Newspapers	350
Magazines	300
Signal length (Morse code)	175
Touch for the blind (Braille)	175
Telegraph	175
Radio	150
Telephone	130
Television	70
Satellite	*60*
Subliminal signals	*50*

(Continued)

Table 1.3   *(Continued)*

Communication Channels	Approximate Number of Years Prior to 2013
Sleep learning	40
Ultra-low frequency sounds	35
Internet	30
Devices for the deaf (cochlear implants)	30
Electronic books (e-books)	25
Lasers	25
Automatic language translation	25
Intranet	20
Avatars in simulated worlds	15
Blogs	12
Webinars or podcasts	12
Wiki sites	10
Social networks	10
Animated multisensory methods	5

Over the centuries, the human species has developed scores of interesting and useful methods for conveying information. Often, there is a need to transmit information over very long distances. Until recently, carrier pigeons were used for messages between distant locations.

However, military organizations have long recognized that visible hilltops or other high places could be used to send information over long distances by means of either polished surfaces during the day or fires at night. Recall the famous line from Paul Revere's ride that describes lighting lanterns in the North church tower to warn of the approach of British troops: ". . . one if by land, two if by sea."

Communication with undersea submarines was difficult until the advent of communication by ultra-low frequency sounds.

Codes and secret communications also have a long history of several thousand years. Later chapters of this book will deal with several forms of codes and secret communications during World War II, including the famous Native American "code talkers" who spoke in a code based on Navajo, Choctaw, and other Native American languages.

Awareness of the need to communicate is ancient knowledge. There is a curious passage in a Buddhist sutra dating from about the third century BC, in which the Buddha discussed how his teachings might be transmitted. He mentions casually that, on earth, teachings are transmitted with words, but on other worlds, teachings are transmitted by lights, by scents, or by other nonverbal means.

Storing Information

Table 1.4 lists how information has been stored and accessed. As all scholars and researchers know, once the volume of information exceeds a few books or a few dozen written documents, there is an urgent need for some kind of taxonomy or catalog scheme to ensure that information can be found again when it is needed.

Information storage and access are critical features of modern computers, and modern software has played a huge part in improving information retrieval.

Table 1.4 *Evolution of Information Storage and Access*

Information Storage and Access	Approximate Number of Years Prior to 2013
Personal collections of written information	6,000
Libraries or public collections of written information	4,500
Topical collections of laws and legal codes	2,000
Topical collections such as medical and law libraries	1,200
University curricula for information by topic	1,000
Taxonomy for biological and scientific organization	300
Dewey decimal system for book organization	135
Sequential databases of information	*65*
Random databases of information	*55*
Relational databases of information	*50*
Affinity recommendations based on past preferences	35
Web search engines for selection of keyword information	*25*
Intelligent agents for selection of relevant information	*15*
Big data analytical tools	*10*

Table 1.4 shows topics that have been difficult for large volumes of information for thousands of years and that in fact are becoming worse in the modern world. For most of human history, information collections seldom topped more than 10,000 volumes, even for large libraries. In today's world of almost instantaneous recording of all books, magazines, research papers, images, and other forms of intellectual content, there are now billions of documents. Every week that passes, more and more information is published, recorded, and added to cloud libraries and other forms of computer storage. There is no end in sight.

There is an urgent need for continuing study of the best ways of recording information for long-term survival and for developing better methods of sorting through billions of records and finding and then aggregating topics relevant to specific needs. The emerging topic of "big data" is beginning to address these issues, but the solution is not currently visible and is still over the horizon.

The first and most long-lasting method of storing and accessing data was by means of libraries. Throughout civilized history, many famous libraries have served scholars and researchers. The library of Alexandria, the library of the University of Nalanda, the library of Perganum, the five libraries of Ugarit, the Roman libraries of Trajan in the Forum, and the library of Constantinople were all famous throughout antiquity.

Modern libraries such as the Library of Congress, the Harvard Library, and in fact many large college libraries still serve as major repositories of information for students and researchers.

Books have been used for thousands of years to record and convey knowledge from human to human, especially from teachers to students. Personal libraries of reference books are the normal accoutrements of all professions, including engineering, law, medicine and, of course, software engineering.

More recently, e-books, web search engines, and intelligent agents are making it possible for individuals and scholars to access more data and information at greater orders of magnitude than was possible at any time in human history up until about 25 years ago.

Enabling Computers and Software

Table 1.5 departs somewhat from the direct line of descent between inventions and computers and software. This table deals with some of the *enabling inventions* that later became important when computers and software also became important.

Table 1.5   *Enabling Inventions for Computers and Software*

Enabling Inventions	Approximate Number of Years Prior to 2013
The modern patent systems	800
Boolean algebra	*175*
Plastics for computer cases, screens, connections, etc.	*125*
Vacuum tubes	*120*
Punched cards	*120*
CRT tubes	*80*
Von Neumann architecture	*75*
Paper tape	*75*
Integrated circuits	*70*
Transistors	*70*
Magnetic tape	*70*
High-level programming languages	*65*
Magnetic disks	*60*
Operating systems	*55*
Magnetic ink for bank checks	*55*
Magnetic stripes for credit cards	*50*
Graphics display adapters	*40*
Laser printers	*40*
Floppy disks	*40*
Dot matrix printers	*35*
Ethernet	*35*
LED displays	*30*
Ink-jet printers	*25*
Solid-state memory	*20*
Flash disks	*15*

One of the first enabling inventions is that of the patent system itself. The first known patent in English was granted in 1331 in England to a man named John Kemp. Later, an Italian patent was granted in Florence in 1421. Patents similar to modern patents and enforced by statute appeared in Venice in a law establishing patents in 1474.

The first patent issued in North America was issued by the Massachusetts General Court in 1641 to a man named Samuel Winslow for a method of making salt. The first federal patent law in the United States was passed on April 10, 1790, and had the title of "An Act to Promote the Progress of Useful Arts."

Note

The name "patent" is derived from the phrases "letters patent" and "letters close." The seal on letters close covered the fold and had to be broken in order to read the letter. The seal on letters patent was attached to the bottom of the document so it could be read with the seal intact.

Software patents have had a very convoluted path and were sometimes barred and more recently accepted. But there is no guarantee that software patents will always be accepted by the U.S. Patent Office. In the 1960s, software patents were barred and several lawsuits were filed, with the courts generally concurring that software was not patentable.

In 1981, the U.S Supreme Court became involved in the case of *Diamond vs. Diehr* and decided that, at least in special cases, software was patentable. This forced a change of procedure in the Patent Office. But the situation remained murky and ambiguous and largely decided on by a case-by-case basis without any real guides or fixed rules.

In 1998 in the famous case of *State Street Bank vs. Signature Financial Group*, it was finally decided what forms of software could be patented. This case involved the hub-and-spoke method of processing mutual funds. The Supreme Court decided that business processes, including those embodied in software, were patentable.

A number of other precursor inventions were also important. For example, without transistors and integrated circuits, there would not be any portable computers, embedded computers, or any types of small electronic devices that today all use software.

The inventions that became integral parts of computers include plastic for cases and screens, integrated circuits, transistors, graphics boards, and LED displays.

Other inventions had a strong impact on the use of computers and hence on the software that was created to support those uses. For example, without the 1960 IBM patent on a magnetic stripe that could be applied to plastic, credit cards would not have been developed. Without the invention of magnetic ink, bank checks would still be sorted alphabetically instead of in numeric order and probably sorted by hand.

Key Inventions Relevant to Software

The inventions listed in the previous tables are all important in one way or another. However, in thinking about the inventions that had the greatest impact on software, the inventions discussed in the following section are the most critical.

Alphabetic Languages

Information recorded using pictograms such as Egyptian hieroglyphics is elegant and beautiful and has produced some wonderful calligraphy, but such systems do not lend themselves to rapid data entry and computerization. The same is true of information recorded using ideograms such as Chinese and Japanese kanji (which uses Chinese symbols). There are thousands of symbols, which makes typing extremely difficult.

During World War II, the text entered into the Japanese "Purple" coding machine actually used two American Underwood typewriters and plain text using English characters. Alphabetic languages have the greatest speed for typed entry.

Binary and Decimal Numbers and Zero

Computers and software can process numbers using any base such as binary, octal, decimal, or hexadecimal. However, electronic circuits for performing mathematics are somewhat easier to design using binary arithmetic. Octal or base 8 numbering systems are easily convertible from binary. (Some Native American tribes used octal numbers since they counted by using the gaps between the fingers rather than the fingers themselves.) Several computers were based on octal numbers such as the DEC PDP line.

Hexadecimal or base 16 numbers are also used in computers and are convenient because they match byte capacities. However, the bulk of day-to-day calculations used by humans are based on decimal or base 10 numbers. Decimal numbers are somewhat analogous to the QWERTY keyboard: not optimal but so widely used that switching to something else would be too expensive to consider.

The decimal point seemed to have originated in India during the ninth century, but it was John Napier who made the concept important in Western mathematics around 1620. Napier also invented logarithms and an interesting manual calculator called "Napier's bones." Logarithms were used in the first slide rules and hence are an important background topic for analog computation.

The concept of zero seemed to have several independent sources. It was used in Babylon with base 60 math, but apparently as a placeholder rather than actual calculations. This use was about 2,500 years ago.

The Olmecs and Mayans both used zero as a true number, and it was used for calendar calculations, which were quite complex. This use of zero seems to date to around 400 AD.

The use of zero in India dates to about 458 AD when it was found in a text on mathematics. Whether this was an indigenous invention or inherited from Babylon is not certain. Later in the 600s, the famous Indian mathematician Brahmagupta wrote a paper on the uses of zero, which moved past zero itself into negative numbers.

Decimal numbers, the decimal point, and zero were all important precursors leading to computers and software calculations.

Digital Computers

Later chapters in this book will discuss the evolution of digital computers and associated software from the mid-1930s through 2010, with projections to 2019. Suffice it to say that software was created specifically to operate on digital computers. Without digital computers, there would be no software. Without software, digital computers would have no major purpose and would probably not have supplanted analog computers.

Higher-Level Programming Languages

I started as a young programmer in the 1960s. Programming using both machine language (mainly for patches and bug repairs) and basic assembly language was how I first programmed IBM 1401 computers.

My firsthand experience was that machine language was very error prone and also rapidly fatiguing due to the high attention span needed to deal with it. Assembly language was a step in the right direction, but not a very big step. Having to use dozens of assembly instructions to handle calculations or format printed output was time consuming and actually boring. Higher-level languages, starting with ALGOL, COBOL, FORTRAN, PL/I, APL, and others, reduced coding time, significantly reduced coding errors, and converted programming into a viable occupation.

Random-Access Storage

Sequential storage of data on paper tape, card decks, or magnetic tape had a fairly long and useful life. But it was very inefficient and required far too much movement of tapes to achieve high speeds. The invention of disk drives and random-access storage allowed faster processing, sophisticated search algorithms, and a path that eventually would lead to today's "big data" world with billions of records and millions of files being accessed for specific problems.

Without random access, modern computing and software could handle only a small fraction of important data analysis problems. Random access would also lead to the relational database concept, sorts, and a variety of powerful query languages in the Structured Query Language (SQL) family.

The Impact of Software on People and Society

The time frame in which computers and software have developed has barely been more than 75 years. Yet their impact on individual humans and on societies has been as important as the printing press, airplanes, television, and automobiles.

Beneficial Tools and Applications

The following is a summary of tools and applications that have transformed the way businesses operate; wars are fought; and individuals gather information, communicate, and use their leisure time. It is surprising that these have all originated within the past 50 years. Probably half of these tools and applications are less than 25 years old.

- Business tools
  - Accounting
  - Actuarial studies
  - Advertising via the web
  - Agricultural planning
  - Analytics
  - Bar-code scanners

- Big data
- Budget analysis
- Cloud computing
- Competitive analysis
- Cost and resource tracking
- Cost estimating
- Crowdsourcing
- Customer relationship management (CRM)
- Customer satisfaction analysis
- Customer support
- Distribution optimization analysis
- Electric power grid controls
- Enterprise resource planning (ERP) packages
- Finance
- Governance
- Human resource management
- Inventory
- Investments
- Just-in-time inventory controls
- Legal support
- Marketing
- Oil exploration
- Order entry
- Order tracking
- Planning and scheduling
- Process controls
- Reservation systems

- Risk estimation and analysis
- Robotic manufacturing
- Sales support
- Supply chain management
- Surveys and opinion analysis
- Telephone network controls
- Water purification
- Web retailing
- Databases
  - Graphics and images
  - Music
  - Signals and analog
  - Text and numeric
- Data warehouses
  - Mixed-data forms
- Education tools
  - Comparative education statistics
  - Curriculum planning
  - Customized e-learning for each student
  - Skills inventory analysis
  - Special tools for the handicapped
  - Student research via the web
  - Virtual classrooms
- Embedded devices
  - Automotive engines and brakes
  - Automotive security systems
  - Avionic

- GPS navigation
- Hearing aids
- Manufacturing
- Medical
- Signal processing
- Smart appliances
- Telecommunications
- Government tools
  - Air traffic control
  - Background verification
  - Budget analysis
  - Census
  - Court records
  - Disaster preparedness
  - Economic analysis
  - Employment statistics
  - Environmental monitoring
  - Financial controls
  - Health and longevity statistics
  - Highway siting, design, and construction
  - Identity verification
  - Land management
  - Law enforcement
  - Legislative records
  - Mandates and regulations
  - National defense
  - Patent analysis

- Political records
- Pollution monitoring
- Prisons
- Property assessments
- Redistricting
- Regulatory agencies
- Risk analysis
- Taxation
- Traffic analysis and controls
- Unemployment support
- Voter records
- Water supply controls
- Welfare
- Zoning
- Leisure
  - Blu-ray and digital video
  - Computer games
  - Digital music formats
  - Geocaching
  - Music playlists
  - Online magazines
  - Streaming video
  - Virtual reality worlds
- Medical
  - Coordination in real time among medical teams
  - External devices
  - Implanted devices

- Insurance record keeping
- Lab tests
- Patient hospital monitoring
- Patient records
- Robotic surgical devices
- Statistics: national, global
- National defense
  - Antimissile shields
  - Combat simulation
  - Command and control
  - Cybersecurity
  - Deep ocean monitoring
  - Early threat warnings
  - Encryption and decryption
  - Intelligence gathering and coordination
  - Logistics analysis
  - National Security Agency signal interception
  - Satellite monitoring
  - Secure communications
  - Threat analysis
- Personal tools
  - Blogs
  - Computers
  - Contact lists
  - Daily news feeds
  - Digital appliances
  - Digital cameras

- Digital image processing
- Digital watches
- E-books
- Email
- Graphics
- handheld full-function digital calculators
- Handicap support for the deaf, blind, etc.
- Home finances
- Instant computer chat
- Music
- Natural language translation
- Presentations
- Scheduling
- Search engines
- Smartphones
- Social networks
- Spreadsheets
- Statistics
- Tablet computers
- Text to speech
- Video processing
- Web browsers
- Word processing
- Professional tools
  - Accounting
  - Analytics
  - Animation and graphic arts

- Architecture
- Civil engineering
- Computer animation
- Data mining
- Drafting
- Economic analysis
- E-learning
- Encryption and decryption
- Engineering
- Intelligent agents for web scanning
- Law enforcement
- Legal support
- Math
- Medical support
- Music composition
- Music recording, playback, and mixing
- National security
- Patent analysis
- Pharmaceutical
- Project management
- Property management
- Publishing
- Real estate listings
- Spell checkers and grammar checkers
- Statistics
- Programming tools
  - Application sizing

- Automatic testing

- Complexity analysis

- Configuration controls

- Continuous integration

- Cost and schedule estimation

- Data mining of legacy applications

- Debugging

- Inspection support

- Maintenance and support estimation

- Measurements and benchmarks

- Programming language compilers

- Quality estimation

- Requirements and design analysis

- Requirements modeling

- Reusability analysis

- Risk estimation

- Static analysis

- Test tools (design and execution)

- Virtualization

- Website design and construction

- Protective tools

  - Antispam

  - Antispyware

  - Antivirus

  - Smart alarm systems

- Scientific tools

  - Archaeological analysis

- Astronomical analysis
- Biological analysis
- Chemical analysis
- Computer-enhanced image calibrations
- Computer-stabilized optical devices
- Deep ocean exploration
- DNA analysis
- Epidemiology analysis
- Forensic analysis
- Geological exploration (side-scan radar)
- Linguistic analysis
- Metallurgy
- Meteorology analysis and weather predictions
- Nanotechnologies
- Nuclear device controls
- Physics research equipment
- Self-aiming telescopes for the deaf, blind, etc.
- Simulations of physical phenomena
- Space vehicles, rovers, and satellites
- Visualization

As can be seen from this list, computers and software are making profound changes to every aspect of human life: education, work, warfare, entertainment, medicine, law, and everything else.

Harmful Inventions

Computers and software have also introduced a number of harmful inventions that are listed below, some of which did not exist before. Among the harmful inventions caused by computers and software are identity theft, hacking, and computer viruses. These are new and alarming criminal activities.

- Browser hijackers
- Computer botnets
- Computer keyboard tracking
- Computer spam
- Computer spyware
- Computer viruses
- Computer worms
- Computerized customer support
- Difficulty in correcting errors in computerized data
- Electronic voting machines without backup
- Hacking tools
- Identity theft
- Phishing
- Piracy
- Robotic telephone calls (robo-calls)
- Robotic weapons systems
- Smart weapons: bombs, drones, and missiles
- Spam
- Special viruses attacking industrial equipment
- Spyware
- Stock market software without anomaly shutoffs
- Unintelligible telephone voice menus
- Web pornography

These threats are comparatively new and all are increasingly hazardous in the modern world. Indeed, identify theft has become one of the largest and most pervasive crimes in human history. It is also an example of a new kind of crime where the criminal and the victim never see each other and can be separated by more than 12,000 miles when the crime takes place.

These harmful aspects of computers and software have triggered new laws and new subindustries that provide virus protection, hacking insurance, and other forms of protection.

These inventions have also led to the creation of new and special cybercrime units in all major police forces, the FBI, the CIA, the Secret Service, the Department of Defense and the uniformed services, Homeland Security, and other government organizations. The emergence of the Congressional Cyber Security Caucus is a sign that that these new kinds of cybercrimes are attracting attention at the highest levels of government.

Weighing the Risks

Computers and software are making profound changes to every aspect of human existence. Many readers have thousands of "friends" on social networks. Even more readers follow the daily lives and activities of countless celebrities and personal friends by using "tweets" or short messages. Text messages are beginning to outnumber live telephone calls (and also cost more due to new computerized billing algorithms).

Purchases of electronic e-books recently topped purchases of ordinary paper books. Banks now charge extra fees to provide paper bank statements as opposed to online electronic statements. All of our medical and education records are now computerized and stored in databases.

It would not be possible to book an airline flight or a hotel without computers and software. Indeed, after large snowstorms or hurricanes when power lines are down, many kinds of businesses cease operations because they are no longer equipped to handle manual transactions. Computerized games, including massively interactive games with thousands of simultaneous players, are now the preferred form of entertainment for millions of young people. Modern films use special effects with lifelike realism that are generated by computers. It is even possible to create new roles for actors and actresses who are no longer living by means of computers and software.

The impact of computers and software has been a mixture of good and bad. Certainly, the ability to send emails and text messages and to find information on the web are very useful additions to our daily lives. We use GPS maps on our smartphones almost every time we travel, particularly when we travel to new and unfamiliar locations.

The ability of physicians to communicate instantly with colleagues helps medical practice. Computerized medical diagnostic machines such as CAT scans and MRI equipment are also beneficial. Cochlear implants have restored hearing to thousands of profoundly deaf patients. Robotic manufacturing is cheaper and sometimes more precise than the manual construction of many complex devices.

But the ever-increasing odds of identity theft and the constant need to keep our computers and electronic devices safe from hackers and data theft are a source of continuing worry and also a source of considerable expense.

In evaluating the advantages and disadvantages of computers and software, the weight of available evidence is that software and computers have provided more benefits to the human condition than they have caused harm. Of course, those who have been harmed probably disagree.

But statistically looking at all known uses of computer and software in the modern world, there have been significant benefits in the way we can communicate, transact business, and carry out scientific and engineering work. It is doubtful that any scientist or engineer would want to stop using computers and software. The same is true of many other kinds of work such as health care, law enforcement, accounting, and even real estate.

Summary

This prelude showed the evolution and convergence of many fields that would come together to create modern computers and software. Mathematics, data storage and retrieval, communication methods, and software itself would come together to create the modern era of personal software and personal computing.

Later chapters in this book discuss the evolution of software engineering from the earliest dreams of visionaries in the 1930s through the growth of the largest and wealthiest companies in human history by the end of the 20th century.

Chapter 2

1930 to 1939: The Foundations of Digital Computing

The early years of the 1930s witnessed original papers leading to the design of digital computers. By the end of the decade, several working digital computers proved that electronic computers were possible. Also during this decade, the probability of a major war led to large government investments in military analog computers for fire control, torpedo launches, and bombsights.

The First Innovators of Modern Computing

The decade from 1930 to 1939 was an era without *software* as we know it today. But it was a very fruitful era in terms of both the invention of the underlying logical ideas behind software and also the design of physical computing devices.

Toward the end of this decade, it was obvious that a major war would soon occur. This created a sense of urgency that led to substantial funding for rapid calculation devices that could be used for military purposes, such as ballistics calculations, logistics, and cryptanalysis.

There were significant investments by all countries for analog computers for military purposes such as naval gun control, submarine torpedo aiming, and bombsights. While many such analog devices were built and tested in this decade, it is best to discuss them in the chapter discussing the 1940s when they were actually used for combat.

In 1930, Vannevar Bush developed a *differential calculator*, which was proof that calculating devices could handle a range of mathematical problems instead of a single narrow form of calculation. This was an analog device rather than a digital computer, so it is not in the line of direct descent to today's digital computers.

In 1934, the German scientist Konrad Zuse put forth the idea that a computer or calculating engine would need a control unit, memory, and an arithmetic unit. Zuse was a pioneer of both computing architecture and programming languages. However, his work was not well known in the United States until after the end of World War II. He is a contender on the short list of having built the first computer. His most successful computers were built during the next decade.

In 1935, IBM hired three female employees, among the first for a technology company. The IBM chairman, Thomas J. Watson Sr., announced that IBM would offer equal pay and equal responsibilities, regardless of gender. IBM later did the same for ethnic minorities who were often discriminated against. In future decades, the computer and software industries would be more egalitarian than some of the older technical fields such as mechanical and electrical engineering. It is a matter of sociological interest that computers and software started out with a major company declaring equal rights and equal pay.

In 1936, Zuse started construction on a relay-based computer (similar to the work of the American George Stibitz) called the Z1. This machine was finished in 1938 but proved to be unreliable for mechanical reasons. However, it did feature programmability.

After an intermediate Z2 machine, later in 1941, Zuse finished a more sophisticated Z3 machine that was programmable, with the programs being entered via punched film. Zuse's machines used binary numbers and are viewed as operating precursors of today's computers. There is still some debate as to whether Zuse or Atanasoff and Berry deserve credit for building the first working computer. In fact, both worked independently, and both deserve credit.

In 1936, the famous Alan Turing published a seminal paper titled "On Computable Numbers," which is generally held to be a description of a working computer with an executable program. Turing's work had both practical and theoretical concepts that would lead to impressive future inventions and to working computers used for code breaking.

A *Turing machine* is an abstract depiction of a working computer that sequentially processes instructions and performs mathematical and logical operations. Even today, a standard definition of a successful computer is that it be "Turing complete" or embodies all of the concepts put forth in Turing's seminal paper.

Turing also developed and defined the concept of an *algorithm*, and he contributed important insights into problems that can be solved by a computer and problems that are insolvable. Turing's contributions to the war effort at Bletchley Park will be discussed in the decade from 1940 to 1949.

In 1937, Claude Shannon, while a graduate student at MIT, wrote a thesis that proved that electrical relays could implement the concepts of Boolean symbolic logic. Shannon's work led to the development of successful digital circuitry, which is needed for digital computers to operate.

A Russian investigator, Victor Shestakov from Moscow State University, developed a theory similar to Shannon's as early as 1935. However, the Shestakov concepts were not published until 1941, so Shannon's ideas have precedence.

Both Shannon and Shestakov recognized that symbolic logic, as put forth by the mathematician George Boole in his 1854 book, *An Investigation on the Laws of Thought*, could be dealt with by relays and electronic circuits that could handle logical decisions as well as carry out mathematical operations.

It is the combination of logical processing with mathematical processing that gives modern computers (and software) their enormous breadth of problem-solving capabilities. Computers and software can not only provide rapid mathematical calculations but also handle complex logical problems such as telephone routing.

In November 1937, a Bell Labs mathematician named George Stibitz, working at home on a kitchen table, built a prototype device that used two telephone relays and flashlight bulbs to represent the binary numbers 0 and 1. Stibitz also realized that this experimental device could be extended to handle rapid calculations involving both division and multiplication.

After some initial indifference, Bell executives decided to fund a larger working version of the prototype Stibitz relay machine. At a cost of about $20,000, this eventually became a machine in 1938 called Model 1.

The Model 1 computing machine had about 450 relays that initially could handle multiplication, division and, later, addition and subtraction. This machine used binary numbers to represent decimal values, which of course later became the main way that computers operate today. Stibitz would continue to make improvements that will be discussed in the next chapter.

One interesting aspect of the Stibitz machine was the use of a teletype keyboard for inputs and outputs. This meant that it was not necessary to have the computing device adjacent to the input mechanism. Within a few years, in 1940, Stibitz demonstrated remote input and output via telephone lines over a distance of more than 20 miles. This early demonstration of remote computing would eventually expand into the internet as we know it today.

In 1938, William Hewlett and David Packard founded the Hewlett-Packard Company (widely known by the initials HP). This company started with a variety of electronic equipment such as oscilloscopes and audio oscillators. In later years, HP became a major vendor of notebook computers, printers, and custom software applications.

In 1939, John Vincent Atanasoff and Clifford Berry developed a prototype computer called ABC (named after the initials of the inventors). This machine is often claimed to be the first digital computer in the world, although there are rival claims and considerable debate and even litigation involving the origin of modern computers. The famous lawsuit between Honeywell and Sperry-Univac will be discussed in Chapters 5 and 6.

In 1939, work started on yet another computer at the IBM laboratory in Endicott, New York. This was called the Harvard Mark 1 computer. The official name of this device was the "automatic sequence controlled calculator."

The Mark 1 was designed by the Harvard mathematician Howard Aikin and other colleagues such as Grace Hopper and several IBM engineers. The design of the Mark 1 was influenced by the earlier mechanical computing device designed by Charles Babbage in the 1870s but not completed during his lifetime.

Note

A working Babbage analytical engine was not built until 1991. Until the successful 1991 construction, there had been debate as to whether the analytical engine would work or not. But it did work and was in fact a Turing complete digital computer. After Babbage in the 1870s, the next Turing complete digital computer would not occur until the 1950s.

The Mark 1 was an electromechanical device that used relays, storage wheels, and rotary switches. It could be "programmed" with sequential instructions fed into the computer via a paper tape. Development of this computer was started in 1939 but not finished until 1944, so the main discussion will be in the next chapter.

Small Mathematical Applications

In this decade, very small mathematical applications were the norm. There were no true programming languages, very little storage capacity for either instructions or data, and rather crude input and output devices.

Table 2.1 shows the approximate numbers of worldwide software applications from 1930 through 1939. These are primarily small experimental "programs" created using either a machine language or some form of keyboard entry. As can be seen, scientific applications dominated during this decade.

Computer programming as we know it today did not really exist in the 1930s. Instead, various controls were used to change the assumptions of electromechanical computing devices. The Zuse Z1 machine was intended to be programmable, but it did not work reliably.

Later sections of this book will discuss application sizes, productivity rates, and quality. There is no available data from the 1930s to make this kind of analysis feasible. The later chapters use 1,000 function points as a standard size, which is roughly equal to about 50,000 code statements in a language such as Java.

In the 1930s with the limited capacities of computing devices, probably the largest mathematical applications (there were no other kinds) were less than 10 function points or perhaps 500 code instructions. Most "programs" were in the range of 2 function points or less than 100 code instructions.

From 1930 to 1939, the world was facing a major war. Warfare brings with it a need for many thousands of computations in order to handle logistics, ballistics, and cryptanalysis.

Table 2.1 *Worldwide Software Applications from 1930 to 1939*

Application Types	Number of Applications	Percentage
Scientific	15	60.00%
Military and defense	10	40.00%
Civilian government	0	0.00%
Systems and middleware	0	0.00%
Embedded software	0	0.00%
Commercial	0	0.00%
Information technology (IT)	0	0.00%
U.S. outsource	0	0.00%
Offshore outsource	0	0.00%
Web applications	0	0.00%
Games and entertainment	0	0.00%
Open source	0	0.00%
Total Applications	25	100.00%

In 1939, the British Navy installed an analog gun control computer on the battleship HMS *King George V*. The cost of this computer was about £213,000, which is approximately $20,000,000 in today's money. It would be many years before digital computers received that kind of funding, and it would be many years before digital computers were sophisticated enough to replace analog computers onboard naval vessels and aircraft.

The on-rushing military threats of this decade highlighted an urgent need for rapid and reliable high-speed calculations of mathematics and also for expanding computing devices from pure math into the domain of logical problem solving.

The pioneering theories and papers created by Turing, Shannon, Zuse, Atanasoff, Aikin, Stibitz, and others would soon lead to true digital computers that could handle logic and math problems thousands of times faster than had ever been possible throughout human history.

Some of these concepts would begin to have practical impacts on the outcome of World War II within just a few years.

Summary

At the start of the 1930s, the need for rapid computation was recognized, but practical knowledge about building such devices was sparse. By the end of the decade, impressive research had provided the logical basis for digital computing, and working computers were under development. This decade also witnessed the inclusion of symbolic logic into computer designs, which would soon open up a vast array of new kinds of applications dealing with logical issues such as telephone routing and other forms of decision making. Computers were no longer envisioned merely as fast mathematical calculators but as tools that could help in solving complex logical problems. Several new analog computers were built for military purposes such as naval gun control, bombsights, and submarine torpedo launching.

Chapter 3

1940 to 1949: Computing During World War II and the Postwar Era

The decade from 1940 to 1949 witnessed the first use of computers in warfare in all of human history. The need for high-speed calculations to handle encryption, decryption, logistics, ballistics, and other military purposes led to a rapid expansion in computer and software sophistication. Thousands of analog computers were used for naval gunnery, bombsights, and submarine torpedo aiming. By the end of the decade, computers had become useful and powerful military tools and were poised to expand into the commercial sector in the next decade. When the decade started, the word "computer" was a job title that was applied to human beings who performed complex calculations, sometimes with the aid of mechanical calculators. By the end of the decade, the term "computer" was phased out as a human job description and had shifted to the modern context of an electronic device.

Global Conflict and Computing

World War II was a global catastrophe that left millions of people dead, homeless, and impoverished. But the military need for high-speed calculations and cryptanalysis led to rapid advances in computer technology and to the first software applications that are similar to the ones used today. All of the major belligerents had some research programs into computing: Australia, China, France, Germany, Great Britain, India, Italy, Japan, the Netherlands, Norway, Poland, Russia, and the United States. Analog computers received more funding than digital computers because they were used for ballistics calculations.

The United States and the United Kingdom were the most ambitious and the most successful. The computers designed and developed by Great Britain are the best known due to their success in breaking German codes and for deciphering messages created on the German Enigma code machine.

In 1940, the word "computer" was used as a job description for human workers who performed complex calculations for military and civilian organizations. Both technical companies and military organizations employed hundreds of human computers who worked by using either their own minds or mechanical adding machines and calculators. Some of the calculations were complex differential equations, while others were more mundane calculations of payrolls and costs.

The majority of these human computers were women. The reason for this is that many women were trained in mathematics, but the inequality in pay for women meant that it was much cheaper to hire women computers than male computers. This inequality in pay would not be rectified for several more decades, and indeed it is not fully rectified even today.

When the Electrical Numerical Integrator and Computer (ENIAC) was nearing completion in 1945 at the Moore School of Engineering in Philadelphia, six women computers were selected to learn how to program it. Thus, the evolution of the term "computer" from a human job description to the name of an electronic device was partly due to the fact that human computers became the first programmers of electronic computers.

When the ENIAC was moved from the university to a military base, the six women programmers lost their jobs, apparently because of some gender restrictions in force at that time. Most continued to program but only for civilian companies instead of the military. This problem of gender discrimination also persisted for several more decades. The major role of women in early computer development is underreported in history.

Note

Pay scales for software engineering work were somewhat more equal by gender than for some of the older technical disciplines such as mechanical and electrical engineering. One reason for this perhaps is that in 1935, Thomas J. Watson Sr., the chairman of IBM, announced a corporate policy of equal pay for equal work. Later, when IBM entered the computer business, it continued this egalitarian policy. In the software engineering field, equal opportunities provide a competitive advantage because programming is a difficult task. Equal opportunity employment and compensation increase the pool of personnel with good software skills.

Wartime Innovations

Throughout history, warfare has led to countless inventions that later proved useful in civilian life. A few examples include canned foods (developed under Napoleon, who offered a reward for a method of preserving food), chronometers, ambulances, sonar, radar, screw propellers for naval ships, tractor treads, the use of railroads for logistical movement of supplies, jet engines, high-altitude rockets, satellites, and Quonset huts (developed at the Navy base at Quonset Point, Rhode Island, as a portable building that could be easily transported and rapidly assembled). Operations research was also developed as a method for improving military logistics and optimizing large-scale movements of equipment and troops.

The reverse is also true with civilian innovations often becoming important for military operations. For example, the German General Staff sent observers to the United States to study the way the Barnum and Bailey Circus loaded and unloaded trains when moving from one city to the next. Students of logistics would visit the Circus Museum in Sarasota, Florida, and examine the models used to demonstrate how the circus could set up and take down tents so rapidly.

When a major war, such as World War II, breaks out, there is a huge need for intelligence gathering, encryption, and decryption. There is also a huge need for logistics support in order to optimize the construction of military materials and the shipment and delivery of those materials to the troops that need them. In addition, there is a huge need for other kinds of calculations, such as ballistics predictions or predicting the run of a torpedo under varying conditions.

Before the war started, and indeed throughout the war, many of the calculations needed to support military and manufacturing operations were performed by human computers who were trained in either mathematics or accounting and could handle the calculations needed to support modern warfare.

There were thousands of these human computers employed by all of the belligerents since they all had needs for mathematical support. In the United States and the United Kingdom, many of these human computers were women, because in those days there was no equal pay for equal work.

However, the human mind, even aided by a mechanical adding machine, can only process a few calculations per minute. Human computers cannot work around the clock and they also need rest and meal breaks. When overworked, fatigue would raise the probability of errors in manual calculations. It was obvious to military and industrial planners that much faster and more reliable ways were needed to handle the millions of calculations necessary to support modern armies, navies, and air forces.

Because Germany was the prime aggressor in World War II, many of the computer programs in other countries were aimed at interfering with German military success and breaking German codes.

Analog Computers During World War II

Combatants used analog computers throughout World War II and digital computers only near the end of World War II after about 1943. Analog computers are not "programmed" via separate stored programs; rather, the programming was built in by the designers of their circuits, gears, spindles, vacuum tubes, and other electronic devices.

Note

Analog computers received more funding than digital computers because they were used for ballistics calculations. Most of the belligerents devised analog computers for use on submarines in aiming torpedoes.

Analog computers were small enough and sophisticated enough to handle complex military problems such as naval gun control, bombsights, and submarine torpedo launching. It would be another 30 years before digital computers with embedded software programs would be small enough and reliable enough to replace analog devices onboard ships at sea and in combat aircraft.

The future inventions of transistors, integrated circuits, and dynamic random-access memory (DRAM) would be needed in order to shrink digital computers to small-enough physical sizes and low-enough electric power consumption to be useful on military aircraft and small ships such as submarines. In addition, the invention of better programming languages than basic assembly would be needed to handle the very complex calculations involved in target acquisition and fire control, bomb runs, and naval gunnery.

Better software quality control would also be needed, because the embedded applications used for weapons control were complex and large. Bugs or defects in the embedded software operating weapons systems can be fatal to the crews and vessels using them.

Analog computers would continue to be the workhorses of ships at sea and aircraft in combat on through the Korean War and into the Vietnam conflict. Digital computers and embedded software would not fully replace analog computers as weapons systems until the 1980s.

Those of us in software owe a debt of gratitude to the analog computing engineers and designers who built devices such as the Norden bombsight, the British "bombe" for cryptanalysis, and the Mark III Torpedo Data Computer (TDC) used on American submarines. These analog computers played a major part in the Allied victory of World War II. The history of military analog computers is as important as the history of digital computers.

Computers in Germany During World War II

It is fortunate for the United States and the Allies that the German military did not place a high priority on digital computers, even though one of the major pioneers in the history of computing, Konrad Zuse, lived in Berlin and developed several working computers between 1940 and 1945. He even designed what is probably the first programming language, called *Plan Calculus* (or Plankalkuel in German) in 1945. This language was not supported by a working compiler, however.

Zuse started as an aeronautical engineer at the Henschel Aircraft Company in 1935. Zuse soon left full-time work and set up a computer laboratory in his parents' apartment in Berlin. He continued to work part-time at Henschel. In 1938, Zuse built his first prototype computer, the Z1, to prove the concept of machine computation. This first machine did not work well due to mechanical issues.

In 1940, Zuse built the Z2 computer, which did work and was probably the first operational electromechanical computer built in the world.

In 1941, Zuse built the Z3, which was an operational electromechanical computer based on binary digits. The German military used the Z3 to calculate wing flutter in combat aircraft. Zuse requested funds to build a fully electronic version, but his request was denied as "not being important to the war effort."

In 1945, Zuse completed the Z4, which had a number of technical advances. It used binary arithmetic and could be programmed using paper tape as the input method. The Z4 could also produce printed output. It was used to solve mathematical calculations and could also handle conditional branching logic. The Z4 was a major contender for being the first successful digital computer. Due to the advance of Russian troops on Berlin, the Z4 was shipped to safer locations several times, which slowed final developments. After World War II, the Z4 was acquired by the Swiss Federal Institute of Technology and it continued to solve mathematical problems through 1950.

Although Zuse approached the German government about using computers for military purposes, there was apparently no interest and no recognition of their capabilities. In fact, Zuse proposed to build an encryption computer, but the idea was rejected.

As a result of government indifference, Zuse had to use scrap parts and hire workers, such as invalids, who were not assigned to military tasks. As in other countries, some of Zuse's workers were women.

In retrospect, the German failure to understand the need for high-speed computing harmed German war efforts and benefited Allied war efforts. During World War II, the German government spent more money on occult studies than on computation. However, Germany did build cryptanalysis machines that were successful in cracking Soviet military codes.

As with other countries, Germany did develop a sort of analog computer to aid in aiming torpedoes when they were fired from submarines. There were also German analog computers used for naval gunfire control.

The German V-1 cruise missile and the V-2 rocket also had analog computer guidance systems, as well as gyroscopes and inertial sensors. However, neither the V-1 or V-2 proved to be accurate. Cities were the targets rather than specific locations within those cities. However, random hits did cause deaths and destruction.

These missiles were constructed using slave labor from concentration camps. One report claimed that due to the harsh treatment of the workers, more people died while building V-2 rockets than were killed by the rockets used in combat.

The V-2 did trigger a need for an effective antimissile defense that would later result in satellites and the Patriot Missile. The V-1 could be shot down by fast fighter aircraft, but the V-2 descended almost vertically at more than Mach 3 speed, so there was no effective defense.

An even more sophisticated analog computer developed in Germany during the war was the Lotfernrohr 7 bombsight, which was installed in the world's first operational jet bomber, the Arado AR 234 bomber in 1945.

Analog Espionage

Some of the technology for the German bombsight was based on the American Norden bombsight that had apparently been passed to Germany by the infamous Duquesne spy ring started by Fredrick Duquesne.

Thirty-four people were tried and convicted of espionage in 1941, the largest spy case in U.S. history. (A 1945 motion picture, *The House on 92nd Street*, was based on this spy ring, and it won an Academy Award for original motion picture story.) However, another source on Wikipedia says that the Norden data was passed to Germany in 1938.

The German government largely ignored digital computing, a technology that actually changed the outcome of World War II. Of course, Germany was a pioneer in other military technologies such as jet engines and field artillery. Germany also built the famous *Enigma* cypher machine, which turned out to be less secure than the German government thought it was. The Enigma machine resembled a typewriter and its codes were created with mechanical wheels.

Germany also had another military encoding system named *FISH* that was electromechanical. This was usually reserved for high-level communications between Berlin headquarters and various army headquarters, while the Enigma was used for more frequent operational communications. The FISH machines were less common and less well known than the Enigma machines.

The FISH machines were designed by the company of C. Lorenz in Berlin. The machine used a stream cipher and was built as an attachment to a standard teleprinter. There were several models produced between 1941 and 1944.

The coding system used by the FISH machines was based on a method devised by Gilbert Vermam of AT&T Bell Labs in 1917. The cipher system used methods of symbolic logic from George Boole's work with emphasis on the "exclusive or" function. Several other researchers developed similar codes.

In August 1941, a FISH message of 4,000 characters was intercepted by the British. Using manual precomputer analysis, Brigadier John Tillman and the mathematician Bill Tutte were able to crack the code and reverse-engineer the FISH machine, a remarkable achievement. This work later fed into the design of computers to speed up decryption.

German cryptanalysts managed to break the Soviet military codes, just as the British broke the German codes. After the war, the Germans turned over their cryptanalyst machines to the British and Americans. These German machines (more than seven tons' worth) were transported to Bletchley Park, where they were used by British cryptanalysts during the Cold War to continue to decipher Soviet coded messages.

Germany also had a nuclear program during World War II. The Allies benefited greatly from the folly of German anti-Semitism, which led to the migration of scientists such as Albert Einstein, Edward Teller, and Leo Szilard to the United States. Enrico Fermi also moved to the States to escape Fascism in Italy. John von Neumann also moved from Hungary but in 1930 before wartime repressions had started.

Computers in Japan During World War II

Japan had a strong tradition of mathematics and pioneered building calculation devices as early as 1902. In that year, Yazu Ryoichi built a mechanical calculating machine called the *automatic abacus*. In appearance, this looks a bit like the Curta mechanical calculator, only larger. In 1906, Kawaguchi Ichitaro of the Ministry of Communications and Transportation built a working mechanical calculator powered by electricity.

During World War II in 1944, the aviation laboratory at Tokyo Imperial University built an electromechanical device for solving simultaneous equations. This was not a true computer but was a step in that direction.

Japanese Technology and Intel's First Chip

An important business event occurred in Japan in 1945 that in later decades would cause Intel to become the world's largest manufacturer of computer chips. Although this had no impact on World War II, it was extremely important for the later computer industry and is not widely known.

In 1945, a company called the Nippon Calculating Machine Corporation was founded to build calculators. Later, it changed its name to Busicom. In the 1960s, Busicom patented the first microprocessor and entered into an agreement with Intel to manufacture it. (Intel was founded in 1968.)

An Intel engineer named Ted Hoff improved on the original Busicom design, and Intel's first microcomputer, produced in 1971, was the Intel 4004 microprocessor, which was based on the Busicom patents that were shared with Intel. It is not widely known in the United States that Intel's entry into the microprocessor field was due to gaining access to Japanese patents.

During World War II, the Japanese navy, as most other navies also did, developed an analog computing device for use on submarines to calculate their aiming points. Incidentally, the Japanese *long lance* torpedo was among the most effective at the start of World War II. It had a longer range and was more reliable than Allied torpedoes.

Japan's main development efforts in computers will be discussed in future decades, when the high-quality levels of Japanese companies enabled them to pull ahead in products such as LCD screens, disk drives, and other computer peripherals. Software in Japan also benefited from the contributions of the Americans W. Edwards Deming and J. W. Juran during the postwar years.

Japan developed several cryptographic machines for encoding naval and military messages. These were mechanical devices and not computers. One Japanese device resembled the German Enigma machine (Japan had acquired Enigma machines in 1937).

But another Japanese coding machine was indigenous and used electrical step switches instead of the rotors used by the Enigma devices. This code machine was called "Purple" by Allied intelligence personnel, and it was decrypted by the United States Army Signal Intelligence Service (SIS) by 1939. Some of the more useful Purple messages that were decoded were Japanese foreign office messages by the Japanese Ambassador to Berlin.

One famous decrypted message, which has been shown in several feature films, was the message to the Japanese Ambassador in Washington that Japan was breaking off negotiations on the day of Pearl Harbor, December 7, 1941. In fact, the U.S. officials had the text of this message before the Japanese Ambassador received it.

Later during the war, messages from Ambassador General Hiroshi Oshima in Berlin were translated. These secret messages often included vital military information, including some told to Oshima by Hitler himself.

Computers in Poland During World War II

World War II started on September 1, 1939, when Germany invaded Poland. However, on July 25, 1939, about five weeks before the invasion, there was a secret meeting between Poland, France, and Britain at Pyry in a forest about 30 miles south of Warsaw. At this meeting, several cryptanalysis methods and an actual Enigma machine were turned over to France and Britain by Polish mathematicians.

By good fortune, Alan Turing was one of the British mathematicians who received the Polish information. This fact would become significant as the war continued and the British began to develop decryption computers. As most readers may know, Alan Turing is a famous mathematician who contributed to the fundamental theory of digital computers, and he also contributed practical engineering knowledge to the development of British decryption computers.

Starting in 1932, Polish mathematicians had been working on breaking the codes used by the German Enigma machine. One of the methods used for decryption was a mechanical calculating device called a *cryptologic bomb*, or "bomba" in Polish. This was one of the methods provided by Poland to the Allies, and it later developed into the famous bombe built at Bletchley Park.

The Polish mathematicians probably sped up British decryption efforts by more than a year and hence aided the Allies in deciphering Enigma codes.

Although Poland as a country was occupied by Germany and later Russia, Polish troops in exile continued to serve with the Allies in both air and ground operations. Polish intelligence during World War II was among the most successful of any of the combatants. During 1939 to 1945, about 40% to 45% of all useful intelligence reports from the German-occupied countries were from Polish agents.

Computers in France During World War II

The rapid collapse of France during World War II interfered with many kinds of scientific studies, including computation. However, the French company Groupe Bull would in later years become a major manufacturer of computers and a rival to IBM. This company was founded in 1931 with the name H. W. Egli-Bull (Egli was a Swiss company).

The Bull company had acquired the patents of the late Norwegian inventor Fredrik Rosing Bull, a famous pioneer in punch-card tabulating machines. Bull died of cancer at age 42 in 1925, leaving a rich legacy of patents and intellectual property. Equipment and tabulating machines using punched cards based on the Bull patents were produced in both Norway and France.

In 1933, the Bull company reorganized under new owners and took the name Compagnie des Machines Bull. The Bull company operated during World War II and remained a major producer of punch-card tabulating equipment.

The original Bull punch card had 45 columns and round holes. When IBM began its rapid expansion with tabulating machines, the IBM punch card had 80 columns and rectangular holes.

Civil litigation such as patent suits continued during World War II, even in occupied countries such as France. In the early war years, Bull switched from round to rectangular holes, which triggered a patent lawsuit between Bull and IBM. In December 1941, IBM France won the patent litigation against Bull. Bull also lost an appeal that was decided in June 1942.

In the postwar years, Bull became a major competitor to IBM and operated in more than 100 countries.

Computers in Australia During World War II

The Australian government sponsored an organization called the Council for Scientific and Industrial Research Automatic Computer (CSIRAC). Although the design of an indigenous Australian computer started near the end of World War II, the first computer produced in Australia was tested in November 1949. The team was headed by Trevor Pearcey and Malcom Beard.

Inputs to the CSIRAC Mark I computer were paper tape and outputs were on a standard teleprinter. Versions of this machine operated from 1949 through 1960, and they eventually featured a programming language called INTERPROGRAM that resembled BASIC.

A nonworking version of the CSIRAC Mark I can be found in the Melbourne Museum. The Mark I is perhaps the ninth working digital computer, after ABC, BINAC, COLOSSUS, EDSAC, ENIAC, Harvard Mark 1, MESM, and Z3.

Computers in Russia During World War II

For a variety of reasons, cooperation between the Soviet bloc and the western Allies during World War II did not encompass cryptanalysis or code-breaking computing devices. There was never the same level of cooperation as existed between the United States and Great Britain.

After World War II, the Cold War increased hostility between the former allies, which meant that Soviet work on computers was not known in the West, except perhaps by those military and security officers with very high clearance levels. Russia and other Soviet countries such as Ukraine were fairly active both during World War II and the later Cold War.

Some of the Russian computer pioneers were contemporaries of Turing, Aiken, Mauchly, Atanasoff, and von Neumann in the 1940s, but their names are hardly known in the West. Some of these Soviet computer pioneers included S. A. Lebedev, I. S. Brook, B. I. Rameev, V. M. Glushkov, and others equally unknown in western computer literature.

There is not much information about Soviet computing during World War II itself, but by 1948, Lebedev in Ukraine built the first Soviet computer, the MESM (a small electronic counting machine). The MESM was later used for calculations involving nuclear devices, space exploration, and electrical transmission. This is one of the first indigenous general-purpose computers built on the continent of Europe except for the work of Konrad Zuse in Germany.

Lebedev later transferred his operations from Ukraine to Moscow and continued to build advanced computing devices, some of which pioneered new technologies and gathered useful patents.

In later decades, Russian and Soviet computers would approach western computers in processing power and capabilities.

Computers in Great Britain During World War II

Because of the success of British code-breakers in solving the codes generated by the German Enigma and FISH machines, the work at Bletchley Park has become famous and is described in books and feature films. Not only did Bletchley Park and computers play a significant part in World War II but also one of the greatest pioneers of computing, Alan Turing, worked there during the war.

In the summer of 1939, when it was obvious that war was going to occur, the British government evacuated the Government Code and Cipher School to Bletchley Park, a large manor house located about 50 miles away from London in Buckinghamshire. Although the initial staff at Bletchley was small, by the time the war ended, about 10,000 people were working there and using a variety of temporary buildings called "huts." Alan Turing was located in hut 8, which has become famous.

Many of the mathematicians were from the Women's Royal Navy Service (WRNS). Here, too, women were pioneers in computing and software.

In 1936, prior to joining Bletchley, Alan Turing published his famous paper "On Computable Numbers," which became the logical and philosophical basis for computer architecture. Even today, the concept of computers as being "Turing complete" is used to ascertain if computing equipment can handle all of the concepts in Turing's seminal paper.

In July 1939, Turing was one of the British mathematicians who received secret information from Polish mathematicians about decoding German codes based on the Enigma. In fact, they received a working Enigma machine that could be reverse-engineered.

As mentioned earlier, Turing developed a new and improved form of machine called the Bombe at Bletchley Park. The version developed by Turing was electromechanical. It was a massive machine that was about eight feet high and weighed at least a ton. It used wheels similar to the Enigma machine. The local name at Bletchley for this first Bombe was "the bronze goddess."

Turing was not the only brilliant mathematician and inventor at Bletchley Park. T. H. Flowers was the chief architect of a fast electronic computer that became known as *Colossus* and was aimed at decrypting codes based on the FISH Lorenz coding scheme.

A large team of engineers and mathematicians worked for two years on building the Colossus. When finished in 1943, it was the first operational computer in Great Britain and a contender for being the first operational computer in the world.

Note

In 2006, a working replica of the Colossus was created and was entered in a code-breaking contest against modern notebook computers. Although Colossus did not win, it had very respectable results for a device designed using 1940s technology.

The British code-breaking program was called the *Ultra* program. The derivation of the word "ultra" implied that the secrecy was even higher than top secret, so it was "ultra secret." Some of the information about the Ultra program was not declassified until 1972, which means that early work on digital computers as part of Ultra was not widely known. Senior officers from both the United States and the United Kingdom credit the Ultra program with shortening the war by perhaps two years. A few even state that the war might have been lost if not for Ultra.

In 1946, Alan Turing presented a paper, written in 1945, to the executive committee of the British National Physical Laboratory. The title was "Automatic Computing Engine" (ACE). It described a very sophisticated stored-program digital computer. Because Turing's work was covered by the Official Secrets Act, he was prevented from publishing the paper or making the contents known.

The proposed Turing computer features subroutine calls, which were not in the Electronic Discrete Variable Automatic Computer (EDVAC), described by von Neumann in his 1945 paper. This means that the Turing computer was somewhat in advance of the EDVAC. Turing also defined a programming language in a section of his report titled "Abbreviated Computer Instructions."

Because of secrecy, a working computer based on Turing's ACE concepts was not built until 1950, when it was the fastest computer constructed up until that time. This was named the *Pilot Model ACE* and it became operational on May 10, 1950. This computer used vacuum tubes for computation and mercury delay lines for memory.

A larger version called MOSAIC, which stood for Ministry of Supply Automatic Integrator and Computer, was completed in 1952, and some of the details of this device remain classified even today. It was used to support radar sightings of aircraft and to compute their future flight paths.

Had the British government moved more rapidly and used the Turing paper as a computer architecture in 1946, high-speed digital computers would probably have occurred about five years faster than they did occur.

It is an interesting historical fact that John von Neumann was familiar with Turing's work. Some of the concepts in von Neumann's paper on the EDVAC seem to be similar to Turing's paper, although this may be a case of independent inventions by both Turing and von Neumann.

Although the Colossus is the best known of the wartime British computing systems, various analog computers were also produced. Those who have not served in the military may not be aware of the complex calculations needed during combat at sea and in the air. Analog computers were the most effective solutions for these calculations from World War II through the Vietnam War.

When two ships are fighting at sea, both ships are typically moving in different directions and at different speeds. To aim a shell at an opponent with a good chance of a hit requires integrating data on the direction and speed of both ships, the velocity and trajectory of the shell, and other factors such as the roll of the ship due to wave action and also wind speed and direction.

The first British mechanical naval gunnery computers were installed on the HMS *Rodney* and HMS *Nelson* in 1924. By World War II, improvements made these devices fairly accurate. By the war's end, radar would also be available, which would greatly improve the accuracy of naval gunnery.

These mechanical analog computers were complex to build and quite expensive. For example, the analog fire-control computer on the battleship HMS *King George V* in 1939 cost about £213,000. This is roughly equivalent to $20,000,000 today. Prices stayed high throughout World War II, although so many were built that there were economies of scale.

Note

The Harvard Mark I computer only cost about $1,000,000. The cost of the analog fire-control computer on the HMS *King George V* was roughly equal to the costs of all digital computers put together between 1939 and 1945. Needless to say, these analog fire-control computers were very complex devices.

Surface naval battles involving capital ships can begin at ranges of almost 20 miles, and the ships seldom approach each other at ranges of less than a mile. Ships in combat usually pursue zigzag courses in order to make enemy aiming difficult. Therefore, naval gunnery deals with aiming massive projectiles over very long ranges and involves both a moving gun platform and a moving target. These are not trivial calculations and they cannot be performed manually with anything like the speed and accuracy required.

Prior to the development of analog fire-control computers, almost 400 shots were needed to ensure one hit at ranges of more than three miles. Analog fire-control computers reduced the number of shots down to perhaps 40 shots per hit.

Not only is surface gunnery a task requiring many computations but also launching torpedoes from submarines requires a great many complex calculations that need high-speed computing. Most of the belligerents used fairly effective torpedo-launch analog computers during World War II.

These analog computer torpedo-aiming devices were quite large for submarines: Some were five or six feet tall and perhaps two feet wide and deep. The urgency of the torpedo-aiming challenge explains why such big machines were squeezed into the very small control rooms of World War II submarines. They also required two extra crew members to keep them up and running.

Even more difficult than naval gunnery is the task of shooting antiaircraft guns against enemy planes. Not only are the planes moving much faster than ships at sea, but they can also move in three dimensions and can change directions rapidly.

Thus, antiaircraft calculations involve altitude, direction, velocity, wind speed, wind direction, and rates of change in any or all of these factors. The essential problem is hitting a very small target that might be traveling an erratic course at more than 350 miles per hour at an altitude of more than 25,000 feet. This is not a trivial set of calculations.

As anyone who has tried skeet shooting knows, the shell must be aimed at where it will be when it arrives, not where the shell is currently located. For airplanes, the radius of destruction from World War II explosive antiaircraft cannon shells was only about 30 feet, which meant that the shells had to be very close to the target to be successful.

Equally challenging and requiring sophisticated calculations is the aiming of bombs from moving aircraft. All of the belligerents developed analog computers for bombsights, with probably the most famous being the American Norden bombsight, to be discussed later in this chapter.

Surprisingly, the accuracy of these electromechanical analog computers for naval and air combat was good enough so that they stayed in operation throughout World War II, the Cold War, the Korean War, and indeed into the 1960s and even the '70s. Some even saw service during the Vietnam War. It would be many years after World War II before digital computers and software were good enough to replace analog computers onboard ships and aircraft.

Within the context of aiming cannons or torpedoes at moving targets, the electromechanical analog computers had one of the longest useful lives of any form of computation. They were accurate enough to provide effective targeting through three wars and numerous police actions.

These were not programmable computers in the modern sense. They only covered a specific set of calculations, and the "programming" was built into the devices by the designers in terms of the mechanical wheels, cogs, and electrical relays.

Bletchley Park was not the only British research establishment with an impact on computers and software. Another location that would have an impact on software in particular was the Bawdsey Research Station, where mathematicians and statisticians would pioneer a discipline known as *operational research* in Great Britain and *operations research* in the United States. This new discipline would expand in scope and would soon involve Army, Navy, and Air Force personnel.

Operations research is concerned with optimizing the effectiveness of group activities, and it involves logic and network analysis as well as ordinary math and statistics. A few examples of the problems studied by operations research will show the combination of logic and math needed to handle complex situations.

One question of great importance involved whether a few large convoys of ships or many small convoys would be most effective in escaping German U-boat attacks. Operations research found that avoiding attacks correlated most strongly to the number of available destroyers and armed escorts that could defend the convoy. Large convoys with many armed destroyers and escort vessels proved to be the best solution.

Another question involved what color of paint on the bottom of antisubmarine aircraft would be least visible to German U-boats. It turned out that aircraft with white bottoms were not spotted until they were 20% closer to the target than aircraft with black bottoms.

A related question was the optimal depth for detonating depth charges dropped from aircraft. The initial standard depth was 100 feet. However, it turned out that most diving U-boats did not reach that depth before the depth charge exploded, so they escaped serious damage. A shallow depth of 25 feet was optimal for aircraft depth charge settings.

When World War II started, 20,000 antiaircraft shells were needed to shoot down one airplane. By the middle of the war, based on analog fire-control computers and operations research applied to antiaircraft loading and aiming operations, the number of shells needed per destroyed aircraft was down to 4,000.

Note

The huge ratio of shots to hits explains why surface-to-air missiles (SAMs) with computer guidance systems would replace antiaircraft guns as the best method of air defense in later decades. To be effective, SAMs required compact onboard radar, small analog computers for guidance, and other sophisticated electronics such as heat sensors. These would not come together during the war but arrived in 1947 and became very sophisticated in later decades.

These real-world military problems combine a need for empirical data and statistical analysis with complex calculations performed at high speeds. These are the very problems that digital computers and software would eventually tackle with great success in future decades.

After the war, operations research and digital computers would apply these concepts to a huge variety of complex civilian problems, including queuing theory, telephone network optimization, supply chain management, "just-in-time" manufacturing, freight delivery-route optimization, railroad and airline traffic analysis, and game theory, among many others.

At the level of individual projects, critical path analysis and PERT diagrams were offshoots from operations research. At a higher corporate level, organization dynamics, business process reengineering, and market analysis would also be derived from World War II operations research.

Digital computers and software would eventually be the best tools in history for solving complex logical problems at high speeds, but many more years and many more inventions would be needed before digital computers and software became truly effective tools for complex real-world problems.

Computers in the United States During World War II

Before addressing the developments of digital computers by the United States in World War II, it is important to consider the analog computers used for bombsights, naval gunnery, artillery ranging, and torpedo launches. There were only a few digital computers built during World War II, but there were many thousands of these sophisticated analog computers deployed on all surface ships, submarines, and bombers.

One of the most interesting analog computers developed by the United States during World War II is the famous Norden bombsight used on both Air Force and Navy bombers. This bombsight had a very long service life—much longer than the average digital computer. It continued to be used during the Korean War and into the Vietnam War. The slang name for this bombsight by flight crews was "the blue ox."

Earlier bombsights could compensate for aircraft speed and direction but were still not extremely accurate. They also required a lot of verbal communication between the pilot and the bombardier during the final stages of the bombing run. The Norden bombsight included a linkage to the aircraft's autopilot and actually calculated the bomber's flight path on the final run before the bombardier would release the bomb.

The Norden bombsight was developed by a Dutch engineer named Carl Norden who moved to the United States and worked for the Sperry Gyroscope company. However, he was also a consultant to the Navy, who awarded Norden a contract in 1929 to build a working automatic bombsight. Norden completed a working prototype in 1930.

The Navy accepted the design, and production of the Norden bombsight started in 1931. Norden founded his own company to build these bombsights and was awarded a Navy contract. Later when the Army and Air Force wanted to buy the Norden bombsights, they had to acquire them from the Navy, which caused interservice rivalry.

Prior to the Norden bombsight, bombardiers also needed to use a variety of tables and manually entered data into the bombsight while communicating course directions to the pilot. As might be imagined, the process was sluggish and prone to a variety of errors.

With the Norden bombsight, all of the calculations were handled by embedded analog computers in the bombsight itself. The bombardier only had to make adjustments using two control wheels. The time required for the analog computers to perform their calculations was about six seconds.

The Norden bombsights were complex devices that used gyro stabilization to ensure a level platform. The accuracy of the bomb drops using the Norden bombsight was within 35 feet for best results and about 75 feet for average results. This is not smart bomb accuracy, but it is not bad for iron bombs with marginal aerodynamic qualities.

In a trial run using an obsolete battleship as the target, about 50% of the bombs dropped from 4,000 feet using the Norden bombsight hit the target. Older bombsights had less than a 20% hit rate under the same conditions.

During actual combat operations, the results from the Norden bombsight would be less successful. This is because combat bombing during the war moved to much higher elevations to avoid ground fire. Some B17 bomb runs were made from more than 25,000 feet, while some B29 bomb runs were made above 30,000 feet.

Norden realized that feedback was needed between the bombsight and the aircraft autopilot, so he developed an improved form of autopilot with a direct link to the bombsight. This was called the Stabilized Bombing Approach Equipment (SBAE), and this was also a form of analog computer.

The Royal Air Force approached the United States in 1938 about acquiring the Norden bombsight but was rebuffed. In fact, they were rebuffed several times, and the situation reached a point where in 1938, Neville Chamberlain wrote a personal letter to President Roosevelt, but this still did not achieve a transfer of Norden bombsights.

Technical cooperation between the United States and Great Britain almost came to a standstill because of U.S. reluctance to provide the Norden bombsight to the Royal Air Force. The United States was concerned that if the Norden bombsights were used in British planes over occupied Europe, their design might become known to the Germans if any planes were shot down.

Note

Although this fact was not known during the war itself, as mentioned earlier in the chapter, German spies had passed along information about the Norden bombsight to Germany as early as 1938. Giving the Norden bombsight to Great Britain would not have degraded its security because the Germans were already building a similar bombsight based on stolen technology passed on by German spies.

The impasse between Britain and the United States on military weapons led to the famous Tizard mission of 1940 to try and improve technical information transfer. This mission was named after Henry Tizard, the chairman of the British Aeronautical Research Committee.

Although the Tizard mission did not acquire the Norden bombsight, it did smooth the animosity between British and American military leaders. The United States benefited greatly by receiving information about British jet-engine development, the cavity magnetron which enabled small radar sets, self-sealing fuel tanks, plastic explosives, and other technologies where the United Kingdom was a world leader.

The magnetron was a critical product that allowed radar sets small enough to be placed in fighters and bombers, which greatly improved combat effectiveness. Even better, these airborne radar sets allowed planes to locate submarines at great distances and even at night. Small radar sets operating in aircraft were one of the most important inventions of World War II, and this has had significant civilian benefits as well.

It is an interesting historical fact that both analog and digital computers changed the course of World War II. In fact, the strong British desire for the Norden analog computer yielded extremely valuable technologies that benefited U.S. war efforts, with the magnetron being a key invention that revolutionized air combat by introducing radar to combat aircraft.

Analog computers were the workhorses of World War II computation. Every war ship, bomber, and artillery battery used analog computation as a standard method of operation. These devices increased both the accuracy and the rates of fire of land artillery and naval guns. They also increased the accuracy of bombing and made precision bombing one of the most effective weapons leading to the Allied victory, although not all results were successful.

Another effective analog computer developed by the United States was the Torpedo Data Computer (TDC), used aboard all U.S. submarines. There were a number of models of this device, but the Mark III and Mark IV were the best of those during the war. The Mark III was operational in 1940, and the Mark IV was operational in 1943.

These bulky devices were so important to accurate aiming that they were carried in submarine control rooms and two extra, specially trained crew members kept them operational. The Mark III and Mark IV torpedo-aiming devices are cited as being the best of any country during World War II.

Unfortunately, the American Mark 14 torpedo was not as reliable as the Japanese long lance torpedo when the war started, but it improved over time. The later Mark 18 American torpedo was one of the best in the war.

The Mark 14 torpedo used a form of analog computer as a detonator, called the Mark VI detonator, which included both magnetic sensors and contact detonation. For reasons of cost, the Mark VI detonators were not given live tests prior to becoming operational. A great many American torpedoes hit their targets but failed to explode during the first two years of World War II due to faulty magnetic detonation.

Another problem was that the initial tests of the Mark 14 torpedo used dummy warheads, which were lighter than actual combat warheads. As a result, the Mark 14s in combat ran about 10 feet deeper than programmed, which caused many misses.

It was only in September 1943 that the various problems of American torpedoes were solved. Problems with the torpedoes were often found under actual combat conditions, and the Bureau of Naval Ordnance ignored dozens of reports from frustrated American submarine commanders. The final fixes required that Admiral Ernest King, the Chief of Naval Operations, "lit a blowtorch under the Bureau of Naval Ordnance."

A naval base for spotting German submarines was established in 1942 on a property adjacent to the torpedo testing area in Newport, Rhode Island. The buildings were designed to look like beach houses in order to conceal their purpose from German submarines that might be approaching Narragansett Bay to attack U.S. ships at the Newport naval base.

Note

One of the torpedo test areas and one of the submarine-spotting buildings are visible from the window of the office where this book was written. Even today, unexploded World War II torpedoes are being removed from Narragansett Bay. This property is now used as a training base by the Rhode Island National Guard and is called Camp Varnum after a Revolutionary War general who lived nearby.

It is an interesting historical fact that the last U-boat sunk during World War II was spotted near the entrance of Narragansett Bay and was sunk near Block Island, about seven miles off the coast of Rhode Island.

This boat was the U-853 and it was on its third combat patrol. The U-boat was destroyed by the U.S. Navy after the Battle of Point Judith on May 6, 1945. The U-boat was sunk by depth charges and the entire crew was killed. Later, several German crew members were buried with full military honors in Newport, Rhode Island.

The U.S. ships involved in hunting and sinking the U-853 included the destroyer escorts *Ericsson*, *Amick*, *Atherton*, and *Moberly*. Blimps and aircraft also participated. *Atherton* and *Moberly* were credited with firing the depth charges that sank the U-853, using analog computers for setting the depth of the explosion.

Shortly before being sunk, the U-853 sank a coal ship named the *Black Point*, the last American freighter destroyed during World War II. It was sunk on May 6, 1945, with the loss of 12 crewmen. Another 34 crewmen were rescued. The Battle of Point Judith was the last Atlantic naval battle of World War II. Black Point Park in Narragansett, Rhode Island, is named after the final U.S. ship sunk in World War II.

On May 5, Grand Admiral Dönitz, Commander in Chief of the German Navy, had issued orders for all submarines to cease offensive operations and return to port, since the German surrender was scheduled for May 8. (Dönitz had become chief of state and president of Germany after Hitler's suicide. He held this position from April 30, 1945, to May 23, 1945, when the German government was dissolved by the Allies.)

Apparently, the U-853 had not received the order to cease combat operations, or the captain chose to ignore it. It is unfortunate for both sides that the battle took place so close to the end of the war and one day after all German submarines had been ordered to cease combat. Since the U-853 sank in water that is 121 feet deep, the hull can still be seen by scuba divers who are certified for deep dives, although this dive is dangerous and should not be attempted by amateurs. There may also be torpedoes and naval cannon shells still onboard, which become unstable with time.

There are only a few working examples of digital computers that the United States completed during the war. The first of the U.S. digital computers was not aimed specifically at military uses but rather to solve linear equations. This computer was designed in 1937 by John Atanasoff of Iowa State University. A graduate student, Clifford Berry, assisted in the construction of the computer. It was called the *ABC* computer after the initials of the inventors.

The ABC computer was finished in 1942 but was not programmable and hence was not Turing complete. However, it did use binary arithmetic and featured parallel processing. It had separate memories for intermediate data and instructions. All calculations were electronic, using vacuum tubes, and did not involve wheels or moving mechanical parts. The ABC could add or subtract at a rate of about 30 calculations per second.

As will be discussed in the chapters about the 1960s and '70s, this computer figured prominently in a patent lawsuit between Sperry-Rand and Honeywell. The judge's decision included a statement that the ABC was the first digital computer, which triggered a controversy still not entirely settled in 2013. The judge stated that Atanasoff was the original developer of electronic computers, which cast doubt on the contributions of Zuse, Mauchly, and Eckert.

In 1942, both the U.S. Navy and the U.S. Air Force established formal operations research groups to apply mathematical methods to the analysis of combat operations. The Navy group analyzed submarine warfare and the Air Force group analyzed bombing and fighter operations. These studies led to innovations in combat patrol logistics and also to the most effective formations for combat aircraft. It would not be until later decades that digital computers and software would be powerful enough to contribute to the solutions of operations research problems.

The next digital computer in the United States was the ENIAC. It was started in 1943 in order to calculate artillery ballistics. It was funded by the United States Army Ballistic Research Agency. ENIAC was not completed until 1946 and so missed World War II service. However, once operational at the Aberdeen Proving Ground, the ENIAC worked well until 1955.

ENIAC was a massive machine that weighed more than 30 tons. It used more than 17,000 vacuum tubes, 70,000 resistors, and 10,000 capacitors. There were no integrated circuits or printed circuits in those days, so construction involved more than 5,000,000 hand-soldered joints, according to Wikipedia.

As is common with vacuum tube devices, tube failure was common. In fact, several tubes burned out every day. A partial solution to this problem was to leave the computer running twenty-four hours a day (at great cost for electricity consumption). This is because most vacuum tube failures occur when they are first turned on and are warming up. In 1948, special high-reliability vacuum tubes were developed, which reduced the frequency of tube failures.

The main designers of ENIAC are the famous computer pioneers John Mauchly and J. Presper Eckert of the University of Pennsylvania, although many others participated in the design and construction.

Many of the technical advances for the ENIAC were patented by Mauchly and Eckert. After Sperry-Rand acquired these patents, the company began to charge royalties for computers built using the same features. This led to a momentous patent violation lawsuit between Sperry-Rand and Honeywell, discussed in later chapters.

Mauchly visited Atanasoff and witnessed the ABC computer in operation. There was also correspondence between Mauchly and Atanasoff about the differences between ABC and the proposed ENIAC. This interaction would play a major role in future decades when there were mutual patent lawsuits between Sperry-Rand and Honeywell.

In 1944, Mauchly and Eckert started the design of a more advanced computer called the EDVAC. The EDVAC was not finished until 1949, and John von Neumann was part of the final team. As with ENIAC, the EDVAC was aimed at ballistics calculations and was funded by the Army's Ballistic Research Laboratory.

Both ENIAC and EDVAC came to the attention of nuclear scientists at Los Alamos, who realized that computers would play a role in solving complex nuclear equations. One of these scientists at Los Alamos was John von Neumann. The notes prepared by von Neumann on the design of EDVAC became world-famous as the essence of the architecture of future digital computers.

The decade from 1940 to 1949 was heavily influenced by the work of von Neumann, who was a polymath and who made contributions not only in computer architecture but also in pure mathematics, nuclear energy, set theory, linear programming, and many other fields. He published 150 scientific and mathematical papers on many important topics.

It was von Neumann's seminal paper in 1945 titled "First Draft of a Report on the EDVAC" that established the *von Neumann architecture* as the basis for computer hardware design. However, another paper in 1945 by Alan Turing titled "Automatic Computing Engine (ACE)" is remarkably similar to the von Neumann report, and probably von Neumann had seen the Turing paper or knew of it.

The von Neumann architecture envisioned a digital computer as comprising a processing unit for math and logic calculations, a control unit, internal memory for storing both data and instructions, and a bus or channel for fetching data and instructions as they were needed. There would also be external mass storage and input/output mechanisms.

Although the von Neumann architecture has been visibly successful in hundreds of computing machines, it had one feature that has been questioned. The von Neumann architecture uses a single bus for both fetching data and instructions, which limits performance. This is called the von Neumann bottleneck. Other machine architectures, such as the Harvard architecture, envisioned separate buses for data and for instructions.

Future generations of researchers would also discover that the von Neumann architecture might have security vulnerabilities that hackers could take advantage of.

Another computer started during World War II was known as the Harvard Mark I. The official name was the IBM Automatic Sequence Controlled Calculator (ASCC). This was an electromechanical computer commissioned in 1943 and constructed in 1944. The U.S. Navy's Bureau of Ships issued the contract.

The Harvard Mark I was designed by another famous computer pioneer, Howard H. Aiken of Harvard. The computer itself was built at IBM in Endicott, New York, and transferred to Harvard upon completion in 1944.

Another famous software pioneer who was also part of the Mark I design team was Grace Hopper. She later became famous for the development of COBOL and for becoming a U.S. Navy Admiral at the peak of her illustrious career.

Grace Hopper took a leave of absence from Vassar in 1943 and joined the WAVES, which was the U.S. Navy organization for women personnel. At the time of the Mark I project, her Navy rank was Lieutenant JG.

Note

Grace Hopper's military career was in the Navy Reserve rather than the regular Navy. She was promoted to Rear Admiral in 1985 and at the time of her retirement in 1986, she was the oldest serving naval officer at age 79. She was a polymath who made great contributions to software and computer engineering. I had the honor of attending one of her speeches just before her retirement. She was an excellent public speaker as well as a brilliant inventor and administrator.

As examples of why early computers were expensive, the Harvard Mark I had 500 miles of wire and more than 3,000,000 soldered connections.

The Mark I was followed by other Aiken designs called the Mark II, Mark III, and Mark IV. None of these should be confused with the British Mark I designed in Manchester, which became operational in 1948.

Aiken caused hard feelings at IBM by announcing the Mark I as his sole invention and for failing to name any of the IBM designers and builders other than James Bryce. This annoyed the IBM Chairman, Thomas J. Watson, and led to IBM moving in a different direction.

The direction IBM selected was to build the IBM Selective Sequence Electronic Calculator (SSEC), The design of the SSEC started in 1944, but the machine was not completed until 1947. The SSEC was the very last electromechanical computer completed. After it, all computers were purely electronic.

Wallace John Eckert of Columbia University (no relation to Presper Eckert) designed the SSEC, but it was constructed at IBM Endicott under the supervision of John McPherson using some technology by an IBM engineer, James Bryce. Francis Hamilton and Robert Seeber also contributed to the design.

The SSEC was not Turing complete and was more of a high-speed calculator than a true computer. However, the SSEC did much to make computers known to the general public. The SSEC was installed in New York near IBM and was located in a former shoe store with a plate-glass window that allowed passersby to see the machine.

The SSEC was a large and impressive machine; because it was going on public display, it was designed to look impressive. The SSEC started a trend of glass-wall, raised-floor computer rooms, which hundreds of companies imitated to show off their entries into the computer era. Of course, terrorism reversed this trend, and computers are now located out of sight in secure buildings.

The SSEC was the first operational computer to be put on public display, and it garnered IBM a great deal of favorable publicity. Partly to present a clean appearance to pedestrians passing by, the SSEC computer was the first to inspire the use of raised floors with cables hidden from view.

Several famous software pioneers were programmers on the SSEC, including John Backus, Herb Grosch, and Ted Codd, later to become famous as the inventor of the relational database concept.

IBM filed a patent on the stored-program capabilities of the SSEC; this patent was later upheld and remains a basis for storing programs and data.

Computers in the Postwar Era

Germany surrendered to the Allies on May 8, 1945, which is now called V-E Day and stands for Victory in Europe. Japan surrendered on August 15, 1945, V-J Day (Victory over Japan). These surrenders ended the immediate hostilities between the Allies and the Axis powers, but they did not reduce the need for either analog or digital computers for military use.

Soon after the end of hostilities, tensions began to occur between the Soviet Union and its former allies. By 1947, this tension had started to be called "the Cold War" and this state of mutual hostility lasted until 1991.

A group of computer engineers meeting in New York at Columbia University on September 15, 1947, decided to form the Association of Computing Machinery (ACM), which is an important business association of computer manufacturers. This organization has become one of the largest technical associations in the world. Its original mission statement is still valid today: "The purpose of this organization would be to advance the science, development, and construction and the application of the new machinery for computing, reasoning, and other handling of information." There are currently about 100,000 ACM members and 170 regional and local chapters. Because of the diversity of computer and software technologies, there are numerous special interest groups (SIGs) within the ACM umbrella. Currently, there are about thirty-five of these SIGs.

Many of the SIGs are famous in their own right, and their conferences are often venues where interesting new inventions surface. Among the special interest groups are SIGCOM for communications, SIGGRAPH for graphical topics, and SIGPLAN for programming languages.

There was a subcommittee on large-scale computing within the American Institute of Electronic Engineers (AIEE) in 1946. Another association was the Institute of Radio Engineers (IRE), which had a committee on electronic computers in 1951. The AIEE and IRE would eventually merge in 1963 to become the Institute of Electrical and Electronic Engineers (IEEE), which would include the IEEE Computer Society, whose headquarters are located in Washington, D.C. The IEEE Computer Society has numerous conferences and publishes thirteen peer-reviewed journals.

There are also computing and software associations in many other countries. These include the British Computer Society, the Computer Society of India, the Australian Computer Society, and many more. Computing and software have vast nets of social groups that share information via conferences, journals and, in today's world, the web.

In 1947, two inventors, Thomas Goldsmith and Estie Ray Mann, filed a patent for using a cathode ray tube as a gaming device. This would later explode into a multibillion-dollar game industry within future decades.

The Cold War Begins

In 1949, the Soviet Union detonated its first atomic bomb, and this led to the concept of *mutually assured destruction*, which meant that an atomic war on both sides would probably blast everyone back to the Stone Age. The Soviet atomic bombs helped to keep the Cold War cool, since neither side wanted a full-scale atomic conflict.

The Soviet atomic bomb also had a major impact on computers and software. A direct response to the Soviet bomb was a new and massive air-defense system called SAGE, which stood for semiautomatic ground environment. SAGE will be discussed in the next chapter.

In 1949, Nationalist Chinese forces evacuated the mainland for Taiwan and the Chinese Communist government took over, which also led to tense relations with Western countries.

These tense relationships led to military arms races on both sides, and part of such escalation involved designing and building newer and more powerful computers of both digital and analog forms.

Postwar Computer Development

Two of the more technically important postwar computers were developed at Victoria University in Manchester, England. The first was the Manchester Mark I, also called the Small-Scale Experimental Machine (SSEM), which was operational in 1948.

The second and larger computer was the Manchester Automatic Digital Machine (MADM), which was operational in 1949. The British press called this machine an "electronic brain," and this started a dispute between the engineering side of the university and the medical school. The dispute centered on whether computers could ever be creative.

The MADM led to 34 patents, some of which were later used in the IBM 701 and IBM 702 computers. The designers of the MADM were Frederic Williams and Tom Kilburn.

Kilburn and Williams filed a patent for a special kind of cathode ray tube called the Williams-Kilburn tube. It provided one of the first and fastest memory devices for storing digital data. Some of the early computers that used Williams-Kilburn tubes included the IBM 701 and IBM 702, the Univac Whirlwind, and the Ferranti Mark I.

When a dot is drawn on a cathode ray tube, it results in a positive charge, and the area surrounding the dot becomes negative. The charges spontaneously disperse, but they can be read and manipulated to store data. These tubes permitted random access, which was a major advance that opened up new kinds of computation.

Williams-Kilburn tubes were somewhat troublesome and not fully reliable. They were used during the late 1940s but were soon replaced by magnetic core memory devices in the early 1950s. Magnetic core memory was faster and more reliable.

However, when first introduced, magnetic cores had to be assembled by hand, using retrained garment workers who could deal with very small objects. In the early years of core memory, hundreds of garment workers in Europe and the United States were retrained to build computer core memories. As it happens, automated equipment for garment making occurred at about the same time, so otherwise the garment workers might have been laid off or unemployed.

Later in 1964, Dr. Robert Dennard of IBM's Thomas J. Watson Research Center would receive U.S. patent 3,387,286 for the invention of DRAM, which would supplant older forms of computer memory. Several researchers working on core memory had filed patents, including Forrester and An Wang (who later founded Wang Laboratories). There were several years of patent disputes that were eventually resolved when IBM purchased all of the patents related to magnetic memory cores.

Another technically interesting postwar computer was the Electronic Delay Storage Automatic Calculator (EDSAC). This computer was built at the Mathematical Laboratory at Cambridge University in Great Britain. The designer was Maurice Wilkes and his colleagues. EDSAC was operational in May 1949 and was used to compute prime numbers, among other things.

As the name implies, the EDSAC used mercury delay lines for memory rather than cathode ray tubes. The mercury delay memory did not provide random access but was fairly reliable for sequential access.

An EDSAC programmer named David Wheeler is credited with having received the first Ph.D. in Computer Science in Great Britain. He is also credited with inventing the concept of subroutines. Subroutines would later be important in many programming languages, and they also led to the first creation of reusable code.

Some of the EDSAC library of 87 subroutines included floating point arithmetic, trigonometric functions, and exponentiation. Subroutines also allowed loops, and thus the *do while* loop was a feature of subroutines used on the EDSAC.

One of the most important postwar computers is the Whirlwind computer built by the Massachusetts Institute of Technology (MIT). The U.S. Navy approached MIT in 1944 about building a flight simulator for training bomber crews. The idea was to have a more realistic flight experience than was provided by the mechanical LINK trainer.

In 1947, Perry Crawford and Robert Everett completed the design of the Whirlwind (after prototype analog devices proved inadequate). The Whirlwind digital computer went operational on April 20, 1951.

The engineering team that built the Whirlwind worked for three years and included about 175 personnel, including seventy engineers and technicians. As can be seen, computers constructed from circuits that require hand soldering of connections are not easy to build. This is why the computer industry would be a small niche industry without the later development of integrated circuits in the next decade.

Among the novel features of the Whirlwind was the use of 16 math units operating in parallel, which made the Whirlwind sixteen times faster than computers using serial math.

The Whirlwind initially used mercury delay lines for memory. In a mercury delay line, a tube of liquid mercury had a microphone at one end and a transducer at the other end. Pulses were sent into the mercury and moved through it at the speed of sound until they were received at the other end. The signals were then amplified and sent back again, so the memory recirculated. The speed of sound varied with temperature, so the mercury delay lines did not operate at constant speeds, which caused problems. In addition to erratic performance, mercury is poisonous, so broken tubes were an occupational hazard of some significance.

Both mercury delay lines and cathode ray tubes were too slow and unreliable to be effective as computer memory devices. The project manager for Whirlwind was Jay Forrester. He had read about a new form of magnetic material and ordered samples. He experimented in his spare time at a workbench in the corner of the lab. After several months Forrester developed magnetic core memory. His first prototype consisted of thirty-two cores, each about 3/8 of an inch in diameter.

Forrester turned over the memory core project to a graduate student, and within two years, magnetic core memory was ready to go commercial to replace mercury delay lines and cathode ray tubes as the memory storage of choice for digital computers. Later, IBM developed the magnetic core concept as well as machines to speed up core memory construction.

The Whirlwind computer would be the basis of the SAGE air-defense system in the next decade and some of its technology would also find its way into SABRE, although improved by IBM. (SABRE stands for Semi-Automated Business Research Environment, which is a somewhat convoluted name perhaps selected merely to use the acronym "sabre.")

An informal use of the Whirlwind computer was the development of a "bouncing ball" game in about 1949 by a researcher named Charley Adams. This was a precursor to later games such as Pong that would generate billions in revenue. It is interesting that computer games started to appear almost as soon as computers themselves.

Eckert and Mauchly formed the Eckert-Mauchly Computer Company (EMCC) in 1949 and it later became Univac. This was the world's first pure digital computer company.

Northrup Grumman commissioned EMCC to build a computer for corporate use, and the result was the Binary Automatic Computer (BINAC). This computer had two separate processing units, each of which could hold 512 words. Mercury delay lines were used for memory storage.

Since the computer was commissioned for a client, it can be considered the world's first commercial computer, but that is really stretching the definition of "commercial," which normally implies multiple customers and multiple sales of the same product. The BINAC was definitely the first contract computer, but only one was built and there was only one customer.

As examples of how difficult and small computer programs were in this era, some of the BINAC test programs were each five to seven lines of code, and a "big" program during testing was 23 lines of code. The largest test program prior to delivery was 50 lines of code.

The BINAC was delivered to Northrup in September 1949, but it did not work properly after delivery. Northrup claimed the computer was not packed properly or was damaged in shipping. EMCC stated that the computer had probably not been assembled properly by Northrup, since EMCC personnel were not permitted onsite and assembly was performed by a graduate student without assistance from EMCC.

Historical Contributions of the Decade

The literature and data on early computers are surprisingly ambiguous for such an important technology. This is partly due to independent work in a number of countries where the computer pioneers were unaware of similar work elsewhere. It is also partly due to the fact that a number of models and upgrades were built, often using the nomenclature of Mark I, Mark II, Mark III, and so forth. However, since this nomenclature was used for different computers in different countries, it is sometimes hard to tell which specific "mark" a reference is citing.

Table 3.1 shows the approximate sequence of digital computer construction from 1940 to 1950. There are various sources that often provide different

Table 3.1 *Computers Developed from 1940 to 1950*

Year	Computer Name	Country	Primary Designers
1940	Cryptographic bombe	U.K.	Alan Turing
1941	Z3	Germany	Konrad Zuse
1942	ABC	U.S.	John Atanasoff, Clifford Berry
1943	Colossus	U.K	T. H. Flowers
1944	Harvard Mark I	U.S.	Howard H. Aiken, James Bryce, Grace Hopper
1944	Bell Labs Model 3	U.S.	George Stibitz
1945	Z4	Germany	Konrad Zuse
1946	ENIAC	U.S.	J. Presper Eckert, John Mauchly
1947	SSEC	U.S.	Wallace John Eckert, Robert Seeber
1948	SSEM	U.K.	Frederic Williams, Tom Kilburn
1949	BINAC	U.S.	J. Presper Eckert, John Mauchly
1949	EDSAC	U.K.	Maurice Wilkes
1949	CSIR Mark I	Australia	Trevor Pearcey, Malcom Beard
1949	EDVAC	U.S.	John Mauchly, J. Presper Eckert, John von Neumann
1949	MADM	U.K.	Frederic Williams, Tom Kilburn
1950	MESM	Ukraine	Alexey Lebedev
1950	Pilot Model ACE	U.K.	Alan Turing

timelines for when these machines were completed, so this table provides only an approximation of when these computers were first activated during this decade.

The earlier computers were electromechanical, while the later computers were electronic. None of them used transistors or integrated circuits, because neither of these inventions would be patented until later in the 1950s. Tubes and relays provided the computing power. Mercury delay lines and cathode ray tubes provided the storage. The magnetic core arrived for the Whirlwind in 1951, so it is not shown in Table 3.1.

These early computers were not commercial products but were custom built by hand and required thousands of vacuum tubes and relays and millions of hand-soldered joints. Early computer construction was highly labor intensive in the era before printed circuits and automated assembly lines.

As can be seen from Table 3.1, computer research during the war years and the postwar era was a truly international undertaking, with the United States and the United Kingdom spending the most money on digital computers due to military necessity.

Germany had very early and rather sophisticated computers created by Konrad Zuse but did not think that they benefited the war effort, so little or no funding came from the German government, which is fortunate for the Allies.

Table 3.2 shows the approximate numbers of software applications developed in the United States from 1940 through 1949. Military and defense software dominated during this decade due to World War II and the Cold War.

Table 3.2   *U.S. Software Applications from 1940 to 1949*

Application Types	Applications	Percentage
Scientific	75	37.50%
Military and defense	100	50.00%
Civilian government	10	5.00%
Systems and middleware	10	5.00%
Embedded software	0	0.00%
Commercial	5	2.50%
Information technology (IT)	0	0.00%
U.S. outsource	0	0.00%
Offshore outsource	0	0.00%

Table 3.2   *(Continued)*

Application Types	Applications	Percentage
Web applications	0	0.00%
Games and entertainment	0	0.00%
Open source	0	0.00%
Total Applications	**200**	**100.00%**

During this decade, assembly language and macro-assembly language were the norm. High-level languages would not appear until the next decade.

Building Software in 1945

Function points had not been invented, so all data were measured by using lines of code. Although this example shows software of 1,000 function points, in the 1940s, most applications were all below 100 function points. This is just a hypothetical prediction. Backfiring or mathematical conversion from lines of code (LOC) to function points show these results for a project of 1,000 function points in this decade:

- Source code for 1,000 function points: 320,000 logical code statements

- Programming language: Basic assembly language

- Reuse percentage: 0% to 1%

- Methodology: Mathematicians or engineers, ad hoc programming

- Productivity: 2.5 function points per staff month

- Defect potentials: 7.50 per function points

- Defect removal efficiency (DRE): 75%

- Delivered defects: 1.875 defects per function point

- Ratio of development personnel to maintenance:

  - Development: 97%

  - Maintenance: 3%

The following are the background data for 1945:

- Average language level: 1
- Number of programming languages: 2
- Logical statements per function point: 320
- Average application size: 1 function point
- Average application size: 320 logical code statements

This decade was characterized by custom hardware and limited memory size. Large programs were impossible because computer memory could not store them.

By the end of the decade, digital computers began to show value but were much too large and expensive for general use. Only military organizations and some universities could afford digital computers. The next decade would see major changes in hardware and major expansion of software.

Programming was also poised to expand, with the development of subroutines and reusable code laying the foundation for future high-level programming languages.

Summary

At the start of the 1940s, World War II rapidly engulfed the world in one of the most devastating conflicts in history. The war led to a massive increase in the need for rapid calculations for military ballistics, cryptanalysis, and other military necessities.

As a result of these military needs, the Allies and the Axis powers both increased their spending on analog and digital computers. Digital computers were used by the Allies to break key military codes for both Germany and Japan, which probably shortened the war and raised the odds of Allied success. Analog computers were built by the thousands for naval fire control, submarine torpedo launching, antiaircraft fire control, and also bombsights linked to autopilots.

At the beginning of the decade, the word "computer" was a job description applied to a human mathematician. By the end of the decade, the word "computer" was starting to be used as it is today, as the name for a high-speed electronic calculating device. The rapid advances of this decade due to military needs would lead to computers entering the business world.

Chapter 4

1950 to 1959: Starting the Ascent of Digital Computers and Software

The 1950s witnessed the migration of computers from military and academic purposes into the business domain. It also witnessed the evolution from custom-built, special-purpose computers to commercial computers such as the Ferranti Mark I, LEO I, UNIVAC I, IBM 701, and IBM 650. Even more important, transistors and integrated circuits were patented during this decade and began to be used on production computers. By the end of this decade, computers were being built globally in China, Russia, Poland, Japan, and many other countries. Programming became a significant occupation and the early "high-level" languages of FORTRAN, COBOL, and LISP were created. The term "software" as we know it was coined. The Cold War and the Korean War continued to demand increased funding for both digital and analog computers, and they also increased the importance of software in military and civilian sectors.

Military and Defense Computers in the 1950s

The tense Cold War between the Soviet Union and the United States and its allies continued during the 1950s. The first Soviet atomic bomb was detonated on August 29, 1949. Needless to say, having the Soviet Union join the nuclear club triggered a massive increase in defense funding for both weapons systems and computer technology. U.S. air defenses needed a major upgrade. It was also obvious that manual air defenses could not possibly be effective, so computerization was mandatory.

SAGE

In the previous decade, defense funding for computers was far greater for analog computers for fire control and ballistics than for digital computers. Very early in the 1950s, the balance began to swing toward digital computers with the SAGE system, or semiautomatic ground environment, which eventually became the most expensive computer ever built, and the SAGE software program became the most expensive program to date. These would remain the most expensive until the end of the decade. After SAGE, large systems and large expenses would sweep through both the defense and business communities.

The SAGE air-defense system would soon create the world's largest digital computer and the world's largest military software application. The convergence of computing, software, and defense was about to hit full stride.

The SAGE project was a landmark in several respects. Perhaps the most important is that it marked the transition of digital computers from dealing with a narrow band of specialized problems to tackling huge and diverse problems of enormous complexity. It is not even remotely possible to provide an effective air-defense system for an entire country without the use of fast digital computers to aggregate all of the torrents of incoming data from thousands of sources.

SAGE also marked a transition between *batch* computation, which could take place at a time convenient to the engineers, to *real-time* computation, which processed new data instantly as it occurred. In future decades, real-time computation would lead to new forms of *embedded computers* that were located inside of physical devices such as automobiles and would constantly monitor and control things like brake systems and fuel injection.

Another important transition introduced by SAGE was continuous operation with high reliability 24 hours per day, 365 days of the year. Prior to SAGE, computers would work for a few hours and then be shut down until needed again. With SAGE, the computers were always needed.

The need for continuous around-the-clock operation also spurred a need for much better quality control on all software applications. That led to new features that allowed computers to monitor their own statuses, or the status of attached computers, and alert console operators to potential problems before they occurred. It also introduced the concept of redundancy, or backup, computers that could take over if a computer needed to be repaired or modified.

As a result of SAGE, within a few decades, the Department of Defense would own more computers than any other organization in the world. Every defense department in every major country would begin to use computers as critical components of weapons systems; air defense; and all military operations on land, on sea, and in the air.

SAGE was not just a computer and software. It was a very large and complex hybrid system that used hundreds of radar receivers feeding real-time data into 24 Direction Centers, each of which was a large building housing at least one *IBM AN/FSQ-7 Combat Direction Central* computer.

The SAGE system interconnected all the Direction Centers, and it also connected with the Army air-defense command posts. Many missile launch sites were also included in the SAGE architecture, which could direct the firing of Nike air-defense missiles as well as long-range strategic missiles aimed at retaliation in the event of an attack.

Prior to SAGE, there were numerous radar installations, but they were independently operated. There was also a Ground Observation Corps with 8,000 lookout stations that were only connected by telephones to command centers. A hurricane or a Nor'easter could shut down air defenses because it would interfere with radar tracks, block visual sighting of anything above the clouds, and blow down many telephone lines, thus cutting off vital defense communication.

Development of the SAGE air-defense system started circa 1950 at the beginning of the decade, and the system became operational in 1958. There were a number of upgrades to SAGE computers and other hardware devices over the years until replacement in 1983.

The original SAGE software package consisted of about 500,000 statements in a basic assembly language, which is equivalent to about 15,625 function points. While this was the largest software application at that time, there are now applications that are more than 10 times larger.

The SAGE system operated until 1983, when it was replaced by newer systems using a combination of airborne radar and ground command posts. The total cost of SAGE was not released, but it is estimated to approach $12 billion during the 1960s (or perhaps $100 billion in today's dollars).

The IBM AN/FSQ-7 SAGE computer was physically the largest computer ever built, and that claim is probably true even today because, soon after, transistorized integrated circuits would shrink computers to a small fraction of the size of vacuum tube computers. The IBM SAGE computer had about 60,000 vacuum tubes and weighed about 250 tons.

The SAGE technology, developed by IBM in Kingston, New York, would play a major part in civilian air-traffic control systems in future years and would also be part of the SABRE airline reservation system (or *Semi-Automatic Business Research Environment*). In fact, some of the IBM personnel from SAGE moved into SABRE development later in the decade.

SAGE and SABRE catapulted computers and software from laboratory curiosities used for a narrow band of scientific and military calculations into major tools that would revolutionize both national defense and business operations. SAGE and later SABRE also catapulted IBM to the top of computer companies, a place where it still resides today.

SAGE also started a trend that still continues today. The costs of World War II weapons were a fairly small component of the United States' annual budget. Starting with SAGE and other new weapons systems, military spending became a progressively larger part of the national budget.

BOMARC

SAGE was not the only new computerized weapon system during this decade. In 1959, the Boeing BOMARC supersonic guided missile was added to the U.S. arsenal. It used an analog computer for guidance combined with navigation from SAGE computers.

The name of this missile was a combination of Boeing and the University of Michigan Aeronautical Research Center. The "BO" came from Boeing and the "MARC" came from the Michigan research lab.

This was the first long-range operational air-defense missile in the U.S. arsenal. It had a range of 400 miles in its later forms and could be launched instantly because hundreds were kept in constant readiness. The BOMARC could reach altitudes of 80,000 feet, which was higher than any other combat aircraft at the time. It flew at about Mach 2.5, so it was faster than any contemporary combat aircraft that it might encounter.

The BOMARC missiles depended on navigation instructions from the SAGE air-defense system for their initial trajectory, but their own onboard radar, sensors, and analog computers could handle the final few miles to detonation.

Neither SAGE nor BOMARC were used in actual combat, and that is perhaps one of their virtues. They were considered to be fairly formidable defense systems that could wipe out enough inbound attacking aircraft to make air strikes on U.S. and Canadian territory unlikely to succeed.

Cultural Perceptions of Computers

During the 1950s, computers began to be featured in Hollywood films and in thriller novels. For example, shots of the actual SAGE computers were used in the films *Voyage to the Bottom of the Sea* and *Conquest of the Planet of the Apes*. When

Hollywood took computers to heart, that also bolstered the attractiveness of programming as an occupation.

In 1951, Arthur C. Clarke, the science fiction writer, published a collection of short stories titled *Sentinel of Eternity*. One of these stories would later be expanded in 1968 into both a film by Stanley Kubrick and a novel by Clarke called *2001: A Space Odyssey*, which featured the HAL computer as the chief villain. It is probably not a coincidence that the letters "HAL" are all one letter below "IBM."

By the end of the 1950s, computers had become so powerful that it would not seem unbelievable for HAL to converse with human astronauts.

Innovators of the 1950s

At the start of the 1950s, mathematically trained human "computers" were employed by the thousands to perform both sophisticated scientific mathematical calculations and also to do mundane accounting math for billing, salaries, taxes, and the like.

By the end of the decade, the term "computer" had morphed into meaning a digital computer, and the occupation of computer programmer was starting to occur in significant numbers, while the older occupation of human mathematical "computers" was in rapid decline and would soon disappear.

In the 1950s, universities with strong engineering and science departments began to teach courses on computers and software. For example, UCLA's initial courses in 1950 were taught by Douglas Pfister and Willis Ware. The Institute for Numerical Analysis was formed at UCLA to work with RAND and military organizations on the use of computers. Other universities, such as Princeton, Harvard, and MIT, also began to incorporate computer-related courses into engineering curricula.

During this decade, several major inventions began the expansion of computers and software from being massive and complex laboratory instruments to becoming global commercial products.

Two critical background inventions, among the most important in the history of science, were the development of transistors to replace vacuum tubes and the invention of integrated circuits to replace discrete electronic components. The first silicon transistor was produced by Texas Instruments in 1974. However, a long history led to this result.

In 1947, William Bardeen and Walter Brattan of AT&T Bell Labs developed a prototype semiconductor based on Germanium. The group leader, William

Shockley, participated in expanding the idea. In 1956, Bardeen, Brattan, and Shockley received the Nobel Prize in Physics for the discovery of the transistor effect.

They were not alone; even earlier work by Julius Lillenfield in the 1920s and by Oskar Heil in the 1930s led to both patenting concepts similar to transistors. However, these did not lead to working models.

Incidentally, the term "transistor" was coined by John R. Pierce of Bell Labs from the combination of the words "transfer resistor." Bell Labs was the research arm of AT&T. Fortunately for the industry, Bell scientists recommended sharing and licensing transistor technology. In 1952, Bell Labs sponsored a nine-day transistor technology symposium, which attracted 100 researchers. Of those who participated, 40 each paid a $25,000 license fee to gain access to transistor technology.

The openness with patents and intellectual property in the 1950s is very different from today's fierce patent wars, which are threatening to stifle innovation or at least make new products extremely expensive to build due to artificially high patent license fees. This era was also before the "patent troll" subindustry appeared. The companies in this group buy patent rights not because of their intellectual value but rather because of their use as threats to gain royalty payments.

In 1949, a German scientist from Siemens AG filed a patent for an *integrated circuit* that he envisioned would use transistors. Later in 1952, Geoffrey Dummer from the British Royal Radio Establishment gave a public lecture on the need for integrated circuits.

In about 1950, a Russian researcher, S. A. Lebedev, built a vacuum tube digital computer in Ukraine called MESM to solve equations in nuclear engineering and rocketry. Lebedev moved to Moscow and eventually developed some 15 different computer models.

A few months after Lebedev's MESM was operational, another Russian researcher, Isaac Brook, and his colleagues built the M-1 computer, which used semiconductor diodes instead of tubes. This is claimed to be the first stored-program computer built in Russia.

In late 1951, the first American commercial digital computer went on the market. This was the famous UNIVAC I, designed by John Mauchly and Presper Eckert. In 1951, Remington Rand purchased the Eckert-Mauchly Computer Company and its name was changed to Univac. In the 1950s, Univac and IBM competed in the nascent market for mainframe digital computers.

In 1952, President Harry S. Truman signed a letter that authorized the creation of the National Security Agency (NSA). This agency replaced an amalgamation of separate military security groups, and it expanded its role from military intelligence to true national intelligence.

In later years, the NSA would become the world's most sophisticated user of computers and also the owner of the world's most powerful computers. The NSA itself would contribute to software engineering and the development of encryption technologies.

In 1957, the Japanese Ministry of International Trade and Industry (MITI) placed a 25% tariff on computers and components imported into Japan. This spurred the growth of Japanese computer companies such as Fujitsu, which soon competed with American companies in global markets. Japan also pursued competition in the market for computer components such as transistors and dynamic random-access memory (DRAM) chips.

As is widely known, the Japanese industrial companies were among the first to apply the concepts of W. Edwards Deming and Joseph Juran to industrial quality control. (Deming's contributions started in the 1940s and early 1950s. Juran's started in early 1954.) In 1950, the Japanese Union of Scientists and Engineers (JUSE) invited W. Edwards Deming of the United States to teach a 30-day seminar on statistical quality control. This seminar also paved the way for the later Deming Prize for quality.

The high quality of Japanese products benefited their market shares in a variety of products, including computer chips, computer memory, televisions and portable radios, and automobiles. Eventually, Japan pulled ahead of the United States in these markets due in part to very high manufacturing quality levels.

In 1958, a researcher named Jack Kilby at Texas Instruments demonstrated a working integrated circuit. This idea was patented in 1959 and was soon used by the U.S. Air Force. In 2000, Kilby won the Nobel Prize in Physics for his invention of the integrated circuit.

Suffice it to say that without transistors and integrated circuits, none of the tiny computerized electronic devices that are common today would be possible. Without transistors and integrated circuits, software would probably be a small niche industry that supported a few dozen mainframe computers that use vacuum tubes. Neither personal computers nor embedded devices would be possible without low-power microscopic transistors and integrated circuits.

In 1958, a mathematician and statistician from Bell Labs named John Wilder Tukey used the word "software" in a paper. This was in the context of being a separate entity from "hardware." This is the first known use of the word "software" in a computer context.

Also in 1958, the first local computer was built in mainland China. It was a vacuum tube computer called the 901, and it was constructed by the Institute of Military Engineering at the University of Harbin.

Programming Languages of the 1950s

Three key high-level programming languages were developed in the mid-1950s and their usage expanded during the 1960s: FORTRAN in 1955, LISP in 1958, and COBOL in 1959. Ideas and seeds for other languages such as ALGOL also started prior to 1960. However, for much of the decade, assembly language was the most common language in use.

COBOL stands for "common business-oriented language." FORTRAN stands for "formula translator." LISP's name is derived from list processing. These names reflect the fact that these new languages were becoming specialized for math, business, or other kinds of problems.

While COBOL, LISP, and FORTRAN were developed in the United States, dozens of other languages were developed in other countries and had different names, even though some were variations on older languages. ALGOL was developed jointly between U.S. and European researchers.

Not only do languages have many dialects or variations, but they also change and add features over time. For example, there were ALGOL versions called ALGOL 58, ALGOL 60, and ALGOL 68 and another revision in 1973. There are also dozens of ALGOL-like languages based on some of the defined features, such as SIMULA.

Early computers were coded in *machine language*, which is so highly complex that errors were rampant and hard to find and fix. Assembly languages introduced mnemonic source instructions that were somewhat easier to understand than binary numbers or machine language.

Originally, assembly languages had a one-to-one correspondence with machine languages in that each source statement was translated into a single machine instruction. Later, the concept of *macro-assembly languages* expanded the scope of assembly source-code statements.

A macro instruction was a method that allowed a number of statements to be created and named separately. The collected statements were called *macros*; a macro instruction is still a quick way of adding reusable features to an application.

The First Commercial Computers

A *commercial computer* is a computer that is built specifically to be sold or leased to paying customers rather than for internal use within the organization that built it.

The history of early commercial computers is ambiguous and confusing when you try to pin down who developed the first commercial computer. The U.S. historical literature claims that the UNIVAC I was the first commercial computer sold to paying clients. Some U.K. literature claims that the LEO I computer was delivered a month prior to the UNIVAC I. Another British machine, the Ferranti Mark I, also claims to have been delivered before UNIVAC I.

Table 4.1 shows the delivery dates of early digital computers.

Regardless of who built the first commercial digital computer, the idea of computing as a business tool was rapidly expanding. There would soon be dozens of commercial digital computers on the market, and a wave of startup computer manufacturers would continue to expand for two more decades.

LEO

The British LEO computer has a background that is historically and sociologically interesting. The J. Lyons Company was not a high-technology company but rather one of Britain's largest food-catering and food-producing companies. It also ran tea shops throughout the United Kingdom.

Two Lyons executives, Oliver Standingford and Raymond Thomson, visited the United States in 1947 to look at new business methods developed during the war. While there, they met one of the ENIAC computer developers and saw the potential of computers for aiding large business operations.

Table 4.1   *Early Digital Computer Delivery Dates*

Delivery Date	Digital Computer	Country of Origin
February 10, 1950	Ferranti Mark I	United Kingdom
March 31, 1951	UNIVAC I	United States
September 5, 1951	LEO I	United Kingdom
April 29, 1952	IBM 701	United States
July 14, 1953	IBM 650	United States

Upon returning to the United Kingdom, Standingford and Thomson visited the British EDSAC computer, then under development. Standingford and Thomson reported favorably on computers to the Lyons board, which voted to provide £3,000 to help speed up the EDSAC development.

Not only was funding provided to EDSAC, but the Lyons board also decided to build a business-oriented computer for the company. This was a bold adventure for a food-processing company that operated tea shops.

The new computer was called the *Lyons Electronic Office*, or LEO, I. A radar engineer named John Pinkerton was hired to run the project and design the computer. A Lyons engineer named Derek Hemy would be the new computer's first programmer.

When completed in 1951, the computer's first production job was bakery valuation. It was also used for payroll calculations, inventory management, and order entry. In other words, the LEO I was immediately useful for handling day-to-day business operations faster and more efficiently than could be done manually.

The LEO I also pioneered outsourcing and service bureau operations, because the computer was soon used under contract to process payrolls for Ford Motors in the United Kingdom. Other clients followed. Outsourcing and service bureaus followed almost immediately in the wake of the first commercial digital computers.

Several upgrades called the LEO II, LEO III, LEO 360, and LEO 326 were built. These were faster and more powerful than LEO I. The later LEO computers featured a multitasking operating system that could run 12 programs simultaneously. Some LEO computers stayed in service as late as 1981, processing telephone bills.

In 1954, Lyons formed a separate company to build the LEO computers, called LEO Computers Limited. The LEO company itself merged with the English Electric Company in 1963 and after several more mergers became part of the company International Computers Limited (ICL) in 1968.

The LEO experience shows that far-sighted business executives from Lyons correctly identified digital computers as the best solution for a wide variety of corporate financial and accounting activities. Their pioneering work helped other companies also move into the computer era.

IBM

1953 marked the introduction of the IBM 701, which is asserted to be the first successful commercial computer, although only 19 were ever made. It was among the first computers used by the Department of Defense. (Currently, the Department of Defense owns more computers than most entire countries do.) The 701 was a vacuum tube computer that used magnetic tape for storage. It was meant for scientific and defense calculations.

The IBM 701 triggered the first computer user group. In 1955, a group of IBM customers in the Los Angeles area founded a user association called SHARE, Inc. This association later moved to Chicago and became a nonprofit corporation.

The idea of computer and software user groups was beneficial to both customers and manufacturers. SHARE members influenced IBM in terms of future features and needs. SHARE members also helped each other with technical advice and even the creation of programs and source code.

SHARE's idea of customer user groups would soon lead to many other similar groups associated with both IBM and other vendors. For IBM, the GUIDE and COMMON associations would be formed. In the 1960s, the DECUS group was formed to support digital equipment customers. User associations are now common for many hardware and software products. The larger associations such as SHARE have regional subdivisions and chapters in many cities.

There were several upgraded versions of the 701 family, but the biggest technical advance was the IBM 7090, which was IBM's first computer with transistors instead of tubes. This computer was announced in 1958. Among its interesting features was an early operating system called IBSYS. This would later evolve into much more powerful operating systems that could keep various hardware components operating in concert. One of the first assembly languages was created for the IBM 701 by Nat Rochester.

Another important invention occurred in 1953 when engineers at IBM's San Jose research facility created the first disk drive, which allowed *random access* to data instead of sequential access, which was normally provided by tape drives. The first commercial disk drive was the IBM RAMAC 350 in 1956. Without disk drives and random access to data, computers would have very limited functionality and later database technologies would not have occurred.

In 1953, IBM released the 650, which was aimed squarely at business customers (the earlier 701 was designed for science and defense customers). The IBM 650 was a market success and between the initial release and 1963, more than 2,000 were sold.

The IBM 650 featured a rotating magnetic drum for memory. Programmers had to be sensitive to drum rotation speed to optimize performance. If a read instruction missed a piece of data, the next opportunity would not occur until the data rotated under the read head again. There was also a small amount of magnetic core memory, used as a buffer between the drum and the processing unit.

For external storage, at first the IBM 650 used only punch cards, but later tape drives were added. Disks were not used in the IBM 650. After RAMAC was invented, disk drives would be added to the later versions of the IBM 650.

One reason for the market success of the IBM 650 was because it was backward-compatible with IBM's punch-card calculating machines. For example, an output deck of cards from an IBM 650 computer could be printed on an earlier IBM 402 accounting machine.

The early versions of the IBM 650 were programmed in machine language. But in 1954, Stan Poley of IBM's T. J. Watson Research Center added the *Symbolic Optimal Assembly Program* (SOAP). Eventually, more than a dozen programming languages would become available for the IBM 650, including FORTRAN in 1957.

Before the IBM 650, universities had built a number of computers, but they were used only for a limited range of scientific studies and had no connection to day-to-day university tasks. The IBM 650 started a trend of using digital computers for academic business activities as well as research tools. Columbia University, for example, would later have about 200 users of their IBM 650 computers.

Other Computer Business Implementations

The 1950s saw the creation of a number of other companies that would help to expand computers and software. Among these were Nixdorf in 1952, Burroughs in 1956, Digital Equipment Corporation (DEC) in 1957, and Control Data Corporation (CDC), also in 1957. Remington Rand acquired the older Eckert-Mauchly company, and it was renamed Univac in 1951.

Some of these same inventions began to find their way into consumer products. In 1954, Regency marketed the first transistor radio. This was followed in 1955 by the more famous Sony TR-55.

1957 witnessed the appearance of the Sony TR-63, the first pocket radio (the TR-55 was too large to be carried in a pocket). This Sony radio pioneered modern personal entertainment devices and expanded Sony into a major global corporation.

In the late 1950s, jet aircraft were added to commercial airline fleets. This fact, combined with a growing economy, increased air traffic by more than 1,000% between 1958 and 1977. With such heavy air traffic, it was becoming unsafe to fly because air-traffic control systems were primitive in the 1950s.

In 1956, two planes collided over the Grand Canyon and 128 people were killed. This spurred Congress to pass the Federal Aviation Act in 1958, which created the Federal Aviation Administration (FAA) to oversee air-traffic control throughout the United States. Computers were used experimentally for air-traffic control in the late 1950s, but a true national, computerized air-traffic control system would not arrive until the 1970s.

By coincidence in 1953, the president of American Airlines, C. R. Smith, happened to sit next to an IBM salesman named R. Blair Smith. The two discussed airline reservations and IBM was invited to visit American Airlines and suggest cooperative action.

This chance encounter led to the cooperative development of the SABRE airline reservation system. It was started in 1959 but not completed until 1964. When complete, SABRE was the largest software application system yet created. An article in *Computer World* on May 29, 2004, reported that SABRE had more than 64 applications totaling about 13,000,000 lines of code. That is roughly equivalent to just over 100,000 function points.

Eventually, the SABRE system would come to be used by more than 350,000 travel agents, 400 airlines, 100,000 hotels, 25 car-rental companies, 50 railroads, and 14 cruiseship lines. The growth and success of SABRE illustrate the power of computers and software to make enormous changes in common business practices.

The downside of computerization is that probably more than 100,000 clerical personnel in these various companies lost their jobs. This loss was partially replaced by the addition, usually within those same companies, of perhaps 30,000 software and data center personnel.

Software Applications in the 1950s

In the 1950s, small applications were the norm, in part due to the difficulty of coding large applications in low-level languages such as assembly.

Table 4.2 shows the approximate numbers of software applications developed from 1950 through 1959. Scientific and military applications continued to dominate during this decade.

During the first part of this era, assembly languages and macro-assembly languages were the norm. Toward the end of the decade, higher-level languages such as FORTRAN and COBOL began to supplant earlier low-level languages.

Table 4.2   *U.S. Software Applications from 1950 to 1959*

Application Types	Applications	Percentage
Scientific	350	30.70%
Military and defense	300	26.32%
Civilian government	125	10.96%
Systems and middleware	75	6.58%
Embedded software	20	1.75%
Commercial	100	8.77%
Information technology (IT)	150	13.16%
U.S. outsource	0	0.00%
Offshore outsource	0	0.00%
Games and entertainment	15	1.32%
Artistic and musical applications	5	0.44%
Web applications	0	0.00%
Open source	0	0.00%
Smartphone applications	0	0.00%
Cloud applications	0	0.00%
Total Applications	**1,140**	**100.00%**

Function Points in 1955

Function points had not been invented, so all data were measured using lines of code. Backfiring or mathematical conversion from lines of code (LOC) to function points show these results for a project of 1,000 function points in this decade:

- Source code for 1,000 function points: 320,000 logical code statements

- Programming language: Basic assembly language

- Reuse percentage: 0% to 5%

- Methodology: Unstructured cowboy development

- Productivity: 3.5 function points per staff month

- Defect potentials: 7.00 per function point

- Defect removal efficiency (DRE): 80%

- Delivered defects: 1.40 defects per function point

- Ratio of development personnel to maintenance:

  - Development: 95%

  - Maintenance: 5%

The following are the background data for 1955:

- Average language level: 1.5

- Number of programming languages: 5

- Logical statements per function point: 213

- Average application size: 200 function points

- Average application size: 42,600 logical code statements

This decade was characterized by a burst of intellectual excitement and a number of key inventions, several of which later earned Nobel Prizes.

At the beginning of this decade, discrete electronic circuits and vacuum tubes were the dominant components of computers and other electronic devices. Computer memory was in the form of mercury delay lines or cathode ray tubes. External memory was paper tape or cards.

By the end of the decade, transistors and integrated circuits were well on their way to universal adoption. Magnetic cores were used for internal memory. Magnetic tape and magnetic disks were used for external memory.

The combination of transistors, integrated circuits, and random-access data storage were all on the critical path leading to the huge expansions of computers and software in future decades. Seldom in history have so many important inventions come to fruition in such a short time span.

Summary

At the start of the 1950s, computers were built by hand, and they each used thousands of vacuum tubes. These custom-built early computers were used primarily for military and mathematical calculations. By the end of the decade, computers had become commercial products for both the military and businesses, and they were manufactured using transistors and integrated circuits. Programming these commercial computers was made easier by the early high-level languages of COBOL, FORTRAN, and LISP. The occupation of computer programmer was starting an ascending trajectory that would soon make it one of the fastest-growing jobs in history.

Chapter 5

1960 to 1969: The Rise of Business Computers and Business Software

In 1960, an IBM patent on magnetic stripes triggered the creation of American Express, Visa, and MasterCard credit cards, which revolutionized retail sales. The magnetic stripe also led to automatic teller machines (ATMs) and electric door locks. To meet a growing demand for new business computers and software, companies such as IBM, RCA, GE, Control Data, and many others marketed new computers aimed specifically at business operations. Database technology also expanded rapidly. These technical changes triggered a huge increase in demand for computer programming personnel.

Two major lawsuits that were filed in the 1960s would change the computer and software industries forever: A patent case decided that the ENIAC patent was invalid, therefore moving computer architecture into the public domain. An IBM agreement to unbundle software as a result of an antitrust suit opened the floodgates to the creation of a huge commercial software industry that would not have been possible had software remained tied to computer hardware.

In this decade, computers would arrive on Wall Street and change the stock and financial markets forever, but not always in a healthy way. The Apollo program took computers and software into space and to the moon. The first Turing award was given in 1966.

An Evolving Workforce

After World War II, the U.S. business environment began to evolve from manufacturing to services. This, in turn, led to a rapid increase in clerical personnel.

According to the Early Office Museum (www.officemuseum.com), the number of U.S. clerical workers increased by 286%, while the entire field of professional workers, including clerical workers, increased by only 85% during the years following World War II.

By the start of the 1960s, clerical work was the dominant form of employment in a number of growing and important industries, including banks, insurance, stock trading, and civilian government operations. A significant number of military personnel also performed clerical work.

Computers and software did not eliminate clerical work, as originally hypothesized, but they did change the nature of the work. For example, many clerks handling medical records shifted into being computer data entry personnel. Clerks handling medical billing began to use computers to track bills. Rather than vanishing, clerical jobs absorbed the use of computers and software.

There were some reductions in clerical employees during the 1960s, but there was also a simultaneous increase in computer and software personnel. In fact, large data centers and programming teams changed banking and insurance operations from being purely manual to almost fully automated.

As an example of the remarkable growth of software during this decade, consider the city of Hartford, Connecticut, and its surrounding towns. For various reasons (including favorable taxes), the Hartford metropolitan area was the home of a number of major insurance companies, including Aetna Insurance, Cigna Insurance, Hartford Insurance, Mass Mutual Insurance, Phoenix Insurance, Travelers Insurance, and others.

At the start of the 1960s, most of these corporations in a major industry were just starting to use computers and software. Yet fairly soon, all of these insurance companies would have data centers and software organizations that averaged about 1,000 personnel each, and Hartford would have more than 50,000 software personnel.

Hartford is perhaps unique because of the high concentration of insurance companies, but all major companies that depended on clerical work were experiencing rapid growth in software and data processing.

Every major bank in America, every insurance company, and every stock brokerage built data centers and recruited software personnel. The largest of these companies would end up employing more than 3,000 software and computer personnel, and even the smaller companies would each employ perhaps 250.

The growth of the computer and software industries in this decade was remarkable. The automobile industry, the oil industry, the telecommunications industry, and the aircraft industry also grew rapidly. However, these other fast-growing industries needed computers and software personnel, so their rapid growth also added to the growth of the software industry.

Eventually, every automobile manufacturer, large oil company, telecommunications company, and aircraft manufacturer would each employ at least 1,000 and sometimes as many as 10,000 software and computer personnel.

Companies such as AT&T, ITT, GTE, and Motorola in the United States and Siemens, Nippon Telephone, and Nokia abroad would end up not only using computers and employing thousands of software personnel but also creating new and innovative kinds of software and computerized telecommunications equipment.

This decade witnessed the arrival of packet switching, pulse-code modulation, binary synchronous communication (BSC), and the invention of IBM's Extended Binary Coded Decimal Interchange Code (EBCDIC) and the American Standard Code for Information Interchange (ASCII). These led to high-speed digital telecommunications switching and, of course, more software personnel for the telecommunications industry.

The arrival of credit cards, debit cards, and ATMs in the early 1960s would not have been possible using only manual clerical workers. Computers and software were necessary adjuncts to these major changes because both credit cards and ATM transactions require real-time processing with results needed in not much more than a few seconds.

The combination of credit cards and ATMs caused the hiring of perhaps 100,000 new computer and software personnel nationally to handle the increased data-processing capabilities of these new financial tools.

Early Specialized Outsourcing

Computers alone are not sufficient for handling large collections of records and data. The 1960s witnessed the emergence of database technology and the arrival of commercial database management systems (DBMS). The early DBMS systems were sequential and handled files with fixed-length field structures. Future decades would see relational databases added to the mix. The IBM *information management system* (IMS) first appeared; it was used on the Apollo spacecraft and also became a successful commercial application.

Because the development of computers and software is not the primary business mission of banks, insurance companies, and many other industries, the rapid growth of software and computing was a mixed blessing. Businesses needed computers and software to compete, but they may or may not have been very efficient and effective in running their own software organizations, which required business skills far removed from their traditional focus.

Thus, the rapid rise of computerization and software would soon create another new industry of specialized companies that provided software and computer power to companies that needed these modern capabilities but did not want the burden of running them. One of the archetypes of these new specialized "outsource" companies was Electronic Data Systems (EDS), which was founded in 1962 by the famous entrepreneur H. Ross Perot (who in 1992 was a candidate for the U.S. presidency).

Another growth industry that resulted from the rise of computers and software was that of management consulting. Several of the large accounting companies created software consulting business units. One of the pioneers was the financial accounting company of Arthur J. Andersen. The consulting portion of this company had a fierce rivalry with the accounting portion, and it eventually split off and became the modern consulting and outsource group of Accenture.

Many other companies entered the management consulting arena during this decade. Among them was the Boston Consulting Group (BCG), founded in 1963.

The rise of computers and software not only had direct impacts on U.S. and global business operations, but these tools also created ancillary businesses in the areas of specialized consulting and outsource companies.

Computer Programmers in the 1960s

This decade is of personal interest to me because it is when I entered the computer business and became a programmer. The way this came about illustrates the informal methods used in those early days before computer science and software engineering were fully established. Young software engineers will probably be surprised and perhaps dismayed at the informal selection process for computer programmers in the 1960s.

Becoming a Programmer

As an undergraduate and graduate student at the University of Florida, there were no on-campus computers during my stay from 1956 through 1961. In fact, the engineering school was only just starting to permit electronic calculators, instead of slide rules, to be used during exams.

During my freshman year, I used a Post Versalog slide rule, which was beautifully made from bamboo and white plastic and had a leather case with a belt strap. Having a slide rule attached to your belt was the hallmark of an engineering student in the 1950s. I still have that slide rule and it brings back memories of an earlier and simpler era.

The University of Florida had no computer science or software engineering courses in those days, although some engineering schools such as Cal Tech and MIT did.

After graduation and a range of jobs for a few years, including some government security work, I became an editor for a medical journal published by the U.S. Public Health Service in Washington, D.C. At about the same time, the Public Health Service acquired some IBM 1401 computers and began to advertise for programmers.

In those days, actual trained programmers were scarce, so the method used was to find people, such as myself, who were familiar with Public Health Service operations and then send them to programming schools.

The selection process included an interesting and, I thought, well-designed aptitude test to see whether candidates were qualified. There were combinations of logical questions and some with a smattering of math. This test was called the *programming aptitude test* (PAT), and it was developed by IBM. It took about an hour to complete.

After passing the aptitude test and being hired as a programmer, I was sent to the local IBM school in Washington, D.C., to learn to program the IBM 1401 using a language called Autocoder.

In the 1960s, programming was not usually taught at universities and never in high school. It was necessary to go to private schools run by companies that built computers such as IBM, RCA, GE, Digital Equipment Corporation, and the like. The instructors were actual programmers and their knowledge was practical and down to earth. There was little theory and a lot of practical information.

Since there were few computer science programs at the university level, the majority of programmers in those days had other majors. In my first programming group, one of the best programmers had been a history major. There were several math majors and also music majors and English majors. A facility with music and a facility with the flow of words are congruent with programming because all three skills involve visualizing and expressing logical sequences. One person in the group only had a high school education but turned out to be a good programmer. Our group had no engineering majors because we were tasked with building business applications rather than scientific or engineering software.

Once a young programmer learned an initial programming language, it was fairly easy to learn new languages through self-instruction. I recall later programming in COBOL, PL/I, and various dialects of BASIC just by picking up the language manuals and learning the syntax and keywords. The ability to visualize patterns is the key to successful programming. The syntax of various programming languages is a minor issue that ranges from annoying to moderately helpful.

The applications we were developing were for the National Institutes of Health (NIH), and we had to keep track of records of equipment and personnel. However, my very first program was to recode an earlier application that had been written for an IBM 650 computer, which was removed from service when the IBM 1401s arrived. Apparently, it had not occurred to the department chief who had been running the program that the IBM 650 programs would not operate on an IBM 1401.

The IBM 1401 that my department of the Public Health Service had available only had 4 K of memory (less than a modern wristwatch). To develop some of the larger applications, we had to go a few blocks away and use an 8-K 1401 that had been acquired by the Internal Revenue Service (IRS).

In the 1960s, computer security was fairly casual and we had no difficulty borrowing time on the IRS IBM 1401. Of course, today IRS computers are heavily guarded and IRS software personnel are thoroughly vetted. In the early 1960s, hacking, identity theft, and denial of service attacks were still unheard of.

Computer rooms in those days were signs of technical sophistication, and many organizations still proudly displayed their computers in glass-walled rooms that were visible from the street so passersby would know that the organization was modern.

We developed our programs on lined paper worksheets preprinted with line numbers; we then punched them into IBM 80-column cards on an IBM 026 punch card. This was before the days of fully staffed data centers, so we often had to load and run the programs ourselves if the console operator was busy.

This decade was the archetype of the term "cowboy programming." We were working before structured programming had been defined, and most of us had learned programming only a few months before. In this era, new programmers working on new applications were quite common.

Although IBM and other groups were building large applications, most of the projects we handled were small and done by single programmers. As I recall, about 500 lines of Autocoder or 50 function points was the largest application I did for the Public Health Service before joining the private industry, where we did have larger systems.

There were no trained test groups and no formal quality assurance teams. Even inspections and peer reviews were only just getting started, and they were used mainly on larger team projects rather than smaller one-person projects.

Because our IBM 1401 computers were used for actual Public Health Service applications during the day, the time available for testing was usually late at night. Programming offices and computer rooms in the 1960s were fairly busy places at midnight and afterward.

Due to the shortage of convenient test times, all programmers in this era became proficient at *desk checking*. This was an early and manual precursor to static analysis. We went through our program listings and checked the accuracy of all algorithms and the branching structure to be sure our code went to the right place on every branch.

Although interpreted languages such as BASIC would become available in this decade, the majority of languages used for commercial and government applications needed to be compiled. This means that testing had to be preceded by compilation, and both activities were normally carried out late at night.

Submitting a faulty program for compilation usually meant at least one wasted day because computer time for a new compilation would not be available until the following night. It is obvious why careful desk checking prior to compilation and testing was the first line of defense against bugs.

In today's world, enormous computer capacity is available to all programmers 24 hours a day, 365 days a year. In the 1960s, the situation was different. Programmers needed to queue for available computer time slots and sometimes a programmer might only be allowed 15 to 30 minutes a day for compilation and testing.

The card decks were carried about in special trays, and for large programs they could be quite heavy. Woe betide a programmer who dropped a tray and got the deck out of sequence or the cards bent. If the cards got bent or warped and swollen from spilled water or coffee, repunching the deck was sometimes the only option.

The outputs from our programs were printed on an IBM 1403 printer, which, as I recall, was a chain-driven printer that was quite noisy. The spinning chains had characters on them, and a hammer would strike it through the paper at just the right instant. It was fast and printed at a rate of about 600 lines of text per minute.

These printers had surprisingly clear and pleasing type styles and faces. In fact, the type styles were much better than later dot-matrix printers. It would not be until laser printers and inkjets arrived that the IBM 1403 was surpassed in typographical elegance.

It was possible for a program to have a bug that caused a printer to suck in paper but not print, so sometimes dozens or hundreds of sheets of paper would spew out of the top of the printer before it could be stopped.

When processing blank lines, the IBM 1403 could suck in paper at about 75 inches per second, so a program with a bug in its print routine could easily go through more than 100 linear feet of paper before it was possible to shut it down. I recall seeing blank paper moving through the IBM 1403 printer so fast that the paper shot up three or four feet in the air.

The IBM 1403 printer also needed fairly serious maintenance that included oiling the moving parts. As a result, the area underneath the printer had to have paper towels or mats below it due to occasional oil leaks.

The IBM mainframe printer paper in those days was not individual sheets but rather continuous forms with perforations. They were large sheets with 132 print positions. The left and right edges had a separate perforated band with holes that allowed sprockets to feed the paper through the printer. The printer paper was delivered in large boxes, and the paper was fed into the printer directly from the box itself. These boxes of paper were heavy and were normally moved on wheeled carts.

These printers were so fast and used so much paper that a tidy computer room was not feasible. All of the IBM 1401 computer rooms had boxes of paper ready to be loaded in front of the printers and empty boxes ready to collect outputs at the rear of the printers.

Paper storage was a logistical problem of this era, and it was necessary to set aside rooms just to hold paper and punch cards. These rooms needed air conditioning because moisture could expand the paper and cause mechanical problems with printers and card readers.

Although I enjoyed my time as a programmer for the Public Health Service, private industry was expanding in computers and software so rapidly that I decided to look for other programming jobs outside of government.

A High Demand for Programmers

In today's world, many programmers and software engineers have lived through the dot-com crash of 2000 and 2001 and the recession of 2008 to 2010. Although software engineering has fared better than some industries, jobs are still hard to find, even for qualified software personnel. In the early 1960s, if you were a competent programmer, you could pretty much have your pick of companies and locations because they all were hiring as fast as they could.

This may sound like a bit of an exaggeration, but I recall several times seeing biplanes flying low over major highways and trailing banners that said: "Programmers—call this number: 123-4567." In California, I also recall seeing skywriter planes flying over public beaches and advertising for programmers with streams of smoke that produced letters more than 100 feet high.

Usually the biplanes with banners flew over major roads during business rush hours on weekdays. The skywriters flew over beaches and recreation areas on weekends. I remember seeing these airplanes that advertised for programming jobs all through the 1960s and well into the 1970s. I suspect the software industry will never see those days again.

In those early days of programming, specialized employment agencies, or "head hunters," sprang up to support the burgeoning software business. There were no fees for the programmers to use their services, since all costs were paid by the companies who were hiring.

When you contacted one of these head hunters and described your qualifications, the usual next step was to select what major company you might want to join and what part of the country you preferred. Although I don't know if anyone tried to do this, programmers in those days could probably have all-expenses-paid trips to at least a dozen companies in a dozen states before accepting an offer.

After I had chosen a job in private industry, there remained a few days of wrapping up work before I left the Public Health Service. In those days, the programmers shared a large open office space with perhaps a dozen desks for a dozen programmers. The office phones had a basic number for the department and an extension for each desk.

I remember hearing phones ringing on some of the vacant desks that had no programmers at the time. I answered a few of these and the calls were from the same head hunter I had used. There were so many jobs for programmers that the head hunter was offering anyone who answered the phone an all-expense-paid (and confirm) job interview trip to almost any city in America. The head hunter was not making calls to specific people by name, merely to the programming office space in the hope of attracting other programmers.

These early days of software engineering were exciting and fun in retrospect. The programming and software occupations were growing so fast that software departments were doubling in size in less than a year. So many jobs were available and turnover was rapid.

Programmers could easily get a 15% salary increase just by changing jobs. Tenure in jobs often was no more than a year. Some programmers worked for half a dozen companies in their first five years after learning to program.

Most programming jobs paid well and also had medical benefits and pension plans, and some had stock options, too. Another minor perk from those early days was that programmers could eat in executive dining rooms instead of employee cafeterias if they wished to. Some companies had other perks such as gymnasium memberships.

Other perks may surprise modern software engineers. Even entry-level programmers had moving expenses paid for by the company if they needed to move from another location. For experienced personnel on their second or third jobs, these moving expenses also included brokerage fees on selling homes, shipment of furniture to the new location (including automobiles), and being put up in a corporate apartment or hotel for perhaps a month after arrival at the new job location.

In fact, some companies would even purchase programmers' old homes so the employees did not have to bother with real estate transactions prior to starting their new jobs. Upon purchasing a new home, all of the fees for turning on utilities would be paid by the company.

Some companies paid programmers a "settling in" allowance for expenses such as new drapes or having a new house painted. In order to not have these payments be counted as taxable income, they were booked as loans to the employees, but they had zero interest rates and never had to be repaid.

In retrospect, it is surprising that the IRS did not try to tax some of these perks because in total their value could top $100,000. However, for some reason, companies in the 1960s had perks for programmers that were not taxable.

The attitude among programmers in those early days was that the companies needed the programmers more than the programmers needed the companies. It was fun to be part of this era of rapid expansion and novel applications.

Almost every application being designed in the 1960s was new, unique, and probably had never been done before. In today's world, almost 90% of new applications are replacements for aging legacy software packages.

In the early 1960s, there were only a handful of legacy applications written for the earlier IBM 650 and IBM 701 computers. Even these were not very old and were being reprogrammed merely because they did not run on newer computers such as the IBM 1401 and IBM 1410.

Eventually, specialists such as systems analysts and business analysts would handle most of the interactions with clients, but in the very early days the programmers not only had to handle pure coding but also had to deal with requirements, architecture, design, coding, debugging, and testing. Some programmers also did postrelease maintenance because separate change teams and maintenance groups were still in the future. Even customer support and answering phone calls from users were chores that programmers tackled in the 1960s.

Today, more than 115 different occupation groups are associated with large software organizations. In the early 1960s, there was very little differentiation and we were all generalists who did whatever was needed.

Emergence of the Software Engineer

The phrase "software engineering" had not become popular then nor was it especially appropriate given the ad hoc development methods then in use. Edsger Dijkstra would not publish his famous paper "Notes on Structured Programming" until 1965.

We called ourselves "computer programmers," not software engineers. We had to use "computer" as well as "programmer" to avoid confusion with radio and television programmers. (I can recall friends of my parents asking what radio station I worked for when they learned I was a programmer.)

The term "software" was so new to the general public that some thought it referred to the little Styrofoam peanuts that were used for packing around delicate electronic components.

Although "software" had been defined in 1958, the first notable use of the phrase "software engineering" did not occur until a NATO conference in Garmisch, Germany, on October 7 to 11, 1968. The conference title was "Software Engineering" and the conference chairman was Dr. F. L. Bauer.

More significantly, the conference notes were edited by Peter Naur and Brian Randall and when they were published in January 1969, the urgency of moving from ad hoc methods to more scientific methods for software development began to expand widely.

None of the programmers in my group at the Public Health Service could be hired in today's world. None of us had computer science or software engineering degrees (universities were just starting to offer computer engineering degree programs), and none of us even knew how to program when we were hired as programmers. Our main assets were nothing more than a working knowledge of how the Public Health Service operated and our ability to pass a fairly straightforward aptitude test.

This unusual period started in about 1950 and lasted until about 1970. Before 1950, there were very few professional programmers. After the 1960s, computer science and software engineering graduates began to enter the workforce in sufficient numbers so that liberal arts majors were no longer actively recruited.

Although on the surface liberal arts majors would not seem qualified for software engineering jobs, many were extremely capable and had long and successful careers. In retrospect, the breadth of knowledge that liberal arts graduates, musicians, and writers brought to software often created elegant and efficient programs.

In following up on these programmers from the early 1960s, some left software, and some stayed in programming and became lead or chief programmers. Some entered management and even became software executives. Some became entrepreneurs and started software companies.

Some of us did more than one of these things. For example, I was a software executive in a Fortune 500 company, started two software companies, and even filed a number of patents on software inventions.

A strong software engineering background today definitely makes work easier for the first year or so. After that, on-the-job experiences become more important. After perhaps a dozen successful software projects, academic credentials are no longer major career factors.

The same is true in other fields. A solid educational background is certainly critical for a surgeon performing the first few operations. After perhaps 100 operations, on-the-job knowledge augments academic knowledge.

The computer programming occupation grew from a few thousand at the start of the decade to almost a million at the end. Very few occupations in human history have grown so fast.

IBM System/360

The IBM 1400 series emerged in 1960 and had a good run for about 10 years. However, in April 1964, IBM announced the larger and more powerful IBM System/360 (S/360), which became the main computer of U.S. industry after battling with other vendors for supremacy.

The hardware architect for the S/360 was Gene Amdahl (who later founded a competitive computer company). The software was managed by Fred Brooks, whose experiences were immortalized in one of the most famous computer books ever written, *The Mythical Man-Month*. Thomas J. Watson, Jr., was the IBM chairman and the driving force behind the S/360. John Opel handled the marketing launch. John would later become President, CEO, and Chairman of IBM, and he was a visionary in his own right.

Note

John Opel served on a board of directors with Mary Maxwell Gates, who was a successful businesswoman and the mother of Bill Gates. John Opel and Mary Gates were both on the board of directors of the charitable organization United Way. It was the connection between John and Mary that led to John Opel being interested in Microsoft as a company that might be able to build the operating system for the IBM personal computer in a future decade.

The architecture of the IBM S/360 had features that were unusual at the time, but it proved to be the key to the long-range success of both IBM and the S/360 computer system.

One novel feature was that the S/360 was not designed as a single computer but as a family of related computers that started fairly small and fairly cheap but could be expanded in power and capacity as the need arose. This meant that companies could start with low-end versions such as the IBM System/360 model 20 or 30 and then move up to larger and faster versions. All of the bigger S/360 units were backward-compatible with the smaller units, so they could run the same applications without any changes.

The original series of IBM System/360 computers included models 20, 30, 40, 50, 60, 62, and 70. The low-end models up through 30 were designed to replace the IBM 1401 series, and they included emulators that allowed IBM 1401 software to operate without reprogramming. Models 65 and 75 were added to the high end later, as were the even higher models 85 and 95. There were also a few special models aimed at military or scientific use, such as model 44 for scientific computing. There were so many models it was hard to keep track of them.

In retrospect, this concept of a family of computers turned out to be a brilliant business strategy. It switched the computer business model from one-time leases or purchases to long-term recurring revenues. The clients could start at the low end and expand as needed without expensive reprogramming or even much lost time during the transition.

It was the S/360 that led to the aphorism that "nobody ever got fired for choosing IBM computers." The S/360 led to multiyear, multiproduct engagements that would make some companies continuous IBM customers for more than 40 years. This kind of brand loyalty was unheard of before the S/360 and remains the envy of almost every other company in the world.

Competitors and some software gurus criticized the operating system as being less sophisticated than others, and it was also thought that the hardware should be improved. Even so, the S/360 was the most successful computing line in history and one of the most successful products of any kind in terms of brand loyalty and recurring revenues.

One of the S/360 engineers, Gene Amdahl, left IBM to found a rival company, Amdahl, in order to compete with the System/360. The Amdahl line of computers was compatible with the S/360 and could run the same software. But the Amdahl computers had advantages in being less expensive. They also had some innovative technical features, such as air-cooled chips that did not need expensive chilled water-cooling systems. At its peak, Amdahl had about 8% of the U.S. mainframe market.

As the S/360 line continued to grow and evolve, Amdahl partnered with Fujitsu and eventually withdrew from the U.S. mainframe market but continued in Japan.

Other competitors such as RCA and even Russian companies tried to build competing hardware to match the S/360 line, but none were especially successful and none could overtake IBM's market share.

The Turing Award

In 1966, the Association of Computing Machinery (ACM) issued the first Turing Award for contributions to computing and software. This award is named after Alan Turing, one of the chief theorists of computer and software design. (Turing's accomplishments were described in earlier chapters.)

Table 5.1 shows Turing Award recipients from 1966 through 2012. The awards are given every year and are very important to the history of computing and software; hopefully, readers will not mind the chronological deviation from the 1960s. This list of awards is probably the most succinct possible way of showing software engineering progress from the 1960s through the modern era.

All of the Turing recipients are deserving of the awards. However, a thoughtful analysis of the list shows that software management is somewhat underrepresented. Fred Brooks is present, but probably Dr. Barry Boehm deserves an award for his contributions to measurement and estimation, and Allan Albrecht deserves an award for the invention of function point metrics. I would think that Steve Jobs is worthy of an award for the full suite of Apple innovations under his leadership. A host of useful innovations occurred under Thomas J. Watson, Jr., when he was Chairman of IBM. In fact, Watson personally directed several software-quality initiatives and was the visionary sponsor of the S/360 line.

Table 5.1 *Turing Awards from 1966 to 2012*

Year	Recipients	Contributions
1966	Alan J. Perlis	Programming techniques
1967	Maurice V. Wilkes	EDSAC; program libraries
1968	Richard Hamming	Numerical methods; error detection
1969	Marvin Minsky	Artificial intelligence
1970	James H. Wilkenson	Numerical analysis; linear algebra
1971	John McCarthy	Artificial intelligence
1972	Edsger W. Dijkstra	ALGOL; structured programming
1973	Charles W. Bachman	Database technology
1974	Donald Knuth	The art of computer programming
1975	Allan Newell, Herbert A. Simon	Artificial intelligence; list processing
1976	Michael O. Rabin, Dana S. Scott	Finite automata; nondeterministic machines
1977	John Backus	FORTRAN; structure of programming languages
1978	Robert W. Floyd	Programming language semantics; parsing
1979	Kenneth E. Iverson	APL; language theory
1980	C. Anthony R. Hoare	Definition and design of programming languages
1981	Edgar F. Codd	Relational databases
1982	Stephen A. Cook	Complexity of computation
1983	Ken Thompson, Dennis Ritchie	UNIX; operating system theory
1984	Niklaus Wirth	Computer languages; ALGOL, MODULA, PASCAL
1985	Richard M. Karp	Theory of algorithms; network flow
1986	John Hopcroft, Richard Tarjan	Fundamentals of algorithms and data structure
1987	John Cocke	Reduced instruction set computing (RISC)
1988	Ivan Sutherland	Computer graphics
1989	William Kahan	Numerical analysis and floating point computation
1990	Fernando Corbato	CTSS and MULTICS time-sharing computer systems

(Continued)

Table 5.1 *(Continued)*

Year	Recipients	Contributions
1991	Robert Milner	Multiple achievements
1992	Butler W. Lampson	Distributed computing; networks; security
1993	Juris Hartmanis, Richard E. Stearns	Computational complexity theory
1994	Edward Feigenbaum, Raj Reddy	Large-scale artificial intelligence
1995	Manual Blum	Complexity theory; cryptography
1996	Amir Pnueli	Temporal logic; verification
1997	Douglas Englebart	Inventions leading to interactive computing
1998	Jim Gray	Transaction processing; database research
1999	Fredrick P. Brooks, Jr.	Computer architecture; operating systems
2000	Andrew Chi-Chih Yao	Theory of computation; communication complexity
2001	Ole Johan Dahl, Kristen Nygard	Object-oriented programming; Simula
2002	R. L. Rivest, Adi Shamir, L. M. Adelman	Public-key cryptography
2003	Alan Kay	Object-oriented languages; SMALLTALK
2004	Vinton G. Cerf, Robert E. Kahn	Internetworking; TCP/IP
2005	Peter Naur	Computer programming; ALGOL 60
2006	Frances E. Allen	Optimizing compilers
2007	E. M. Clark, E. A. Emerson, J. Sifakis	Model checking for defect removal
2008	Barbara Liskov	Foundations of programming design; fault tolerance
2009	Charles P. Thacker	Personal computers; Ethernet; tablet PCs
2010	Leslie G. Valient	Theory of computation
2011	Judea Pearl	Calculus for probabilistic reasoning
2012	Silvio Micali, Shafi Goldwasser	Complexity theory applied to cryptography

The Invention of the Credit Card

Several important background inventions occurred in the 1960s. One of these was the AT&T Datanet, the first commercial modem, in 1960. Another was the development of ASCII in 1963; it is the ubiquitous coding system used to allow disparate computers to share common information. The most important perhaps was a major IBM invention in 1960 that would change the way consumers made purchases.

IBM had developed a technology for a kind of magnetic tape that could be affixed to small plastic cards. In 1960, the American National Standards Institute (ANSI) made the IBM magnetic tape a U.S. standard. In 1962, the International Standards Organization (ISO) also issued a global standard.

Once the new IBM magnetic strip was a global standard, credit card companies and credit card purchases expanded rapidly. The impact of credit cards on computing and software was enormous. Banks and credit card companies rapidly expanded their data centers and many created large internal software groups.

However, credit cards also created new opportunities for crime. In later decades, cybertheft of credit card numbers would become one of the most frequent targets for computer hackers.

Note

The first popular credit card, Diners Club, had been introduced in 1950. But it was a cardboard card without a magnetic stripe. The original Diners Club card only worked at 27 restaurants in New York, which explains why "Diners Club" was the chosen name.

Credit card purchases rank as one of the most important retail business changes in human history. But without fast computers and reliable software, credit card processing could not have taken off as rapidly as it did.

The first credit cards from Diners Club and American Express were proprietary, closed systems, which meant that only customers, retailers, and the card companies were involved in the transactions. Banks were excluded. These cards also required full 100% payment of balances at the end of every month. Revolving credit was introduced in 1959, with substantial interest payments and fees for late payments.

In 1966, Bank of America entered the credit card world by forming BankAmerica Services Corporation. The business idea of this unit was to franchise credit cards to hundreds of banks nationally and internationally. This would soon lead to the Visa card.

Also in 1966, another group of banks formed the InterBank Card Association (ICA). This group issued MasterCard credit cards, which competed directly with Visa.

Both the Visa and MasterCard services opened the gates to interbank transfers and cooperation between member banks. These cards were popular, so smaller banks began to issue credit cards. Eventually, hundreds of companies, such as airlines, retail chains and, in later years, web companies such as Amazon, issued Visa or MasterCards in their own names.

The magnetic stripes on plastic cards not only created the modern credit card business, but they soon proved useful in other areas. For example, many door locks (usually used by hotels) are now opened by use of magnetic cards.

Note

Alarmingly, the Congressional Cyber Caucus sponsored by Congressman James Langevin of Rhode Island reported in December 2012 that a hacking device for magnetic-lock hotel doors has surfaced, and this has been used in thefts of computers and personal property from rooms at several major hotel chains.

Needless to say, the rapid expansion of credit card usage was mirrored by a rapid expansion of computer capacities and software applications to process the card payments. Because small banks could not afford their own software groups, third-party companies got into the credit card business as service bureaus or outsourcers who ran or developed credit card applications for banks that did not have the capacities themselves.

Automation and New Professions

1960 marked the introduction of the IBM 1401 computer, which for 10 years was the dominant business computer and would greatly expand software from its scientific and military origins into the business world. In 1964, it was joined by the IBM System/360 line, which would become the most popular computer line in history.

1960 also marked the introduction of the Digital Equipment Corporation (DEC) Programmed Data Processor-1 (PDP-1), which would play a significant role in the development of computer games, the UNIX operating system, and even computer hacking.

As the IBM 1401 and other business-oriented computers began to be used by banks and insurance companies, hundreds of clerical employees were phased out of their jobs as automation began to take over. Another position that was phased out due to electronic computers was the human "computer" who handled mathematical calculations.

Digital computers introduced major sociological change that is still far from complete. Some of the displaced clerical workers became data entry specialists, program librarians, or part of the administrative teams that surround software and data center operations.

While thousands of clerical jobs disappeared, companies began to build internal software organizations that eventually would employ thousands of skilled workers. In general, computers and software reduced clerical employment but added new kinds of knowledge work and new kinds of skilled workers. In many cases, the clerical workers were shifted into computer work and therefore learned useful new skills.

In the fullness of time, software organizations in large companies would employ more than 115 new occupation groups, such as business analysts, database analysts, software engineers, webmasters, database administrators, and the more recent scrum masters and Agile coaches.

As software personnel expanded in numbers, academic departments for computer science and software engineering opened up and rapidly increased both in enrollments and in graduations. After the 1960s, formal training would be a requirement for computer programmers and the period of casual entry into programming would end.

The DEC PDP-1

The DEC was founded in 1957. By coincidence, the DEC headquarters building was in a converted mill factory in Maynard, Massachusetts, just a few miles from my home in the 1970s and 1980s.

The DEC PDP-1 was built and released in 1960. It updated an older computer called the TX-0 that had been built at the MIT Lincoln Lab. The DEC PDP line was a pioneer in what was called *minicomputers*, or smaller, cheaper computers aimed at companies and universities who might not be able to afford IBM mainframes.

The PDP-1 used modified IBM Model B typewriters (with type bars rather than balls) for printed output devices. Larger and more robust typewriters called *Friden Flexowriters* were also used. Because these printers used regular typewriter paper and had letter-quality printing, several early word-processing programs were developed for the PDP-1. One of these had the provocative name of *Expensive Typewriter*.

The earlier TX-0 computer at MIT had attracted programmers to write experimental games in their spare time. When the PDP-1 replaced the TX-0, gamers at MIT developed one of the first interactive games called Spacewar. This happened circa 1961.

Later, in 1969, Ken Thompson and Dennis Ritchie were interested in porting a game called Space Travel to a PDP-7. In the process of doing this port, Ritchie and Thompson ended up developing the UNIX operating system. It is a topic of historical interest that a game program was the main reason for the port, and it was perhaps the first UNIX application after the port.

The C programming language was developed in a UNIX context and would eventually become one of the most widely used languages in history. C programs had access to computing hardware and so were useful for operating systems and other applications that controlled physical devices. Although C would not become available until the next decade, the design of C started circa 1969.

Programming Languages of the 1960s

The decade from 1960 to 1969 was fruitful for programming languages and led to the development of many new languages, including, but not limited to, the following:

- ALGOL 60
- ALGOL 68
- APL
- BASIC
- BCPL
- COBOL 61
- COMIT
- CORAL 66
- DIBOL
- FORTRAN 66

- InterLisp

- JOSS 1

- LOGO

- Mark IV

- MUMPS

- PL/I

- RPG

- Simula 67

- SNOBOL

- Speakeasy 2

- TRAC

Not only did this decade witness the invention of many new programming languages, but it also saw the start of a very common trend that would become commonplace in later decades: the use of more than two languages in the same application.

Early examples of multiple languages in one application included job control language (JCL), COBOL, and SQL. More recent examples include Java, HTML, and .NET languages.

This plethora of programming languages would eventually lead circa 2013 to a grand total of more than 2,500. This raises an important question that is not yet fully answered: Is this huge number of programming languages a sign of software engineering sophistication, or are software engineers building new toys to play with?

While some of these programming languages are helpful in developing specific kinds of applications, the full set of programming languages has several harmful effects on software engineering that have been more or less ignored by the software engineering literature:

- Aging and obsolete languages raise the difficulty of maintaining legacy applications.

- Aging and obsolete languages have few programmers who know them.

- Multiple languages in the same application make debugging difficult.

- There are no firm guidelines for language selection; the reasoning resembles that of a cult.

- Security flaws appear to be endemic in a majority of popular languages.

This book is not the proper place for dealing with the issues surrounding the existence of so many programming languages and the absence of real proof that these numerous languages are helpful to the software engineering domain.

Other authors and other books can prove that so many languages are either helpful or harmful to software engineering. I think that all these languages may be doing more harm than good, but that is a subjective opinion from casual observations and not based on solid data.

JCL was another ubiquitous language developed in this decade in several dialects and varieties. It was used to schedule the execution sequences of applications under the various IBM operating systems. JCL is not a true programming language but rather was the forerunner of scripting languages that control execution sequences. No less a luminary than Dr. Fred Brooks called JCL the ugliest language ever developed.

Leaving languages, in the middle of the 1960s, Martin Goetz filed the first software patent in 1965, and this introduced the first known commercial software package, Autoflow, also in 1965.

The early 1960s also witnessed the initial development of database technology, which later became a primary use for digital computers. The CODASYL data description and the IBM IMS database were both released circa 1962. Relational databases would not occur until the following decade.

Based on research at MIT, Ivan Sutherland published an early paper on object-oriented programming in 1963. Later, in 1967, the Simula programming language introduced classes and instances, or objects. Many other object-oriented languages would follow in the next decades.

The programming languages of APL, BASIC, and PL/I were developed during this decade. The acronym APL stands for *a programming language*. This is a highly mathematical language developed by Ken Iverson with Adin Falkoff of IBM. The language concepts stem from a report in 1957, but the first working version of APL was not ready until 1960.

Note

I worked with Dr. Charles Turk to create IBM's first software estimation tool in 1973. This tool was called the Interactive Productivity and Quality model (IPQ), and it was coded in APL by Dr. Turk.

The PL/I language was also developed by IBM. (The abbreviation used a Roman numeral "I" instead of an Arabic "1" for marketing reasons.) The S/360 computer was envisioned as being suitable for both business and scientific purposes. Up until this time, programming languages had either been oriented toward math and science, such as FORTRAN (which stood for formula translator), or for business, such as COBOL (which stood for common business-oriented language).

With the S/360 being marketed as a general-purpose machine for both business and scientific uses, IBM wanted a companion programming language that could also be used for both business and scientific applications. The first definition of PL/I appeared in 1964.

The PL/I language was powerful and effective but did not become the standard language for everything as IBM had hoped. The PL/I language was still in use in 2012.

The history of the family of BASIC programming languages is well known. The first dialect of BASIC was developed by John Kemeny and Thomas Kurtz of Dartmouth College in 1964. The BASIC language was aimed at computer users who were not mathematicians and who needed a fairly simple language to complete their tasks. BASIC aimed, and succeeded, in being easy to learn and easy to use.

In later decades, when the use of personal computers exploded, BASIC dialects were the tool of choice for millions of hobbyists and casual programmers. Still today, there are more than a dozen dialects of BASIC, including some like Visual Basic from Microsoft that are used to create commercial and industrial software as well as for personal applications.

The Computer Business of the 1960s

Computers began to expand rapidly as business tools. The initial expansions took place in industries with high volumes of paperwork and large clerical staffs. Banking, insurance, and stock trading are prime examples of paper-intensive industries that would soon benefit from using computers and software.

During the latter part of the 1960s, the computer trade press began to use an unflattering name, "IBM and the Seven Dwarves," for the companies in the computer business. There were actually more than seven computer companies, but the name had such a provocative ring that it became popular. The companies included in this set were:

- Burroughs

- Control Data Corporation (CDC)

- GE
- Honeywell
- National Cash Register (NCR)
- RCA
- UNIVAC

During this decade, the computer and software business was exploding in size and capabilities. In later decades, the business climate would change and most of the smaller computer companies would be acquired, withdraw from computers, or go out of business, as will be discussed in later chapters. The competition between IBM and these companies is interesting in its own right but only of peripheral interest to the history of software engineering.

Other computer companies not included in the "seven dwarf" list were somewhat specialized and included the following:

- Amdahl
- Apollo
- Cray
- Data General
- DEC
- Ferranti
- Fujitsu
- Groupe Bull
- Hitachi
- Mitsubishi
- Nixdorf
- Olivetti
- Scientific Data Systems (SDS)
- Sun
- Wang
- Xerox

Not all of these appeared in the 1960s, but it is clearer to list them all in one place rather than scattering them through several chapters.

In addition to digital mainframe computers, there were also a number of specialized analog-digital hybrid computers mainly used for engineering and scientific problems. These are not as well known as pure digital computers. Two examples of hybrids were the HYCOMP desktop analog/digital hybrid from 1961 and the larger HYDAC 2400 analog/digital computer from 1963. Others included the Beckman hybrid from 1960 and the EAI 680 scientific hybrid used in engineering.

Pure analog computers remained in widespread military service as bomb-sights, torpedo guidance computers, and missile-navigation systems. Analog computers would dominate military weapons for more than another decade. The use of digital computers on the Apollo spaceships would soon pave the way for digital computers to take over from analogs on aircraft and missiles.

Portable computers and notebook computers will be discussed in later chapters. However, although commercial notebook computers did not exist in this decade, Alan Kay created an early concept of a notebook computer called *Dynabook* in 1968. His idea was to provide schoolchildren with portable learning devices.

An article published by Kay in 1972 showed a device that looked remarkably like a cross between a modern tablet computer and a notebook. This was a visionary idea that would later grow into powerful concepts at the Xerox Palo Alto Research Center (PARC) in California where Kay worked. Xerox PARC will come up again in the next decade due to the impact that Xerox technologies had on Steve Jobs and Apple Computer.

The need for computers as business tools was clearly shown by what happened to Wall Street. Between 1965 and 1968, shares of stock traded on Wall Street increased from about 5,000,000 to 12,000,000, which stressed back office clerical work to the breaking point. Clerical staffing increased rapidly.

One of the reasons for the increase in stock sales was a reduction in the percentage of a stock's price that needed to be paid to acquire it. The rates were reduced from 100% of the stock's value down to 70%, which naturally led to increased sales volumes.

But in 1969 and 1970, stock trading declined abruptly, cutting into brokerage revenues and causing layoffs and financial distress among brokerage houses. About 100 Wall Street firms went out of business or merged, which was a shrinkage of about 17%. For Wall Street companies, this was the worst crisis since the Great Depression.

Many of the Wall Street companies that failed did so in part because they had lost control of their back office financial records due to huge clerical workloads. About 90% of the operating costs of Wall Street firms in this decade were tied up in clerical work. Clearly, Wall Street was ready for a move into computerization, which would occur in the 1970s.

Litigation Changes the Computer World Forever

The 1960s witnessed several major lawsuits that would change the nature of computing and software in unanticipated ways. The first of these major lawsuits were two patent violation cases filed by Sperry-Rand against Honeywell and a countersuit filed by Honeywell against Sperry-Rand. Both suits were filed on the same day, May 26, 1967. Honeywell filed a few minutes before Sperry-Rand, which later turned out to be important.

Honeywell charged Sperry-Rand with being a monopoly and asked that the patent on the ENIAC, owned by Sperry-Rand, be invalidated. The impact of the ENIAC patent was that Sperry-Rand was claiming ownership of the main features of all digital computers and therefore charging license fees. This patent was a clear bottleneck to the expansion of the computer industry.

This lawsuit and several predecessor lawsuits were the longest trials in American history and accumulated thousands of pages of data and information about computer technology and the history of digital computing. In total, more than 150 witnesses were involved.

Not only was this case important for the computer and software industries, but it happened to be the first major lawsuit where computerized legal files were used.

The fact that Honeywell filed first led the case to be tried in Minneapolis rather than in Washington, D.C. At the time, Honeywell was the largest employer in Minnesota, so the outcome of the case was important locally.

The case was not decided until the 1970s, so it will be discussed again in the next chapter. The importance to the industry and to this book is that the eventual decision invalidated the ENIAC patent. This had the effect of putting most of the technology used to build digital computers into the public domain. This, in turn, led to a significant expansion in computers and companies building computers.

Another momentous event for the software industry occurred in 1969, when IBM unbundled software as a result of an antitrust suit. Prior to 1969, IBM computers came with the software bundled and not priced separately. Bundling or providing software for free was a barrier to entry, and unbundling led to the creation of today's vast software market.

The IBM antitrust lawsuit was filed at the end of the decade on January 17, 1969, by the Department of Justice. It would not be decided until the 1980s, but by then unbundling was long established. (The case was eventually withdrawn by William Baxter in January 1982. Baxter was the Assistant Attorney General in charge of antitrust.)

There were some noncomputer pure software companies during this decade, and they concentrated on applications packages that were not closely tied to any specific computer brand or model. One of the most successful and longest-running software companies was Cincom, which was founded in 1968 by Thomas Nies, Tom Richley, and Claude Bogardus. All three founders had worked for IBM prior to founding Cincom. (The unusual name of the company is based in part on the fact that it was started in Cincinnati, Ohio.)

In those days, IBM provided operating systems and systems software and compilers, but client companies were expected to write their own applications. Having clients write their own software applications explains the huge increase in software personnel during this decade.

The Cincom vision was to commercialize common kinds of software applications that were widely used and needed. One of these areas of common need was the database. The Cincom TOTAL database package entered the market in 1970 and was a pioneer in commercial DBMS. Cincom was and is a successful software company that has outlived many of its competitors.

Computers and Software in Space

On July 20, 1969, the Apollo 11 spacecraft landed Neil Armstrong and Buzz Aldrin on the moon. This was one of the greatest scientific achievements in human history.

The Apollo spacecrafts pioneered the use of digital computers and software for the space program. The physical computer used on the Apollo program was among the first to combine integrated circuits and low-power transistors. It was named the Apollo Guidance Computer (AGC).

The AGC utilized a special kind of read-only memory (ROM) called a *core rope*. A magnetized strand passed through hollow cores. Up to 64 separate wires could pass through a core, and each carried software information. The advantage of core ropes was high-density storage—about 18 times more data than conventional magnetic cores could hold.

These core ropes were actually woven by female seamstresses. This gave rise to a slang term for the memory of "LOL," or "little old lady."

Although the Apollo team included many famous engineers and scientists, Charles Stuart Draper was one of the Apollo computing pioneers. The famous MIT lab in Cambridge, Massachusetts, is named for him.

IBM was also a participant in the Apollo program, and the famous IMS database was first created for the Apollo program, but it was also marketed commercially.

The Apollo software was programmed using both an assembly language and an interpreted language. A special real-time, multitasking operating system was developed for the Apollo program. While the Apollo computer was slow and limited compared to today's computers, it was a great step for computing, just as landing on the moon was a great step for mankind.

Alarmingly, during the descent to the moon, a number of error conditions and error messages appeared, indicating computer or software problems. Apparently, too many tasks were executing concurrently and exceeding the system capacity.

Fortunately, the software had priority scheduling algorithms and it was possible to eliminate low-priority tasks so that the actual guidance of the descent operated perfectly. One of the Apollo guidance controllers, Steve Bales, received a Presidential Medal of Freedom award in recognition of his successfully ensuring the Apollo landing.

The Apollo computer and software systems were important precursors to "fly-by-wire" systems that would become the norm on future aircraft and the space shuttle. The near disaster during the Apollo 11 descent, and the even greater problems with later Apollo missions, emphasize the fact that onboard software for aircraft and space vehicles needed to approach zero-defect quality levels.

Computer and Software Growth in the 1960s

As the decade neared its end, computer programming was evolving toward software engineering, with improved standards and better quality control.

I went to work for IBM at their lab in Boulder, Colorado. During a 12-year tenure, I was fortunate to meet a number of IBM colleagues who would contribute important insights to the software engineering field.

Among my technical colleagues were Dr. Harlan Mills of "clean room" and "chief programmer" fame; Dr. Ted Codd of relational database fame; Dr. Ken Iverson, the inventor of APL; Dr. Charles Turk, the codeveloper of IBM's first software cost-estimating tool; and Dr. Gerald Weinberg, the author of *The Psychology of Computer Programming*.

Among my management and executive colleagues were Jim Frame, who managed the IBM Santa Teresa Lab; Ted Climis, the head of the Systems Development Division; Dr. Fred Brooks, who was in charge of the OS/360 and later wrote *The Mythical Man-Month*; and T. J. Watson, Jr. Watson personally sponsored an initiative to improve the quality of IBM software, and he was the executive who sponsored the S/360 line.

By the late 1960s, computers were also starting to have an impact on sports. In 1968, a golf pro named Jim Healy built the first computerized tool for calculating golf handicaps. Later, this kind of software would become the industry standard for amateur and professional golfers.

The original tool was a one-off build using a custom microcomputer. Later, in the 1980s, the software migrated to personal computers starting with Radio Shack Model II and then moving to Apple and IBM personal computers.

The decade also witnessed the development of the UNIX operating system by AT&T Bell Labs in 1969. The same year, the Department of Defense Advanced Research Projects Agency (DARPA) introduced ARPANET, which was the forerunner of today's internet.

There were cowboy development, low-level languages such as assembly and later macro-assembly languages, and then mid-level languages such as COBOL and FORTRAN.

Small applications were the norm at the start of the decade, but size increased by the end of the decade. Toward the end of the decade, several newer languages such as ALGOL, LISP, COBOL, and FORTRAN started to be increasingly used.

Table 5.2 shows approximate numbers of U.S. software applications for the 1960s. The number of applications was starting to expand across all kinds of software applications. Software was no longer restricted to scientific and military endeavors but indeed was moving into every aspect of human life.

All of the major business categories have software applications, and even games and artistic activities are starting to use software. This would accelerate in later decades.

Table 5.2   *U.S. Software Applications from 1960 to 1969*

Application Types	Applications	Percentage
Scientific	1,000	15.94%
Military and defense	2,500	39.84%
Civilian government	1,250	19.92%
Systems and middleware	500	7.97%
Embedded software	250	3.98%
Commercial	125	1.99%
Information technology (IT)	500	7.97%
U.S. outsource	100	1.59%
Offshore outsource	0	0.00%
Games and entertainment	25	0.40%
Artistic and musical applications	25	0.40%
Web applications	0	0.00%
Open source	0	0.00%
Smartphone applications	0	0.00%
Cloud applications	0	0.00%
Total Applications	**6,275**	**100.00%**

Function Points Backfired for 1965

Function points had not been invented, so all data were measured using lines of code. Backfiring or mathematical conversion from lines of code (LOC) to function points show these results for a project of 1,000 function points in this decade:

- Source code for 1,000 function points: 160,000 logical code statements
- Programming language: Macro assembly
- Reuse percentage: 0% to 5%
- Methodology: Unstructured cowboy development
- Productivity: 5 function points per staff month
- Defect potentials: 6 per function point

- Defect removal efficiency (DRE): 83%

- Delivered defects: 1.02 defects per function point

- Ratio of development personnel to maintenance:

  - Development: 90%

  - Maintenance: 10%

The following are the background data for 1965:

- Average language level: 2.0

- Number of programming languages: 10

- Logical statements per function point: 160

- Average application size: 600 function points

- Average application size: 96,000 logical code statements

Note

The phrase "language level" was developed within IBM circa 1968 and refers to the power of a language relative to basic assembly language. Thus, for a level 2 language, it would require two statements in basic assembly language to produce the functionality of one statement in the target language. The level concept is still in use today. For example, Java is ranked as a level 6 language. Levels are based on logical code statements, not physical lines of code.

By the end of the decade, applications grew in size and complexity. It was obvious that the LOC metric was no longer useful. In 1970, many IBM publication groups exceeded their budgets due to basing document costs on a percentage of coding costs. When Programming Language/Systems (PL/S) started to replace assembly code, all of the document departments using a percentage of PL/S coding costs exceeded their budgets. As a result, IBM began the studies that led to function point metrics a few years later.

Summary

At the start of the 1960s, software was bundled with computers and given away with the hardware. The ENIAC patent made it difficult for other manufacturers to build computers without heavy royalty payments. Eventually, legal case decisions resulted in the unbundling of software and led to the commercial software industry, putting computer architecture into the public domain. This decade also witnessed thousands of businesses buying computers and starting to use them to replace labor-intensive tasks such as record keeping. Software development organizations and corporate data centers began to appear at the start of the decade and expanded rapidly. Many new computer and software companies were created in this decade, but few would have long lives.

Chapter 6

1970 to 1979: Computers and Software Begin Creating Wealth

Thanks to the unbundling of software by IBM in 1969, the 1970s would witness the creation of several companies that would later expand into the largest and wealthiest companies in U.S. history: Apple, Microsoft, and Oracle are three examples. The rapid expansion of computer use led to the very rapid expansion of companies that created commercial software that benefited both corporations and individuals. It was not anticipated at the beginning of this decade (and confirm) that software would eventually cause Bill Gates to become among the wealthiest persons on the planet and Apple Computer to become among the wealthiest companies.

By the end of this decade, computers and software would be among the fastest-growing and most profitable industries in human history. The settlement of the patent case between Honeywell and Sperry-Rand invalidated the patent on ENIAC and essentially put computer architecture into the public domain. During this decade, software began to diverge into a number of subcategories such as business software, embedded software, middleware, and many others.

Software Evolution in the 1970s

The field of software engineering grew faster than almost any occupation in history during this time. The decade also witnessed the creation of many different subfields of software such as business applications, project management applications, personal applications, systems software, embedded software, middleware, scientific and mathematical software, communications software, manufacturing software, database software, and software for games and entertainment.

Trends in Software

A popular trend during this decade was the emergence of *vertical markets* among both computer and software vendors. A vertical market refers to selling complete packages that support all data-processing needs for a particular business function or industry. Banks, insurance providers, and health-care companies are good examples of target vertical markets because all three depend on complex and somewhat specialized calculations using large volumes of data.

In all three industries, there are hundreds of companies with data-processing needs that are close to being identical. Insurance claims handling is pretty much the same whether it is completed by Hartford, Farmers, Aetna, Prudential, GEICO, or American Commerce. Dealing with transactions through an automated teller machine (ATM) is similar for Bank of America, Wells Fargo, Citizens Bank, and hundreds of others. Vertical markets make sense when there are a great many companies in the same business sector with similar data-processing needs.

The concept of *time sharing* was also popular during the 1970s. Time sharing had originated in earlier decades but became a major technique for lowering the costs of computer usage during the 1970s. This was the decade of mainframe computers and some minicomputers, but before the internet and before personal computers.

Time sharing allowed multiple users to be connected to a single mainframe and use it when other applications were paused or quiet. Thus, the rather high costs of the mainframe lease and software could be apportioned across multiple users. Time sharing for multiple companies was often offered by service bureaus that acquired and owned the computers and rented time for a weekly or monthly fee. In the 1980s, after the arrival of the IBM personal computer and the Apple II, time sharing would begin to fade away and personal computers would take over.

Toward the end of the 1970s, security and protective software emerged as a subindustry in the wake of increasing numbers of viruses and cyberattacks.

This was a very dynamic decade with rapid growth in the number of software engineers and also rapid acceleration of several companies toward enormous size, wealth, and influence.

At the beginning of this decade, universities did not offer degrees in software engineering. By the end of the decade, almost all major universities had software engineering curricula available and degrees were being offered.

There was also the start of the huge market share by U.S.-based companies for commercial software due primarily to IBM up until the middle of the decade. In future decades, Apple, Microsoft, Cullnane, Computer Associates, Oracle, and other U.S.-based companies would dominate world markets. SAP in Germany is an exception to the rule and is a major power in enterprise resource planning (ERP) applications.

Political Failures

Outside of software, the decade was rocked by two political events that shook U.S. citizens' confidence in the federal government and lowered respect for their highest officials. On October 10, 1973, Vice President Spiro Agnew resigned in disgrace due to accusations of accepting bribes, some of them in his vice presidential office.

The second and even more discouraging event was the August 9, 1974, resignation of President Richard Nixon in the aftermath of the famous Watergate scandal. Had he not resigned, Nixon would have faced an impeachment trial.

Note

Watergate involved a break-in at the Democratic National Committee (DNC) headquarters in the Watergate Hotel. Eventually, 43 trials and convictions occurred, revolving around several of Nixon's staff. The famous hidden tape recorder in Nixon's office provided evidence of a coverup. There was a mysterious 18.5-minute gap in the recordings where one of the tapes had been erased. Neither the gap nor the missing information was ever fully explained. After resignation, Nixon was given a blanket pardon by President Gerald Ford.

There have been other scandals in the past, but these two resignations by the Vice President and President less than a year apart raised serious doubts about the integrity of politicians. Even today, confidence is low for members of Congress and other national officials.

These doubts are often justified for a divisive Congress that frequently issues partisan diatribes with no substance or data. Time and again, Congress has stalled until a day or two before some major catastrophe such as a fiscal cliff (massive tax increases) or sequester (massive spending cuts) takes place.

Both of these problems were caused by a failure by Congress to perform due diligence or to use any predictive analytics of the consequences. Indeed, Congress failed to act to prevent the sequester, and neither the House nor Senate properly assessed the potential harm from this failure.

Without an operations research group, Congress cannot properly apply predictive analytics to financial and economic issues. This often results in the passing of legislation that can be harmful and have little benefit. The Congressional Budget Office (CBO) should be such an organization, but it is not always listened to and is not always on target.

Rapid Rise of Computer Companies

Before the 1970s, the bundled software provided by IBM constituted the majority of systems software and a significant percentage of applications software used in the United States and throughout the world. After unbundling by IBM, the software industry began to show the classic patterns of older industries.

There were numerous small companies with one or two software applications; a group of midsized companies with up to a dozen software applications; and a few large companies with dozens or, in a few cases, hundreds of software packages. There were rapid rises and equally rapid declines of companies within the sector.

It is an interesting phenomenon that the life expectancy of an American corporation is less than the life expectancy of an American citizen. The life expectancy of software and computing companies seems to be worse than other industries, with many companies dying within a few years of being incorporated.

These rapid deaths are especially true for venture-backed companies, which are often pushed toward such fast growth that research and development of new products can't keep up. At the opposite end of the spectrum, some companies, such as Apple, Microsoft, Oracle, SAP, and Google, have soared to unexpectedly huge market shares and enormous wealth.

The oldest of the computer and software companies is IBM, which alone is more than 100 years old, having been formed (under a different name) in June 1911. As will be discussed in later chapters, IBM had some rough times during the Depression and also in the 1980s, but it managed to recover in both cases.

Note

The oldest American technology company seems to be Consolidated Edison, which was formed in 1823 to provide gaslights long before the invention of electricity. The world's oldest company is a Japanese company named Kongo Gumi. It was started about 1,430 years ago to build Buddhist temples. It remained in one family until 2006, when it was acquired by Takamatsu, a larger Japanese construction company. Until 2006, Kongo Gumi was also the world's oldest family-owned business.

A declining stock market during 1970 and 1971 slowed the growth of commercial software companies, but this accelerated the growths of internal software groups within many companies as they acquired computers and began to automate their business operations.

Major Companies Formed During the 1970s

Several important companies that used computers in new and interesting ways were created or expanded rapidly during the 1970s, including FedEx, NASDAQ, and Southwest Airlines.

FedEx

Federal Express was formed in 1971 by Frederick Smith and soon became a giant of freight transportation due to developing the "hub-and-spoke" model of air transportation centering on Memphis, Tennessee.

It is most efficient to move goods to a central facility (the hub) along a direct route (a spoke). Goods are then moved from the hub to the final destination. Attempting to ship directly from destination to destination without a hub would lead to impossible combinatorial complexity.

The FedEx computerized routing and tracking software became a model for other companies involved with the distribution of goods. This was an excellent example of operations research applied to optimizing the shipment of goods. FedEx became one of the most cost-efficient cargo companies in history, and it continues to use computers and software to fine-tune operations.

NASDAQ

The NASDAQ stock exchange was also created in this decade, and it became an important stock exchange for computer and software companies when they decided to issue an initial public offering (IPO). The name of this exchange is an acronym derived from *National Association of Securities Dealers Automated Quotations*.

NASDAQ started operations on February 8, 1971. It was the first computerized and automated stock exchange, so clearly software and computers were important enabling technologies. At first, NASDAQ was a kind of bulletin board rather than a true exchange. But as it grew and evolved, it became the first computerized online stock trading exchange in 1987.

Southwest Airlines

Another company with an effective business model was Southwest Airlines, which was founded in 1967 by Herb Kelleher but did not change its name to Southwest Airlines until 1971.

As an example of using computers to aid business operations, Southwest was the first airline to have a website starting in 1995. Southwest continues to have more website visits than any other airline and does more business through its website than any other airline. Southwest was also a pioneer in *fuel hedging*, or contracts that buffered the airline against increasing fuel costs.

Southwest eventually became powerful enough to cause the repeal of the Wright amendment, which had limited the airline's ability to fly to states other than Texas. Southwest is now the largest, most successful, and most profitable U.S. airline.

Younger readers may not have been aware that three of the most successful modern companies in America—FedEx, NASDAQ, and Southwest Airlines—are all relatively young and began their growth to dominance during the 1970s. All used computers and software in interesting ways to help them grow and become cost effective.

Computer and Software Companies Formed During the 1970s

Many companies that have played important roles in software development were founded during the 1970s. There are many others besides the ones mentioned here, but these samples run the gamut of companies that either grew to become enormously wealthy or quickly passed from view. Both extremes reflect the history of software.

Several companies later to become famous in the computer and software sectors started out as something else: consulting companies or making some other kinds of electronic products. It was the excitement of the burgeoning computer and software domains that attracted so many startups that migrated toward computers and software.

When looking at the companies in software and computers that were formed during the 1970s, readers will notice that many of them were created in "Silicon Valley," which is essentially the Santa Clara valley in California.

The original towns included in Silicon Valley ran north from San Jose up past Palo Alto. This region included Stanford University and was not far from

U.C. Berkeley on the other side of the Bay. Steve Jobs, the cofounder of Apple, for example, lived in Cupertino, California, which is fairly near the center of Silicon Valley. Dozens of software and high-technology companies are still located in the region, as are many of the venture capital companies that funded the startups.

Other fruitful areas for software startups are on the East Coast centering on Cambridge, Massachusetts, and in the state of Texas. But successful software companies have occurred in many geographic regions, including Cincinnati, Ohio; Seattle, Washington; Portland, Oregon; and Jacksonville, Florida.

This decade witnessed a number of lawsuits either between software and computer companies themselves or filed by governments. Several antitrust suits, patent infringement suits, copyright infringement suits, and other kinds of modern litigation against computing and software companies seemed to accelerate during this decade, and they have scarcely slowed down in later decades. Business tends to be litigious, and the software business is no exception.

The following sections are a sampling of the computer and software companies that formed in the 1970s.

Altair Computers

The Altair 8800 computer was one of the first *personal computers*. It is famous because Altair Basic was the initial product developed by Microsoft. The company that built Altair was the Micro Instrumentation and Telemetry Systems Corporation (MITS), founded in 1969 in Albuquerque, New Mexico, by Forrest Mims, Ed Roberts, Stan Cagle, and Bob Zaller.

MITS did not start with computers but rather with model-rocket equipment (which explains the somewhat complex name of the company). Computers came later in the 1970s. The Altair 8800 came out in 1975 and was featured in *Popular Science* magazine, which made it quite a best seller, with thousands of units selling in the first month. Paul Allen and Bill Gates moved to Albuquerque, founded Microsoft, and developed applications for the Altair 8800, including Altair Basic.

The Altair 8800 was technically sophisticated for the era, using an Intel 8080 chip and creating what later became the S-100 bus, a de facto industry standard. This computer was the enabling device that started many other important companies and inventions.

Apple Computer was founded in part due to Steve Jobs's and Steve Wozniak's desire to improve on the Altair 8800 by offering a full computer. IMSAI computers were also introduced soon after with the idea of improving on the Altair.

IMSAI is probably the first "clone" that was advertised as being plug-compatible with the Altair 8800.

Apple Computer

Steve Jobs and Steve Wozniak finished building the famous Apple 1 computer on April 1, 1976, and incorporated Apple on January 3, 1977, in Cupertino, California. Apple would grow to become one of the world's wealthiest corporations.

En route to this milestone, Apple would adopt Objective C as its main programming language; pioneer elegant and popular devices such as the iPod, iPhone, and iPad; and develop scores of innovative software applications.

Other popular technologies by Apple would involve creating the most successful online music business, creating a set of popular Apple stores throughout the world, and in general innovating across a broad range of computer and software technologies.

Readers interested in the deeper history of Apple can read Walter Isaacson's book *Steve Jobs: The Exclusive Biography*, published by Simon and Schuster. This book is a fascinating biography of a brilliant but decidedly erratic individual.

Baan

The Baan Corporation was created in 1978 by Jan Baan in the Netherlands. It started as a consulting company, but Jan and his brother Paul soon built an interesting software application in the ERP sector.

For a while, Baan grew rapidly and acquired many other software companies. It had a good technical reputation for its fast and capable database and ERP packages. Baan became a public company in 1995 and was listed on NASDAQ.

In 1998, Baan got into financial trouble and began to lose its market share. After a string of consecutive losing quarters, Baan was acquired in 2000 by a British company named Invensys. One of the reasons for the sale was that Baan had been accused of exaggerating sales volumes, which lowered its reputation and value.

Computer Associates (CA)

CA was founded in 1979 by Charles Wang and Russell Artzt in Islandia, New York. CA was a pioneer in the *business-to-business* (B2B) software domain. CA specialized in a variety of business software applications such as accounting, finance, order entry, and the like.

CA tried to develop personal computer packages such as security and antivirus but decided to leave that line and stay focused on larger business applications sold to corporations rather than to end users.

They had a large software development staff and created quite a few inventive applications. In fact, CA holds more than 400 patents and has hundreds more pending.

Over time, CA also grew by acquisition and acquired so many software companies that the Department of Justice began to examine whether or not CA might own so many in the same field as to perhaps constitute a potential monopoly. Some of the companies CA acquired were well known, such as Applied Data Research (ADR), Cullinet, Capex, Sterling Software, the Ask Group, and UCCEL. CA has acquired nearly two dozen software companies.

CA was the focus of a number of government investigations on topics of insider trading, executive compensation, and accounting methods. For various reasons, CA had an unusually numerous set of lawsuits involving customers, competitors, and the federal government. One of the lawsuits was between CA and another giant, Electronic Data Systems (EDS), in 1996.

Note

As disclosure, I was an expert witness in a customer lawsuit against CA, but I retired before the litigation finally settled.

One of the government investigations was for using accounting practices that inflated revenues by booking them before they had been paid. This case involved the Securities and Exchange Commission (SEC) and the Department of Justice. It resulted in a 2004 settlement under which CA paid $225 million to shareholders and revised its accounting methods. This was a serious issue, and former CA executive Sanjay Kumar, the CEO and Chairman, received a 12-year prison sentence. Eight other CA executives pleaded guilty to fraud charges.

One government concern was that in 1999, Charles Wang received the largest corporate bonus ever issued by a public company in history during a time of business slowdown. The stock options awarded in this bonus amounted to about $670 million, which is certainly a notable bonus.

In spite of intermittent legal problems, Computer Associates has grown fairly steadily and is one of the largest pure software companies in the world. The hundreds of CA patents and the large number of software engineers who perform research and development in CA show that the company was serious about software engineering.

Cray Computers

In 1972, the well-known computer designer Seymour Cray left Control Data Corporation (CDC) and started his own company, Cray Research. The research labs were in Chippewa Falls, Minnesota, and its corporate headquarters was in Minneapolis, Minnesota. The first Cray-1 supercomputer was installed in 1976 at the Los Alamos National Laboratory.

Cray computers were among the first *supercomputers* and, indeed, the Cray-1 was the fastest computer of the time. Seymour Cray soon dropped out as CEO and became an independent consultant, starting several more companies. His original company filed for bankruptcy in 1995.

The technologies used in the Cray computer lines were advanced for the era and pioneered a number of innovations. The high-cost, high-speed innovations of the Cray line became prestigious, and major companies and national governments were proud to be known as Cray computer users.

The idea of superfast computers resonated through the industry. Cray triggered a number of competitive companies in later decades and more or less pioneered the supercomputer.

Supercomputers were used for very difficult problems that required intensive and rapid calculations: weather predictions, nuclear physics, fluid dynamics, logistics, and other complex problem areas.

Eventually, monoprocessor supercomputers such as the Cray line began to encounter competition from massively parallel arrays of computers. Because fast monoprocessors were expensive, while small parallel computers were cheap, the market for supercomputers began to shift toward parallelism.

Because a major feature of computers is high processing speed, computer manufacturers often compete for speed records. In 1976, when the Cray-1 high-speed computer was first built, it established a world speed record for the era by calculating at a rate of 160 megaflops (a megaflop is one million floating point operations per second).

Over the years, IBM, Fujitsu, Cray, and other companies would have heated competition for these high-end supercomputers.

Cullinane

Cullinane was formed in 1968 by John Cullinane and Larry English. It was located in Westwood, Massachusetts. The company is cited in this chapter because it went public in the 1970s.

The Cullinane IPO was the first for a pure software company. It was also the first IPO handled by Hambrecht and Quist, who would later handle many others. It was also the first software IPO where a software company was valued at more than a billion dollars. Later, Cullinane became the first software company to run an ad during a Super Bowl.

The main software applications for Cullinane were in the database management area; its Integrated Data Base Management System (IDMS) was its main database product. This competed successfully with several others, including IBM's Information Management System (IMS). IDMS was based on the CODASYL data model and would eventually lose ground to relational databases.

In 1982, IBM announced the 4300 series of computers and told clients that the Cullinane IDMS database product would not run on the 4300, so IMS was the only choice. Unfortunately for IBM, it turned out that Cullinane was able to port IDMS to the 4300 series by changing only one single instruction! This, of course, embarrassed IBM and put them on the defensive.

After many ups and downs, Cullinane (whose name was changed to Cullinet) was acquired by CA in 1989.

During the 1970s and 1980s, database products were a fairly hot component of the software market space, and many companies and products entered the market. Database applications remain important today. Among the numerous database applications and query methods are Access, dBASE, DB2, Easytrieve, Filemaker, FoxPro, IDMS, IMS, Informix, Ingres, MySQL, Oracle, Sybase, and many more.

Database technology is also a hot pure research topic, and at least a dozen navigation models have surfaced, including sequential, CODASYL, relational, entity-relationship, and many more. This book only deals with a few surface issues, but the database literature is large and has many excellent sources.

Digital Research

The company now known as Digital Research was founded by Dr. Gary Kildall and his wife, Dorothy, under the name Intergalactic Digital Research in 1976 in Pacific Grove, California.

The original name was an attempt at humor that was not uncommon in the era, as shown by the 1975 creation of a journal originally called *Dr. Dobb's Journal of Tiny BASIC Calisthenics and Orthodontia*. Both the company and the journal changed their names when their ideas started to be taken seriously. Dr. Dobb's evolved into a respected technical journal and has a website that is still widely read by software engineers.

Digital Research created the famous *control program for microprocessors* (CP/M) operating system that was used on many computers running Intel chips. For several years, it was the dominant operating system for computers that used the Intel 8086 and 8088 chips.

It is the stuff of legend that IBM originally asked Digital Research to develop the operating system for the IBM personal computer in 1980. For one reason or another, Digital Research declined, which allowed Microsoft to create both the IBM disk operating system (DOS) and, later, Microsoft Windows. One possible reason is that Gary Kildall did not want to sign the IBM nondisclosure agreement, but there have been different stories about why Digital Research declined IBM's offer.

Note

It is interesting that when first approached by IBM, Bill Gates referred IBM to Gary Kildall of Digital Research as a professional courtesy. When IBM was rebuffed, Microsoft got the contract.

Digital Research later built a competitive operating system for the IBM PC called DR DOS that competed head to head with MS-DOS. Some computer companies offered both. However, Microsoft gave such good licensing terms to computer manufacturers that included MS-DOS on every machine sold that sales of DR DOS dried up. This led to an antitrust suit against Microsoft in 1994 and another in 1996.

When Microsoft developed Windows, the original DOS application was under the covers. However, the Digital Research DR DOS was not supported. Indeed, one of the claims in the 1996 antitrust suit was that Microsoft detected the presence of DR DOS and caused system crashes to give the impression that DR DOS was unstable. Microsoft paid $150 million to settle the 1996 suit and a condition of the settlement was that evidence from the suit be destroyed.

Eventually, Microsoft expanded into the world's largest software company, while Digital Research drifted along until being acquired by Novell in 1991.

Galorath Incorporated

Galorath was started by Dan Galorath in 1979 as a consulting organization aimed at improving software development, which was a common concern during this decade. The company later incorporated in 1987 in Marina Del Rey, California. Galorath is one of a number of organizations that build parametric software cost-estimating tools. The main product of Galorath is called SEER, and it has software, hardware, and manufacturing flavors.

Parametric estimation for software projects is more accurate than manual estimation, and the accuracy is even better for large applications with more than 1,000 function points where few project managers have extensive data or experience.

Parametric estimation should have been a mainstream technology used on all major software projects. But for some reason, the parametric companies have stayed comparatively small and also independent rather than being scooped up by larger global companies.

Note

Companies named after their founders often encounter problems if the company is sold, as can be seen in the discussion of Ed Yourdon's company later in this chapter. The company retained the founder's name long after it had gone on to something else.

IMSAI Computers

In 1973, William Millard started a home business called Information Management Associates (IMS) in San Leandro, California. In 1974, the company began to design a special workstation for General Motors auto dealerships, but it did not finish this.

In 1976, IMS brought out a clone of the Altair 8800 called the IMSAI 8080. Like the Altair, it used the Intel 8080 chip and even copied the S-100 bus. The IMSAI came out in 1975 and sold well for a few years, perhaps delivering as many as 20,000 units. However, sales declined and financial problems mounted. IMSAI was acquired by two former employees, Thomas Fischer and Nancy Freitas, after IMSAI filed for bankruptcy in 1979.

The IMSAI computer would serve as a model to the dozens of clones that would mimic the IBM personal computer in future decades. Once a salable product shows signs of a large market, dozens of fast followers plunge in behind, as can be seen by the current markets for smartphones and tablets.

It is a curious phenomenon that getting venture funding for a truly new and original concept is very difficult. But if the concept succeeds in gaining market acceptance, it is quite easy for the next 10 clones to get venture funding. This is perhaps because the venture community does not quite understand technology itself but is pretty good at seeing what sells once it is developed.

InterSystems Corporation

InterSystems was founded in 1978 in Cambridge, Massachusetts, by Philip T. Ragon. InterSystems is a privately held corporation that has turned a vertical market in the health-care area into a multibillion-dollar business. In fact, Ragon is a software billionaire.

The health-care industry (including the medical records for the Veterans Administration) was an early adopter of a special language called MUMPS, which stands for *Massachusetts General Hospital Utility Multi-Programming System*. MUMPS originated in 1966 by Neil Pappalardo and colleagues at the Massachusetts General Hospital. It is a somewhat quirky interpreted language that features an integral database technology aimed at medical records.

InterSystems was a pioneer of using MUMPS and is one of its original vendors. Later, InterSystems built its own proprietary database called CACHE. InterSystems is a major vendor serving hospitals and medical records groups.

In 2008, InterSystems filed an unusual lawsuit against Microsoft, which had offices in the same building in Massachusetts. The suit tried to prevent Microsoft from expanding and renting more office space. As mentioned elsewhere in this chapter, the software industry is somewhat litigious.

In the modern era, InterSystems remains a major player in health-care applications. As a private company, it is not as well known as public companies such as Apple and Microsoft, but it is a very successful enterprise with a strong vertical market. It provides proof of the concept that vertical markets can be successful.

Lawson Software

Lawson was formed in 1976 in St. Paul, Minnesota. The founders were two brothers, William and Richard Lawson, together with John Cerullo as Chief Technology Officer (CTO).

The Lawson Company was a pioneer in ERP packages, where they competed with SAP, Oracle, PeopleSoft, and others. Lawson was successful enough to go public in 2001.

Microsoft

In 1975, Bill Gates and Paul Allen founded Microsoft in Albuquerque, New Mexico. The future history of Microsoft would be a key element of the growth of the software industry in this decade and in all future decades. The name "Microsoft" was developed by Paul Allen as a combination of "microcomputer" and "software."

The first Microsoft product was a BASIC interpreter for the Altair 8800 computer built by MITS. This later evolved into the well-known Microsoft

BASIC, which was a major language of the 1970s. In 1979, Microsoft moved from Albuquerque to Bellevue, Washington, where its world headquarters still remains.

It is interesting that Gates and Allen approached MITS rather than the other way around. The first BASIC for the Altair was written by Gates in about eight weeks.

Note

Bill Gates's mother, Mary Maxwell Gates, and John Opel, the CEO of IBM, were both on the executive board of United Way. This contact was how IBM first became aware of Bill Gates and Microsoft.

Oracle

In 1977, Larry Ellison, Bob Miner, and Ed Oates founded the company that would later become Oracle. However, its first name was Software Development Laboratories and it was not renamed as Oracle until 1995.

Reportedly, Oracle was chosen as the name because it was a code name for a CIA project that Ellison had worked on. In fact, the CIA and the Air Force were early customers of the Oracle database.

Larry Ellison became interested in relational databases after reading materials published by Ted Codd of IBM, the famous inventor of the relational model. Oracle also became a leader in ERP, and it eventually went on a buying spree and picked up many other software and hardware companies.

Oracle was a model of software success and eventually became a major player in both the database world and the ERP world. Ellison himself became famous due to his interest in yachting and yacht racing. He was also famous for his strong opinions, one of which was a dislike for Microsoft. Ellison was reported to be the highest-paid CEO of any U.S. company and not just in software. This is another example of software creating vast wealth. Oracle annual sales are in the $10 billion range.

There were many competitors in both the database and ERP domains, such as Informix and Sybase. A major ERP competitor was the German company SAP. Oracle filed a software piracy and copyright violation lawsuit against SAP. In 2010, Oracle was awarded a total of $1.3 billion by the court. This was the largest copyright award of any lawsuit. Needless to say, there was an appeal and more legal wrangling. As of 2012, the award was reduced to around $272 million, but it is uncertain whether there will be further suits or changes in the amount.

Oracle grew by acquisition as well as by its own development efforts. Some of the famous companies and products now under the Oracle umbrella include Sun Microsystems, the famous Java programming language, and the Open Office suite that competes against Microsoft Office but is free to users. Oracle also acquired Siebel, JD Edwards, and PeopleSoft.

Oracle has become sort of a software conglomerate with database packages, ERP, business tools, development tools, and several other kinds of software packages.

Price Systems

Price Systems designs and builds parametric hardware and software cost-estimating tools, primarily for military and defense software applications. It was founded as a division within the RCA Corporation in 1975 in Cherry Hill, New Jersey.

Frank Freiman was the original founder and one of the developers of the initial estimation tools together with Robert Park. The current president is Tony DeMarco, also a pioneer in software cost estimation.

When RCA began its withdrawal from the computer business, Price became an independent company. Later, in 1998, there was a management buyout, which moved the company to Mount Laurel, New Jersey. The management team included Anthony DeMarco, Bruce Fad, Earl King, and George Teologlou.

Because the military and defense communities often build large software applications with more than 10,000 function points or 1,000,000 lines of code, parametric estimation is often used. (A study that I conducted found that the accuracy of manual estimates became progressively worse with application size and was always more optimistic than the actual costs and schedules when the projects were completed.)

Price is now one of a number of companies that design and build parametric estimation tools. All of these companies are roughly the same size and all are independent, even though several started within large corporations.

Parametric estimation companies have also been subject to a curious reversal of startup sequencing. Many software companies started as small independent companies that were later acquired by major corporations. Parametric estimation, on the other hand, tended to start in major corporations such as IBM, RCA, and TRW and were then spun off into independent companies later.

Prime Computers (Pr1me)

Prime Computers was in the sector of building minicomputers. It was founded in 1972 in Natick, Massachusetts, by a team of several entrepreneurs, some of whom had worked on the MIT Multics project. The first Prime computers were patterned after Honeywell computers and are sometimes called clones.

Note

While "Prime" is spelled using the letter "i," the company's logo uses the numeral "1." This is an awkward situation for discussing the company, so "Prime" with all alphabetic characters is used in this book.

William Poduska was the Vice President of Software and became an important figure in the history of software engineering. Poduska eventually left Prime and founded Apollo Computers.

Prime was one of the companies that achieved success with vertical marketing: banking was the industry chosen by Prime, and it did well. By the mid-1980s, many banks were using Prime hardware and the Prime database. Prime peaked during the late 1980s when its equipment was used by over 330 Fortune 500 companies.

Prime also tried to diversify and had several interesting computer-aided design (CAD) products. In later years, Prime fell behind in processing speed and technology. For example, unlike high-end IBM equipment, Prime computers could be exported to Russia and the Soviet countries because the U.S. government did not consider them to have any technologies that might be stolen.

Eventually in 1998, Prime stopped most of its manufacturing and shut down many operations. The remaining pieces were renamed Computervision and were acquired by Parametric Technology.

Systems Applications Programs (SAP)

An important kind of software application and an important company emerged circa 1972. This was the German company *Systemsanalyse und Programment-wicklung*, or Systems Applications Programs (SAP), which was a pioneer in ERP applications. The original name meant systems analysis and program development.

SAP was founded in Mannheim, Germany. Later, the company kept the same SAP acronym but changed the legal name of the company to *Systeme, Anwendungen, und Produkte in der Datenverabeitung*. This newer name meant Systems, Applications, and Products in Data Processing. The five founders were Detmar Hopp, Klaus Tschira, Hans-Werner Hector, Hasso Plattner, and Claus Wellenreuther. (These founders were all former IBMers. For about 100 years, IBM has been a fruitful source of entrepreneurs who form their own companies.)

The technology used by SAP had a convoluted path. Some of the software and ideas were originated by Xerox. When Xerox decided to leave the computer business, it hired IBM to transition some of its software onto IBM platforms. One of the packages was called SDS/SAPE and was used in SAP. But there is more to the story. IBM gave the software to the five founders of SAP in exchange for founders' stock in the company in the amount of about 8%.

SAP was also interested in vertical marketing. As SAP grew and prospered, it was able to enter quite a few vertical markets at the same time. Among these were manufacturing, process control, finance, government operations, consumer products, and services.

SAP grew to become the world's third-largest software company, and en route to this rank it also acquired other companies such as Sybase and SuccessFactors.

SAP also started an interesting academic program that allows university professors and students full access to SAP. The SAP University Alliance Program now includes around 1,200 universities and about 250,000 students. The idea of a strong university program pays off with future customers who learn to use products as students and want to continue after graduation.

As mentioned in the section of this chapter on Oracle, in 2010, SAP lost a $1.3 billion copyright infringement suit filed by Oracle. There are still ongoing changes and adjustments, so the litigation and final amounts may not yet be settled.

Tandem Computers

Tandem was founded in 1974 by Jimmy Treybig, James Katzman, and Michael Green, with the help of the venture capitalist Jack Loustaunou and others in Cupertino, California. The founders had worked for Hewlett-Packard and broached their ideas for fault-tolerant computing but, at the time, HP was not interested.

The technical idea behind Tandem was important then and is still important now. For many kinds of critical software packages such as ATMs, stock exchanges, telecommunications, and hospitals, failures and outages are disasters.

Tandem designed computers that were intended to operate in a nonstop mode and to not fail. Obviously, to operate without failing, redundant components were needed, along with a method of quickly switching from a failing component to an alternate component without losing time or data.

Tandem carried redundancy to new heights. All of the components were redundant and separate from each other so that the failure of any would not impact the others. They communicated by sending messages back and forth.

Tandem also created a kind of monitor or watch-dog software feature that kept track of the reliability of every component and issued warnings as soon as problems were detected.

In addition, Tandem developed methods of swapping out or changing components while the rest of the computer continued to operate. These were important concepts for computers and software that needed high reliability.

At the time Tandem was founded, computer reliability measured in terms of mean time to failure (MTTF) and averaged only a few days. Tandem stretched out the MTTF window by at least 100-fold.

The markets served by Tandem recognized the value of what they were doing, and Tandem became a darling of Silicon Valley with one of the fastest ascents to Fortune 500 status of any company.

Tandem also had an interesting corporate culture, which engendered both enthusiasm and loyalty among Tandem employees. (Tandem was one of my consulting clients in the 1980s. The Tandem managers and technical personnel were very enjoyable to work with, and all seemed very capable.)

Tandem used a number of unique and proprietary software and hardware designs. One of these was the Tandem operating system. Unfortunately, when Tandem tried to enter the PC market in the mid-1980s, its product was not fully IBM-compatible and not compatible with many boards and physical devices either. As a result, it was unsuccessful.

Note

Many companies learned to their sorrow that being only semicompatible with IBM was not enough to succeed, as shown by the ITT and AT&T personal computers, the Tandem personal computer, and the DEC Rainbow personal computer. The IBM personal computer architecture had become a de facto global standard and only rival computers that were 100% compatible, such as Compaq, were able to stay in business.

By the 1990s, Tandem experienced a slowdown in sales and some financial issues. Tandem was acquired by Compaq, who hoped to achieve success in the higher ends of the computer market but did not do so.

Compaq also acquired Digital Equipment Corporation (DEC), which had also fallen on hard times when personal computers replaced minicomputers and their VAX line, and DEC was late to the personal computer market.

The amalgamation of Compaq with other computer companies was not successful, so in 2001, the whole combination was acquired by Hewlett-Packard. Tandem became a line of servers within HP.

One of the reasons for the lack of success of Compaq with Tandem is because of differences in marketing and sales strategies. Compaq computers were stand-alone devices that could be acquired and used at once. They did not require a lot of onsite discussions and negotiations in order to make sales.

Tandem computers, on the other hand, were often acquired to tackle mission-critical tasks where very high reliability was needed. Therefore, the sales cycle involved many visits to executives and technical personnel to show how the Tandem computers would fit into the overall business architecture of the potential clients.

The Tandem products and the Tandem corporate culture are part of the Silicon Valley legends and deserve to be studied. The basic Tandem ideas of aiming at ultra-high nonstop reliability were sound and solved previously unmet market needs. But technology changes so rapidly in computers and software that it is not easy to keep pace.

Yourdon, Inc.

Yourdon, Inc., was founded by the famous software author Ed Yourdon in 1974 in New York. As discussed elsewhere in this chapter, software applications were becoming large and complex. It was obvious that something more rigorous than unstructured cowboy development was needed for applications as big as operating systems.

Yourdon's interesting new company was among quite a few startups from this decade that actually made a difference in how software was developed. Yourdon is one of the pioneers of *structured development* and also one of the most prolific authors (together with Dr. Gerald Weinberg) of books that introduced thousands of young software engineers to better methodologies. Yourdon has written dozens of books, but his most famous, due to its striking title, is *Decline and Fall of the American Programmer*, published by Prentice Hall in 1992.

When Yourdon ran his company, it grew to about 150 people with offices in the United States and Europe. Yourdon provided training and consulting to hundreds of companies and thousands of software engineers.

In 1986, Yourdon was sold to CGI Informatique, a French company that later merged with IBM. After the sale, Yourdon had some difficulty in extracting his own name for personal use, which is not uncommon for companies named after famous individuals.

Yourdon's company did not build either computers or software directly, but it provided extremely valuable information via books and training to those who did build computers and software. The company was a pioneer in a valuable niche.

Yourdon also created a famous magazine called *American Programmer*, which later was acquired and changed its name to the *Cutter IT Journal*. This remains one of the better journals associated with software engineering.

The Impact of Companies Founded During the 1970s

The companies cited in this chapter show how important computers and software had become to corporate operations during this decade. FedEx, NASDAQ, and Southwest Airlines all used computers and software to achieve excellence in customer service and to take their respective businesses in new directions probably not achievable without computers.

Of the computer and software companies cited in this chapter, four grew to become among the largest and wealthiest companies on the planet: Apple, Microsoft, Oracle, and SAP.

A number of the entrepreneurs who started these companies also became vastly wealthy, with Bill Gates being the world's wealthiest man for several years. Other entrepreneurs such as Paul Allen, Steve Ballmer, Steve Jobs, and Larry Ellison also became personally wealthy, as did Charles Wang, Jeff Bezos, Sergey Brin, Terry Ragon, and quite a few others.

Other leaders from this decade published scores of books that transformed software development from an unstructured cowboy style to a more predictable structured style. Some of the authors whose work was influential include Fred Brooks, Gerald Weinberg, Ed Yourdon, James Martin, Carma McClure, and Larry Constantine.

The computer and software industries have been attractive for entrepreneurs in part because these industries have created many of the more recent billionaires and hundreds of millionaires. In a comparatively short time span, the computer and software industries have created enormous wealth and made permanent changes in business and government operations and even in our personal lives.

The Troublesome Growth of Software Applications

As software became more pervasive during the 1970s, applications became larger and more complex. This led to pioneering studies in improving software engineering. It also led to the publication of two landmark books, among the most famous software books to date: *The Psychology of Computer Programming* by Gerald Weinberg in 1971 and *The Mythical Man-Month* by Frederick Brooks in 1975. Both authors were colleagues at IBM, which was a hotbed of software engineering research during this decade.

Other notable books from this decade include *The Art of Software Testing* by Glenford Myers in 1979 and *Structured Design* by Edward Yourdon and Larry Constantine, also in 1979.

As it happens, my first book, *Program Quality and Programmer Productivity*, was published in 1977. In those days, the term "software engineering" was not yet widely used and those of us who built software were still just called programmers.

As can be seen from the book titles and publication dates, software began to be studied as a technical discipline that needed formal methodologies in place of cowboy programming using random techniques. These books were written in response to the expansion of software, the increase in size of software systems, and the mounting numbers of quality problems that began to attract attention.

Brooks's classic book *The Mythical Man-Month* dealt with an issue that first became important during this decade and that still remains important. The issue is that as software applications began to get large, software bugs or defects and the volumes of software paperwork increased at a faster rate than size itself measured using either function points or lines of code. The IBM operating system discussed in the book, the S/360, was the first IBM application to top 1,000,000 lines of code, or roughly 10,000 function points.

IBM had not planned on keeping the S/360 for more than about five years. In the middle of the 1970s, IBM was working on a new operating system to be called *Future System*, or FS for short. This would have been at least ten times larger than the S/360. However, it was recognized that even IBM would have trouble building such a massive system to meet the planned schedule and making it reliable enough to meet IBM's stringent quality standards.

While doing some work on the IBM Future System, I became interested in the size of the requirements and specifications. When they were scaled up from the size of similar materials for the S/360, the number of pages in total would take 40 years for an IBM employee to read. One of the endemic problems of a big system is that the volume of paperwork grows faster than the code size.

Numerous Fragmented Software Subcategories

The decade saw the overall software industry begin to fragment into a number of subindustries, each of which would become large and profitable in its own right.

Younger readers probably take these categories for granted because they have used computer-controlled devices since early childhood. Older readers born before World War II have seen the creation of the entire gamut of applications discussed here because none of them existed until the 1950s and many did not exist until the 1970s or later.

The following subsections provide short summaries of these software categories. These are some but not all of the major forms of software that emerged during the 1970s.

Advanced and Experimental Software

The kinds of applications that are deemed "advanced" change over time. In the 1970s, the fields of artificial intelligence and natural language translations were being pioneered and were certainly advanced for the time. Later, mind/machine interfaces and robotics would become topics of advanced research. Virtual reality was also an advanced topic. Software that aids astronomers and physicists is often both advanced and experimental. Medical diagnostic software is also an advanced topic.

Some specific advanced topics from the 1970s included embedded medical devices such as the software used in cochlear implants; GPS mapping, which would later become the dominant method for navigation and map making; natural language translation; robotic manufacturing; and artificial intelligence.

Business Software

Business software includes software that handles banking and financial transactions, personnel transactions, order entry, accounting, insurance processing, airline and hotel reservations, and many other kinds of general business transactions.

Business software evolved from earlier accounting and financial packages that used tabulating machines rather than true computers. When digital computers began to replace tabulating machines, the class of *management information systems*, or MIS, applications began to emerge. These soon shifted from using punch cards to using magnetic tape to using disk drives.

The advent of business MIS software led hundreds of companies to create internal software development groups and also large data centers for their mainframe computers. By the end of the 1970s, some of these software and data center combinations employed more than 5% of the total corporate workforce.

The comparatively high costs of such groups and their tendency to run late and have cost overruns led to the development of software outsource companies, specialized management consulting companies, and the development of tools such as parametric estimating tools that could help keep software projects under control. CA was founded in 1979 and is an archetype of a company that marketed business MIS applications for finance, accounting, fixed assets, and other common business purposes.

Some specific kinds of business software include accounts payable, accounts receivable, order entry, payrolls for exempt and nonexempt employees, inventory management, and customer data.

Communications Software

Software and computers quickly moved into standard telecommunications and led to the creation of digital switches and eventually to digital handsets and smartphones. Software also had a major impact on data communications and led to the creation of email, instant messaging, and other forms of data transfer.

Specific kinds of communications software include network management, central office switching systems, private branch exchange (PBX) switching systems, cell phone routing, and many others.

Cybercrime and Hacking Software

Computerized storage of valuable information such as bank accounts, social security numbers, birth records, criminal records, medical records, and other vital data has caused cybercrime to become an alarmingly large and profitable subindustry. There are now many groups of organized hackers involved in stealing and selling personal, business, and even government data.

Specific kinds of cybercrimes are too numerous to cite here and are discussed in Chapter 12. However, cybercrimes include botnets, viruses, worms, hacking, identity theft, phishing, keystroke logging, and many others.

To counter cybercrime and hacking software, a number of defensive categories have emerged, including firewalls, antivirus and antispam programs, and some newer programming languages such as E that are intended to raise the resistance of software to external attacks.

Database Software

Computers and software quickly became the tools of choice for storing and analyzing large volumes of records and business data. This would not be possible without special kinds of software applications for storing data in ways that allowed fairly convenient random access to specific records and fields. Database technology is one of the most important byproducts of digital computers and software.

As a result of database technology, millions of books, vast collections of laws, and huge volumes of data are available for analysis in unprecedented ways. This is becoming known as *big data* and is a concept that will be discussed in later chapters.

Currently, there are at least a dozen database schemas such as hierarchical, relations, entity-relationship, etc. There are also dozens of commercial database engines and query tools such as Access, DB2, SQL, MySQL, NoSQL, Oracle, and many more. This is a major subfield of software engineering and has been an active topic of research for 50 years or more.

Education Software

In one of their final meetings before Steve Jobs passed away, one of the topics of conversation between Steve Jobs and Bill Gates was a shared disappointment that computers had not had as great an impact on education as they both had wished.

Note

Readers of this book will probably find *Steve Jobs: The Exclusive Biography* by Walter Isaacson a very rich source of information about computers and software between the mid-1970s and about 2010. Isaacson's book includes many interviews with software luminaries and gives their firsthand opinions.

There are some very good education tools available for both normal educational purposes and also special education for blind, deaf, or handicapped students. However, ordinary public schools tend to use software for logistical purposes, such as schedules and payrolls, more than for educational purposes. Even in high school, software is more or less used in the background, except in some schools that do teach programming.

In some states such as Pennsylvania, there are corporations that have pooled their resources to acquire computers and software, which are then donated to inner-city schools that may lack the funds to acquire such tools. Some of these corporate donors also invite groups of students to visit offices and see what it will be like to work at one after graduation. These groups also fund field trips so grade school students can visit universities, because many young children have no idea at all what college life would be like.

On the other hand, outside of schools, children start using smartphones and computers from a very early age. In fact, a number of self-taught hackers have been found who are no older than 15.

Several school districts, such as those in California, are beginning to replace paper textbooks with e-books on Amazon Kindles, Nooks, or iPads. However, computers and software could probably be more effective and more widely deployed than they are today. Conservatism on the part of school administrators and the fact that school boards and many teachers are themselves not fully computer literate may be causative factors.

Embedded Software

One of the major subindustries of the software world is that of embedded software within physical devices. Some of the more important forms of embedded software applications include software in medical devices, software that controls automobile engines, avionics software that controls aircraft during flight, and hundreds of embedded applications in consumer products ranging from televisions to telescopes.

There are probably more embedded applications installed than any other known form of software. This is because some embedded applications are used in millions of physical devices. As an example, almost every modern automobile now uses embedded software for antilock brakes, and many also use embedded software for fuel injection. Millions of "smart" appliances such as television sets, washing machines, microwave ovens, and even alarm clocks and wristwatches now are controlled by embedded applications. In industrialized countries, an average college-educated white-collar worker probably uses at least 50 embedded devices on a daily basis, often without even knowing it. If we have medical problems, such as deafness or a heart malfunction, embedded devices may be implanted in our bodies. Over the past 35 years, embedded devices have been used in almost every kind of modern appliance and piece of complex mechanical equipment.

The widespread use of embedded devices is not without new and modern problems. Lawsuits have been filed due to brake failures or unintended automotive acceleration. When a computer-controlled device breaks, it is no longer possible to make repairs; instead, it is now necessary to swap the defective embedded device for a new one, often at considerable expense.

A final problem based on our recent dependence on embedded devices is that some can be hacked or accessed remotely by cybercriminals. Worse, an electromagnetic pulse (EMP) caused by a nuclear explosion, and possibly by strong solar storms, can shut down or damage embedded devices, possibly beyond repair.

Gaming and Entertainment Software

The computer game industry is one of the most striking new kinds of businesses in all history. The idea of millions of humans interacting in virtual environments was not even a science-fiction dream until these games started to appear in real life. Computers and software have also transformed filmmaking and have led to amazingly realistic special effects and almost photographic realism of images that are purely computer generated. Music composition and music performances have also been impacted by computers and software. Indeed, almost every teenager has access to thousands of downloaded songs at any time.

Some specific game and entertainment software include replicas of board games such as chess and backgammon; hundreds of card games; single-player games such as the classic *Doom*; and, more recently, massively multiplayer online role-playing games (MMORPGs).

Computerized animation is now the dominant tool for cartoons and full-length films. Computerized music services such as Pandora use sophisticated algorithms to classify composers and musical types; composers and performers can now write music and record it using embedded devices and computers. Music synthesizers are older than computers, but all of the modern ones use embedded chips and software.

Manufacturing Software

For hundreds of years, assembly lines and machine tools were controlled manually by skilled operators. During the 1970s, computers began to be applied to assembly lines and repetitive operations. Eventually, this would lead to fully robotic manufacturing with very few humans involved in the process at all. Not only hardware manufacturing but also chemical, pharmaceutical, and oil manufacturing would become more and more automated.

Today, many companies practice *just-in-time* manufacturing, and the whole sequence from ordering raw materials through final assembly is controlled by computers. Robotic manufacturing has cut down on shop-floor labor in the automotive and aerospace sectors, as well as in the area of smart appliances and smartphones.

Middleware Software

Computers and software are symbiotic. The hardware is inert unless controlled by special kinds of software termed *operating systems* that handle disk drives, communication ports, and other physical attributes. The applications that customers use and care about sit on top of the operating systems, but not directly on top. In between the operating systems and the user applications is a layer called *middleware* that sends requests from applications to the operating system, distributed computing, web request processing, and other services. The exact nature of middleware is somewhat ambiguous.

Some specific examples of middleware include game engines that help game developers interface with graphic chipsets, libraries of services that handle multimedia, and the multimedia home platform within smart television sets.

Military Software

Starting with SAGE in the 1950s, the Department of Defense and the military services have been leaders in usage of both computers and software. In fact, even before digital computers, the military had a long and successful history with analog computers. These were used for bombsights, torpedo targeting, shipboard gun controls, anti-aircraft targeting, and numerous other purposes. In fact, analog computers were the dominant military computing engines through the end of the Vietnam War. Digital computers are now major operating components of all sophisticated weapons systems, including combat aircraft, guided missiles, warships, battle tanks, and essentially any complex device.

Of course, weapons systems are not the only kinds of software used by the uniformed services. Hundreds of other kinds of applications are needed for logistics, planning, communications, medical records, personnel records, payrolls, purchasing, and normal kinds of business functions. The U.S. Department of Defense is currently the world's largest owner of software, which is starting to age and have significant maintenance costs.

Some of the largest software systems in history have been built by the U.S. Department of Defense and the uniformed services. One of these was the World-Wide Military Command and Control System (WWMCCS), which reportedly topped 300,000 function points or more than 21,000,000 lines of code.

In recent years, the military services have created cyberwarfare units for protecting U.S. cyberassets and for coming up with possible future offensives against enemy cyberassets in the event of a physical war.

The U.S. strength in computers and software is a strong military asset. However, other countries are attempting to catch up, with China being the number two country in usage of computers and software for military purposes. In fact, China currently has a larger cyberwarfare unit than the United States.

Open-Source Software

Surprisingly, the field of open-source software has grown about as fast as other new software fields. Even more surprising, the quality of open-source packages often compares favorably to commercial software applications, some of which are quite expensive.

The open-source topic is included in this chapter on the 1970s because one of the founders of the concept, Richard Stallman, began to share software developed at MIT with other universities from 1970 forward.

The phrase "open source" means that the source code of the software is available to the user community and users can modify the code if they wish. The category of *open source* overlaps but is not identical to the category of *freeware*. As the name implies, freeware is distributed at no cost. However, not every freeware application provides source code.

Some open-source software ranks among the most widely used applications of the modern era. Several examples of open-source applications with millions of users include Mozilla Firefox; the Android operating system; and the Open Office suite of tools that includes a word processor, a spreadsheet, a slide program, a drawing package, and more.

Many programming languages and their compilers and tools are also open source, such as Perl, PHP, Python, and Ruby. The Linux operating system is also open source.

Just because an application is open source does not give users unlimited permission to do anything they want with the application and its source code. Many open-source products are distributed using the well-known GNU General Public License (GPL), which was created by Richard Stallman of the Free Software

Foundation. The GNU license allows users to modify the code, but products using either the original or modified code must also use the GNU license. This is called *copy left* as opposed to *copy right*.

There are websites and services that list open-source and freeware tools. SourceForge.net is such a site. There are currently around 50,000 available open-source applications, roughly half of which use the GNU GPL license.

The domain of open-source software has a growing number of interesting and useful applications and a fairly sophisticated way of developing the software, releasing it, and fixing bugs. Open source is by no means chaotic, but neither is it strict and regimented.

An interesting book on the open-source movement is *The Cathedral and the Bazaar*, written by Eric Raymond in 1997. This book was subtitled *Musings of Linux and Open Source by an Accidental Revolutionary*. The theme of the book is that conventional commercial software is built like a cathedral with careful plans and a formal organization. Open source, on the other hand, operates like a bazaar with scores of vendors more or less cooperating under general guidelines.

Personal Software

The 1970s would be only the beginning of applications for personal use, which would not come to fruition until the arrival of portable computers and handheld smart devices in future decades. However, applications such as calendar management, word processing, and spreadsheets did arrive during this decade.

In today's world, a variety of extremely sophisticated software packages are available. Some handheld smartphones have voice-activated commands that can tell their owners useful information such as the names of nearby restaurants. GPS maps are endemic and can point out optimal routes by car, bicycle, or on foot. Among those with an interest in astronomy, star maps provide a wonderful view of every major star, planet, and constellation in every direction, including through the earth. Many of us no longer keep manual telephone lists or address books because our personal records are online.

If we want to buy something, our computers, tablets, or smartphones can provide information and addresses of local stores. They can also show the comparative prices of specific products in local stores. If we don't need the item today, we can buy it over the web and probably avoid paying local or state taxes.

Computers and software have made a very big impact on our personal lives and communication styles. Many of us have many more "friends" on social networks than we have in real life. We may spend more time texting with our real friends than we spend in actual conversation with them.

Programming Tool Software

As software engineers or programmers became more numerous, markets appeared for specialized tools such as debugging tools, trace tools, and interactive development environments (IDEs).

The very oldest programming tools appeared in the 1950s in the form of assemblers and early compilers for higher-level languages. In today's world, modern programmers have more than 50 kinds of tools, including requirements tools, design tools, inspection support tools, test case generators, test library support tools, automated testing tools, debugging tools, reengineering tools, documentation tools, defect tracking tools, and too many more to name.

Project Management Software

The technical parts of project management involve scheduling, resource allocation, cost estimation and cost data collection, change management, status reporting, and quality analysis. Computers and software have long been useful for project managers in every field. The 1970s witnessed the arrival of parametric software estimation tools.

In today's world, this type of software is used by millions of project managers to handle topics such as staff allocations, progress tracking, budgets, cost estimating, quality estimating, project office operations, and proposals for new business.

For software projects, there are a number of powerful parametric estimating tools that are in general more accurate than manual estimates. These include COCOMO II, Cost Xpert, KnowledgePLAN, SEER, SLIM, Software Risk Master (SRM), and TruePrice.

All of these predict software development costs. Some also predict quality. One, SRM, has special estimates for venture-backed software startups and also for the probability and costs of litigation between outsource contractors and their clients.

Scientific and Mathematical Software

Computers were created to speed up complex mathematical operations required by scientists such as astronomers, chemists, and physicists. Specialized software for statistics and mathematical operations has now become so easy to use that it is available to high school students.

Ordinary spreadsheets can handle various common calculations. More specialized packages such as SAGE, SAS, MatLab, Mathematica, and at least 50 more are available. Some are freeware, some are open source, while others are fee-based products. One other example is the R programming language, which is free and widely used for statistical applications.

Security and Protective Software

The arrival of hacking, viruses, worms, and denial of service attacks created a critical new subindustry of companies that develop and market antivirus tools, firewalls, and other kinds of protective software. There is a heated technical race going on between cybercriminals and cyberdefenders.

Major threats include viruses, worms, spyware, botnets, denial of service attacks, identity theft, and many others.

Major defensive products include firewalls and over a dozen malware and antivirus tools such as AVG, Avira, Bitdefender, Kaspersky, McAfee, Microsoft Security, Norton, and many more.

Social Network Software

Social networks have millions of members in essentially every country in the world. The most common social networks today are Facebook, Twitter, LinkedIn, and the older America Online (AOL). Not exactly social networks per se but having a similar impact on daily lives are craigslist and Angie's List, used by millions of consumers to find products and reviews of services. Wiki sites are another new form of social network, which has led to *crowdsourcing*, which is when disparate groups of people can address some fairly complex issues in one place on the web.

Social networks derived from earlier technologies such as bulletin boards and email. They gradually added features such as instant chatting, images, photographs, and other newer features such as audio.

More than 100 major social networks appear on the web and probably one or two new ones spring up every month. YouTube, MySpace, SecondLife, and Friendster are other examples of social networks. Massively multiplayer computer games are not pure social networks, but they overlap that field because the players are in contact with one another.

Facebook is the largest with 200 million subscribers. However, dozens of social networks each have more than 10 million subscribers.

Social networking is a phenomenon that started less than 30 years ago, but the combined memberships of all social networks is probably equal to perhaps one seventh of the global population.

Users of social networks vary by age, occupation, and other variables. Schoolchildren through college levels are intense users of social networks. People under the age of 25 typically are members of several social networks and use them daily. People older than 65 may not use social networks at all, and some don't know anything about them.

Survey Tools Software

One of the more common uses for computers in the modern era is to find out what people think about various topics. Prior to the internet and the web, surveys were printed on paper and distributed by mail, both of which are fairly expensive. In today's world, surveys are easy to design and build, and they can be distributed globally or to any selected target audience almost instantly via the web.

A web search of online survey tools found more than 50 of them, ranging from freeware to fairly expensive commercial products. A few samples include Survey Crafter, Survey Monkey, Limesurvey, QuestionPro, Keysurvey, Formsite, SurveyGizmo, and Google Forms.

Utility Software

The generic term "utility software" includes a variety of tools that manipulate data, code, and other artifacts. Sort programs are a major example of utility packages. Some common software utility programs include disk drive defragmentation, clutter cleaners such as CClean, Norton Utilities, registry fixers, and file transfer programs. There are probably more than 100 utilities, but there is no exact definition for what a utility actually is because it does so many things.

As can be seen, the overall field of software engineering, like medical and legal practice, is forming a large number of specialized fields and disciplines. The taxonomy in this section shows 20 different kinds of software applications.

Prior to the 1970s, there were only two common kinds of software: scientific and military. All of the other diverse forms of software began to grow and expand at the end of the 1960s but expanded with great rapidity during the 1970s.

Younger readers have probably used these kinds of software since childhood. Older readers born before World War II may have been active participants in creating these categories of software.

A Lawsuit That Changed Computer History

In April 1973, the longest federal business lawsuit in U.S. history was finally decided. This was the patent litigation between Honeywell and Sperry-Rand. This was a complex case with charges and countercharges, hundreds of witnesses, and thousands of pages of discovery documents covering the full history of the computer industry.

A patent application had been filed on the ENIAC computer in 1947 but not issued by the patent office until 1964. The ENIAC had been built by J. Presper Eckert and John W. Mauchly, but the patent had been acquired by Sperry-Rand.

Because the patent covered the essential design and features of digital computers, other companies such as IBM were required to pay royalties for all digital computers that had the same or similar features as those covered by the patent. Some of the companies facing royalty charges included Burroughs, Control Data, General Electric, Honeywell, National Cash Register, Philco Ford, and RCA. (IBM did not face charges because it had a patent-sharing arrangement with Sperry-Rand.)

The federal judge for the case was Earl R. Larson and his decision was issued on October 19, 1973. The gist of the decision, which was itself a very large document, essentially found that the ENIAC patent was unenforceable and invalid for a wide variety of reasons.

One aspect of the decision was and still is controversial. The judge stated in passing that the inventors of the digital computer were not Eckert and Mauchly, but rather John V. Atanasoff, whose ABC computer was discussed in Chapter 3.

As it happened, Mauchly had visited Atanasoff and had seen the ABC computer and also written a letter about it. The ABC and ENIAC computers were different in many respects, so the judge's opinion remains controversial even today.

In any case, the decision that invalidated the ENIAC patent opened a path for dozens of companies to start building digital computers without paying royalties to Sperry-Rand. The implications of this decision are significant to the growth of the computer and software industries.

It is quite possible that if royalties had remained in force, small companies such as Apple, Altair, Atari, Commodore, Data General, Prime, Sun, Tandem,

Tandy, and Wang would never have been started because the royalties demanded from each company ranged from $20 million to $250 million.

If the lawsuit had gone the other way and the ENIAC patent had been confirmed, the computer and software industries today would probably be quite different than they have become. Large companies would dominate, and probably the diversity of hardware and software offerings would be much smaller.

Background Enabling Inventions

Without some convenient method of storing software, it would be difficult to have a true software industry. One of the critical background inventions of the modern software world was the development of the floppy disk and the floppy disk drive in 1971.

The first floppy disk was eight inches in diameter and only held about 80 kilobytes of information. But the floppy disk was a success and became a standard feature of IBM's S/370.

Modern readers who use flash drives or external disk drives that weigh only an ounce or two would be surprised at how big and heavy the early eight-inch disk drives were. A disk drive sometimes weighed 40 pounds.

Even so, floppy disks provided an effective medium for storing, transporting, and marketing software, without which there might not be a software industry.

Note

I once had an eight-inch drive connected to an early Tandy Radio Shack TRS-80 computer. It was a large box about 18 inches wide and deep and 12 inches high. I had to put the drive on the floor because it was too bulky and heavy to sit on a desk.

The older storage media of punch cards, paper tape, and magnetic tape were not suitable for widespread software distributions. Punch cards and paper tape were short-lived and susceptible to damage from humidity and water. Magnetic tape was bulky and subject to fairly rapid magnetic degradation. Mainframe disk drives existed but were too heavy and large for home use.

Equally important, Ted Codd from IBM in San Jose began to publish descriptive information about the relational database model, which would lead to vast improvements in data access and data access speed. Relational database technology also opened up markets for a number of new vendors such as Ingres and Sybase, as well as IBM's own System R.

The quartz movement used in modern watches dates back to the 1920s, but it needed semiconductors to move into small personal timepieces. The Centre Electronique Horloger (CEH) built a working quartz analog watch in 1967. Sony built a successful quartz watch, the Astron, in 1969.

In 1972, Hamilton introduced the first digital watch, the Pulsar. This watch cost about $2,100 when it first came out. Earlier, Hamilton had built a digital clock that appeared in the movie *2001: A Space Odyssey*.

In today's world, digital quartz movements are inexpensive and dominate timekeeping. Billions of timekeeping and timing devices are available in watches, timers, medical devices, military devices, and anything else that needs accurate timekeeping.

1970 marked the start of the UNIX operating system, which would become one of the most popular software applications in history.

This decade also witnessed the rise of minicomputers and the rise of specialized computers for word processing and office tasks. Among the companies in this niche were DEC with its PDP and VAX computers, Wang with both specialized word processing machines and small computers, and Prime Computers.

The physical reduction in the size and weight of computers from mainframes to minicomputers made it obvious that it would soon be possible to have computers that were small enough to carry around and be portable.

The IBM 5100 computer, released in September 1975, was the first computer that could be carried from place to place, although it required some physical strength because it weighed about 55 pounds.

In 1976, this "portable" computer was followed by the NoteTaker from Xerox Park, which was a prototype that would later be the pattern for the Osborne and Compaq portables in the next decade. These portables each weighed about 26 pounds.

In the 1970s, the need for portable computers was seen, but the technology to shrink computers down to a truly portable form factor would not surface until later decades.

Also in 1976, the mathematician Tom McCabe developed the *cyclomatic complexity metric*. This measures the control of the paths through a software application. It has remained a key metric for more than 35 years.

This decade also saw the use of embedded software in an ever-growing family of physical devices. For example, the first widely used cochlear implant was developed in 1972. Cochlear implants surgically embed wires that replace damaged cochlea, and sound quality is adjusted by software in the embedded device.

In October 1978, Al Albrecht of IBM in White Plains gave the first public speech on function points at the joint IBM/SHARE/GUIDE conference in Monterey, California. (After the conference, Al's paper was republished in my first book, with the permission of Al and the conference organizers. This first publication of Al's paper in *Programming Productivity: Issues for the Eighties* by the IEEE Computer Society Press was the first of many articles and books about function points.)

In 1979, Dan Bricklin and Bob Frankston introduced the VisiCalc application for Apple computers, which greatly expanded the use of personal computers for personal finance and easy mathematical modeling. VisiCalc was also released for the IBM PC in 1981.

This decade saw the evolution of higher-level languages. Some of the languages created in this decade include Pascal and Forth in 1970; C, Smalltalk, and Prolog in 1972; COMAL and EML in 1973; ELAN in 1974; Scheme and RATFOR in 1975; and SQL in 1978.

These joined COBOL, FORTRAN, and PL/I, and the explosion of languages was well under way. From this decade forward, new languages appeared almost every month, and the total number of languages now tops 2,500.

The explosion of programming languages seems to be more of a sociological phenomenon than a true technical need. The existence of so many programming languages makes maintenance of legacy applications complex and difficult. Indeed, the life expectancy of a large application is sometimes longer than the life of the language used to create it.

Another phenomenon also occurred in this decade, and it is still expanding in the present decade. Applications began to use multiple languages such as COBOL and SQL or, more recently, Java and HTML. From my collection of data, an average software application contains about 2.5 different programming languages. I have noted that the maximum number of programming languages in a single application is 15, and quite a few applications use more than half a dozen.

The plethora of languages is not necessarily beneficial to the industry. Development may be aided somewhat, but the task of maintenance and enhancement of legacy applications written in dead or dying languages has become a major cost driver for the software industry.

The 1970s also saw the early evolution of structured programming and the birth of object-oriented programming. The decade witnessed the rapid migration of computers and software from the scientific and military domains into the business domain.

Table 6.1   *U.S. Software Applications from 1970 to 1979*

Application Types	Applications	Percentage
Scientific	4,000	13.33%
Military and defense	10,000	33.33%
Civilian government	2,000	6.68%
Systems and middleware	4,000	13.33%
Embedded software	3,000	10.00%
Commercial	1,000	3.33%
Information technology (IT)	5,500	18.33%
U.S. outsource	350	1.17%
Offshore outsource	100	0.33%
Web applications	0	0.00%
Games and entertainment	50	0.17%
Open source	0	0.00%
Total Applications	**30,000**	**100.00%**

This decade, one of explosive growth of software in all industry segments, also witnessed IBM's rise to become one of the world's major providers of computers and software. Table 6.1 shows the approximate numbers of applications during this decade.

Function Points in 1975

Function points were invented by IBM in White Plains by Al Albrecht and colleagues circa 1975 and were published outside of IBM in 1978.

Formal inspections were developed by IBM during this decade by Mike Fagan, Ron Radice, and colleagues in IBM Kingston. During this decade, IBM pioneered dozens of software engineering technologies and established an excellent reputation for quality and reliability of both hardware and software.

For the same application of 1,000 function points, the results would be the following:

- Source code statements for 1,000 function points: 91,426 logical code statements

- Programming language: C

- Reuse percentage: 0% to 10%

- Methodology: Unstructured waterfall

- Productivity: 6.00 function points per staff month

- Defect potentials: 5.00 per function point

- Defect removal efficiency (DRE): 85%

- Delivered defects: 0.75 per function point

- Ratio of development personnel to maintenance:

  - Development: 80%

  - Maintenance: 20%

The following are the background data for 1975:

- Average language level: 3.50

- Number of programming languages: 100

- Logical statements per function point: 91

- Average application size: 950 function points

- Average application size: 86,450 logical code statements

The combination of better programming languages and increased development rigor was responsible for the productivity and quality gains. However, large software projects continued to have cost and schedule overruns and far too many bugs. Canceled projects with more than 10,000 function points remained an endemic problem.

Summary

The unbundling of software by IBM in 1969 opened the floodgates to the creation of hundreds of commercial software companies. The patent decision in 1973 that invalidated the ENIAC patent opened up paths for new computer companies as well, including small companies such as Apple and Commodore.

At the start of the 1970s, computers and software were minor niche industries with uncertain futures. By the end of the decade, computers and software were on their way to creating wealth beyond imagination and making Bill Gates the world's wealthiest individual and Apple Computer the world's wealthiest company. The jobs of computer programming and software engineering continued to expand rapidly.

By 1979, computers and software were well on their way to becoming the dominant tools for business and government operations, and they were also on their way to becoming major personal tools as well.

After this decade, the impact of computers and software would permeate every aspect of business, government, military, and personal activities. The world was changing, and computers and software created huge networks that spanned the globe.

Chapter 7

1980 to 1989: The Rise of Personal Computers and Personal Software

The 1980s witnessed a major business change in history. The arrival of the IBM personal computer and the continued expansion of the Apple line turned computers and software from pure corporate business tools into sophisticated personal tools. The hardware changes were accompanied by a huge expansion in new commercial software packages aimed at the personal computer market. Indeed, "commercial off-the-shelf" (COTS) software began to displace custom-built software in many industries on both mainframe and personal computers.

The explosion of personal computers had a negative impact on minicomputers, which had been a growing business up until this time. Mainframes and supercomputers continued to be critical tools in major corporations and large government agencies. By the end of the decade, minicomputers were a dying industry.

The advent of personal computers led to a major expansion of software for personal use such as office suites, calendars, and home finance.

By the end of the decade, notebook computers were arriving, as were even smaller devices called personal digital assistants (PDAs). Portability became a new market force as many companies competed for combinations of light-weight and long-battery-life personal devices. (During the 1980s, I visited several companies working on prototypes of small computers and handheld devices that would emerge in later decades.)

This decade also saw the expansion of *outsourcing* as companies realized that their internal software groups were large, expensive, and not necessarily capable of building software well.

Another major advance in this decade was the creation of the *World Wide Web*, which would change human communications forever.

Rapid Changes in Computing

The beginning of the 1980s witnessed a world-changing event: the release of the IBM personal computer in 1981. The marketing power of IBM and the ease of use of the IBM PC opened up the markets for commercial software because almost every citizen would soon use a computer for personal tasks.

The IBM PC catapulted Microsoft to become a major player in the software industry, and Bill Gates became the world's wealthiest man for many years. The famous *disk operating system*, or Microsoft DOS (MS-DOS), had been ordered by IBM in 1981, and the first version was released to outside customers in 1982. DOS was the main operating system of the early PC era.

The Windows operating system was originally an extension to DOS, but by the time of Windows 2 in 1982, it began to have a graphical appearance with overlapping screen images.

Early in the decade, Apple selected the Objective-C programming language as its main language for Apple products. The language was originally developed by Dr. Tom Love and Dr. Brad Cox at ITT, and it was acquired by Stepstone Corporation when ITT sold its telecommunications business to Alcatel. Objective-C is still used in Apple products, making it one of the longest-lasting industrial programming languages.

This decade saw the incorporation of the Software Engineering Institute (SEI) in 1984 and increasing rigor of software development. Software assessments as designed by Watts Humphrey were offered by SEI, and assessments plus benchmarks were offered by Software Productivity Research (SPR), starting a year before SEI. Both methods expanded rapidly in this decade.

Programming languages began to explode in numbers and variety with new languages such as Ada, Quick Basic, Pascal, C11, Objective-C, and dozens of others appearing. New languages came out at a rate of more than two per month during this decade.

This decade witnessed the arrival of the internet and what would later facilitate the World Wide Web. The *internet* is a collection of protocols that connects computers and networks to each other. The term "world wide web" was coined by Tim Berners-Lee and is a set of services that use the internet. It would be the next decade before the World Wide Web actually became global.

The internet derived from the older ARPANET and several other similar networks in Europe. Other enabling technologies were needed; among them was the famous internet protocol suite TCP/IP. The TCP/IP standard facilitated the emergence of a new commercial business of "internet service providers," or

ISPs as they are commonly called. (Other enabling inventions such as hyper-text markup language [HTML] are discussed in the next chapter dealing with the 1990s.)

The International Function Point Users' Group (IFPUG) moved from Canada to the United States in 1986. Soon after, the IFPUG began to offer certification examinations to ensure accuracy in function point counts.

The initial examination was developed by Al Albrecht, who was at SPR at the time, having retired from IBM. In later decades, the IFPUG would become the world's largest software metrics organization with branches in more than 25 countries.

Function point metrics began to replace older metrics such as "lines of code" and "cost per defect" for economic studies. The lines of code (LOC) metric ignores requirements and design and penalizes high-level languages. The cost per defect metric ignores fixed costs and penalizes quality. Function points are the most accurate metrics for software economic analysis.

The SPQR/20 estimation tool in 1984 was the first commercial estimation tool built around function point metrics. It was also the first estimating tool with integrated sizing. It produced sizes of source code volumes for 30 languages and sizes of various paper documents such as requirements, design, and user manuals.

This decade witnessed the rise (and fall) of numerous computer- and software-related companies. Some of these achieved bursts of glory but eventually succumbed to technical malaise. Some of the names of companies that thrived during this decade include Amdahl, Digital Equipment Corporation (DEC), Burroughs, Control Data Corporation (CDC), Wang (a pioneer in word processing), Data General, Tandem, the RCA computer line, the Honeywell computer line, the Bull computer line, the Xerox computer line, the AT&T personal computer line, the ITT personal computer line (not fully IBM-compatible), and quite a few others. Some companies that grew rapidly in this era still prosper, such as Hewlett-Packard. Others such as Sun were acquired, in this case by Oracle.

The rise and fall of companies in the computing and software industries is an interesting story. Some of the issues that caused business failures included the rise of IBM, attempts to lock clients into proprietary hardware and software, and a widespread failure to recognize the importance of personal computers as a world-changing event in business operations. For example, DEC was late in bringing out a personal computer, and when it did, its computers were not fully compatible with IBM's, which by then was on its way to being the main tool of millions of corporate personnel.

Although the fundamental technology was designed in the previous decade, Sony and Philips combined to bring out the very successful "compact disk read-only memory" (CD-ROM) in 1983. The first music recorded on a CD was Richard Strauss's Alpine Symphony in 1981. On March 2, 1983, CD players and several disks were released in the United States, which started a boom.

These disks were soon applied to personal computers, although briefly competing devices such as the Bernouli Box and the Iomega Zip Disk competed but were soon bypassed by CDs that could be written on as well as read from. The huge storage capacities of these CDs allowed whole software packages such as Microsoft Office to be delivered on a single disk, as opposed to dozens of floppy disks.

In the next decade, the even higher-capacity "digital versatile disks" (DVDs) would become popular for both movies and very high-capacity computer storage devices.

Although not a pure software organization, the famous Project Management Institute (PMI) was founded in 1984. It has become well known for its certification programs in various management disciplines. It has also created a large library of books and papers called the PMI "body of knowledge," or PMBOK.

Companies Formed During the 1980s

Table 7.1 shows a sample of companies that were founded during the 1980s. This is a representative sample but far from complete. Thousands of local companies serving a single geographic area were also created.

Table 7.1 *Sample of Companies Founded from 1980 to 1989*

Company	Year
Accenture	1989
Adobe	1982
Advanced Business Solutions	1983
Amadeus IT	1987
America Online (AOL)	1983
Apollo	1980
Ashton-Tate	1980
AutoDesk	1982
Avira	1986

Table 7.1 *(Continued)*

Company	Year
BASIS	1985
BitStream	1981
BlackBerry	1984
Borland	1983
Broderbund	1980
Capcom	1983
Central Point	1980
CGNET	1983
Cisco Systems	1984
Cognex	1981
Compaq	1982
Computer Aid, Inc. (CAI)	1982
Cutter Consortium	1986
Dell	1984
Digital Consulting Institute (DCI)	1982
Fox Interactive	1982
Intuit	1983
KeySoft	1989
KPMG	1987
Leading Edge	1980
Level 9	1983
Logitech	1981
Lotus	1982
McAfee	1987
MicroGraphX	1982
NeXT	1985
Pegasus	1981
PeopleSoft	1987
Peregrine	1981
Quest	1987
Sage	1981

(Continued)

Table 7.1   *(Continued)*

Company	Year
Sapien	1986
SciSys	1980
SEI	1984
SPR	1983
Stepstone	1984
Symantec	1982
Tata	1989
Trilogy	1989
Unisoft	1981
Vero	1988
Wind River	1981
Wolfram	1987
Wyse	1981

Table 7.1 is only a sampling of companies that became large enough to be mentioned specifically here. There were thousands of smaller local companies that were also created during the 1980s.

This decade did see some major corporations created such as Accenture, Cisco, and KPMG. But the previous decade was when the largest software giants originated: Microsoft, Oracle, and SAP. Many of the companies created in the 1980s would provide products and services that filled in the gaps around offerings from companies such as IBM and Microsoft.

Future decades would see another wave of major companies when the web opened up new technical possibilities. The web would lead to modern giants such as Amazon, Google, and Facebook.

The impact of computers and software has occurred so rapidly that many of the companies and products we use every day not only did not exist 25 years ago but the companies themselves also did not exist. Many of the technologies these companies market did not exist either.

Computers and software have triggered a major new form of industrial revolution where automated methods are transforming not only manufacturing and business operations but also communications and knowledge sharing.

Recall that in the 1980s, computers were more or less isolated from each other except by rather slow and primitive connections such as modems. Later, when the web became a global communication channel and all computers were connected, huge new business opportunities would appear.

Not all of these new web-based businesses would succeed, as will be seen later when the dot-com bubble is discussed.

There are too many companies to discuss them all, but the ones that had interesting business models or created novel products are discussed here.

Accenture

The rapid growth of the software industry during this decade and the prior decade opened up new opportunities for both outsourcing and consulting. Major companies needed computers and software but were inexperienced and often blundered. Accenture was able to become one of the largest software consultancies in the world by providing aid to thousands of companies in dozens of countries.

The history of Accenture is long and too complex for a full discussion, but it has been used in many business school case studies. Accenture originated as the consulting wing of the former Arthur Andersen accounting company back in the 1950s. In 1989, Andersen Consulting split from the accounting side of Andersen and became a separate business unit, which is why it is cited in this chapter.

The split between the accounting and consulting groups exacerbated internal political and finance issues between the two sides, which eventually led to a famous arbitration and a complete divestiture of the consulting organization, which became a separate company in 2001.

As part of the split, the consulting company needed to stop using any form of the "Arthur Andersen" name. An internal contest resulted in the name "Accenture" being selected. It had been submitted by an employee from Denmark.

Also in 2001, Accenture had a successful IPO. Since then, it has grown to more than 250,000 employees worldwide. Accenture provides consulting and outsource services to almost 75% of Fortune 500 U.S. companies and about 90% of the Global Fortune 100 companies.

Accenture is successful due to the universal adoption of computers and software by hundreds of major companies that are not necessarily skilled in either computers or software.

When complex technologies such as computers and software become mainstays of corporations and government agencies, there is a huge need for expert consultants who can assist groups that may not have sufficient internal expertise to be effective. This is a niche that Accenture has managed to dominate. Accenture is not alone, of course, but it was certainly among the best known by corporate CEOs, CFOs, and CIOs in every industrialized country.

It is of both social and technical importance that the original Arthur Andersen accounting company was found guilty of criminal charges due to the way it audited the Enron books (Enron went bankrupt in 2001 amid a flurry of criminal investigations). Arthur Andersen voluntarily gave up its license to perform accounting in 2002. Although the U.S. Supreme Court later overturned the guilty finding, by then Arthur Andersen had lost its reputation and most of its employees and assets.

This was a sad ending for a company whose founder, Arthur Andersen, was a pioneer in both accounting education and accounting ethics. He was among the first to provide on-the-job training during business hours. He was also instrumental in creating accounting standards and the concepts of generally accepted accounting practices. His personal motto was "think straight, talk straight." He was known to be so honest that he turned down business from clients that wanted to wiggle with accounting standards.

Adobe

Adobe was founded in San Jose, California, in 1982 by John Warnock and Charles Geschke. Both were former employees of the famous Xerox PARC research laboratory, which invented many advanced topics but was never successful in marketing them. The name of the company is taken from Adobe Creek, a seasonal creek that ran behind the founders' homes in Los Altos, California.

Adobe's first product was the PostScript page-description language used on millions of laser printers. Adobe also brought out a family of type fonts for computers but ran into competition from Apple in that business.

Later, Adobe came out with Adobe Illustrator and Photoshop for the end-user personal computer markets on both Macintosh and IBM platforms.

Among their most ubiquitous products was the almost universal *portable document format*, or PDF, file, which is now a global standard (ISO standard 3200-1/2008). Adobe also controls the TIFF graphics format for compressed files.

Adobe was slow to enter the desktop publishing market with its own product, but it had so much money available that it eventually acquired competitors in this field such as Aldus and Macromedia.

In 2010, Adobe and Apple had a fairly public dispute due to Apple's claim that Adobe was insecure and could not be used on several Apple products. Adobe countered with a claim that Apple only wanted to keep Adobe away from its platforms.

Adobe stock has been traded on NASDAQ since 1996. It remains a large and innovative company with numerous applications and products centering on digital typography and graphics. Probably almost every reader of this book uses one or more Adobe products such as PDFs, TIFF files, Photoshop, and many others.

America Online (AOL)

AOL was founded in 1983 under the name of Control Video Corporation. It changed its name to America Online and then to AOL. The original founder was Bill Meister. The company's first product was a modem and a connection to the Atari 2600 computer-game console.

Later, it brought in new technical and management leaders and change strategy. After some other name changes and direction changes and the departure of the founder, the newly named America Online began the service that later made it famous: a network that was graphically based, easy to use, and provided rich and varied content to subscribers.

AOL as a corporation was a pioneer in both emails and social groups, which later became known as "social networks."

At its peak in around 1995, AOL had about 10 million members. However, AOL charged for email and other services ($19.95 per month) at a time when free email services were starting to appear. Also, response time and even access were often sluggish, leading to customer dissatisfaction and departures.

AOL also had an erratic history as a corporation with both ups and downs, mergers, divestitures, and other corporate changes. Between 2000 and 2009, AOL was owned by Time Warner Corporation, an arrangement that apparently satisfied neither side. AOL was spun off into a separate company in December 2009.

As other social networks and email services eroded AOL's key business, it was necessary to change directions. The new strategy, which thus far seems to be helping, is to concentrate on "content" as opposed to the network and network services. For example, AOL acquired the *Huffington Post* and MapQuest.

In April 2012, the *Huffington Post* won a Pulitzer Prize, becoming the first online journal to do so. David Wood was the reporter who won the prize based on his series about the postwar experiences of U.S. soldiers back from Afghanistan and Iraq.

AOL also began a push for generating revenues via online advertising. AOL continues to experiment with content and ads, which will hopefully keep it profitable.

Avira

Avira is a successful antivirus company that was founded in Tettnang, Germany, in 1986. Avira currently has about 100 million customers and is a major player in the antivirus industry. Avira is one of a number of companies that have an interesting business model. Avira provides a basic antivirus package for free but also offers more sophisticated versions for a fee.

As with many specialized niche industries, the antivirus world has frequent reviews and rankings of relative performance. Avira normally gets good reviews.

Other players in the antivirus market include AVG, Norton, Trend Micro, McAfee, Kaspersky, and many more. There is a hot race between the virus producers and the antivirus defenders.

Note

Avira's CEO, Tjark Auerbach, supports a number of charities and nonprofit art groups through his Auerbach Foundation. Quite a few software executives have a strong interest in social and charitable issues. Others include Bill Gates of Microsoft and Tony Salvaggio of CAI. Given the accumulated wealth of the software industry, its social and charitable impact has become significant.

BlackBerry (Research in Motion, or RIM)

The BlackBerry product is a pioneering smartphone. The company itself was founded in Waterloo, Ontario, in 1984 by Mike Lazaridis. Apparently, he named the company Research in Motion (RIM) because he liked the phrase "poetry in motion." The name "BlackBerry" is due to a slight resemblance of a computer keyboard to the surface of the actual blackberry fruit.

Some state governments provide seed money for software companies. The Canadian government played a significant role in funding the RIM startup. In the United States, venture capitalists provide all the seed money rather than the federal government. Private investors also provided initial funds for RIM.

The first product from RIM in 1998 was a paging device that competed with Motorola. The first BlackBerry smartphone came out in April 2000. For several years, the BlackBerry smartphones did well and their sales, customers, and revenues climbed quickly. Having a BlackBerry was a status symbol among both executives and technical geeks.

However, in 2007, the Apple iPhone arrived on the market and the RIM business prognosis took a turn for the worse. The BlackBerry Storm model came out in 2008 with a touchscreen, but it suffered from poor reviews and dissatisfied customers.

The proprietary BlackBerry operating system, QNX, also suffered from competition with Android. In its first year on the market, Android pulled ahead of BlackBerry in U.S. customers. Indeed, BlackBerry had a net decline in U.S. customers due to Android competition.

Worse, in September 2011, BlackBerry's network had a massive network failure that disconnected U.S. customers for several days and garnered huge amounts of negative publicity. This was front-page news and was even mentioned on national television news shows.

In spite of increased competition and significant layoffs, BlackBerry continues to be a major player in the smartphone business. Its newest models are getting good reviews. In 2013, RIM changed its name to BlackBerry.

The history of RIM and BlackBerry shows that having a good idea and a good invention do not ensure long-range success. Companies such as RIM need to keep current with industry trends and hopefully stay ahead of them. They also need to keep up with quality and reliability, since poor quality is a market killer.

Borland

The history of Borland is a sort of microcosm of many Silicon Valley software companies, with a few unique factors as well. Borland was founded in Scotts Valley, California, in August 1981. The founders were three Danish citizens: Niels Jensen, Ole Henricsen, and Mole Glad. The most famous founder, Philippe Kahn, joined forces with Borland later. Kahn was Chairman, President, and CEO from 1983 until 1995, when he left.

The company's first product was a CP/M add-on, but Borland soon got into a different niche that was more successful. Its 1983 products of TurboPascal and SideKick had large sales and made Borland one of the more successful programming language companies. SideKick was a forerunner of features that later appeared on PDAs to keep track of calendars, address books, phone numbers, and so on.

Borland had a successful IPO in 1989 and again in 1991. Both were oversubscribed and generated substantial capital.

Through a combination of acquisitions and internal development, the Borland products expanded to include Turbo C, Quattro Pro, dBASE, and Paradox.

Borland had an unusual copyright lawsuit with Lotus, which had charged copyright violations over the Quattro spreadsheet. This was one of the first "look and feel" infringement cases. The case was decided in favor of Borland by the First Circuit Court of Appeals in Boston, Massachusetts.

What happened next was unusual. Lotus appealed to the U.S. Supreme Court. One of the nine justices, John Paul Stevens, recused himself, leaving only eight to hear the case. The eight justices tied 4 to 4 in their decision, which left the original decision intact. Having a tied decision in a Supreme Court case is extremely rare.

In the late 1990s, Borland had declining sales and some issues with products that were aging and hard to port to Windows. It tried to compete with Microsoft Office by partnering with WordPerfect, but that was not a success.

Borland also attempted, with some success, to build software development environments with products such as JBuilder and Delphi. However, the open-source subindustry targeted the same field with free products such as Eclipse, and these were much more successful.

Borland also tried application life cycle management (ALM), but while it had strong pieces such as StarTeam, Caliber, and Segue (which was a test tool suite), the integration of the pieces was spotty. In the meantime, IBM Rational, Microsoft VSTS, and HP Mercury arrived to compete in the same space.

Between its revenue peak in the early 2000s and its final acquisition by Micro Focus, Borland experienced a string of revenue and earning losses and seemed to have no strategy to turn things around (or at least not one that worked).

After several changes of CEOs and still more changes of direction, Borland decided to move toward enterprise applications rather than personal applications. This led to an ill-conceived name change from Borland to Inprise. The name change was not a success. Nobody knew what Inprise did because the name was unknown, and many people thought Borland had gone out of business when it stopped being mentioned in ads. In 2001, the company became Borland again.

After a number of different direction and management changes that are very complex, Borland was finally acquired by Micro Focus in 2009. The price was about $1.50 per share, or $75 million.

The history of Borland is a cautionary tale for software entrepreneurs. Changing business direction is hard to do successfully. Changing business direction almost every year confuses customers, investors, and employees. A rapid sequence of acquisitions and divestitures also makes it hard to have a solid core business.

In retrospect, if Borland had continued to grow its language products and personal assistant products, it might have continued to grow. Attempting to compete with Microsoft in the office suite world and getting into the database market without really understanding it was not a path to success. Changing executives and business plans so often that it is hard to keep track of them is also troubling.

The Borland experience shows that the 1980s was a period of technical fragmentation combined with lots of companies going after "hot" markets such as development environments. Increasing competition in niche markets was part of the reason for Borland's decline.

Computer Aid, Inc. (CAI)

CAI is primarily a midsized software outsource group, but with some unique attributes. It was founded by Tony Salvaggio and Winslow Hill in 1981 in Allentown, Pennsylvania. Of the two founders, Salvaggio was a former IBMer and Hill was from Bethlehem Steel, which was located only a few miles from Allentown.

CAI is one of many startups created by former IBM personnel (including the author of this book). Other famous companies created by former IBM personnel include Amdahl and Electronic Data Systems (EDS).

CAI grew initially by outsourcing software maintenance of legacy applications. This is a task that many outsourcers perform better than their clients, and CAI is no exception. As with many other outsource groups, CAI expanded globally and has a large team of software personnel located in the Philippines as well as in Europe and the United States.

The CAI executives, including Tony Salvaggio, recognized that the software industry needed more and better information. CAI created a wholly owned subsidiary called the Information Technology Metrics and Productivity Institute (ITMPI). The ITMPI group has provided seminars, webinars, a monthly electronic journal, and an increasingly large library of articles and reference materials. Some of the courses are certified by the PMI. ITMPI is a valuable information resource for the software industry.

Creating an organization that offers high-quality speakers and authors who are industry gurus and not corporate employees was a bold and innovative step. I have participated in a number of ITMPI events and found them to be very well managed and popular with attendees and clients. The ITMPI library has become one of the richer sources of software information for many corporate software groups.

CAI is also unusual for an outsourcer in that it developed several successful software packages. One of the recent software tools is the Automated Project Office (APO), which handles various project and portfolio measurement, monitoring, and governance functions.

A unique feature of the APO is the ability to integrate third-party software tools that are called "cartridges" and are intended as useful plug-ins. One of these is a risk cartridge.

CAI is confident in the efficacy of its proprietary internal tools and methods, so it offers a number of fixed-price contract options. Given the uncertainty of cost and schedule results in the software industry, fixed-price contracts require better-than-average capabilities and project-planning discipline.

Another unusual aspect of CAI is its interest in and support of public schools, especially inner-city schools. CAI has founded a group of companies in Pennsylvania that provides equipment and support for inner-city schools.

Some of the services this group provides include donating equipment, letting employees have time off for tutoring and mentoring students, sponsoring field trips to universities to show children what college life is like, and inviting students to the corporate offices to see what business life is like.

These educational programs are carried out as public services and are not for profit. It is unusual for a company to demonstrate this kind of social consciousness, and the CAI executives are to be congratulated for their assistance to inner-city schools and education.

Cisco Systems

Cisco Systems is another legendary saga from Silicon Valley. Cisco is not a pure software company but rather is a company that uses embedded software in routers and communications devices to allow computers to communicate and also to create wireless networks. However, Cisco does have some "pure" software business such as the well-known WebEx internet conference hosting service for providing webinars and meetings via the World Wide Web.

Cisco was founded in 1984 in San Jose, California, by a married couple who had worked at Stanford University, Leonard Bosack and Sandy Lerner. Shortly after starting, they were joined by Richard Troiano.

The Cisco logo is an abstract representation of the San Francisco Bridge. The name of the company itself is the "cisco" portion of "San Francisco."

Cisco went public in February 1990. The success of its routers and communication devices was such that for a while, Cisco was the wealthiest company in the world with a market capitalization of around $500 million in 2000 (its peak). Even today, Cisco remains a wealthy and successful company, even though Apple has pulled far ahead of everyone else.

Cisco supports both corporate mainframe and client-server communications and also personal computer communications with devices such as the Linksys routers. The communication and router business is highly complex and in rapid technical evolution. These products are partly electronic and contain embedded software, which allows them to be upgraded in the field.

The wealth and success of Cisco are built on the facts that computers and software are used by all companies and government agencies and by a majority of private citizens as well. In order to communicate among all of these diverse and heterogeneous systems, products such as those offered by Cisco and its competitors are needed in every computer installation.

Digital Consulting Institute (DCI)

Digital Consulting Institute is an interesting example of an ephemeral market that was strong and growing at the start of the decade but that found that advances in technology steadily eroded the size of the market.

DCI was a seminar and education company founded by George Schussel and his wife, Sandi, in 1982 in Andover, Massachusetts. During this decade, there was a rapid expansion of programming personnel combined with a growing interest in structured development. Professional seminars and courses were a high-growth subindustry. Academic education was still somewhat lacking for corporate needs, so DCI and several other seminar groups offered a large number of courses for both technical and management personnel.

After 10 years or so of growth, DCI jumped into larger multispeaker events and also started to do trade shows with vendor showcases. These larger events attracted audiences in the hundreds and required larger conference halls at major hotels. At its peak, DCI had hundreds of top speakers and thousands of clients, many of whom worked for Fortune 500 companies.

Some of the speakers are familiar names and are cited in several other chapters in this book: Steve Jobs from Apple; Larry Ellison from Oracle; Ted Codd from IBM; Fran Tarkenton, the former football quarterback; Ed Yourdon, the famous software author; and John Cullinane are samples of the top names in the DCI stable of speakers.

Note

In the interest of full disclosure, I taught a number of seminars for DCI during the 1980s and the next decade, too, because I had lived in Massachusetts not far from where DCI had its facilities.

The successes of DCI and Schussel were significant enough so that in 1998, Schussel was named an entrepreneur of the year by the IEEE Computer Society. To show the esteem in which he was held, the other recipients in 1998 included Bill Gates, Paul Allen, Steve Jobs, and Steve Wozniak (the A-list of Silicon Valley entrepreneurs).

Later, in the 1990s, the internet began to erode the stand-up seminar business. Online "webinars" became popular and live events declined. After the terrorist attacks on September 11, 2001, many companies cut back on air travel and many professionals became reluctant to fly. In fact, air travel became much less enjoyable than it had been due to increased security, which necessitated arriving at airports hours prior to departure.

However, worse things were in store for DCI. In 2004, Schussel was indicted by the IRS for tax evasion. The IRS claimed that about $8 million in unreported income had been diverted to a Bermuda subsidiary and then put into other accounts without being reported as income. Although Schussel pleaded innocent, Ron Gomes, who had been President of DCI, pleaded guilty to income tax evasion. There were other indictments, too. Schussel was eventually found guilty and sentenced to three-and-a-half years in federal prison.

In part because of these criminal proceedings and in part because the internet had eroded seminar training, DCI, after a change of names, ceased operations in 2004.

Note

While running DCI, Schussel had been something of a philanthropist. His experience in federal prison showed him how difficult it was for ex-convicts to reenter normal life and find work outside of prison. As a result, Schussel began a series of blogs and other efforts to assist former prisoners in finding work and a new place in society.

When DCI was founded, no one realized how powerful the internet would become and how it would change normal classroom and seminar training.

The demise of a company due to IRS criminal charges is unique in this book, although no doubt it has happened many times in many industries.

Huawei

Huawei is not a U.S. company but is included to illustrate that computers and software became global business sectors during the 1980s. It is also cited because the telecommunications industry was a pioneer in both computers and software and also in software quality control.

Huawei was founded in 1988 in Shenzhen, Guandong, China, by a former military officer named Ren Zhenfei. Huawei was originally a private company that was owned by its employees, which would have been an unusual business model in the United States. Another unusual aspect of the Huawei business model is that about 46% of the company's approximate 140,000 employees works in research and development. This harkens back to the glory days of Bell Labs when it was one of the world's premier research organizations that developed many of the devices used today, such as transistors in 1953. Huawei currently has 20 R&D laboratories located around the world in many countries, including the United States.

Huawei is a global corporation that manufactures communication devices, networking equipment, cell phones, and other products. Huawei became the world's largest manufacturer of telecommunications equipment circa 2012, when it pulled ahead of Ericsson.

Huawei started operations as a marketing company that sold private branch exchange (PBX) switching systems developed by a Hong Kong company. After several years, Huawei began to build its own PBX switches aimed at hotels and corporations that needed their own telephone systems.

In 1997, Huawei began to expand outside of China. In 1999, Huawei joined the International Telecommunications Union (ITU), which is a business necessity for global telecommunications companies. Huawei's global business grew so rapidly that by 2005, global sales were larger than sales in China for the first time.

As companies grow rapidly, their organization structures also need to grow and stay flexible. To assist in this rapid growth, Huawei contracted with IBM from 1998 to 2003. Huawei has also entered into a variety of joint ventures with U.S. companies such as Motorola and Symantec.

As many readers know, cell phones are becoming a major target of computer hackers and identity thieves. The joint venture between Huawei and Symantec is aimed at improving the security of cell phones and other forms of communication from remote hacking and theft. This collaboration led to a new company called Huawei Symantec, Inc., located in Chengdu, China.

Corporate organizations in China differ from those in the United States. Huawei is considered to be a collective rather than a corporation. The distinction is outside the scope of this book but is of social interest.

For Huawei, as for all other telecommunications companies, software is now a critical component of all devices and networks. Cell phones, modems, routers, and other equipment are all controlled by embedded software. Central office switching systems and PBX switches are also controlled by software. Billing, administration, and network management are also controlled by software, usually running on larger computers and sometimes on custom computers.

Quality Control in Telecommunications

For historical reasons, the telecommunications industry had sophisticated quality control back in the days of electromechanical switches. When computers and software began to be used for telecommunications, the industry was among the first to have formal software quality assurance groups. It was also among the first to use pretest inspections of requirements, design, and source code in order to raise defect removal efficiency (DRE) up to the 99% range.

Telecommunications companies were also early adapters of Tom McCabe's "cyclomatic complexity" metric from 1976 to examine code complexity. They also quickly adopted various code coverage analytical tools to show testing effectiveness. Motorola became famous for its Six Sigma quality program. Suffice it to say the telecommunications industry is among the top industries in software quality control.

In the modern world, quality remains a central focus of the world's telecommunications companies, and security has been added to the set of quality concerns. Huawei is a good example that illustrates the technical and social impacts that computers and software have had on major industries. Recall that in the early days of telephones, routing calls from one subscriber to another took place in central offices staffed by live telephone operators. Some of these were so large that supervisors used roller skates to move from operator to operator when there were troubles or requests that needed special attention. Needless to say, these manual telephone exchanges were highly labor intensive and costly.

The History of the Telephone

The history of the telephone is ambiguous. In the United States, Alexander Graham Bell patented the first telephone in 1876, and he is widely regarded as the inventor of the telephone. But, in fact, about half a dozen other people also claim to have invented the telephone: Elisha Gray from the United States, Antonio Meucci from Italy, and Johan Philip Reis from Germany also built telephones or telephone-like devices at roughly the same time as Bell. However, patents tend to win out, and Bell was indeed the first to patent the telephone.

But a phone by itself has little social value. It is necessary to be able to connect a subscriber's phone to those of other subscribers. Therefore, telephone switching is a critical component of modern telephone networks.

A Hungarian engineer named Tivadar Puskas seemed to originate the idea of a telephone switchboard while he worked for Thomas Edison on a telegraph exchange. The world's first commercial telephone exchange opened on January 28, 1878, in New Haven, Connecticut, with 21 subscribers. For more than ten years, manual switching of telephone lines by live operators would be the norm.

The first electromechanical telephone switch, called the "stepping switch," was invented in 1891 in Kansas City, Missouri, by Almon Brown Stowger. What is interesting is that he was not working in the telecommunications field but was in fact an undertaker who ran a funeral parlor.

The reason that Stowger was interested in a better method of routing calls is because the wife of the owner of another funeral parlor happened to be the town's telephone operator. Stowger was losing business when people tried to call his company because some of the calls would be connected to the other funeral parlor.

The idea of automated telephone switching was sufficiently important that Stowger and various friends and relatives founded the Stowger Automatic Telephone Exchange Company. Its first switch was installed in La Porte, Indiana, in 1892 and had 75 subscribers. It is of considerable social interest that one of the world's largest industries was created due to lost customers whose calls were being routed to a competitor by a live telephone operator.

The modern telecommunications industry employs millions of workers in every country in the world. It is one of the largest and most sophisticated industries in terms of computer and software usage and also in total software personnel. It is also an industry with many large companies in many countries: Alcatel, Apple, AT&T, Bell Northern, Ericsson, GTE, Huawei, HTC, Motorola, Nokia, Samsung, and Siemens are only a few examples.

Intuit

Intuit is a very rare example of a small company competing successfully with Microsoft. In fact, Microsoft even withdrew from the personal finance market space partly due to the success of Intuit. The failure of Microsoft Money to compete with Intuit Quicken is a very rare example of a small company taking market share from Microsoft.

This company was founded in 1983 by Scott Cook and Tom Proult in Palo Alto, California, in the midst of Silicon Valley, although legally it is a Delaware corporation. The first product of Intuit was its flagship application Quicken, which is a personal financial package that keeps checkbooks balanced and can handle other personal finances such as those generated by rental properties. The IBM personal computer version was written in BASIC and the Apple version was written in Pascal.

There were competitive products early on, but by 1988, Quicken was the top-selling personal finance tool. In 1991, Microsoft decided to compete in this space and brought out Microsoft Money.

Intuit had a successful IPO in 1993 and began to acquire companies in related fields such as income tax preparation, including the well-known TurboTax. In 1994, Microsoft approached Intuit about acquisition, but the Department of Justice stopped the merger on the grounds that it might create a monopoly. That left Microsoft and Quicken as the top competitors in a narrow niche.

Intuit is primarily a commercial vendor in the finance and tax areas. It also has some free services, some of which have received favorable reviews. Intuit has an online research application dealing with taxation called the Tax Almanac that was launched in 2005. Articles and materials are prepared by tax professionals and are available free to academics and other tax preparation groups, as well as to consumers. The Almanac was listed as one of the more useful websites available as of 2005.

Not every aspect of Intuit's business operations receives favorable comments. For years, banks had downloaded consumer financial data in a format called QIF, which stands for Quicken Interface Format. This was available free of charge. Quicken developed another proprietary format called QFX that was fee-based, and it then dropped support for the older QIF format. In fact, Intuit has received bad reviews for dropping support for older versions and requiring customers to buy new versions of software and services.

Intuit also spends quite a bit of money lobbying, and some of the things it lobbies for are not necessarily good for consumers. It lobbied to eliminate free online tax filing for low-income residents of California, and it lobbied to keep consumers from filing income tax returns directly with the IRS.

Microsoft competed with Intuit in the personal financial space, but in June 2009, Microsoft began to withdraw from that market. Microsoft stated that the market for personal financial software had declined, but Intuit with Quicken is still successful in that market.

Intuit is still the major vendor of personal financial software and also of accounting packages such as QuickBooks for various kinds of companies, including nonprofits. However, it is not usually beneficial for consumers to have only one major source for fairly important applications such as personal finance.

KPMG

The early history of KPMG dates back to 1870 and the early days of accounting and auditing companies. Because computers and software were applied to accounting and finance almost as soon as they were invented, accounting companies became computer experts before most other industries. This expertise soon led to accounting companies forming separate management consulting groups to aid clients in dealing with their own computers and software.

KPMG is the result of a complex set of mergers and acquisitions that are too baroque for discussion in this book. The company is cited in this chapter because two accounting and financial firms (KMG Group and Peat Marwick) merged to create KPMG during the 1980s. The combination was then called KPMG in the United States. This company has had a lot of name changes: over half a dozen, in fact. Without doing an exhaustive check, KPMG has probably had more name changes than any other company cited in this book.

Today, KPMG has three main lines of business: auditing, tax preparation, and advisory services. The first two are the older, traditional kinds of business that date back to the 1870 era. Advisory services is a more modern business based on computers and software.

The KPMG advisory groups also have three broad ranges of service: management consulting, risk assessments and management, and restructuring.

Note

The term "risk" is an important word that is in rapid evolution. Up until the computer era, about 1970, risks were either financial or legal. In today's world of hacking, viruses, and denial of service attacks, computer and software risks are now a critical component of risk management.

KPMG is a microcosm of the history of auditing, accounting, and management consulting. The companies in this group have frequent mergers and name changes. They play a major role in corporate operations because an annual audit is a critical milestone that is important for stockholders and business activities such as venture funding or future mergers. Readers should read the section on Accenture in this chapter to learn what can happen when audits are not done well. (Arthur Andersen had to give up its license as a result of the Enron audit.)

KPMG's advisory services have become large and well respected and serve many major corporations. It is a multinational organization, but its corporate structure is intricate and complex. The KPMG groups in each country are separate legal entities that are part of a cooperative organization headquartered in Switzerland. The reason for this perhaps is to provide liability protection. In any case, KPMG is an interesting case study for business schools.

Lotus

Lotus shows that Silicon Valley was not the only venue for software startups. Lotus was incorporated in Westford, Massachusetts, in 1982 by Mitch Kapor and Jonathan Sachs with financial support from the venture capitalist Ben Rosen. Jim Manzi started as a consultant and soon joined to become the President of Lotus. Mitch Kapor had previously worked on the pioneering VisiCalc spreadsheet at VisiCorp, where he was head of development (VisiCorp was yet another pioneer company).

As background software application interfaces evolved from command lines to graphics, a new form of input called "what you see is what you get" (WYSIWYG) began to emerge.

The first product of Lotus had the awkward name of Lotus 1-2-3. The unusual name is because the product was not only a powerful spreadsheet but also had graphics capabilities and could be used as a database (i.e., it was three products in one). This product was released on January 26, 1983. The "Lotus" part of the name refers to a meditation posture called the "Lotus position." (Mitch Kapor used to teach transcendental meditation, although the Lotus position is common in many Eastern religions that use meditation.)

The timing for Lotus was perfect. The IBM personal computer had come out in 1981 and was about to become one of the best-selling technical products in history. Spreadsheets had just come out and were about to enable almost anyone to have sophisticated mathematical and statistical power at their fingertips.

As a result of this synergy, Lotus expanded far beyond the original marketing plan. In fact, Lotus was briefly the largest independent software vendor in the world.

Lotus brought out other products such as Jazz and Symphony (continuing a policy of eclectic names). These were only marginally successful. They had mediocre reviews and did not sell well. However, the Lotus Notes email package did well and would later be a reason why IBM acquired Lotus in 1995.

Lotus was also a pioneer in "look and feel" copyright lawsuits that tried to expand copyright law into new directions. (The section about Borland in this chapter cites the most interesting look and feel case, which was highly unusual in that the U.S. Supreme Court had a four-to-four tied decision, which means that the arguments on both sides could not be decided.)

The success of Lotus Notes led to another unusual business situation. IBM made a hostile acquisition offer in 1995 for $60 a share at a time when Lotus stock was selling for $32 per share. After some wrangling back and forth, IBM acquired Lotus for a cost of $54.50 per share, or about $3.5 billion.

Lotus personnel were apprehensive about being part of IBM due to their rather famous corporate culture and also to their very superior benefits program. Among the benefits offered by Lotus to employees were a day-care center, same-sex partner insurance benefits, and quite a few others that were not common in the 1980s.

Note

The history of Lotus reminds us of the fact that there are only two common exit strategies for software corporations or any other corporations: they fail and go out of business or they are acquired by a larger company. Two other options occur for the luckier ones: they generate enough revenues to go public, or they generate stable revenues and can operate forever as private companies.

NeXT

The history of NeXT is also part of the history of the famous entrepreneur Steve Jobs, who founded both Apple and NeXT. The excellent biography of Steve Jobs by Walter Isaacson provides the details of how Jobs was forced out of Apple and started NeXT. While the politics of Jobs's leaving Apple are fascinating, what he did at NeXT is the topic of this section: primarily the NeXT software and to a lesser degree the hardware.

Jobs had been interested in the concept of specialized workstations for education and professional scientific work, because ordinary Apples, Macs, and IBM computers were not fast enough and lacked high-end graphics.

After being forced out of Apple in 1985, Steve Jobs founded NeXT in Redwood City, California, the same year. He was also able to get several of his former Apple colleagues to join him. (Apple had an unusual employment agreement that allowed employees to own some of the software they developed at Apple, unless it had been released. This fact would be useful at NeXT.)

However, the departure of several key Apple players for NeXT put a kink in the immediate plans when Apple sued. The suit was eventually settled out of court and the former Apple personnel were allowed to continue their design work for NeXT.

The prestige of Jobs and his past successes meant that other entrepreneurs had confidence in him. For example, Ross Perot, the founder of EDS, invested $20 million in NeXT and acquired 16% of its stock.

The first NeXT computer came out in 1988 and was called "the cube" because of its physical dimensions. The case was in fact a cube made of magnesium and sized 12 inches on each side. While it was elegant, it had some design and performance problems.

The NeXT introduced an unusual magneto-optical drive from Canon as its primary input and storage medium. This was slower than a hard drive. Worse, there was only one drive on the NeXT, so there was no way to transport files from the NeXT to any other computer without a network, because the single drive needed to run the software.

Because NeXT was aimed at being a high-end professional workstation, it is technically and socially important that it was in fact used for several important inventions. Tim Berners-Lee used a NeXT computer to build his first web browser in 1991, so NeXT was instrumental in building the World Wide Web. Also, the game designer John Carmack used a NeXT computer for two games whose realistic graphics were among the best of the era: *Doom* and *Wolfenstein 3D*.

The NeXT hardware was elegant and innovative, but it was the software that persisted after the hardware manufacturing was closed down in 1993 (with layoffs of several hundred personnel).

Steve Jobs had acquired the Objective-C language at Apple and it was used at NeXT to create the NeXTStep operating system. A variant of this, called OpenStep, was done with Sun.

While this was happening, Apple was considering a replacement for its aging Mac operating system. After quite a lot of thought and due diligence, Apple concluded that NeXTStep might be the best choice to create a new OS. Rather than license the software, Apple decided to acquire NeXT. It is financially interesting that while other NeXT shareholders received $429 million in cash, Steve Jobs received 1.5 million shares of Apple stock.

The acquisition of NeXT by Apple took place in 1996. After a 12-year hiatus, Steve Jobs returned to Apple originally as a consultant, then as interim CEO, and then as formal CEO in 2000.

The NeXTStep operating system became the nucleus of the later generation of Apple operating systems. Objective-C continued as the main programming language, and the object-oriented concept flourished.

While NeXT was not a commercial success with its hardware products, it was technically sophisticated and served as a model for other high-end workstations. The software created by NeXT has persisted long after most of the NeXT workstations were moved to museums or recycled for their magnesium cases.

PeopleSoft

The advent of computers and software led to a number of specialized niche applications. One of these niches is *human resource management systems* (HRMSs), which encompass a variety of personnel records. PeopleSoft, as the name implies, was a pioneer in HRMSs. It was founded in 1984 in Walnut Creek, California, by Dave Duffield and Ken Morris.

At first, PeopleSoft concentrated on HR applications but evolved into an enterprise resource planning (ERP) company after a merger with competitor JD Edwards in 2003.

PeopleSoft is somewhat unique in that it built a proprietary software development methodology called PeopleTools and even a proprietary programming language called PeopleCode.

As often happens in the software business, the success of PeopleSoft attracted the attention of a larger competitor, in this case Oracle. Starting in 2003, Oracle attempted a hostile takeover of PeopleSoft for about $13 million, but the bid was rejected. The U.S. Department of Justice stepped in and claimed that if Oracle acquired PeopleSoft, it might lead to a monopoly. However, this claim was rejected by a U.S. federal judge.

After a series of negotiations, Oracle did acquire PeopleSoft in 2004 for about $10.3 million. Soon after the acquisition, Oracle laid off about 6,000 personnel out of the 11,000 who had worked at PeopleSoft.

Oracle decided that the JD Edwards name was more popular than the PeopleSoft name, so several PeopleSoft products were rebranded as JD Edwards products.

Note

The history of PeopleSoft shows that hostile takeovers are a common social phenomenon in the software business. Some of these takeovers are because the technology is valuable and doing well. Some hostile takeovers are done to eliminate competition and remove competing technologies from the market. Oracle has continued to enhance and maintain many PeopleSoft applications.

Although the PeopleSoft name is a brand within Oracle, the more recent products are fusions of the technologies from PeopleSoft, JD Edwards, and Oracle itself. In fact, the name "Fusion Applications" is what the product or products will be called. Mergers between competitors are sometimes successful, sometimes not successful. But mergers are a fact of life in the software business.

Rational

Rational is now part of IBM, but it had an eventful history prior to being acquired. Rational was incorporated in 1981 by Paul Levy and Mike Devlin in Westford, Massachusetts. Its name at the time of incorporation was Rational Machines and, in fact, Rational had hardware as well as software.

The original business plan for Rational was to improve software development practices centering on the new Ada programming language combined with iterative methods. But code alone is not the only thing that needs to be done well, so Rational also tackled architecture, requirements, design, quality control, and testing and made useful innovations in all of these disparate fields. It also had a kind of Ada metalanguage called *DIANA*, which stood for Descriptive Intermediate Attributed Notation for Ada (certainly on a short list of complicated names).

The initial *Rational Environment* was a combination of a suite of software tools and a custom workstation called the R1000. Recall that in the early 1980s, high-end commercial workstations had not yet appeared. When Rational began to port their tools and methods to other platforms and downplay their own custom hardware, the company changed its name to just Rational and dropped the "Machines" part.

There were various concepts and tools under the Rational umbrella, but they came together into a powerful suite of methods and supporting software called the Rational Unified Process (RUP). Some of the RUP concepts originated in an older tool called *Objectory* by Dr. Ivar Jacobsen, who later joined Rational when his company merged in 1995.

RUP had a pragmatic and empirical basis that it was necessary to concentrate on risk abatement and quality control (historically weak for software). The RUP concepts codified many of the principles of iterative and structured development and surrounded them with tools for requirements analysis, design, coding, testing, and governance.

Although RUP was developed in the 1990s, it still ranks as a top methodology today when quality and productivity are accurately measured. For major applications larger than 1,000 function points, RUP is one of the best methodologies even compared to Agile, which has become the most popular method of the current decade.

Agile tends to run out of steam when an application has more than 100 users and is larger than 1,000 function points. With hundreds or thousands of users, no single embedded user can possibly understand all of the requirements.

With large systems, no one understands more than about 10% of what the system will do. Therefore, more formal architecture and requirements methods that combine the thoughts of many decision makers are needed, and RUP has both the methods and the tools to consolidate the diverse requirements for major software packages.

Among the concepts embedded in RUP is a design representation method called the *unified modeling language* (UML), which is the most widely used set of requirements and design approaches.

The technical and social history of UML is an interesting story in its own right. UML combines the contributions of three researchers who had similar goals. They had each developed new forms of representations for software architecture, requirements, and design. The three were James Rumbaugh, Grady Booch, and Ivar Jacobsen. When all three began to cooperate on UML, they became known in the software literature as "the three amigos" after the Steve Martin comedy.

Dynamic Modeling

One effective feature of UML was visual modeling. Clearly, graphical representations are superior to text for complex and abstract concepts such as major software applications. In my view, UML could be extended in today's world to include dynamic 3D models in full color that can show two forms of change that are not included in today's UML.

One form would represent and model the application when it is executing and show the dynamics of inputs, outputs, and processing in visual form. Relative speeds would be realistic but, of course, slowed down for the benefit of human observers. Dynamic models would help to eliminate performance bottlenecks and also reveal security flaws.

A second form of dynamism would show the continuous growth of requirements during development and after release. Development requirements change on average about 2% per calendar month and tend to be messy. Once software is delivered, it still changes so long as there are active users. Postrelease changes average between 8% and 14% per year after release, sometimes for more than 20 years.

Requirements changes are usually not well defined and tend to degrade the structure of software architecture as they accumulate. The industry needs better and more dynamic visual representations of software in motion. Software applications are obviously the most fast-moving products ever built, and they also evolve continuously over many years.

Another use of dynamic models would be to simulate various kinds of virus attacks and other cyberthreats which, of course, only occur when the software runs. Back doors might also be identified.

As Rational grew and evolved, it acquired several companies that added to the Rational technology stack. However, the most important change occurred in February 2003, when Rational was acquired by IBM and became known as IBM Rational.

Some acquisitions by large companies benefit both, and some are not so successful. In the case of Rational and IBM, there appears to be a useful synergy.

Rational has continued to add new tools and methods, and IBM has benefited from the Rational technology stack. Rational has also benefited from the effectiveness of the IBM marketing and sales engines.

An endemic problem of the software industry is the tunnel vision of too many companies and consultants that offer "solutions" to software problems. For example, the static analysis companies concentrate only on static analysis. The automated test tool companies only think about testing. The Agile coaches only think about Agile.

Rational has perhaps the widest range of tools and methods of any company that concentrates on improving software development. They have requirements tools and methods, architecture, design, code, static analyses for both text documents and code, integration, defect tracking, and many more. It is refreshing to see a group that recognizes that good software requires a combination of many partial solutions and not some kind of silver bullet. If the solutions are cohesive and work well together, that is even better.

SEI

During the 1980s, the Department of Defense (DoD) continued as the world's largest user of computers and software. The DoD and the military services also built very large applications, some of which topped 100,000 function points in size or more than 10 million source code statements. These big systems had a distressing tendency to be late and not work well when delivered.

To help improve the technologies of software engineering, the Defense Advanced Research Projects Agency (DARPA) funded the creation of SEI in 1984. SEI was located partly on the campus of Carnegie Mellon University in Pittsburgh, Pennsylvania.

SEI was not a normal venture- or equity-funded company but rather a federally funded research and development center. SEI became an important software research group serving initially the DoD and military contractors, but it eventually expanded to other software industries outside of defense.

The most famous of the SEI software approaches was the widely used *Capability Maturity Model* originally called by its initials (CMM) and later adding the word "integrated" to become CMMI when it expanded to include system engineering. CMMI is a method of assessing software organization capabilities by means of a formal questionnaire that examined *key process areas* (KPAs).

The CMM is based on methods used by IBM in the East Coast labs, which is not surprising because IBM's former director of software engineering, Watts Humphrey, moved to SEI and developed many of their concepts.

Five-Point Ranking Scale

A prominent feature of CMM and CMMI was a five-point ranking scale that evaluated the relative sophistication of the organizations being studied. The original CMM scale had a distressingly high number of companies that were not very sophisticated. Table 7.2 shows the early distribution.

The older assessment method developed by the author was based on the IBM West Coast assessment approach. This method also used a five-point scale but with very different meanings and rankings. Table 7.3 shows the assessment scale used by SPR since 1983.

The two scales both attempted to capture software team capabilities but used different numbering systems, which indeed ran in opposite directions. As the SEI assessments became popular, a mathematical conversion tool was developed by the author that could do bidirectional conversions between the SEI and SPR scales. Another estimating tool was developed that could show the time and expense from moving up the CMMI ladder from Level 1 to any higher level. (The ascent could take more than six months per level and cost more than $5,000 per capita.)

The SEI assessment approach was generally successful in leading to process improvements among those who used it thoughtfully. Mechanical adherence was less successful. In spite of statistical evidence that ascending the CMMI ladder is

Table 7.2 *Five Levels of the SEI Capability Maturity Model (CMM) Circa 1990*

SEI Maturity Level	Meaning	Frequency of Occurrence
1 = Initial	Chaotic	75.0%
2 = Repeatable	Marginal	15.0%
3 = Defined	Adequate	8.0%
4 = Managed	Good to excellent	1.5%
5 = Optimizing	State of the art	0.5%

Table 7.3 *Five Levels of the SPR Excellence Scale*

SPR Excellence Scale	Meaning	Frequency of Occurrence
1 = Excellent	State of the art	3.0%
2 = Above average	Superior to most companies	18.0%
3 = Average	Normal in most factors	54.0%
4 = Below average	Deficient in some factors	22.0%
5 = Poor	Deficient in most factors	3.0%

(Continued)

(Continued)

beneficial, there are still occasional lawsuits against Level 5 organizations. Many small companies that are Level 1 or don't use the CMMI at all can do a good job. There are also other proprietary methods used by companies such as Apple, IBM, and Microsoft that achieve results equal to CMMI Level 5 but don't use the CMMI at all.

As the SEI research programs gathered speed, the SEI assessments expanded the range of topics considered, and a "people CMM" dealing with personnel factors was developed by Dr. Bill Curtis and colleagues and published by SEI in 1993.

There are also other research studies carried out by the SEI staff. One recent study was on estimation. A major study group is that of computer security called the Computer Emergency Response Team (CERT).

When SEI was first created, it was uncertain if it would accomplish tangible results or merely be yet another government think tank that published reports but had little practical impact on daily activities. Fortunately for the software industry, the methods developed by SEI had a pragmatic basis, and those corporations who ascended the CMM and CMMI levels from 1 to above Level 3 also tended to improve quality and productivity.

More than 30,000 people have been trained as SEI assessors, and they work globally. The SEI research personnel have published more than 50 books through Addison-Wesley, with many of them containing valuable contributions.

SEI now has international affiliates and has just created a commercial subsidiary that will expand the core concepts to a broader range of industries than defense. Other sources of nongovernmental funding will occur as well.

Overall, SEI has benefited the software community and has been a prime example of a well-run government-funded research establishment that has achieved practical results.

Software Productivity Research (SPR)

I founded Software Productivity Research along with my wife, Eileen, in 1984 in Acton, Massachusetts. I had designed IBM's first two software estimating tools in 1973 and 1974 and later three software estimating tools for ITT.

When the ITT Corporation sold its telecommunications business and closed its research labs, I decided to become an entrepreneur. SPR was a classic "sweat equity" startup that began in the home.

As the company grew, it moved into offices in Cambridge, Massachusetts, and then to larger offices in Burlington, Massachusetts. At its peak, SPR had offices in Burlington, London, San Francisco, and Chicago.

Note

The original offices in Cambridge were in the Henderson Carriage building, which at one time housed an actual carriage factory. This company had been commissioned to build the chariots for the first filmed version of *Ben-Hur*, set in ancient Rome, and a working replica of a Roman chariot had a prominent place in the lobby.

Having designed proprietary software estimating tools for IBM and ITT, it seemed like a good business idea to bring out an advanced commercial software estimating tool.

I had studied the economic problems associated with the LOC metric and knew that this metric was inadequate for either estimation or economic analysis of software.

Al Albrecht and his colleagues at IBM in White Plains had developed function point metrics in the mid-1970s, and IBM had placed its metrics into the public domain in 1979. With function point metrics, noncoding tasks such as requirements, design, and user documentation could be both measured and estimated.

The first commercial estimating tool developed by SPR was called SPQR/20. The name stood for *software productivity, quality, and reliability*, with the number 20 being the number of input questions needed to generate estimates.

SPQR/20 was the first commercial software estimation tool based on function points. It was the first to include sizing of source code and text documents. It was the first to include quality and reliability predictions, and it was the first to predict 5 years of postrelease maintenance. SPQR/20 could predict source code size for 30 programming languages ranging from basic assembly through PL/I and Ada through application generators.

SPR came close to receiving venture capital, but the venture group attempted to change the terms of the agreement the day before the planned signing date. The revised terms were unacceptable, so my wife, who was also on the board, and I rejected the venture terms.

As an alternative to venture funding, SPR opened up a profitable consulting practice that combined software process assessments with software benchmark data collection. It is socially and technically interesting that SPR was carrying out formal software process assessments 1 year before SEI was incorporated.

Upon his retirement from IBM, Albrecht, the inventor of function points, came to work at SPR in 1986. Function point metrics were just beginning their expansion, and IFPUG had just moved from Canada to the United States.

SPR used function point metrics for both estimating and software benchmarks, with considerable success in both domains. While working at SPR, Albrecht developed the first certification examination for IFPUG function point analysts. This exam has, of course, been updated as the counting rules have changed but remains in use today.

SPR continued to be a hybrid company with a consulting group and an estimating research and development group. The data collected from consulting eventually led to a third business: carrying out expert witness tasks in litigation for breach of contract lawsuits or for cases involving taxation of software assets.

For example, a major tax case involved the value of the software portfolio of EDS when it was acquired by General Motors. A major breach of contract case was between the State of California and Lockheed over a system that was supposed to keep track of payments for dependent children. Still another interesting case was between Accenture and the Canadian government over an increase in requirements, which led to a payment dispute. Function points were used in this case to prove that the extra features had indeed been commissioned by the client and that the costs were indeed outside the scope of the original contract.

Charles Douglis was brought in as Chief Financial Officer of SPR and was soon made President, while I served as Chairman of the board. Charles's excellent financial background led to ten straight years of profitable growth, culminating with the sale of SPR to Artemis Management Systems in 1998.

SPR is fairly typical of hundreds of startups that grow using the founder's own revenues rather than external venture funding. Friends and colleagues who started venture-backed companies in the same year that SPR was founded all eventually left and their companies filed for bankruptcy due in part to questionable decisions made by the venture groups.

Some venture-backed companies succeed and grow to become major corporations, but many others are pushed too fast in the wrong direction and end up failing.

Although I retired from SPR in 2000, the company is still doing well and is expanding into South America. The current commercial estimation tool of SPR is called KnowledgePLAN, and it includes very detailed activity- and task-based estimation.

One unusual aspect of SPR after the sale to Artemis is that when Artemis itself encountered a business slowdown, the employees of SPR acquired the company, with Doug Brindley as the current President. Doug had been the GM corporate contact in the tax litigation involving EDS, so he was familiar with the SPR technology.

The assessment and benchmark consulting business started at SPR was so successful that two former SPR Vice Presidents of Consulting started their own companies and continue to operate in the areas of function point analysis and benchmark data collection. These two companies are the David's Consulting Group and the Quality/Productivity Management Group.

Stepstone Corporation

Stepstone Corporation was founded in 1983 in Newtown, Connecticut, by Dr. Tom Love and Dr. Brad Cox with other colleagues who had worked at ITT Corporation's Programming Technology Center in nearby Stratford, Connecticut. It was originally called Productivity Products International (PPI).

Note

ITT sold its telecommunications business to Alcatel, which closed down the U.S. research labs in Shelton, Connecticut, and Stratford, Connecticut. I had worked at the ITT research lab in Stratford and his wife, whom he met while at ITT, had worked at the ITT research lab in nearby Shelton. The Shelton lab was a telecommunications research laboratory and the Stratford lab was a software engineering technology center. Tom Love was the Director of the Advanced Technology Group at the Programming Technology Center (PTC), and he hired Brad Cox into that group at ITT.

The main product of Stepstone Corporation was a powerful object-oriented programming language called Objective-C. The ideas for this language started at ITT and were stimulated by the August 1981 issue of *Byte Magazine*, which was devoted to Smalltalk. Brad Cox saw the opportunity to develop an extension of the C programming language based upon reading this magazine. His ITT work was published as a 1983 SigPlan Notices paper titled "The Object-Oriented Precompiler: Programming Smalltalk—80 Methods in C Language." This original language was referred to as OOPC. A second generation of the language was built from scratch at Schlumberger Research and then a third language was built from scratch at a startup company started by Tom Love and Brad Cox called Productivity Products in June 1983.

The Objective-C language became one of the most important languages in the software industry when Steve Jobs and his technical staff decided to make Objective-C the primary language for all Apple software products (which came about because Steve Jobs had selected Objective-C for the NeXT computer and its operating system, as discussed in the section on NeXT).

One might think that having Apple (and NeXT) select the language as a key tool for all future products such as the Macintosh operating system, the iPad, the iPhone, and others would be sufficient to catapult Stepstone to Fortune 500 status. This might have happened had the original agreement between NeXT and the Stepstone Corporation stayed in effect, because it called for a payment of $5 to Stepstone for every Apple device or workstation that contained Objective-C code.

However, Stepstone had received venture funding, and contracts were no longer in the hands of the founders but rather in the hands of officers selected by the venture capitalists. For reasons that do not make any business sense, NeXT acquired full rights to Objective-C for a single one-time payment of less than $100,000.

According to one source that analyzes use of programming language on the internet, the Objective-C language is currently the third most widely used programming language on the planet.

Symantec

Symantec is now a major vendor of security packages to protect personal computers. It was founded in 1982 by Gary Hendrix in Mountain View, California, which is one of the central Silicon Valley communities. Symantec was funded by a grant from the National Science Foundation (NSF).

At first, Symantec built artificial intelligence tools and a natural language database application that ran on DEC computers. These proved to be difficult to port to personal computers, so Symantec more or less had no product, but they still had some interesting and valuable intellectual property.

Symantec was acquired by another company called C&E Software founded by the entrepreneurs Dennis Coleman and Gordon Eubanks. They decided to keep the name Symantec for the merged business. Their products included word processing, file management, and a natural language query tool called *The Intelligent Assistant* that was a pioneer in database queries and report generation. Their combined database and word processing tool was called Q&A for "question and answer."

To increase sales, Symantec started a very unusual sales program called *six pack*. Every employee was asked to work 6 days a week, visit six dealerships per day, and train six sales representatives per store. To keep costs low, they were asked to stay with friends or use a Motel 6 in keeping with the six-pack theme. For a while, Symantec's revenues were so low that the Chairman and President received zero salary, vice presidential salaries were cut 50%, and other employees' salaries were cut 15%.

In 1986, Symantec formed a subsidiary division called Turner Hall that marketed third-party software plus add-ons that supported other products such as Lotus. As revenues increased, Symantec made an acquisition of Breakthrough Software, the developer of the TimeLine project management tool. In 1989, Symantec had a successful IPO.

As a result of the merger plus the Turner Hall subsidiary, Symantec had three fairly autonomous business units, which seemed to fit the corporate culture and business model of growth by acquisition. One of the important acquisitions was the Peter Norton Computing Company in 1990. Norton Utilities was a well-regarded suite of applications that tuned up personal computers and eliminated junk.

Symantec had developed antivirus software for the Mac platform before its acquisition of Norton. But the Norton name was so highly regarded in the industry that Symantec released its PC antivirus package under the name Norton AntiVirus, even though it had been internally developed at Symantec.

Because antivirus protection is technically sophisticated and must deal with moving targets, Symantec established a formal antivirus research group with about 400 personnel. Although consumer antivirus packages are perhaps best known, Symantec also has corporate and enterprise security packages as a result of acquiring Veritas. Symantec and the Chinese telecommunications company Huawei have also created a joint company for cybersecurity research and analysis named Huawei Symantec.

Symantec is a good company for business school case studies because it changed directions several times. Its unique "six pack" sales program, which involved almost every single employee, is also a novel approach that merits business school attention.

Not all reviews of Symantec have been favorable. For example, in an attack on the *New York Times* software and network, only a few of the threats were detected by Symantec tools. Symantec itself was hacked in 2012, which is embarrassing for a security company.

Symantec had acquired VeriSign, which supposedly verified websites and issued security certificates. After VeriSign was hacked and had some data stolen in 2010, the validity of these services came into question. Also, VeriSign was criticized for delays in reporting the hack.

A final issue with Symantec is that it has not received very high reviews from consumers or journals for customer support.

Some of the security attacks and issues against Symantec illustrate an important point. Hackers and computer viruses are growing more sophisticated and therefore antivirus companies need to work hard to stay ahead of the game.

TechSoup Global

TechSoup Global is a nonprofit organization under the 501(c)(3) regulations. It was started in 1987 in San Francisco, California, by Daniel Ben-Horin under the name The ComputerMentor Project. The organization changed its name to TechSoup Global in 2008, becoming another of the hundreds of software and support companies and organizations to have multiple names as it grew.

This organization is itself a nonprofit, and its mission is to support other nonprofits and charitable organizations by providing donations of software, computers, and other technologies, charging only a small administrative fee. The TechSoup organization also supports libraries. Many charitable organizations are staffed by volunteer workers and have small budgets for computing and software resources, but they are vital to their operations.

Nonprofits in Computing and Software

As an example, my wife, Eileen, is deaf but has cochlear implants that restored her hearing. She started a nonprofit foundation called the Gift of Hearing Foundation (GOHF) to help make cochlear implants available to those without insurance, especially small children. The entire board operates on a volunteer basis.

Much of the work of GOHF involves databases of clients, hospitals, surgeons, audiologists, insurance companies, and other associations who aid the deaf and hard of hearing. In order to assist an uninsured patient in receiving a cochlear implant, at least a dozen groups need to be contacted and agree to work together. There are numerous forms, applications, and other documents involved. Without computers and software, the manual effort devoted to paperwork might cost almost as much as a cochlear implant itself.

The original name of ComputerMentor was apt because the founder and his colleagues did provide mentoring and training to nonprofit personnel who needed computers and software but were not trained in software engineering or technical skills. Although it started as a local organization in California, TechSoup grew and expanded so that in the current decade, it supports nonprofits and charitable groups in 190 countries.

As mentioned several times in this book, major software companies have created enormous wealth, and quite a few have decided to use some of that wealth for charitable and public service projects. In order to provide software and equipment to charitable groups at lower than retail prices, the major vendors need to make their products available via donations for charitable licensing. A number of major companies participate with TechSoup in aiding charitable organizations by means of donations. Among the companies that support charities are Microsoft, Cisco, Symantec, Sun, and Adobe.

TechSoup Global now has a network of partner groups in 40 countries, and it offers a number of services, including recycled and refurbished computers, training, manuals, and other assistance all aimed specifically at other nonprofits and charitable groups.

Just as computers and software have become the main operating tools of business and government, they are also vital to charitable organizations. For example, every charity needs a database of the clients it supports and the donors who contribute. All charities have to keep normal financial records, which in many ways are more burdensome than the financial records of profit-making companies. Nonprofit taxation is remarkably complicated. (Intuit has a special version of QuickBooks for nonprofit groups.)

Overall, TechSoup Global has provided assistance to more than 197,000 charitable and nonprofit organizations with a combined retail value of software and computers that approaches $3.5 billion.

Without the donations and assistance of TechSoup and other charitable support groups such as Freelanthropy, many charities and nonprofits would probably not be able to support as many people as they do because manual methods of record-keeping would not be sufficient. Charitable groups and nonprofits need software and computers as much as Fortune 500 companies do, but in general they have very small budgets and depend on volunteer software and support personnel.

TechSoup Global also provides some specialized services to large organizations that provide grants and funding to charities and nonprofits. Many of these are located in other countries, and TechSoup helps in ascertaining if their legal status is equivalent to nonprofits in the United States. This is called *equivalency determination*.

Needless to say, the groups that offer grants, the vendors who donate software and computers, and tax authorities such as the IRS want to be sure that the recipients of grants, donated software, and donated computers are authentic charities and nonprofit organizations.

TechSoup Global occupies a very interesting market niche that needs much more study than it ordinarily receives in the academic software literature. In fact, business schools should consider case studies of the benefits and impact of computers and software in charitable organizations.

Wolfram Research

Wolfram Research was founded by the mathematician Stephen Wolfram in 1987 in Champaign, Illinois. The two main products of this company are important, pioneering, and powerful.

One product is Mathematica, which is an advanced mathematics package widely used by astronomers, physicists, chemists, biologists, and other researchers who need to perform sophisticated mathematical calculations. It is also used by many college students and essentially anyone who needs more mathematical power than a spreadsheet or scientific calculator can provide.

The second major product is Wolfram Alpha, which is a pioneer *intelligent agent* that scans the web and returns with an analysis of results rather than just lists of websites that contain information.

There are other products besides these two, such as Wolfram System Modeler and Wolfram Workbench. The company also developed the Computable Document Format (CDF), which is similar in concept to the PDF but is used for only interactive documents.

Many of the founders of software systems have interesting backgrounds and personalities, and Stephen Wolfram is no exception. He was something of a child prodigy and was known to do mathematical homework for his fellow students for a fee. He matriculated through several major schools, including Eton, Oxford, and Cal Tech, where he received a Ph.D. in physics at the age of 20. Prior to that, he had published a number of highly regarded papers on physics topics such as heavy quarks while still a teenager.

Note

Stephen Wolfram is also a consultant for *Numb3rs*, a television mystery show about the use of mathematics to solve criminal cases.

It should be recalled from the first chapter of this book that a need to speed up mathematical calculations was the impetus that led to dozens of mechanical calculating devices and finally to analog and digital computers. Wolfram's Mathematica is one of the most advanced mathematical packages in history, and it shows pretty much everything computers can do for math.

The search engine Wolfram Alpha is also a pioneering tool. When a user poses a question where factual answers are possible, Wolfram Alpha gives a useful return. For example, a question such as "How many protons are in a hydrogen atom?" will yield the return answer "1." This is not just a pointer to a document or website, but a true answer.

More sophisticated questions are also answered. For example, a website about Wolfram Alpha had a sample question of "Tell me about Big Mac nutrition," meaning the hamburger sold by McDonald's. The response to this question is an itemized list of ingredients plus information on calories, saturated fat, polyunsaturated fats, protein, carbohydrates, and basically everything else.

Wolfram is doing continuous research on knowledge capture, taxonomies for knowledge classification, and other advanced research topics.

The ideas behind Wolfram Alpha can become a major new field of intellectual research as well as software engineering research. Potentially, Wolfram Alpha can become a kind of worldwide knowledge web that synthesizes facts and turns them into useful and readable information.

Needless to say, the technology in Wolfram Alpha has implications for military, defense, and security systems as well as for business and science. A military question such as "Tell me about North Korean air-defense capabilities" should yield interesting information. Another question of interest might be "Tell me which countries initiate the most cyberattacks on the United States."

It is fairly easy to search the web and find out factual information. But to synthesize factual information from hundreds of sources and produce a reasoned analysis is a much harder undertaking. Wolfram Alpha is a true pioneer in a field that is likely to have a global impact.

There are numerous business questions that an intelligent agent such as Wolfram Alpha might soon be able to answer, too. Among these would be "Which Fortune 500 customers use the Oracle ERP package?" or "How many copies of the KnowledgePLAN parametric estimating tool are installed in South America?"

Wolfram Research remains a private company that has not gone public or had an IPO. However, the value of the Wolfram Research intellectual property seems to be enormous. No doubt many large corporations such as Google or IBM that have research laboratories would find Wolfram Research to be a highly attractive acquisition target.

The companies cited in this decade are only samples. Many other companies were also formed during the 1980s. This decade saw the almost universal adoption of computers and software as the key business tools of all major companies and government agencies. The use of personal computers as private tools also grew rapidly thanks to the IBM PC (and its many clones) and the Apple computer.

The Growth of Software During the 1980s

Software continued to grow explosively during this decade. Table 7.4 shows the approximate numbers of software applications developed in the United States in the 1980s.

Results for 1,000 Function Points Circa 1985

The results of the same application of 1,000 function points would be the following:

- Source code for 1,000 function points: 58,182 logical code statements

- Programming language: COBOL and SQL

Table 7.4   *U.S. Software Applications from 1980 to 1989*

Application Types	Applications	Percentage
Scientific	24,000	8.00%
Military and defense	60,000	20.00%
Civilian government	28,000	9.33%
Systems and middleware	36,000	12.00%
Embedded software	39,000	13.01%
Commercial	16,000	5.33%
Information technology (IT)	90,000	30.00%
U.S. outsource	4,200	1.40%
Offshore outsource	1,600	0.53%
Web applications	0	0.00%
Games and entertainment	1,150	0.38%
Open source	50	0.02%
Total Applications	**300,000**	**100.00%**

- Reuse percentage: 0% to 15%

- Methodology: Iterative and structured development

- Productivity: 7.0 function points per staff month

- Defect potentials: 4.5 defects per function point

- Defect removal efficiency (DRE): 87%

- Delivered defects: 0.58 defects per function point

- Ratio of development personnel to maintenance:

  - Development: 70%

  - Maintenance: 30%

The following are the background data for 1985:

- Average language level: 5.50

- Number of programming languages: 750

- Logical statements per function point: 58

- Average application size: 1,100 function points

- Average application size: 63,800

During this era, the sizes of software applications rapidly increased. Prior to this era, only a few applications, such as mainframe operating systems, were larger than 10,000 function points. In the 1980s, a number of major defense applications and civilian systems began to push past 100,000 function points.

The increase in application size led to an alarming problem that still exists: about 35% of major applications with greater than 10,000 function points are canceled without completion. This is because poor quality leads to such major cost and schedule overruns that the ROI becomes negative.

Summary

At the beginning of the decade, software and computers were still somewhat experimental in many companies. By the end of the decade, software and computers were well on their way to becoming the main business tools of every company and government agency in the world that has more than a few employees.

The growth of computer and software usage by companies who might not have a sufficient quantity of skilled personnel led to the rapid growth of several ancillary subindustries such as management consulting, software book publishing, seminars, and commercial education shops such as Digital Consulting.

Still other high-growth subindustries of this decade were management consulting groups such as Accenture and outsource groups such as CAI. This decade also witnessed rapid increases in commercial COTS and the arrival of some open-source packages.

This was the last decade before the internet and the World Wide Web changed the fundamental nature of human communications and social interaction. During the 1980s, people still had more live friends than remote friends known only by web contact. They still used their telephones more for conversations than for texting. Smartphones were still in the future.

Chapter 8

1990 to 1999: Expansion of the World Wide Web and the Rise of Dot-Coms

During the 1990s, the rapid expansion of the internet and the World Wide Web changed human communications and social life forever. New companies began to emerge and carve out new kinds of markets by selling products remotely over the web.

The exuberance and excitement of vast new global markets based on the internet led to an enormous explosion of companies and products marketed over the web by companies termed *dot-coms*. They were known as dot-coms because their website addresses ended in a period followed by the term "com," which was the official web term for commerce.

Early in the next decade, the dot-coms bubble would burst, and many of these new companies disappeared into bankruptcy, but the 1990s witnessed a huge global expansion of communications and remote commerce.

This decade also saw the arrival of online banking and new ways of purchasing articles remotely. It was also a fruitful decade for computer games, which grew in number and complexity and began to offer realistic backgrounds and high-resolution graphics.

In 1999, the new euro currency arrived and began circulation. This caused changes to thousands of banking and financial applications as they were updated to reflect the new currency. The euro became official on January 1, 1999, although notes and coins did not begin circulation until 2002.

In the last half of this decade, the "Y2K" problem would emerge and divert substantial software resources toward converting two-digit dates such as "99" into four-digit dates such as "1999." The reason was that when the year 2000 appeared, the "00" format would damage sort sequences for time-sensitive information such as taxes and corporate earnings.

Toward the end of the decade, some applications were approaching 20 years of use, so "maintenance" began to replace new development as the dominant software work. Legacy applications needing geriatric care were large components of the euro and Y2K problems.

Emergence of the World Wide Web

The development of the internet itself was discussed in the previous chapter. Recall that the internet is the network and network tools that allow computers and other networks to communicate with each other. The World Wide Web is not the same thing as the internet. The web is a collection of tools and services that uses the internet but that focuses on sharing documents and information. A central tool for the web is hypertext, which allows marked phrases in a document to lead users to other pages and other websites.

In 1990, Tim Berners-Lee coined the term "World Wide Web." He was very influential in its development and created several enabling inventions, including the famous hypertext markup language (HTML), the hypertext transfer protocol (HTTP), the first web browser, and several other inventions. Probably every reader of this book uses the letters "HTTP" on a daily basis as an integral part of web addresses. Not as many readers know that it is a fairly recent invention.

Because the web consists of millions of hypertext pages, the invention of HTML ranks as a major human invention in communications. In a hypertext page, selected phrases are "live" and navigate a computer to another page and another website. Anyone who uses Wikipedia or other web documents will notice that the live phrases are usually colored blue or underlined so that they stand out from the normal black text.

When Tim Berners-Lee developed the first web browser, the computer he used was a NeXT computer designed by Steve Jobs, which was discussed in the previous chapter.

The web browser is a critically important invention because it helped convert the web into history's most important research tool. The history of browsers and the so-called browser wars would make an interesting book—probably a thriller.

Tim Berners-Lee published a summary paper of the World Wide Web project on August 6, 1991. This is usually considered to be the date of the birth of the World Wide Web.

Senator Al Gore, later to become the Vice President, was the sponsor of an important bill called the High Performance Computing and Communications Act of 1991, which was also termed "the Gore bill." This bill was passed and signed by President George W. Bush. The Gore bill allotted $600,000 for the creation of a *National Research and Education Network*.

Gore is also credited with coining the term "information superhighway." Gore was computer literate enough to publish an article in a special issue of *Scientific American* in September 1991 titled "Communications, Computers, and Networks." *Scientific American* was and remains a prestigious scientific journal.

The Mosaic web browser first appeared in 1993. This was not the first web browser, but for several years, it was the most popular. Mosaic was developed at the National Center for Supercomputing Applications (NCSA) at the University of Illinois campus in Urbana-Champaign.

Mosaic supported several older internet protocols, had a pleasant interface and good cosmetics, and ran on IBM personal computers. Basically, it made the web fairly easy to use by consumers instead of a network used by technical specialists. But there would soon be many more browsers.

Some of the Mosaic developers also worked on the Netscape browser, which was another popular tool for web surfing.

The phrase "surfing the web" was created in 1992 by a librarian named Jean Armour Polly from Liverpool, New York. She used the phrase in an article she wrote called "Surfing the Internet."

Computers and software have made substantial changes to our everyday working vocabulary. Hundreds of new terms or new definitions for older terms have been due to the influence of computers and software. A few samples include application, big data, binding, browser, botnet, bug, computer (the device), cybercrime, database, deadlock, function point, google (as a verb), hypertext, hypervisor, interface, internet, malware, object, object-oriented, patch, program, programmer, relational database, software, URL, virtual, virus, workstation, and worm.

A special technical vocabulary associated with a scientific or technical field is called an *argot*. The software engineering argot is one of the largest to date and is still growing rapidly. New terms are being created probably on a weekly basis.

Suffice it to say that there was much competition and eventually litigation in the important field of web browsing, including tough competition between Netscape and Windows Explorer. In the fullness of time, a number of powerful browsers were established, including Google Chrome, Firefox, Opera, Safari, and Windows Explorer.

The "browser wars" ran throughout this decade and were not finally resolved until the results of an antitrust lawsuit against Microsoft were implemented in the next decade. On May 18, 1998, the Department of Justice filed an antitrust suit against Microsoft. The claims of this suit were that since Internet Explorer was included in every copy of Windows, that method of distribution was anticompetitive.

This was a very messy case with strong opinions on both sides. The decision by Judge Thomas Penfield Jackson might have split Microsoft into two companies. However, upon appeal, the split was not required. Microsoft was required to publish application program interfaces (APIs) and to permit certain third-party applications to connect to Windows.

The case itself has been controversial, with some saying Microsoft was given monopolistic powers as a result of the appeal. These are legal issues that I am not qualified to discuss, but there are many articles by lawyers who examine a number of issues outside the scope of this book. The Microsoft antitrust suit was front-page news at the end of the decade and into the following decade.

Bill Gates testified and apparently did not make a good impression due to numerous instances of forgetfulness so that he could not answer specific questions. The entire case was very messy, and almost everyone who participated ended up with tarnished reputations.

In the aftermath, open-source software has been able to compete successfully against the browsers of major companies such as Microsoft and Apple. For example, Firefox and Google Chrome are now both highly successful competitors against Internet Explorer.

Other Innovations of the 1990s

Another innovation in this decade was the development of the Linux open-source operating system by Linus Torvalds and colleagues. Linux was an important technology and also served as a useful model for open-source development.

One major invention that greatly expanded the use of computers for research was the development of the Google search engine by Larry Page and Sergey Brin in 1997. Search engines have made it possible to find information about any conceivable topic on the web in a matter of seconds.

The year 1993 witnessed Windows 3.1, which departed from older versions in not being built on the older disk operating system (DOS) but rather on a new kernel.

The first of the "modern" versions of Microsoft Windows was Windows 95, which was released in 1995 as the name implies. However, many more releases and versions were soon to follow.

In 1995, a combination of electronics companies—Philips, Sony, Toshiba, and Panasonic—brought out a high-capacity optical disk storage device called a *digital versatile disk* or *digital video disk* (commonly called a DVD). These had much higher capacity than the older compact disks (CDs) from the previous generation.

The DVD format would lead to a subindustry of home theater equipment that included a DVD player and a high-end audio system with either five or seven channels of sound. The DVD format held so much information that it was no longer limited to mere stereo sound. These home theaters were filled with embedded software and indeed probably could not operate successfully without embedded software. DVD drives also showed up on computers, but in a computer context, the older CD drives were still the norm.

In 1997, the International Software Benchmark Standards Group (ISBSG) was formed in Australia. The ISBSG is one of the most convenient sources of software benchmark data and is also fairly inexpensive. Its data collection of more than 6,000 software projects is widely used in every major country.

In or about 1997, Electronic Arts commissioned studies that used GPS satellites to map a number of golf courses. This mapping led to both simulated computer golf games such as Links and later to the ability to download highly accurate GPS maps of thousands of golf courses onto handheld and even wristwatch-sized devices.

Technology Changes the Sport of Golf

Golf is a sport that has been changed significantly due to software and microcomputers. Computers and software also led to the development of golf-course design packages that allow both amateurs and professionals to model highly realistic golf courses. These are often add-ons to computerized golf games but are also used to design real golf courses.

In today's world, golfers can buy a variety of small GPS devices, including several that are worn as wristwatches. These provide useful information such as the exact distance from any point to the next tee. Some also caution about hazards and obstructions and will even keep score.

The end of this century witnessed the first use of the phrase "big data," which refers to the ability of analyzing large databases with millions or even billions of records.

This decade saw a rapid increase in higher CMM levels of 3, 4, and 5. It also witnessed the development of the Rational Unified Process (RUP) and the increased usage of Joint Application Design (JAD) and the unified modeling language (UML). Web applications exploded in numbers. Viruses and cyberattacks likewise began to explode in frequency. Identity theft became a national problem.

The number of programming languages topped 1,750, with Java, Visual Basic, PHP, JavaScript, and Ruby becoming the best known. Global outsourcing exploded during this decade, with India, China, Russia, the Philippines, and other low-cost countries absorbing U.S. software projects. Commercial off-the-shelf software (COTS) began to approximate 50% of corporate portfolios. Massive enterprise resource planning (ERP) applications were added to portfolios because older stove-pipe applications could not easily share corporate data.

The last few years of the decade witnessed two interesting problems that caused changes to millions of software applications on a global basis: the rollout of the euro in 1999 and the Y2K problem at the century's end when the calendar changed from 1999 to 2000 and two-digit abbreviations for years would no longer sort properly.

Companies Formed During the 1990s

Table 8.1 shows many of the companies that formed from 1990 to 1999.

Table 8.1   *Companies Formed from 1990 to 1999*

Company	Year
Agilent	1999
Akamai	1998
Amazon	1994
The Analysis Group	1990
Apache	1999
AVG Anti-Virus	1991
CAST Software	1993
Cognizant	1994
Digital Playground	1993
eBay	1995

Table 8.1 *(Continued)*

Company	Year
Expedia	1995
Geek Squad	1994
GoDaddy	1997
Google	1998
Hasbro Interactive	1995
Heartland Payment Systems	1997
Insight Venture Capital	1995
ISBSG	1997
ITT Technical Institute	1994
Macromedia	1992
MCC	1992
Monster.com	1999
Mosaic	1993
NetBank	1996
Netscape	1994
PALM	1992
PayPal	1998
Priceline	1997
R Systems	1993
Red Hat Software	1993
Red Storm Entertainment	1996
Sapiens	1990
SegaSoft	1995
SilverLake	1999
Sirius Satellite Radio	1990
Starfish	1994
Symbian	1998
Taligent	1992
ThoughtWorks	1993
Visio	1990
VMware	1998

Table 8.1 is interesting in that it shows the evolution of software and computer use. Many of the companies in prior decades such as Microsoft and Apple were creating new languages and new tools for building software. Although there were tool and software companies created during the 1990s, the majority of companies formed used computers and software to create new kinds of businesses. For example, Amazon is a successful pioneer in web marketing, PayPal and NetBank were pioneers in remote financial transactions, Google was a pioneer in search engine technology, and Sirius was a pioneer in internet radio broadcasts from satellites.

In the 1990s, computers and software had already become universal tools for running businesses, government agencies, and "brick and mortar" retail stores. In this decade, new forms of web-based business models started to blossom and expand. Some of these, such as Amazon, are still successful today, but many did not make it past the dot-com bubble burst of 2000.

As with the other chapters, there were many additional companies created besides the ones shown here. For example, at least a dozen game companies were created. However, game companies tend to have their own culture and seldom commission studies of quality or productivity, so very little data, other than revenues, are available.

Some of the companies with unusual or interesting business models created during the 1990s are discussed here.

Akamai

Akamai was founded in 1998 in Cambridge, Massachusetts, by MIT graduate student Daniel Lewin and MIT professor Tom Leighton. (On a sad note, Lewin was one of the passengers on American Airlines Flight 11 and was killed during the September 11, 2001, terrorist attacks.)

This is an interesting niche company. It speeds up web browsing by mirroring sites and web content on very fast servers. There are a lot of servers, and one of the Akamai value-added features is a set of mathematical algorithms for optimizing traffic. (The two founders were both mathematicians.) Akamai has more than 100,000 servers in 78 countries. Although Akamai provides services to users, their clients are major corporations that want to provide fast and secure content to their customers.

Amazon

Amazon was founded in Seattle, Washington, in 1994 by entrepreneur Jeff Bezos. It went public in 1996. Amazon is currently the world's largest online retail store. This company, like Apple, was formed in the garage of the founder. The name is derived from the Amazon River and was selected because Jeff Bezos wanted the company to have "A" as the first initial so that it would appear toward the front of catalogs and phone books.

Amazon started as a bookstore, and it obviously competed with thousands of brick-and-mortar stores all over the country. The advantage that Amazon provided was that it offered more content than local stores. Costs were low because there was no physical warehouse. There were no sales taxes either, but that advantage is under fierce attack by numerous state governments.

Amazon's business plan called for slow growth, and indeed the company lost money from its inception through the fourth quarter of 2001. However, Amazon's stable sales volumes and low operating costs kept it in business through the dot-com bubble burst of 2000.

Amazon later expanded from books to other kinds of products. Amazon now brings to mind the older Sears Roebucks catalogs from the 1950s when Sears sold a huge variety of products. Today, Amazon sells computers, cameras, all forms of electronics, DVDs, perfume and, of course, books and e-books. The diversity and marketing success of Amazon caused *Time Magazine* to name Jeff Bezos person of the year in its 1999 special edition.

In recent years, Amazon was a pioneer in e-book publishing and also brought out a line of e-book readers called Kindles, which compete with Apple and other tablet vendors.

One of the useful features of Amazon is a ranking system where customers can rank products and also the suppliers of the products. The rankings use a star system, with five stars being the top rank. This is such a useful feature for purchasing items such as books and DVDs that it is surprising that traditional brick-and-mortar stores do not do the same thing. However, the rankings are sometimes suspect and can become skewed and raised by favorable ratings placed by friends or employees or even by made-up reviews.

Amazon is also a web host for a number of other companies because its server farm is so large.

Amazon is currently facing numerous challenges from state governments because, in many states, no sales taxes are collected on goods sold online. The reason for this is that Amazon does not have a physical presence and hence is immune from taxation. This issue is not going away because many states foolishly gave huge pensions and unsustainable benefits to unionized workers, which is now driving states toward bankruptcy. Needless to say, the states are looking at taxation of internet sales as a method of providing new revenues.

When the state of Rhode Island attempted to tax Amazon sales, the response from Amazon was to sever business ties with local companies that had been partners. Individual consumers could still purchase from Amazon. So far, attempts by state governments to tax Amazon and other web businesses have not been fully successful and seem to have caused more harm to local companies than good.

Apache

Today, most computer users utilize Apache servers, but very few know this. The origin of the name is ambiguous and either is an homage to the Apache Native Americans or is derived from the term "patchy" because the first product was created by patches to an older product.

The company was formed in 1994 by Robert McCool, more or less. He had been working on HTTP protocols at the NCSA. When he left, a number of suggested patches circulated in email form. As they were implemented, the group doing the code gradually became known as the Apache group.

The Apache group later formed a nonprofit foundation in 1999 called the Apache Software Foundation. Having software created and offered by a nonprofit foundation is an interesting social phenomenon of the software era. The software created by the foundation is free and open source but controlled by an Apache foundation license. The Apache Software Foundation has a board of directors but no actual employees. Instead, software is developed by a network of more than 2,600 volunteers. This is an interesting business model that deserves to be studied in business schools.

The main products of the Apache Software Foundation are systems for controlling web servers. In 2009, the Apache server farm became the first to host more than 100 million websites. By the end of 2012, almost 64% of global websites ran on Apache servers.

The web has evolved a fascinating social history as well as an interesting technical history. It is hard to envision any other field where critical services are provided to more than 100 million users by unpaid volunteers.

Craigslist

Craigslist is an interesting tale of an entrepreneur accidentally creating a successful company out of a part-time hobby. The company was started as a pastime in 1995 in San Francisco, California, by Craig Newmark. As it happens, he was a computer programmer at the time. He was new to San Francisco and thought a list of local events was a good way to research interesting local topics and possibly meet new acquaintances.

He started an email list to friends and colleagues of local events and topics of interest in the San Francisco Bay area. Later, he ported the list to the web. In 1999, craigslist was incorporated in California as a for-profit company.

Although craigslist started as a source for local events, it soon transformed into a host for job wanted ads, sales of automobiles and other products, and even a dating service. (In fact, there have been problems with offensive materials and adult advertisements.)

Note

A famous murder case involved a medical student named Philip Markoff who posted a fake job ad on craigslist to lure victims. He murdered Julissa Brisman, who responded to the ad, and he became known in the media as the "craigslist killer." Markoff later committed suicide while in jail awaiting trial.

In 2000, Jim Buckmaster joined craigslist as Chief Programmer and CTO. He introduced a number of technical changes, such as self-posting of ads, screening for offensive materials, and interface improvements.

In 2004, eBay bought 25% ownership in craigslist, but the transaction apparently was not a happy one because eBay and craigslist entered into litigation in 2008.

Craigslist is currently ranked as the tenth most widely visited website with about 50 million monthly visitors. Income is derived from charges for various kinds of ads, such as $75 for a job ad in the San Francisco region.

The success of craigslist as opposed to ads in local papers shows the social impact of the web on modern commerce. Suppose you live in a small town with a population of perhaps 20,000 and you want to sell a luxury automobile such as a Lexus. The local paper and local ad brochures will only reach a few dozen potential buyers, mainly in your own local community. This is the way business has been done for more than 200 years.

An ad on craigslist, on the other hand, will also reach people in surrounding towns and even adjacent states. Instead of a few dozen potential local buyers, craigslist may reach several hundred potential buyers within a 75-mile radius. The web and companies such as craigslist were expanding former neighborhood services into wide-area services.

Digital Playground

Digital Playground was founded in 1996 in Van Nuys, California, by an adult filmmaker named "Joone." One of the unanticipated subindustries associated with computer and software was the advent of internet pornography, which has become a major business.

Although Digital Playground makes adult videos, it is also a pioneer in a number of technical topics. For example, Digital Playground was a pioneer in holography and 3D filming. They were also among the companies that chose the Blu-ray format as their choice for high-definition films. They also pioneered interactive videos where a viewer could seemingly communicate with an actress. The software technology of Digital Playground and other adult internet companies is surprisingly sophisticated.

The company was acquired in 2012 by Manwin, a larger adult-film company located in Luxembourg.

The porn industry is now a major computer subindustry on a global basis with dozens of companies and thousands of technical workers as well as thousands of actors and actresses. The industry has its own culture and even has annual awards for best picture, best actor, best actress, and other categories. This subindustry is seldom discussed in the mainstream software engineering journals and books, but any software industry that employs thousands of workers and generates billions in income is significant.

eBay

eBay is a prime example of a Silicon Valley success story in which a basically sound idea was parlayed into a billion-dollar company, more or less by accident. It was started in San Jose, California, on September 5, 1995, by a computer programmer named Pierre Omidyar, who was born in France and whose family was Iranian. The original name of the company at its foundation was Auction Bid. It became eBay in 1997. It is an interesting social phenomenon that many startup companies later change their names for one reason or another. Without a careful count, more than 25% of the companies cited in this book have had more than one name.

eBay started as a web-based auction house. This is an excellent example of how a traditional business such as auctions evolved into a much larger web-based business as a result of having access to millions of possible clients.

A web history of eBay has an interesting tale of one of the first products sold: a broken laser pointer, which sold for $14.83. The eBay founder Pierre Omidyar emailed the buyer to be sure he understood that the pointer was broken and inoperative. The response was "I collect broken laser pointers." At that point, Omidyar realized that web auctions could sell almost anything.

At first, eBay sold physical objects but later expanded into selling services as well, such as airplane tickets. In today's world, it sells dozens of services and thousands of products.

eBay had an initial public offering (IPO) on September 28, 1998, and the founder became a billionaire, along with Meg Whitman, who had been hired as President. eBay also grew by acquisition and, among other properties, it acquired the Skype computer-based telephone conference facility and the PayPal company for handling online payments.

Once PayPal was acquired and part of eBay, the company began to mandate PayPal as the sole source of payments, which cut out credit cards from a number of products. (PayPal will be discussed later in this chapter.)

Although eBay sells a wide variety of products, it does not sell everything. For a combination of legal, business, and ethical reasons, eBay does not sell alcoholic beverages, tobacco products, firearms, drugs, medicines, bootlegged or stolen products, harmful products, lottery tickets, and a number of others.

One interesting feature of eBay is the ability of clients to rank sellers using a five-point star system. In a reversal of roles, eBay itself was compared and ranked among a set of 15 web vendors.

Another unusual feature of eBay is that it donates a percentage of revenues to charitable organizations. In fact, users and clients can name specific charities for the donations. This is an unusual aspect of a business plan but laudable. Other wealthy software companies might follow the same pattern.

Note

A number of software entrepreneurs are philanthropists and donate funds, corporate support, and energy to worthy charities. The Bill and Melinda Gates Foundation is perhaps the largest charitable organization started by a software entrepreneur. The software industry has become one of the most significant sources of funds for nonprofit charitable organizations. This fact is of both social and historical importance.

Like other web sales and services organizations, eBay is in the spotlight for not charging taxes in locations where it does not have a physical presence. Many state governments are trying to get around this limitation.

A final interesting aspect of eBay is that its new corporate office in San Jose was designed to be environmentally friendly. Solar panels on the roof provide almost 20% of the power to run computers and office equipment in the building. The lighting system also detects and responds to ambient light. Instead of constant light output, the building adjusts brightness based on outside light.

eBay has become a diverse company with many business partners and many forms of business. It is no doubt a key company for business school case studies. eBay also demonstrates the power of computers, software, and the web to forge new kinds of remote businesses out of the traditions of older businesses such as auction houses.

GoDaddy

GoDaddy is an interesting niche company that is based on the existence of the World Wide Web and the fact that web addresses need to be unique.

The company was founded in 1997 in Phoenix, Arizona, by an entrepreneur named Bob Parsons. The original name at founding was Jomax Technologies. Here, too, name changes are very common among software startups. It was originally a private company that almost had an IPO in 2006 but decided not to. In 2011, about 65% of the company was sold to a group of venture capitalists for a ballpark figure of around $2.25 billion.

Bob Parsons had already been a successful entrepreneur with an earlier company called Parsons Technology, which he had sold to Intuit, and then retired. GoDaddy was created when he left retirement to become an entrepreneur for the second time. In an industry populated with young entrepreneurs such as Steve Jobs, Sergey Brin, and Mark Zuckerberg, it is interesting that GoDaddy was founded by a former Marine who had already sold one company and came out of retirement to start a new one.

The name "GoDaddy" was apparently decided in a casual meeting with employees who were not happy with the previous Jomax name for some reason. A similar name, Big Daddy, was suggested but was already in use. (Had this been an East Coast firm, the name might have been "Big Papi" after the Red Sox player David Ortiz.)

The main business of GoDaddy is entirely dependent on the existence of the internet and World Wide Web. It could not exist without these. After the web was created and companies began to build websites, it quickly became obvious that each site needed a unique name. In order to do this, it was necessary to create a formal registry of names, which are called *domain names*.

The alphabetic or alphanumeric domain names are only the surface. These are mapped to a mathematical and numeric internet protocol (IP) address that allows automatic jumps from one domain to another. The analogy that comes to mind is the relationship between human names in a phone book and their numeric telephone numbers.

Note

The original Domain Name System (DNS) was developed in 1983 by Paul Mockapetris.

In the early part of the decade, the registry of domain names was kept by the National Science Foundation (NSF). In 1993, the NSF decided to privatize domain registration.

GoDaddy was not the first company to provide name registration: that was Network Solutions. The domain name business now has a number of companies that share the master registry and compete with each other. GoDaddy is one of the larger competitors, with about 50 million names in their registry.

DNS naming and control are critical aspects of the internet and World Wide Web, but the specific mechanism is beyond the scope of this book. Suffice it to say that keeping track of billions of web pages is not trivial and the math is complex.

GoDaddy achieved a kind of social fame due to its somewhat risqué advertisements. GoDaddy hired a number of attractive female models who became known as "GoDaddy girls." One of these is the famous racing driver Danica Patrick.

GoDaddy also garnered quite a bit of social commentary due to its fairly unconventional ads placed during various Super Bowls. For a company to be big enough to advertise during a Super Bowl, it needs to be big indeed and profitable. GoDaddy also sponsored a postseason college football bowl called the GoDaddy Bowl.

Although the advertising strategy of GoDaddy may seem eccentric, the company has achieved a good reputation. It was cited among *Fortune Magazine*'s list of the 100 best companies to work for in 2012. It received a similar award for being among the best companies in Phoenix from the *Phoenix Business Journal* in 2011.

GoDaddy also makes a number of significant charitable contributions. Among its supported charities are those aiding disabled children; avoiding domestic violence; and researching solutions for Parkinson's disease, homelessness, and breast cancer. GoDaddy also contributes to Toys for Tots, the local Humane Society, and the Phoenix Children's Hospital. GoDaddy makes many corporate contributions and encourages employees to participate in charitable work as well.

Google

The history of Google is a classic entrepreneurial legend. Two graduate students developed an interesting mathematical method for searching the web and parlayed it into a multibillion-dollar corporation a few years later. Adding to

Silicon Valley's reputation as an incubator for startups, Google was incorporated by Larry Page and Sergey Brin on September 4, 1998, within a friend's garage in Menlo Park, California. Menlo Park is near the epicenter of Silicon Valley.

Note

The name "Google" is derived from a mathematical term "googol." That term was created in 1938 by a nine-year-old boy named Milton Sirota. A googol was defined by Sirota as 10^{100} power. But Milton Sirota also proposed a bigger number called a *googolplex*. That was first defined by Sirota as "one followed by writing zeros until you get tired." Sirota was the nephew of the well-known mathematician Edward Kasner, who narrowed the googolplex value to $10^{10^{100}}$. No matter how they are defined, googols and googolplexes are very big numbers.

In 1996, Page and Brin were graduate students at Stanford University in Menlo Park. They were working on an interesting project called the Stanford Digital Library Project. The goal of the project was to create an integrated universal digital library.

As part of the research on the Stanford library project, Page and Brin explored web links and developed interesting and powerful algorithms for web searching based on back links. They were not quite alone in the field since another researcher named Robin Li had a similar idea. Later, Li would patent his algorithms and create Baidu, his own company and search engine in China.

There were other and competing methods of web searching besides Google, but Google tended to provide good results quickly, and it gained prominence. Google also began to generate serious revenues by allowing ads that were related to specific keyword searches. Although Brin and Page had originally opposed ads, they finally decided that revenues were needed and ads were the most effective way of getting it.

Google had several rounds of private and venture funding prior to going public with an IPO. Most Google employees were also stockholders, so the reporting requirements for Google were already quite strenuous.

On August 19, 2004, Google had a successful IPO and sold more than 19 million shares at $85 per share. Google was on its way to becoming a software giant. By the end of 2004, Google and its partners were processing almost 85% of all web searches. There were competitors such as Yahoo, but Google was the elephant in the room. Later, Microsoft would create its own Bing search engine. Yet other sophisticated forms of search engines are emerging such as Wolfram Alpha.

Google continued to grow rapidly both by acquisitions and by expanding into other fields. For example, Google Gmail is now a major email service. Google's office suite, Google Docs, competes against Microsoft Office. The

Google Chrome browser competes with Internet Explorer, Firefox, Opera, Safari, and several more.

Microsoft became a fierce competitor of Google. In fact, Microsoft sued Google to stop its key executives from joining Google, on the grounds that their knowledge of Microsoft applications would benefit Google and be a violation of employment agreements. This case settled out of court.

Google became famous for a somewhat quirky corporate culture and for a tendency to be very eclectic rather than pursuing only a single business path. Its business strategy is often hard to gauge because it seems to zigzag from one technology to another.

Like many other software companies, Google has a large nonprofit philanthropic wing and it started this off with a billion dollars in funding. Google supports many charities and nonprofits in areas of poverty abatement, climate change, and various public health programs. This is yet another example of software entrepreneurs with social consciences using some of their large profits for charitable causes. Fortunately, this is not uncommon in the software business.

Staying on the cutting edge of software engineering research and equipment research is one of Google's main focuses. The new Google Glass concept of eyeglasses with an embedded computer is getting good and bad reviews. The Google development of a hybrid electric vehicle is far from conventional software but technically interesting.

Several Google products such as Sky Map and Google Maps are now among the most widely used applications on smartphones. The recent flap caused by Apple attempting to replace Google Maps with its own flawed mapping program was front-page news for several weeks.

Google is one of the fastest moving and most rapidly changing companies cited in this book. It seems to crank out new inventions and products at a very rapid clip. Many are useful and exciting, but not all. In any case, Google has added a great deal of excitement to software engineering and is pushing software in many interesting new directions. Among these is Google's research on secure programming languages and better ways to prevent cyberattacks.

Heartland Payment Systems

Heartland Payment Systems was founded in 1997 in Princeton, New Jersey, by Robert O. Carr. Its main business is processing credit card payments.

Credit cards were based on IBM's magnetic stripe that could be pasted onto plastic cards. Soon after the stripe's invention in 1960, Visa, MasterCard, American Express, and others would make credit card purchases universal.

Heartland is one of several companies whose main business is actually processing the card payments from thousands of merchants and small retail organizations. These companies are more or less invisible to consumers but provide the "engines" that make credit cards useful. They all use software and powerful computers because they process millions of transactions per day. Heartland currently processes credit card data for around 250,000 businesses that generate about $120 billion per year in credit card payments.

In 2009, Heartland made front-page news due to a massive cyberattack that stole credit card data from the magnetic stripes of thousands of individual consumers' credit cards. The actual theft occurred in 2008. A man named Albert Gonzalez was arrested and indicted and later convicted and sentenced to 20 years in federal prison.

The attack was seemingly based on SQL injections, which introduced back-door traps that diverted user data to false addresses so information could be extracted. Once the data are stolen, they can be magnetically encoded onto phony cards. Similar attacks and other indictments were issued for attacks against the retail store T. J. Maxx and the Dave and Buster's restaurant chain.

The Heartland cyberattack is a cautionary tale that in the modern world, data stored on computers are more valuable, and sometimes easier to steal, than gold. In the aftermath of the attack, Heartland introduced new and improved security methods that include full encryption of all data.

Insight Venture Partners

As can be seen by the number of multibillion-dollar software companies cited in this book, the software industry has generated enormous wealth. This wealth is often created when startup companies become successful. Insight Venture Partners specializes in funding software startups.

The company was founded in 1995 in New York by Jeff Horing and Jerry Murdock. In total, Insight has invested in about 170 software companies, including some famous ones such as Twitter, Tumblr, and Quest Software. About $5 billion has been invested by Insight.

Insight Venture Partners is not a software company itself but has provided the seed money for many software startups, of which 21 later became large enough to have IPOs. It is of social and historical interest that the enormous wealth the software industry has created needed venture funding to get started. Without venture funds from groups such as Insight Venture Partners, many of the companies cited in this book would not have gotten started.

The ISBSG

The ISBSG is an interesting niche company that began as a loose cooperative of metrics organizations in five countries. It was founded by Terry Wright in 1994, and three years later Peter Hill joined as President and registered the company in Melbourne, Australia. The ISBSG is organized as a nonprofit group and it provides a very useful service to the software community.

The ISBSG collects benchmark data for software productivity and quality. Today, the volume of available benchmarks exceeds 6,000 projects, and hundreds more come in on an annual basis. The ISBSG benchmarks cover a variety of software types from a variety of industries. More than 20 countries have provided benchmark data to date.

All of the benchmarks in the ISBSG repository use functional metrics. Both International Function Point Users Group (IFPUG) function points and COSMIC function points are represented. Some of the other functional metrics such as NESMA and FISMA are also included.

Function Points and Other Metrics

The plethora of function point variants is not really helpful to economic understanding. The rival claims among the function point variants for being "more accurate" are also not helpful. Function points in all flavors are counted using a complex set of rules, and there are variances in counts even by certified counting personnel. There is no "cesium atom" or absolute standard against which benchmark accuracy can be compared.

However, function points are the only available metric that provides useful economic data and can successfully normalize results. The older *lines of code* metric penalizes modern programming languages and makes requirements and design invisible. The widely used *cost per defect* metric violates standard economic assumptions and also penalizes quality, achieving the lowest cost per defect for the buggiest software.

Other metrics such as story points for Agile projects are not standardized and vary so widely from group to group that statistical analysis is pointless.

Use-case points are more stable (although not standardized) but are only good for projects that actually design software with use cases. They have no value for cross-methodology comparisons.

Function points in all flavors are the best and most reliable metrics yet developed for software benchmarks and for software economic studies. The ISBSG is a major source of data using functional metrics.

(Continued)

(Continued)

One caveat about functional metrics is that manual counting is so slow and so expensive that functional metrics are seldom used on systems larger than about 10,000 function points. Manual function point counting averages about 500 function points per day for certified counters. The costs of manual function point counts range between about $2.50 and $5.00 per function point counted.

Large systems in the 100,000 function point range (such as operating systems, defense systems, and ERP packages) are almost never counted with function points and therefore are not included in the ISBSG repository.

There is a mathematical technique called *backfiring* that can convert counts of logical code statements into equivalent function point counts, but this method is not accurate due to wide variations in individual programming styles. Backfiring was first developed in IBM by Al Albrecht and his team, who invented function points in the early 1970s at the IBM location in White Plains, New York.

There is also a modern and patented high-speed sizing methodology based on pattern matching that can size applications in fewer than two minutes regardless of their nominal size, but this method is so new that no data using it are in the ISBSG repository. This method is owned by Namcook Analytics LLC.

Another new method of *automated function point* has been announced as a standard by the Object Management Group (OMG), but no data are yet available using this approach.

The IFPUG issued a new size metric in 2012 that measures nonfunctional requirements. An example of a nonfunctional requirement would be for special features that improve security or performance but are not counted using function point analysis. This new approach is called SNAP metrics. Because it is so new, empirical data and measured results are just starting to appear in 2013. No doubt these data will be added to the ISBSG repository in the future as they become available.

The ISBSG's data collection method uses a relatively sophisticated questionnaire that captures useful information about software methodologies, programming languages, and other factors that influence software project results.

The ISBSG business model provides the input questionnaire to all clients free of charge, so there is no charge to have data submitted to the ISBSG repository. There are charges for extracting data from the repository, but they are not excessive.

The ISBSG data can be sorted and selected to show a number of subtopics of interest. For example, there are data on new projects and maintenance and enhancements; there are data on large systems and small applications; there are data on Agile projects and waterfalls; there are data on COBOL applications and C11 applications. The ISBSG provides a number of useful filters so that clients can extract specific data. Data can also be shown by industry such as banking, insurance, telecommunications, manufacturing, and others.

It happens that self-reported data from clients are not always 100% accurate. Leakage and data errors are not uncommon among the companies that have provided data to the ISBSG repository. Several consulting companies that go onsite and interview software development teams may have more accurate data, but there are substantial consulting fees for onsite data collection, while the ISBSG data are gathered for free. Also, the consulting companies charge a great deal more for their data than does the ISBSG.

Overall, the ISBSG benchmark repository is a valuable resource for the software industry. The data are widely used by many companies to calibrate estimates and to compare methodologies. The ISBSG data are also published in various articles and books. There are also special reports that might, for example, cover an in-depth study of a major bank.

The software industry needs the kind of data that the ISBSG provides, and this organization has become a valuable resource for academics, corporate researchers, and government researchers.

Monster.com

Few companies discussed in this book are better exemplars of the power of the internet and web for influencing human life than Monster.com. Monster.com has become the largest employment website in the world, with more than 1 million résumés uploaded to it and almost 65 million job-seeking visitors per month. A company like this could not have existed 20 years ago because the enabling technologies of the internet, the web, databases, and combinatorial search logic are all necessary to make it work. Because this book covers social phenomena as well as technical topics, the success of Monster.com is one of the most significant job-seeking and job-posting evolutions in human history.

Monster.com was formed in 1999, but it was created from a merger rather than as a single-company startup. The two pioneering employment sites that merged were the Monster Board (TMB) and the On-Line Career Center (OLC). Jeff Taylor was a founder and CEO of the Monster Board. The organization started in Framingham, Massachusetts, but moved to Maynard, Massachusetts, where it occupied space in the former office complex of Digital Equipment Corporation (DEC). (As it happens, I lived only a few miles from the Maynard complex in the next town over, Acton, Massachusetts.)

The early history is complex and involves multiple mergers and acquisitions. It started with an older company called Telephone Marketing Programs (TMP)

Worldwide that was formed in 1967 and started as a print-based "yellow pages" firm. In 1993, TMP started a recruitment division. In 1995, it acquired the Monster Board and the On-Line Career Center, the two companies that would later merge. Monster.com itself is owned by Monster Worldwide, Inc.

Monster was a pioneer in web-based job searches and had one of the first job-search websites in 1994, not long after the web began to function internationally.

Although Monster.com is very popular with job seekers and companies seeking new employees, not everything was smooth as the company grew. In 2007, Monster.com was hacked, and personal information for thousands of job-seeking candidates was stolen from its databases. Although Monster said it would improve security, there was another hack in 2009 at the U.K. Monster data center, which may have resulted in as many as 4.5 million records being stolen.

In 2006, the Attorney General's office of the State of New York began an investigation on assertions of back-dating stock options. Monster started its own internal investigation and reported some irregularities, which resulted in restating earnings from 1997 through 2005. There were some personnel terminations as well.

The parent TMP Worldwide company went public in 1996 and is traded on NASDAQ. In spite of hacks and legal issues, Monster.com remains a pioneer in online employment searches and job postings, and it is also a company that created many innovations in personnel systems.

Netscape Communications

Netscape was a pioneer among web browsers and was also one of the combatants in the famous "browser wars" by competing against Microsoft. The company was founded in Mountain View, California, on April 4, 1994, by Jim Clark and the famous Silicon Valley entrepreneur Marc Andreesen. Originally, the company was Mosaic Communications Corporation, but as with many software startups, the name of the company changed.

Many of the same people who developed the original Mosaic web browser also worked on the development of the Netscape web browser, but the source code of the two was different. Netscape also created the famous JavaScript programming language and originated the *Secure Sockets Layer* (SSL) protocol.

At its peak, Netscape had about 90% of the browser market but eventually lost market share to Microsoft's Internet Explorer. This led to an antitrust suit against Microsoft in 1998 since Internet Explorer was provided as part of Windows and was not marketed separately.

Netscape was acquired by America Online (AOL) in 1999 for stock and equity worth perhaps $10 billion.

In the first browser war, Internet Explorer achieved a dominant place, while Netscape's usage declined. However, Netscape decided to make its browser source code an open-source platform, and that helped create the Mozilla Foundation. The later Firefox browser by Mozilla is a descendant of the original Netscape browser.

Note

The browser wars continue today and new players have joined the fray. Current browsers include Apple Safari, Google Chrome, Internet Explorer, Mozilla Firefox, Opera, OmniWeb, Shira, and a number of others. In today's world, browsers also operate on smartphones and tablets as well as on computers. The history and technology of web browsers are among the most complex but interesting topics in the larger history of software engineering. The browser wars are leading to rapid increases in browser capabilities and features as the various browser companies seek to pull ahead of their rivals.

Netscape itself went from being an independent company to being owned by AOL to being closed by AOL in 2003. However, the name "Netscape" still continues, as does the browser. A search for "Netscape" on the web leads to the site of an internet service provider (ISP).

Priceline

Priceline was founded in 1997 in Norwalk, Connecticut, by the software entrepreneur J. S. Walker. The Priceline business model is interesting and unusual. Priceline is a conduit for various products and services such as airline tickets, hotel rooms, and vacation packages. Users specify a price range, and Priceline then reports back on what companies can match the user's stated price. The actual names of the hotels or airlines are concealed from customers until they make a no-refund purchase agreement. Priceline receives its cut from the vendors of services that were sold. Priceline has now added a more traditional business model where the names of the vendors are shown prior to purchase.

Priceline became famous due to its commercials featuring a former *Star Trek* actor, William Shatner. Later ads also featured his costar Leonard Nimoy, who played Mr. Spock. Shatner was given equity in Priceline in exchange for his presence in the ads.

Priceline is a good example of a company and a business model that is entirely driven by computers, software, the internet, and the World Wide Web. All of these are needed to match the requests from millions of consumers to thousands of products and services. The Priceline company could not have been created prior to the 1990s because all of its enabling technologies are part of the internet era.

Red Hat Software

Red Hat Software is interesting because its business model centers on open-source software, which is an important phenomenon of the software engineering world. The company was founded in 1995 in Raleigh, North Carolina, by Bob Young and Mark Ewing, who merged two Linux and Unix companies to create Red Hat. The name "Red Hat" derives from a Cornell University lacrosse hat given to Bob Young by his grandfather, although he himself attended Carnegie Mellon University.

Red Hat is the largest contributor to the Linux kernel, and it licenses other software under the GNU open-source licensing agreement. Red Hat Enterprise Linux is one of the most widely used Linux versions. Like many open-source companies, Red Hat offers software itself for free, but it charges for consulting, training, and support. The company also receives voluntary donations from satisfied users.

Although the phrase "open source" brings up an image of nerdy hackers working alone, in fact quite a bit of open-source development is done by professional staff and uses professional quality assurance. Red Hat has more than 600 personnel in North Carolina, for example.

Open-source projects compare favorably to regular commercial software. In fact, open-source developers pioneered the usage of static analysis tools. The open-source business model is worthy of business school case studies because it is popular and seems to be successful.

Red Hat shows that quite a bit of money can be made from the open-source model. Red Hat had an IPO on August 11, 1999, that was the eighth largest first-day gain in the entire history of Wall Street! (Their stock is sold on NASDAQ.)

In 2005, *CIO Insight Magazine* ranked Red Hat number one in vendor value. On July 27, 2009, Red Hat replaced CIT Group in the Standard and Poor's 500 stock market. This is a first for an open-source company. Also, in 2012, Red Hat became the first open-source company to top $1 billion in revenues, receiving about $1.25 billion that year.

Since their IPO, Red Hat has acquired a number of other companies and services and has also opened new offices and facilities in other countries, such as India. Red Hat is proof of the concept that the open-source phenomenon can be a successful way to run a software business.

Red Storm Entertainment

Red Storm Entertainment is a computer-game company founded in 1996 by Tom Clancy and Doug Littlejohns in Morrisville, North Carolina. Tom Clancy is the famous adventure and military novelist, and Doug Littlejohns was a submarine captain in the British Navy.

This company is a good example of the increasing sophistication of computer games and the growth of the whole computer-game industry. Computer games originated as fairly simple games such as Pong. Later, they evolved into more sophisticated role-playing games, simulations of board games such as chess, sports games such as tennis and football and, finally, massively multiplayer online role-playing games (MMORPGs) where thousands of participants wander as avatars through artificial worlds. In some games, it is even possible to build buildings, acquire real estate, and simulate actual urban growth.

The Red Storm games center on the books and concepts that originated in Tom Clancy's novels. Some of the Red Storm games include Rainbow Six, Eagle Watch, Ghost Recon, and Rogue Spear.

In 2000, Red Storm was acquired by the larger game company Ubisoft. Computer games may seem unimportant, but in fact they are often on the cutting edge of computing and software technologies. The rendering engines for realistic backgrounds have expanded from games to other forms of business such as animated films.

Computer Games as a Major Industry

The computer-game business entirely depends on computers and software and could not exist before they became widely used and popular. Modern games have expanded from being played on computers to operating on special game consoles such as the Nintendo Wii and Microsoft Xbox, tablets, special handheld devices such as Gameboy, and smartphones.

Some of the MMORPGs are played by hundreds or thousands of participants, and the games operate 24 hours per day, seven days per week. This is a new and interesting social phenomenon that would not occur without computers, software, and the web. Computer gaming has also created major new forms of software technology. Some game systems such as the Wii feature physical attachments that resemble tennis rackets, golf clubs, and other sports equipment. These allow fairly realistic simulations of actual sports.

There is some concern among psychologists and medical professionals that violent computer games may lead to violence in real life. There is also concern

(Continued)

(Continued)
among medical professionals that games may be somewhat addictive and that excessive computer-game playing can lead to obesity and lack of muscle strength due to passive physical posture with no exercise.

The sophistication of computer-game algorithms reached a new high on May 11, 1997, when IBM's Deep Blue supercomputer beat the world chess champion Gary Kasparov. The match was close, but Kasparov apparently made a mistake during the opening moves of game six. This was the first time a computer had beaten a world-champion chess player. However, ordinary computer chess games on personal computers play well enough to be tough competitors for unranked amateur chess players and even for fairly serious ranked players.

Sirius Satellite Radio

Sirius Satellite Radio was founded in July 1990 in Washington, D.C., by the attorney and entrepreneur Martine Rothblatt. It is currently headquartered in New York. This was not an ordinary company startup because before it could begin operations, Rothblatt had to petition the Federal Communications Commission (FCC) to gain its approval for using part of the 2300-MHz band. While embedded software is what drives the Sirius operation, it is the politics of getting the company started that is the most interesting and is also unique in this book.

Fortunately, Rothblatt was not only an attorney but also a specialist in communications laws. She demonstrated a prototype from ground-based transmitters to the FCC in 1992. Getting government approval for Sirius was not a trivial undertaking. The legal and public policy issues were more complicated than the technology issues.

Rothblatt was not a novice in satellite communications, having previously founded the GeoStar satellite navigation system and the PanAmSat television broadcast group. Clearly, she knew a lot. Rothblatt left Sirius in 1992 due to her daughter's illness, and she founded a medical research organization.

Five more years of lobbying and politics would be needed to gain regulatory approval. Two CEOs followed her: Robert Briskman, a former NASA engineer, and then David Margolese, who had funded Sirius. Needless to say, opposition from conventional ground-based broadcasters was fierce. Probably the politics of starting Sirius are more complex than any other company cited in this book.

The FCC had shifted from assigning frequencies to auctioning them. In 1997, Sirius successfully bid $83 million to gain access to the frequencies originally requested in 1990. The FCC also sold a license to a competitor, XM Radio.

It was also necessary for Sirius to build satellite radio receivers and to negotiate with major automobile companies to put satellite radios in automobiles, without which there was little likelihood of a successful business model. Before Sirius could become a viable company, several more daunting tasks were needed. First, Sirius had to launch three satellites and construct a coast-to-coast transmitter network.

In total, starting up Sirius Satellite Radio took about $2 billion in total funding. This meant it was the most expensive startup cited in this book as well as the most expensive startup of any company in history!

As is common and mentioned often in this book, there were several name changes along the way, including CD Radio, which did not attract enthusiasm. Prior to acquiring XM, the final name was Sirius Satellite Radio; it is now called Sirius XM Radio.

Sirius was a startup company, but it also basically invented and founded an entire new industry. Sirius engineers had to design custom satellites, calculate optimal orbits, design custom computer chips, and develop custom software. They also had to lobby the FCC and Congress and even build custom broadcast studios with glass walls. From the first petition in July 1990 until the first broadcast on Valentine's Day in 2002, almost 12 years and more than $2 billion were needed to get Sirius off the ground.

The business model of Sirius was to offer fee-based high-definition music without commercials. There are commercials on Sirius, and plenty of them, but not while music is actually playing. (In the interest of disclosure, I have been a Sirius customer for several years.)

In 2007, Sirius acquired the competitive XM satellite radio after gaining Securities Exchange Commission (SEC) and FCC approvals, which involved another complex political process.

Sirius does not just broadcast derivative or common materials. Quite a few broadcasts are unique, and Sirius has forged relationships with entertainers and also sports teams and leagues. For example, Sirius broadcasts many college and professional football games to national audiences. However, it is a curious legal issue that restricts major league baseball games only to XM and not to Sirius, even though the two are now merged. That is a legal issue outside the scope of this book.

Sirius would make a very interesting case study for business schools because it not only created a new industry but also technical issues were strongly intertwined with political and regulatory issues. While software is critical to Sirius and XM operations, it is the combination of politics and technology that makes the story unique.

ThoughtWorks

ThoughtWorks is an interesting example of a software company aimed at improving software itself. The company is also unusual in that it has a strong social commitment.

In the 1980s, an entrepreneur named Roy Singham started a management consulting company in Chicago, Illinois, called Singham Business Services. As so often happens in the software business, Singham changed the name of his company. Singham incorporated under the name ThoughtWorks in 1993, also in Chicago.

The new ThoughtWorks company concentrated on trying to improve software development methods and practices, certainly a laudable goal. The company has both a consulting portion and a software tool portion called ThoughtWorks Studios. ThoughtWorks also commingles commercial applications with open-source applications, which is an interesting and unusual business model.

The well-known software engineer Martin Fowler joined ThoughtWorks in 1999 and became its chief scientist in 2000.

ThoughtWorks pioneered some interesting technologies on its own and was also an early contributor to the Agile methodology. Indeed, Martin Fowler was one of the signatories of the Agile Manifesto in 2001. Thought-Works is also working on continuous development and continuous integration, or attempting to convert software from discrete releases several months apart to a kind of process-control flow of rapid releases of new functions as they become ready.

One of the more interesting aspects of ThoughtWorks is its strong commitment to social issues. According to its website, the company mission has three key elements:

- Run a sustainable business

- Champion software excellence and revolutionize the IT industry

- Advocate passionately for social and economic justice

The third element is both unusual and laudable.

The ThoughtWorks support of social issues includes providing technical aid to nonprofit and charitable groups that need technical assistance. ThoughtWorks also allows employees to provide nonbillable time to charitable groups. Thought-Works also contributed an application that allowed emergency donations to flood victims in Australia.

Another unusual aspect of the ThoughtWorks social program is that employees are allowed to contribute open-source code that they have developed. This is a very unusual concept, and it should be studied by business schools.

Currently, ThoughtWorks has more than 2,000 employees and has offices in Chicago; London; Bangalore; Brisbane; Calgary; San Francisco; and Porto Alegre, Brazil.

Visio

Visio was an interesting niche company that developed a sophisticated graphics package that used predefined shapes and links. Visio supported various software diagramming methods such as flowcharts and UML diagrams. It also supported other forms of scientific and technical graphics.

This company was formed in Seattle, Washington, in September 1990. The founders included Jeremy Jaech, Dave Walker, and Ted Johnson. All of the founders had worked together at Aldus Corporation.

As so often happens with software startups, there were several name changes. Visio started with the name Axon Corporation. In 1992, it changed its name to Shapeware. In 1994, it changed its name to Visio 1, and when it did an IPO, the name was Visio.

I was a Visio client in the late 1990s before Visio was acquired by Microsoft in 2000. The current name of the company is Microsoft Visio. The acquisition was in the form of a stock swap and amounted to about $1.5 billion. This was Microsoft's largest acquisition at the time.

The graphics technology of the Visio products uses vector graphics and a proprietary file format, so Visio diagrams cannot be read or opened by many other software applications. However, Visio can open other graphics formats. (The Libre Office suite can open Visio files and in fact may be an industry leader in opening more file formats than other office suites.)

Although Visio is cited in this book primarily because it supports software engineering diagrams, it is in fact a very eclectic tool that can produce diagrams for many scientific and engineering fields, including electrical engineering, chemistry, and even botany.

The shapes and diagrams are organized as stencils and templates, and it is fairly easy to scroll through Visio catalogs. In addition, third-party vendors offer custom stencils and templates for Visio. For example, the networking company Cisco has a library of Visio stencils for various kinds of networks and products such as optical networks, routers, security flow, and many more.

Visio is a good example of a "niche" software company that provides a special kind of tool for special purposes, but graphics design is a pretty large niche with millions of potential engineering and scientific customers. Visio is not alone and has many competitors, such as SmartDraw and even the open-source Libre Office. However, Visio has a large market share in a variety of scientific disciplines. With Microsoft's powerful marketing engine, Visio has become a major player in the computer software industry.

VMware

VMware is another company whose business is exclusively dependent on computers and software, and it could not exist without them. The name is a compression of "virtual machine," and that is an interesting technology.

The VMware company was founded in 1998 in Palo Alto, California, which is in the midst of Silicon Valley. The group of founders included Diane Green, Mendel Rosenblum, Scott Devine, Edward Wang, and Edouard Bougnion. Mendel Rosenblum was Chief Scientist and Diane Green was President.

Software runs on specific computers and specific operating systems. A virtual machine is a software package that imitates a hardware/software combination so that applications can be run on computers and operating systems different from the ones originally intended.

VMware was acquired by the larger EMC Corporation in 2004 for about $625 million. In 2007, EMC had an IPO for part of the VMware stock, which opened at $29 per share and ended at $51 per share.

In 2007, Diane Green was terminated by the board, and later Mendel Rosenblum resigned. Things were apparently not happy inside the VMware/EMC merger.

VMware has both commercial and open-source applications. This is an unusual combination but is becoming more frequent in the software industry.

VMware's products include several forms of *hypervisors*, which allow guest operating systems to run on artificial, virtual hardware platforms. VMware also supports dual-boot systems, or running two different operating systems on the same platform.

Virtual machines offer some significant cost savings for commercial software development companies and also for large software users. Suppose a software vendor was building an application that was planned to be released in versions for Microsoft Windows, Apple Macintosh, and Linux. Without virtualization, the vendor would need separate hardware devices for each. With virtualization, a single computer can be made to appear as though it were three different machines.

There are many other companies besides VMware in the virtualization business sector. This is an interesting example of a new kind of market niche that exists only because of computers and software.

In general, the software companies cited here are expanding the uses of computers and software into new directions. Several of the companies cited could not have existed 20 years beforehand because the internet and the World Wide Web were needed in order to carry out their business models.

Mass Updates and Aging Legacy Software

Business and commercial software applications began to expand in numbers by 1975. By the middle of the 1990s, some applications, such as IBM's operating systems, had been evolving and used for more than 20 years. The same was true for other industries and applications that had been early adopters of computers and software: banks, insurance, telecommunications, and a number of others.

The increasing age of many important software packages introduced a new phrase into software engineering: "legacy applications." The large volume of aging legacy applications would soon play a part in a new kind of software problem called *mass updates* that require changes to thousands of legacy applications simultaneously. (Mass updates occur when problems, such as the one that Y2K posed, that affect thousands of applications need to be changed at the same time.) This type of problem is going to stay with us from now on and will get worse in the future.

The task of maintaining aging legacy applications would grow rapidly and by 2000, software maintenance would absorb more software engineering time than software development. This is not unexpected and has occurred in other industries. By the time automobiles had been in use for 30 years, there were more mechanics who maintained automobiles than there were assembly line workers building new automobiles.

Consider the software world as it neared the end of the decade, say from 1995 on. The new euro currency was about to be introduced in 1999. The famous Y2K problem would occur as the calendar changed from 1999 to 2000 at midnight. Neither of these issues is a problem for new applications, but both were serious problems for the huge inventory of aging legacy software packages.

Both of these topics would impact thousands of legacy applications that had been running for many years. They would require the diversion of thousands of software engineers and millions of staff hours to modify aging applications.

These are among the first instances of mass updates. Mass updates had never happened before, but they will happen again, with ever-increasing costs and difficulty because legacy applications are continuing to grow faster than they can be replaced.

Many problems associated with the insufficient numbers of digits will occur during the next 50 years, too, but when these issues will pop up is somewhat unpredictable.

An interesting report by Dr. Clifford Kurtzman notes that the population of the United States will exceed the capacity of unique ten-digit phone numbers for all callers before the year 2025 and perhaps as early as 2015 due to the huge increases in multiphone families brought about by smartphones. Already, there is a need to reassign area codes to help solve this problem.

In 2038, the internal Unix clock will overflow, causing a kind of mini-Y2K problem for Unix systems.

The availability of unique U.S. social security numbers (each nine digits long) may be exceeded by about the middle of the century, say 2050. Other similar problems are ISBNs, which now have 13 digits rather than just 10 digits, and IP addresses.

The cumulative costs of expanding numeric fields as their capacity is exceeded will erode many of the economic advantages derived from using computers and software. It is obvious that a more permanent general schema must be developed before numeric-field maintenance expenses in legacy applications become severe.

None of these numeric- and date-related software updates will add useful new features or functions to applications. Their main purpose is merely to allow the applications to continue to operate when dates or numeric information exceed the available sizes of the fields originally set aside to store the information.

The software industry is currently dealing with each problem individually as it occurs, rather than seeking general solutions to the fundamental problem. It might be time for an international symposium on the problem of dates and computers in order to address the root causes of such problems.

Four possible solutions can be envisioned for the fundamental problem of inadequate date and numeric field sizes:

- Developing standard formats for dates that will not expire in short periods

- Developing methods for finding hidden or indirect dates with high efficiency

- Developing mass-update tools and technologies that can make changes rapidly

- Developing improved testing methods to minimize the risks of missed dates

Unfortunately, the current international standards for dates are not adequate and do not support scientific dates or any long-range date calculations. There are no proven methods for finding indirect dates or dates embedded in other fields, such as part numbers. Much of the work of finding and repairing date fields remains manual and labor intensive.

Further, testing of software has never been 100% effective, and testing for date and numeric fields has seldom been more than 95% efficient and often worse. Looking back at the Y2K problem, almost a third of the reported Y2K problems occurred in applications that had been repaired, tested, and put back into service.

Incompatibilities of International Date Formats

For centuries, the way in which dates are represented when they are printed has varied from country to country. These variations presented no real problem until the advent of the computer era. Even with computers, the problems were fairly minor, but it was obviously necessary to know which date format was used in order to ensure correct date calculations.

For example, in the United States, a format of month/day/year such as 10/6/98 for October 6, 1998, is used. In much of Europe, the same date would be printed using the format of day/month/year or 6/10/98 for the same day. The European form might be misinterpreted as June 10th in the United States, or the U.S. format might be misinterpreted as June 10th in Europe if the software assumed the wrong alternative.

To facilitate international trade and commerce using computers and software, the International Organization of Standards (ISO) has proposed a standard date format that expands the number of year digits from two to four. This is the well-known ISO standard 8601: 1988(E). This same format is supported by the American National Standards Institute (ANSI) and by the National Institute of Standards and Technology (NIST).

The ISO date format puts the year first, then the month, and then the day using the format yyyy/mm/dd. Thus, the date of October 6, 1998, would be represented as 1998/10/06 using the ISO standard. (Note that the slash symbols "/" are not part of the date standard but are simply used here to enhance legibility on the printed page.)

Unfortunately, the most common date format used in the United States works in the opposite direction and puts the year last. This is the default representation on various Microsoft products, although Microsoft's products can support the ISO format, too.

As it happens, the four-digit ISO standard for date formats is not fully adequate. Both the ISO standard and the normal U.S. date representation share a common failing when trying to deal with dates and computers. Both of these date formats exhibit unconscious attempts to conserve storage space without realizing that this is causing unnecessary problems.

By adding at least one extra digit to the ISO date format, any date representation could be accommodated by using the extra digit as a key (shown as "x" in the examples) to identify whether the ISO date format (x-yyyy-mm-dd) or the U.S. default date format (x-mm-dd-yyyy) was intended.

The key could also identify other alternatives, such as the normal European date format (x-dd-mm-yyyy) or even Julian dates, which record the number of days from the beginning of a year starting with 1 and running to 365 or 366. Even the traditional Japanese dates based on Imperial reigns could be accommodated.

Using an extra digit (or digits) as a key with the meanings listed in Table 8.2 would make identifying which date format is intended a lot less messy than what is currently used. Today, ascertaining which of the many possible date formats might be used in software applications either requires advance notification to programmers and users or extraordinarily complicated algorithms for deriving dates, with no absolute way of knowing if the date format selected is the right one without inspection or testing. Consider how versatile date logic would be if one or more extra digits were utilized.

The examples shown in Table 8.2 illustrate what might be done using only a single extra digit. For many date and timekeeping purposes, it might be desirable to include not only century, year, month, and day information but also

Table 8.2 *Possible Date Format Key That Uses One Additional Digit*

Key	Definition	Format
1	ISO date format with four digits for year	(yyyy-mm-dd)
2	U.S. default date format with four digits for year	(mm-dd-yyyy)
3	Normal European date format with two digits for year	(dd-mm-yy)
4	Normal European date format with four digits for year	(dd-mm-yyyy)
5	Normal U.S. date format with two digits for year	(mm-dd-yy)
6	Julian date with two-year digit	(yy-ddd)
7	Julian date with four-year digit	(yyyy-ddd)
8	Astronomical time starting from January 1, 4713 BC	(ddddddd)

weeks, hours, minutes, seconds, and even milliseconds. Thus, if a date key is used to identify which format is being utilized, even the following 16-digit date format could be used if needed:

x-yyyy-MM-ww-dd-hh-mm-ss

In this 16-digit format, x is the date code; yyyy represents the year; MM represents the month; ww represents the week of the year; dd represents the day; hh represents the hour; mm represents the minute; and ss represents the second. Even 16 digits are not enough precision for some uses, so the schema could be extended down to the nanosecond level. If it takes 20 digits or more, any known date format might be incorporated into the schema, but then conservation of space is irrelevant.

For a universal date format, there may be hundreds or even thousands of date variants that would need specific keys. Therefore, a four-digit key followed by 20 digits of date information should be able to accommodate any known calendar and to operate over arbitrarily long time periods.

The ISO standard date format is not adequate for scientific purposes. For dealing with geological and astronomical time periods, spans of millions of years must be accommodated, and most of this time would be in the BC era and hence require negative numbers. For astronomical time, billions of years must be accommodated. Indeed, for astronomical purposes, the calendars of other planets such as Mars may eventually need to be accommodated.

We need an effective method for storing dates in computers in an era where unlimited optical storage is the rule. Storing dates and printing them or displaying them are not the same issue.

Many standard date formats attempt to use the same format for both date storage and for date representation. This triggers unexpected problems for computers and software. If we can develop an effective storage method for dates and time, then we can display and print the information in any format that we choose.

Let us design a computerized date-storage format that can last indefinitely, support scientific as well as business dates and time, and support all of the older date-format variants. As the situation now stands, there are no current or proposed date standards by ISO or anyone else that are fully adequate even for business if it is transacted by computers, to say nothing of scientific purposes.

Under current date formats, it is almost impossible to utilize technologies such as data mining and online analytical processing (OLAP) for scientific data associated with geology, archaeology, or astronomy. This is because the dates involved exceed the ranges of standard date formats and, in many cases, they exceed the date-handling ability of normal business software applications such as spreadsheets and database packages.

Adding extra key digits to date formats in computers would allow any conceivable date format to be included in the general schema so that geologic and astronomical time, Julian dates, the Chinese calendar, the Jewish calendar, or even the Aztec calendar could be utilized as needed.

The date key would not have to be printed or appear onscreen, but the presence of a date key would enable software applications to handle calendar calculations with far greater ease and flexibility than has ever been possible since computers became business and scientific tools.

It should be noted that the general solution of using a key field to identify which specific numeric or alphanumeric format follows can be used to deal with other problems besides dates. This same method might be used to handle the international variations in zip code formats or the international variations used for social security numbers (or their equivalent) in other countries.

An expanded date format would require changes to software applications and databases and would be expensive to implement. But between the Y2K problem, the UNIX date rollover, and other date problems, we are already going to spend several billions of dollars in software date changes, so we might as well invest in a permanent solution.

Some of the proposed new replacement dates have the same kind of problem as the current dates. For example, the new ISO format does not have enough digits to handle scientific date purposes. The ISO format will overflow in the year 10,000 and hence can't be used for scientific purposes.

Computer date storage is far more important than printing or displaying dates. It would be enormously valuable if a truly effective date-storage standard could be developed. The heart of this proposal is to separate the way dates are stored from the way they are displayed. How dates are displayed can be a matter of personal or national preference. But how dates are stored in computers needs to be global and suitable for both scientific and business purposes.

Right now, none of the current date standard formats are going to accomplish anything but cause more long-range problems for software and computer vendors and a continuing need for tricky and error-prone date calculations.

The treatment of dates may be something of a non sequitur in a history book, but date problems first became troublesome and expensive with the Y2K issue at the end of the 1990s.

The Expansion of Outsourcing

The rapid expansion of software and the increasing volumes of aging legacy software packages caused many companies to rethink whether it was cost-effective to employ large data-processing staffs when their core businesses had little to do with software.

The 1990s witnessed a rapid increase in both domestic and international outsourcing, with many companies reducing or eliminating internal software staffs and transferring their software projects to outsource vendors. Maintenance outsourcing was the most common, but development outsourcing also grew rapidly.

Growth of Software Applications During the 1990s

The numbers of software applications continued to climb during the 1990s, but the rate of growth was starting to slow down because so many applications were already in use. Table 8.3 shows the approximate numbers of applications created in the United States during the decade.

Table 8.3 *U.S. Software Applications from 1990 to 1999*

Application Types	Applications	Percentage
Scientific	96,000	6.40%
Military and defense	240,000	16.00%
Civilian government	280,000	18.67%
Systems and middleware	180,000	12.00%
Embedded software	312,000	20.80%
Commercial	80,000	5.33%
Information technology (IT)	265,000	17.67%
U.S. outsource	26,000	1.73%
Offshore outsource	15,000	1.00%
Web applications	1,000	0.00%
Games and entertainment	4,500	0.37%
Open source	500	0.03%
Total Applications	**1,500,000**	**100.00%**

Perhaps the most interesting and technically important change in application patterns during this decade was the emergence of web applications, which were just starting their own explosive growth path.

The arrival of web applications led to the start of the dot-com bubble, which saw the creation of hundreds of venture-funded companies whose market plans were based on web sales, such as Amazon. The bubble would burst early in the next decade, and most of these companies are now gone.

Amazon was incorporated by Jeff Bezos in 1994 and went online in 1995. Its original market plan was to rapidly expand its client base regardless of profits. Indeed, Amazon ran at a loss for several years, and its stock declined sharply during the dot-com bust. However, Amazon persevered and eventually became the world's largest retail establishment.

Results for 1,000 Function Points Circa 1995

During the 1990s and the following two decades, many function point "clones" were developed. The original IBM function point was taken over by IFPUG in the 1980s. From that point on, alternative functional metrics appeared, including Mark II function points, COSMIC function points, FISMA function points, NESMA function points, fast function points, engineering function points, and the pseudo-functional metrics story points and use case points. The Mark II function point metric in the United Kingdom by Charles Symons was the first known alternative to IFPUG function points.

Productivity and quality for the same 1,000 function point application would be the following:

- Source code for 1,000 function points: 53,333 logical code statements

- Programming language: Java

- Reuse percentage: 0% to 25%

- Methodology: RUP

- Productivity: 8.00 function points per staff month

- Defect potentials: 4.0 defects per function point

- Defect removal efficiency (DRE): 90%

- Delivered defects: 0.40 defects per function point

- Ratio of development personnel to maintenance:
  - Development: 60%
  - Maintenance: 40%

The following are the background data for 1995:

- Average language level: 6.00

- Number of programming languages: 1,600

- Logical statements per function point: 53

- Average application size: 950 function points

- Average application size: 50,350 logical code statements

This decade still experienced far too many cancellations and overruns for large software applications. It also saw a rapid increase in global outsourcing.

Summary

The 1990s witnessed the arrival of the dot-com era, when the internet and World Wide Web introduced new ways of doing business by selling products and services remotely. Some companies prospered and created entirely new forms of business. Others tried but would fail during the dot-com bust early in the next decade.

By the end of the 1990s, hundreds of applications were aging and in need of geriatric renovations. The double impact of the euro rollout in 1999 and the Y2K problem at the century's end showed that mass updates to legacy applications would be troublesome, and there are many future mass updates just beyond the horizon, when unique digit combinations will run out for telephone numbers and social security numbers.

As software applications grow older, software maintenance begins to move ahead of software development as the main form of software engineering work. This is not surprising, considering a similar situation where there are more mechanics fixing automobiles than there are assembly-line workers building new automobiles.

This was the first decade of the internet and the World Wide Web. In this decade, this technology started to change the fundamental nature of human communications and social interaction. During this decade, some people began to interact more with remote acquaintances than with their families and friends.

Social networks would blossom in the next decade but had already begun. A new subindustry of massively interactive computer games had begun and would continue to grow in the next decade.

Chapter 9

2000 to 2009: The Rise of Social Networks and Economic Crises

From 2000 to 2009, social networks such as Facebook and Twitter would enroll most of the planet's population to create the largest human online networks in history. By the end of this decade, many people would have more virtual friends on social networks than real friends in their daily lives. They would also spend more time communicating with virtual friends via social networks and smartphone texting than in actual face-to-face or even phone conversations. This was also a major decade for computer games with the emergence of more than 50 game companies.

One interesting new form of research was created in this decade. The advent of the Wikipedia encyclopedia demonstrated the value of *crowdsourcing*, or having thousands of minds address common topics. To my surprise and perhaps to the surprise of readers, Wikipedia has become the largest and most widely used encyclopedia in history.

Wikipedia has more than 25 million articles written by 39 million contributors. No other "book" in history has had so many coauthors. It is used by more than 80 million people each month in the United States alone.

Two major economic crises disturbed the growth of technology companies in this decade. The first was the bursting of the dot-com bubble in 2000, which sent many startup companies into bankruptcy and essentially stopped the flow of software venture capital for a few years.

The second was the Great Recession of 2008, which saw the bursting of the housing bubble and the need for government bailouts of numerous banks. This was a major setback for many companies, and software personnel were laid off in a number of industries, which is unusual because software personnel had been growing steadily for four decades.

In spite of the dot-com bubble bursting and the Great Recession, software startups continued at a surprisingly fast pace through both crises. But instead of wildly speculative internet companies, many of these startups had serious business plans and were aiming at unexploited niche markets. Two examples are Zillow, which provides national real estate data, and PerfectMatch, which used computer models to create a web-based dating service.

By about 2005, maintenance and enhancement of legacy applications would pull ahead of new development as the main activity of software engineers.

The Dot-Com Bubble

In the 1990s, the expansion of the internet and the World Wide Web created what was called "the new economy" when companies used the vast reach of the web to try and sell products and services to millions of people rather than selling locally in brick-and-mortar stores. Some of these dot-coms were Amazon, eBay, and Priceline, all of which had interesting and effective business plans.

However, the excitement of the web led to many startups whose business plans were not well thought out. There are many products that are suitable for remote web marketing, but others are best served by local stores.

The venture capital community is not really very sophisticated in risk and market planning, and it invested unwisely in companies that proper due diligence would have led them to avoid. The inevitable result of the rush to the web was an artificial bubble of dot-com startups, many with inflated market values. This bubble started to expand during the 1990s, but it could not continue forever.

Speculative bubbles are common economic phenomena and have occurred many times over hundreds of years. Indeed, a second speculative bubble, housing, would crash later in 2008.

The dot-com bubble reached its peak on March 10, 2000, when the NASDAQ technology stocks peaked at 5,132.52. This was about double the stock value from a year before. Many of the technology companies whose stock prices were soaring were losing money, and a few had no revenues at all. The speculative bubble was about to burst.

The Super Bowl in January 2000 featured 17 advertisements by dot-coms, each of which had paid at least $2 million. This was a unique phenomenon to have so many young companies with enough cash on hand to commission Super Bowl ads.

On April 4, 2000, a decision in the Microsoft antitrust litigation was announced, and Microsoft was found to be a monopoly. NASDAQ dropped to a low of 3,649 but rebounded to over 4,000 at the end of the trading day.

Barron's Magazine had run an alarming article that stated that of the 371 dot-coms trading on NASDAQ, many had never made a profit and would probably fail when they burned through their venture funds. From that point on, the bubble shrank rapidly through 2000 and 2001 and into 2002. Dozens of dot-coms disappeared, and many others saw their stocks drop precipitously.

The dot-com bubble had collateral damages as well. Many network and telecommunication companies had expanded their own networks to support the anticipated growth due to dot-coms. For example, WorldCom became overextended and declared bankruptcy. Many cities and states tried to attract high-technology companies with tax breaks, business parks, and technology centers and were left with empty offices and unused auditoriums. In total, the dot-com bubble burst lowered technology stock values by about $5 trillion compared to their peak value.

Two more recent examples of collateral damages show that effects are still occurring even today. The first was in 2009 when the city of Port St. Lucie, Florida, offered substantial incentives so that the graphics art company Digital Domain would move a development lab to the area. A massive 115,000-square-foot office and studio complex was constructed on the western side of Port St. Lucie and was occupied by about 300 software and graphics personnel early in 2012.

However, in spite of an IPO in 2011, Digital Domain soon declared bankruptcy in September 2012 and closed its Port St. Lucie facility, with a loss of hundreds of jobs. The city of Port St. Lucie is now trying to sell or rent the huge office complex, currently without results. The only space in it being used today is an auditorium for church services.

Digital Domain was not a novice startup with unproven talent. The parent company had won seven Oscars for special effects in films, including *Titanic* and *What Dreams May Come*. It employed some of the top computer and software graphics artists in the world.

After the bankruptcy, quite a lot of the intellectual property of Digital Domain was acquired, but that did no good for the huge vacant offices in Port St. Lucie, which are now being maintained at municipal expense and may push the town toward its own bankruptcy.

The second recent collateral damage example was Studio 38, which was given a $75 million loan by the Economic Development Commission of Rhode Island in 2005. This was an animated game company started by former Boston

Red Sox pitcher Curt Schilling. In return for the loan, the company moved to Providence and began operations with about 250 employees.

As is common with software applications in the $75 million startup range, the main product of Studio 38 ran behind schedule. As is also common with startups, the company itself ran low on funds and fell behind in its payments to the state.

In the absence of fresh capital from film credits, external investors, the state, or other sources, the company missed payrolls, ran out of funds, laid off the entire staff, and then declared bankruptcy.

The bottom line is that urban and state governments are not necessarily qualified to judge whether a given company will actually add jobs, as they all promise, or will merely occupy space until financial problems overcome them. The software and high-tech industries are attractive to novice investors because it is true that a number of these companies have become enormously successful and wealthy. But it is also true that a much larger number of these companies have failed and gone bankrupt.

The software engineering personnel who had been working for these companies found themselves out of work and facing a declining job market for the first time in software history. Even admissions to software engineering curricula in colleges and universities declined when it became obvious that software jobs would not expand rapidly forever.

The Great Recession

Although the dot-com bubble was a serious crisis for software and technology companies, it was not the only bubble to burst during this decade. Starting at the end of 2007 and running through 2010, the country and much of the world encountered what has come to be known as the *Great Recession*, which is an echo of the Great Depression, which started in 1929.

The recession rippled through the entire economy and affected thousands of companies and millions of individuals. However, the burst of the housing bubble and the severe reductions in real estate costs had the greatest human impact on ordinary consumers.

Real estate bubbles have occurred so many times over history that they have even been statistically analyzed, but the big bubble burst circa 2008 was particularly severe. It was caused in part by speculative building of homes for "flipping" or purchases by investors rather than by homeowners who wanted to live in the homes. In some communities in Florida and Nevada, there were actually more houses on the market than there were people to live in them.

Overall, the Great Recession was caused by a very complex set of interlocking events and mistakes. In approximate chronological sequence, they run as follows:

1995

- Opening too many subprime mortgages to home buyers with low incomes. This was due to the urging of the U.S. government to increase home ownership among low-income citizens.

- Basing subprime mortgages on variable interest rates. Thus, when interest rates went up, thousands of subprime mortgages became unaffordable.

- Reducing oversight of financial institutions due to the mistaken belief that financial markets would be self-regulating. This lack of oversight resulted in a host of new and complicated financial transactions with increasing risks.

2000

- Dividing and repackaging mortgages into complex financial bundles and selling the pieces. These bundles were classified as low risk, which was a serious mistake due to lack of oversight and inadequate audits. Repackaging and reselling mortgage segments in bundles makes renegotiation of mortgages very complicated because there is no longer a one-to-one relationship between homeowners and banks or mortgage companies.

- Overbuilding homes and condominiums due to escalating real estate costs. Many homes were built for "flipping" rather than occupancy, so the United States soon reached a surplus of about 500,000 more homes than there were people to live in them. This surplus was not troublesome when prices were going up, but when the bubble burst, the surplus caused prices to drop more quickly than might otherwise have happened.

2008

- Allowing Lehman Brothers to fail in September 2008, which triggered an abrupt and startling global financial crisis.

- Providing Troubled Asset Relief Program (TARP) funds to banks and financial institutions without oversight. Although the TARP was intended to restore financial flexibility for consumers and homeowners, the lack of oversight resulted in decreases in lending by TARP recipients but no decreases in bonuses and compensation for officers.

2009

- Providing stimulus money to states without adequate oversight. As a result, a significant amount of stimulus money was used to pay the pensions of retired workers and the salaries of current workers rather than being used to create new jobs and remove unemployed citizens from welfare.

- Failing to provide really effective stimulus aid for thousands of homeowners who were facing foreclosures but who did not qualify for any of the new programs.

The results of these mistakes soon led to numerous business and personal bankruptcies, thousands of foreclosures, and thousands of layoffs. It also led to huge losses in the stock market. There is more that can be said about the Great Recession, but its impact on software companies was a reduction in sales volumes and an increase in layoffs of personnel. In order to save money, there was also an increase in offshore outsourcing to countries with low labor costs such as India, China, the Philippines, and Ukraine.

The interlocked factors of the Great Recession are what physicists call a *linked oscillating system*. That is, so many things are interrelated that changes in any one of them ripple through all of the others. Here are some examples:

- Every layoff of a worker who is also a homeowner raises the possibility of one more foreclosure.

- Every foreclosure puts one more home on the market and increases the surplus of vacant homes that already totaled more than 10% of all U.S. houses at the peak of the recession in 2010.

- Every foreclosure lowers the property values of surrounding homes and drives prices down. The more foreclosures there are in a town or neighborhood, the greater the loss of value for the entire community.

- Many foreclosures of rental properties have the unintended consequence of putting renters on out the street, even though they had been paying their rents on time.

- Every foreclosure costs banks more money than they gain by seizing the property. As a result, foreclosures also raise the risk of bank failures. Renegotiation of loans would be more profitable for banks than foreclosures, but the mortgages are scattered among various institutions so that simple renegotiations are no longer possible. Banks seem not to have grasped the essential math that renegotiation would have been more cost-effective than foreclosures.

- The combination of job losses and foreclosures cut consumer spending by more than 25% compared to the peak of 2007, which caused serious damage to retail stores, automobile dealers, restaurants, and other businesses.

- The cutback in retail sales also caused cutbacks in manufacturing, in international sales, and in shipping and transportation. These cutbacks reduced the profits of shipping companies, railroads, airlines, and trucking companies.

- The combination of job losses, foreclosures, and business shrinkage lowered the stock market by unprecedented amounts, although a partial recovery took place during the spring of 2009. Full recovery was not seen until early in 2013.

- The reductions in retail sales, manufacturing, and transportation coupled with job losses have seriously reduced tax revenues at town, state, and national levels. Almost every state and a majority of towns had serious budget deficits in 2009. Some of these continued into 2013 due in part to excessive largess in pensions and health care for retired government workers.

- Due to high unemployment rates and numerous foreclosures, state and municipal tax revenues continued to decline from about 2008 through 2011, but there were some increases in 2012.

- Attempts to increase tax revenues via "tax-the-rich" methods backfired and caused reductions in tax revenues. The very wealthy are highly mobile, own properties in several states, and have attorneys and tax accountants far more sophisticated than state officials. There have been no successful revenue increases in any state that has attempted tax-the-rich programs. In spite of the failure of this method, many states and the federal government continue to try and push through these programs without understanding that revenues will decline rather than increase.

- Attempts to tax internet sales by individual states (such as Rhode Island) backfired and reduced tax revenues. This is because major internet vendors such as Amazon and Overstock cut ties to Rhode Island companies, as will most of the other major players. The result is damage to Rhode Island companies without any corresponding increases in tax dollars.

What is technically interesting about the dot-com bubble, the Great Recession, and the housing bubble is that these issues could have been predicted and modeled using a combination of historical data and predictive analytics. It does not require really sophisticated math to predict that if more houses are built than there are people to live in them, prices must come down. It is also easy to predict that when home prices fall below average mortgages, there will be many foreclosures because homeowners can no longer sell their houses for a profit. Municipal and state governments and the federal government need better skills in operations research and in economic modeling than they have today.

A combination of predictive analytics and intelligent agents that bring back relevant data from web sources allows the construction of powerful economic planning tools that can chart risks for municipal governments, state governments, the federal government, and corporations in many key industries.

Innovations of the 2000s

Leaving behind the two burst bubbles, we now return to other interesting software issues that occurred between 2000 and 2009.

In 2000, IBM began to market a new storage method called *flash drives* or, more popularly, *thumb drives*. These are small solid-state devices with persistent memories that can hold information indefinitely without needing electric power. These devices normally plug into a USB port.

The invention of thumb drives occurred in the prior decade, but their commercial entry was in December 2000. Several companies and inventors have rival claims to being the true inventor, and a number of lawsuits have been filed, some of which are still unresolved. IBM; an Israeli company, M-Systems; Trek; and Netac all have filed various patents and patent disputes. The bottom line is that thumb drives are now the most popular method of storing information on computers since they are easier to use than disks and much smaller.

January of 2001 witnessed the introduction of a new form of research tool and a new method of creating such tools. This month marked the date that Wikipedia first went online. Earlier research by Rick Gates and Richard Stallman contributed, but Wikipedia itself was started by Jimmy Wales and Larry Sanger, using concepts originated by Ward Cunningham.

More or less to the surprise of everyone, Wikipedia has grown to become the largest and most widely used encyclopedia in the world. The method of having the entries created by thousands of unpaid volunteers turned out to be extremely effective and has since grown into a method for dealing with other kinds of problems and issues.

The first years of this decade witnessed the final results of an antitrust lawsuit against Microsoft by the Department of Justice, which is fascinating in its own right. The gist of the final decision was that Microsoft would no longer give away Internet Explorer with Windows.

Microsoft also agreed to provide competitors with application program interface (API) data and to stop interfering with attempts to connect third-party browsers and software to Windows. This was a major decision for Microsoft competitors and for dozens of commercial software vendors who needed their packages to operate under Windows in order to market them.

February of 2001 witnessed an important moment in software history. This was the meeting at the Snowbird Lodge in Utah, which led to the publication of the famous Agile Manifesto. The 17 participants included Kent Beck, Mike Beedle, Arie van Benekum, Alastir Cockburn, Ward Cunningham, Martin Fowler, James Grenning, Jim Highsmith, Andrew Hunt, Ron Jeffries, Jon Kern, Bran Marick, Robert C. Martin, Steve Mellor, Ken Schwaber, Jeff Sutherland, and Dave Thomas.

This decade saw the creation of the Information Technology Metrics and Productivity Institute (ITMPI) by Computer Aid, Inc. The ITMPI began a series of seminars and webinars to expand knowledge of software engineering principles. Eventually, the ITMPI had a stable of perhaps 50 top-tier software experts and public speakers whose topics were recorded for later use.

The year 2004 witnessed the arrival of Facebook by Mark Zuckerberg to the web, although earlier versions were experimented with. Facebook started the social network explosion, which is still occurring today, although not every new social network succeeds. The 2010 film *The Social Network* is an interesting account of the creation of Facebook, as well as a warning about litigation.

The year 2006 saw the arrival of Jack Dorsey's creation Twitter on the web, and the site had expanded to 500 million users by 2012.

In 2008, the Brazilian government issued a new regulation that affected all government contracts. Contractors were required to stop using "effort hours" and switch to formal metrics. This was the IN04 directive. Although the directive did not mandate function points, the overall impact of the regulation was such that the International Function Point Users Group (IFPUG) function points became the normal metric for both government and commercial contracts in Brazil. A number of IFPUG executives have been from Brazil, including a past president.

The governments of Italy and South Korea also use function points for government contracts, and they may pass regulations similar to those used in Brazil. Function point metrics are definitely the most reliable metrics for software contracts and business purposes.

Function point metrics have comparative data available from more than 50,000 software projects. The nonprofit International Software Benchmark Standards Group (ISBSG) by itself has more than 6,000 projects measured with function point metrics.

By comparison, the sum total of other metrics such as story points, use case points, RICE objects, lines of code, and so forth is only about 1,000 projects.

This decade saw the expansion of Agile methods such as Scrum and Extreme Programming (XP). It also saw the expansion of Watts Humphrey's Team Software Process (TSP) and Personal Software Process (PSP). Many more new programming languages popped up.

The end of the decade witnessed the resurgence of Apple in the market due to the success of its famous iPhones and iPads. Indeed, Apple became the company with the highest market value in the United States, which capped a remarkable turnaround.

Apple seems to have fostered a culture of innovation, and this has brought forth a string of new kinds of products that sometimes change the direction of the entire high-technology business sector.

By the end of the decade, identify theft, hacking, and denial of service problems were major international concerns. Indeed, "cyberwarfare" was becoming a global concern, as many attacks are traced to foreign governments.

The phrase "cyberwarfare" started to be widely used by the middle of the decade. Indeed, apparent cyberattacks involving national governments are becoming increasingly common, as demonstrated by the attacks on Iran and by the discovery of hacking attacks on U.S. electric power facilities in 2009.

Earlier in 2007, the McAfee Company reported evidence of 120 countries gearing up for cyberwarfare, with financial systems and electric power systems being the targets of choice.

Static analysis tools were added to the quality arsenal in the 2000s, with good results, although the basic technology of static analysis dates to the 1980s. However, both open-source and commercial static analysis tools expanded in numbers and sophistication.

It was during this decade that a major shift occurred: More than 50% of the U.S. programming population worked on maintenance and enhancement of legacy applications rather than new development. New languages included C# and Visual Basic Net, and Microsoft's suite of languages evolved and added features.

Toward the end of this decade, cloud and software as a service (SaaS) applications began to expand in numbers. In addition, smartphone and tablet applications entered the arena and are now on an explosive growth path. As of 2010, the world total of programming languages topped 2,500.

The topic of "big data" (or heterogeneous collections of large volumes of information) would start to attract interest during this decade, as would the field of predictive analytics. In fact, big data and predictive analytics form a synergistic combination.

Companies Formed During the 2000s

In spite of the economic damages caused by the two burst bubbles of this decade, many new companies were founded, including Facebook and Twitter, which both grew rapidly to have millions of customers and earn billions of dollars. Table 9.1 shows a representative sample of companies started from 2000 to 2009.

Table 9.1 *Companies Formed from 2000 to 2009*

Company	Year
AbsolutData Research	2001
Aconics	2000
Advice Interactive Group	2008
Agito	2003
Andreesen Horowitz	2009
App Dynamics	2008
Archon Information Systems	2008
BAE Systems	2005
Barracuda	2003
BMI Gaming	2009
The Book Depository	2004

(Continued)

Table 9.1   *(Continued)*

Company	Year
Booker Software	2007
Canonical Ltd.	2004
Charge Smart	2008
Cloud Fire	2009
Cofio Software	2006
CoSoSys	2004
Cybertrust	2004
Data Market	2008
DigiCert	2003
Digital Risk	2005
DreamWorks	2000
EHarmony	2000
Etheric Networks	2000
Facebook	2004
Fidelity National Information Services	2006
Freelanthropy	2004
GIANT Company Software	2000
Global Insight	2001
Guidewire	2001
The HIVE Group	2000
Huawei Symantec	2008
IKnowWare	2002
Image Metrics	2000
Intellectual Ventures	2000
The Internet Marketing Association (IMA)	2000
Internet Security Alliance	2001
IT-Block	2001
JIVE Software	2001
Kobo, Inc.	2009
L-1 Identity Solutions	2006
Lite Speed Technologies	2002
Matrix Knowledge	2005

Table 9.1 *(Continued)*

Company	Year
MAXUM Games	2001
Meeting Zone	2002
METALOGIC Software	2001
Microsoft Studios	2002
MicroTask	2009
Mind Genius	2008
Moody's Analytics	2007
Moody's Corporation	2000
Mozilla Corporation	2005
My Medical Reports	2008
Natural Insight	2004
Neato Robotics	2009
Open Source Development Labs (OSDL)	2000
Opera Solutions	2004
Oversight Solutions	2003
PerfectMatch	2003
PIER Systems	2000
Point Judith Capital	2001
Rightware	2009
RPX Corporation	2008
ScanSafe	2004
Semantic Web Company	2004
Sirius XM Radio	2008
Skyfire	2007
Skyhook Wireless	2003
SocialFlow	2009
SolveIT Software	2005
SpaceX	2002
SpamCube	2003
Sumtotal Systems	2004
Survey Gizmo	2006

(Continued)

Table 9.1   *(Continued)*

Company	Year
TASC, Inc.	2009
Team and Concepts	2003
Tesla	2003
TrustPort	2008
Twitter	2006
Umbra Software	2007
Verizon Wireless	2000
Vizio	2002
Wiki Spaces	2005
Wikipedia	2001
Working Point	2007
Xbox Live Productions	2008
YouTube	2005
Zillow	2005

In collecting the information for Table 9.1, at least 50 computer-game companies were noted to have started during the decade, but most are not shown in the table. Gaming is an important but specialized industry. The computer-game companies have a tendency to be ephemeral and either merge with others or change their names. Only a few game companies are discussed in this book. (I have never been commissioned to study either productivity or quality within game companies or within the game divisions of larger companies such as Microsoft.)

Some of the companies with interesting or unusual business models that were created in this decade are discussed here.

AbsolutData Research

AbsolutData Research is an interesting company that focuses on using the power of predictive analytics to help major companies with decision making. This company was founded in India, but it has global clients, including many U.S.-based Fortune 500 companies.

The company was started in New Delhi, India, in 2001 by Anil Kaul, Suhale Kapoor, and Sudeshna Datta. Since its foundation, AbsolutData Research has doubled its revenues every year; it opened a new head office in Alameda, California, near San Francisco, as well as offices in New York and Los Angeles. The main research laboratory is located in Gurgaon, India.

In 2012, Fidelity Growth Partners in India committed $20 million to help the company expand into big-data analytics. AbsolutData Research has been ranked high on various lists of analytics companies and also on lists of fast-growing businesses such as Asian-American companies by Deloitte. The company employs about 150 analysts.

Two of the newer "hot topics" to emerge in the 2000s are *big data* and *predictive analytics*. In fact, the two are strongly related because without predictive analytics, big data by itself has little value.

Andreesen Horowitz

The entrepreneur Marc Andreesen and the venture capitalist Ben Horowitz were well known in Silicon Valley as private investors who liked interesting technology startups. Andreesen himself is a software engineer who developed some of the Mosaic browser features, and he cofounded Netscape. Horowitz was also a technologist and CEO of Opsware, which was sold to Hewlett-Packard.

On July 6, 2009, the two joined forces to create the Andreeson Horowitz investment venture capital company in Menlo Park, California. What sets them apart perhaps from other investors is that both are experts in software and technology products and hence have an edge in understanding the kinds of new products and companies that are likely to succeed.

At a time when venture capital was shrinking, Andreesen Horowitz was able to attract more than $1.2 billion for technology investments. Among the well-known companies they invested in are many of the top social network organizations, including Skype, Twitter, Facebook, and Groupon.

Because of the technical sophistication of the founders, Andreesen Horowitz is not afraid to tackle early-stage investments for true startups that are just getting started. They have invested in 66 startups and a total of about 156 companies. This is one of the advantages of having proven software entrepreneurs as venture capitalists.

Andreesen Horowitz is an interesting niche company that helps the software industry by funding startups as well as larger investments in midstage companies that want to grow faster. Without companies such as this, the software industry would be smaller and less eclectic.

Archon Information Systems

Archon Information Systems is an interesting niche company, and the niche it occupies is municipal tax collection. Archon was founded in New Orleans, Louisiana, in January 2008 by Brian P. Barrios, Beau L. Button, and William D. Sossamon. All three had worked in law firms in New Orleans that were involved in tax matters.

The Archon business is driven by software, and its packages are widely used by municipal governments. Its brand is *CivicSource*, which currently includes CivicSource Administrator for property taxes and CivicSource Auctioneer for supporting municipal auctions of foreclosed properties, which has had a distressing increase in frequency due to the Great Recession and the bursting of the real estate bubble. A third component is CivicSource Services, which supports routine matters of municipal tax offices.

This company illustrates the fact that software is moving into every aspect of corporate and government activities. As software expands in use, more and more niches such as property taxation are opening up for software entrepreneurs. This decade is filled with new niche companies and new niches.

Canonical, Ltd.

Canonical is yet another niche company, and its particular niche involves the Ubuntu operating system and open-source applications centering on the Ubuntu version of Linux.

Canonical was founded in 2004 in London, England, by Mark Shuttleworth, who was born and educated in South Africa. He had founded and sold a domain-name registration company, which provided about $75 million in funds for other business opportunities. Shuttleworth became famous by becoming a private astronaut who took an eight-day trip on a Soyuz spaceship to the international spacestation for a cost of about $20 million. He invested about $10 million into the creation of Canonical.

At first, Canonical operated as a virtual company, with the staff working from their own homes. However, in 2005, offices were acquired in London and later in Montreal, Canada. Today, there are Canonical offices in about 30 countries, including locations in Boston, Lexington, London, Taipei, Shanghai, Saõ Paulo, and the Isle of Man. Its total employment is about 500.

Note

The Ubuntu operating system is a popular variant of the Linux operating system. The name "Ubuntu" is apparently based on a word in an African dialect that means something like "kindness and compassion to all others."

The open-source business model is to distribute various software packages for free but to charge for support, consulting, and other various related services. Sometimes this strategy is profitable, as demonstrated by Red Hat Software (discussed in the previous chapter). In the case of Canonical, revenues seem to be moving toward $30 million, which is the approximate break-even point for Canonical.

Although Ubuntu is the flagship product, Canonical has many other packages and also many services. Among the packages are Bazaar for revision control; Malone (named after Bugsy Malone) for bug tracking; Rosetta for natural language translation and localization of software packages; and Blueprints, a planning tool.

Open-source software has become an interesting and unique aspect of the larger software industry. It is hard to think of any other industry where products are given away for free and revenues derive entirely from support and ancillary services.

Facebook

Before discussing Facebook the company, readers are urged to watch the interesting movie *The Social Network*, which describes in some detail both the excitement of software startups and some of the hazards, including being sued. The film is broadly based on the creation of Facebook with, of course, some artistic license. It shows the intellectual excitement in Cambridge, Massachusetts, when software was a high-growth industry. (I also founded a company in Cambridge, although 10 years prior to Facebook.)

Facebook was founded in February 2004 by Mark Zuckerberg and his Harvard roommates Eduardo Savarin, Andrew McCollum, Dustin Moskowitz, and Chris Hughes. The company was actually incorporated in Florida. The idea of Facebook was that it would be a social website where fellow Harvard students could share ideas, photographs, and topics of local interest.

Zuckerberg had started an earlier website in 2003 called FaceSmash. This was a somewhat tactless website where people could compare photographs of two people and vote for "hot" or "not hot." Some of the photographs were acquired by hacking, and later Zuckerberg would face university charges for violating security and copyright infringement. Eventually, these charges were dismissed. Had they not been dismissed, he might have been expelled from Harvard.

Zuckerberg also tried a more socially correct form of website. For a class, he uploaded about 500 images and pictures of ancient Rome and let people share comments about them. This received a high grade from the professor, and some of its features were later used in Facebook.

In 2004, Zuckerberg began work on a project called "thefacebook," which would later morph into Facebook. This had the nucleus of later features such as posting pictures and allowing commentaries. Somewhat surprisingly, about 1,200 people registered on the site on its first day. Within a short time, about half of the students of Harvard were using "thefacebook."

However, future legal problems began to surface. Three senior Harvard students, Cameron and Tyler Winklevoss and Divya Narenda, asserted that Zuckerberg had agreed to help them create a similar project to be called Harvard Connection.

At first, Facebook was local to Harvard but soon expanded throughout the Ivy League and then to many other colleges in the United States and other countries. In 2004, operations were moved to Palo Alto, California, and the name was changed to Facebook after that domain name was purchased for $200,000.

Note

Incidentally, buying and selling domain names has become a minor subindustry of the web, and it is not always an ethical industry. Many potential domain names, especially those with the names of famous people, are registered purely to be sold for a profit. Sometimes domain names sell for many thousands of dollars.

Facebook kept expanding, adding high schools and international universities. Then, memberships were offered to several high-tech companies, including Microsoft and Apple. In September 2006, Facebook was opened to anyone over the age of 13 with a valid email address.

In recent years, Facebook has added corporations as well as living people. In fact, a Facebook page is something of a status symbol for companies, along with being "followed" on Twitter.

It is of sociological interest that some of the Facebook features such as "friending" and "unfriending" have been widely discussed and are seemingly important to many users. There is some anxiety that "unfriending" a difficult person may have personal repercussions.

It is also interesting that Facebook created an unusual way of hiring software engineers. Using Facebook itself, a set of quizzes and questions was distributed, and those who did well in solving them were recruited by Facebook.

The site's popularity continued to grow, and Facebook is now the largest photo repository on the web, with more than 100 million images and 350 million users.

Facebook planned for an IPO in 2012. Legal problems occurred shortly before the planned IPO when Facebook was sued by Yahoo over patent infringement. The suit was filed on March 12, 2012.

As Facebook grew, it needed additional funding, and it received both angel investment funding and several rounds of venture capital funding. Several companies also approached Facebook about partnerships or even acquisition, including Google, Microsoft, and Yahoo. However, Zuckerberg was cool to acquisition. The reason additional funding was needed is because Facebook was operating at a loss.

In 2008, Facebook hired Sheryl Sandberg as Chief Operating Officer, and the company began to plan ways of expanding revenues. Advertisements were chosen as the optimal solution to higher revenues. This seemed to be effective, and in 2009, Facebook's revenues became positive instead of negative. Later in 2012, Facebook had about $3.7 billion in advertising revenues and a profit of about $1 billion.

Facebook filed for an IPO on February 1, 2012. The price was set at $38 per share. The IPO itself was May 18, 2012. At first, the IPO seemed successful because it raised $16 billion and was the third-largest IPO in U.S. history. However, at the closing bell, the stock was only selling for $38.23. By May 25, 2012, the stock had declined about 16.5% down to $31.91 to the dismay of early investors.

The IPO was soon followed by complaints and investigations about whether the underwriting banks had improperly shared information with only a select few clients. The State of Massachusetts also subpoenaed Morgan Stanley over the same issue. Several lawsuits, including class-action lawsuits, were filed. Since these events are quite recent, the way they will turn out is not yet known.

Facebook is an interesting business case for how the web has expanded human communications and shared the interests of millions of people in every portion of the globe. Facebook also served as a model for a number of other social networks. Indeed, the social network space is becoming very crowded, and probably not all of the new social networks will last for very long.

Getting venture funding is often difficult for true startups forging unique or novel businesses. But once the initial startup company has proven to be successful, venture money flows into the next dozen or so startups in the same sector.

The appeal of social networks will probably lead to interesting theses and dissertations by psychology students. It is not immediately apparent why people enjoy them so much that they can spend hours each day involved with social networks as opposed to interacting with living people.

Freelanthropy

Freelanthropy is also a niche company, and the niche appears to be one with some value to charitable organizations and nonprofit companies. This company was founded in 2004 in La Canada Flintridge, California, by Dan Sheehy. There were some corporate changes, and the company was formally organized as Freelanthropy LLC in 2006.

The business model is unusual and interesting. With Yahoo and other browsers, Freelanthropy builds custom toolbars that are stated to improve client interactions and generate revenues. There is also a search portal using Yahoo Search and Ask. About 1.3 million nonprofits are supported.

The toolbars provide a "shop and give" option in which some funds go for product or service purchases and some go to a charity or nonprofit. These funds are divided 50/50 between the charity itself and Freelanthropy.

The Freelanthropy tools use the *pay-per-click* model, which is yet another unique form of doing business that has only come into existence based on the World Wide Web. When a potential customer clicks on a specific ad in order to move to its website, the advertiser pays a small fee to the hosting website. Unpopular ads have little or no costs. The most popular ads pay the most, so the pay-per-click model is proportional to the popularity of the sites. The model can have either fixed or variable costs based on bids. The actual methods are outside the scope of this book.

Note

The first recorded pay-per-click business activities took place in 1996 for a website called Planet Oasis. At first, the method was viewed with suspicion, but fairly soon more than 400 companies were paying in the range of $0.005 to $0.25 per click. Soon, larger vendors such as Google and Microsoft were also offering pay-per-click services.

A number of vendors of products and services have agreed to provide a small percentage of sales to various charities through Freelanthropy. The toolbar and search portal make it easy to direct customers to these vendors.

Freelanthropy's site is not without a few technical problems. One user complained that his browser was hijacked and kept returning to the site. But since that complaint seemed unique, it was probably some form of technical glitch and not an intended diversion.

Global Insight

Global Insight is also a niche player, but it is a major figure in a very important niche. Global Insight is the world's largest commercial economic-study organization, with a staff of more than 700 and a client base of more than 3,800 organizations. Global Insight uses computers and software as an integral part of both data acquisition and data distribution.

The founder and President was Dr. Joseph Kasputys in Lexington, Massachusetts. Global Insight was formed in 2001 by a complex merger of a number of formerly independent companies: Wharton Econometric Forecasting Associates, Data Resources Inc., Primark Decision Services, and others. Global Insight is now a subsidiary of IHS, formerly Information Handling Services. Global Insight also acquired a number of companies.

The Hoovers Business Guide reports that Global Insight has data from more than 200 companies and 170 industries. The company has 25 offices in a dozen countries. One well-known client is Wal-Mart. Global Insight developed its new ad slogan of "Save Money, Live Better," which replaced the older ad "Always Low Prices."

This company provides consulting and data to probably a majority of U.S. Fortune 500 companies and many global companies as well. The parent company of IHS is also an interesting niche company in the information-gathering business. The entire field of information gathering and dissemination has been transformed by the internet, the World Wide Web, and the vast increase in converting books and paper text documents for online storage.

HIVE Group

The HIVE Group is another small niche company that specializes in the visualization of complex information using a patented method called *tree mapping*, developed by Ben Shneiderman of the University of Maryland.

The tree-mapping visualization method uses rectangles of various sizes and colors to show hierarchies and relationships among data elements. This is hard to explain in words, but a visit to the HIVE Group's website will reveal quite a few interesting examples.

The HIVE Group was founded in Richardson, Texas, in 2000. The chairman is H. William Jesse and the CEO is Jim Bartoo. Ben Shneiderman, the inventor of tree mapping, is a corporate advisor. He is also a professor at the University of Maryland.

Ben Shneiderman has a long history of invention in the areas of visualization of information. He is credited with inventing the method of highlighting text phrases that would allow users to jump from one website to another based on the specific text. This is now the most widely used method of navigation during scientific research. The word "hypertext" is used for these phrases with active web links.

Visualization of complex information is one of the more common uses of computers. The tree-mapping method is now widely used by government agencies and major corporations to improve the understanding of complex topics.

Although tree mapping is successful, the technology exists in the current era to move beyond static diagrams and into the realm of animated, full-color, and even three-dimensional representations of complex information.

The HIVE Group is an example of a company built around a single innovation, but one that has enough interest to keep the company growing and profitable.

Intellectual Ventures

Intellectual Ventures is very controversial and has an interesting business model that is based on patented intellectual property. Many of the patents are in the computer and software domains, but there are also patents from other technical disciplines such as biology, medicine, physics, and all forms of engineering.

The company was founded in Bellevue, Washington, in 2000 by former Microsoft executives Nathan Myhrvold and Edward Young, with a number of prominent later cofounders.

The main business of Intellectual Ventures is either filing patents based on their own internal research or acquiring patents from other inventors and companies. A visit to the website provides information on how to have a patent reviewed.

The company also has its own research facilities called Intellectual Ventures Labs. Quite a few famous scientists work at these internal labs, and the disciplines include medicine, biology, physics, software, nanotechnology, and others. Researchers also study global warming and have patented a potential (but possibly harmful) method of reversing global warming by creating an artificial shield over the earth that would partially block sunlight. (If this method failed, it might reverse global warming enough to create a new Ice Age.)

Intellectual Ventures is a private company that seems to be well funded with perhaps more than $5.5 billion from a variety of external sources. Some of the investors are major companies such as Microsoft; Intel; Sony; Nokia; Google; and a variety of other high-tech, medical, science, and bioengineering groups. Some venture funds are also invested.

It is one of the largest holders of patents in the United States. Intellectual Ventures owns more than 30,000 patents in total, including 2,000 filed by internal researchers. It is now filing close to 500 new patent applications per year.

The controversy that flows around Intellectual Ventures centers on a new term: "patent troll." That term refers to a company that acquires patents not to produce new products but rather to gain revenues by litigating other companies for patent infringements.

Note

Claims of patent trolling are legal issues outside the scope of this book. I am not an attorney and have no legal training, so the information discussed here comes from web and journal articles and other second-hand sources. Readers should discuss patents and other legal issues with qualified attorneys.

In 2010, Intellectual Ventures filed patent suits against a number of prominent companies. However, patent litigation today seems to be endemic for the software and computer industries and also for equipment manufacturers such as Apple, Samsung, Motorola, and the like. There are a lot of ongoing patent suits, and the impression is that many companies are using patents as business weapons to attack competitors.

Patent Litigation in Recent Years

It would be interesting to look at the statistics of patent litigation filed each year for the past 15 years. Apparently, the numbers of patent cases are accelerating. In 2011, President Obama signed the Leahy-Smith America Invents Act (AIA), which introduced major changes into U.S. patent law. The gist of the new legislation is that the patent filing date seems to take precedence over the actual invention date.

The full impact of the law has many legal issues and should be discussed with qualified patent attorneys. The impacts are beyond the scope of this book. A new method of calculating patent awards called the Nash Bargaining Solution (also outside the scope of this book) has also begun to appear. The bottom line is that 2012 was a record year for U.S. patent litigation, either due to the new law or to some extrinsic reasons that are hard to quantify.

Looking at trends since 1991, the number of patent lawsuits filed seems to follow more or less the trends of patents granted each year, and both are increasing. Patent sales are also increasing, especially in the telecommunications sectors as various phone companies jockey for position, sue one another, and buy up patent portfolios from older telecommunications companies. Buying and selling patents is not specifically related to software and computers, but both are part of larger patent trends that include more litigation and very active patent acquisition.

In any case, the business model developed by Intellectual Ventures of buying and creating patents seems to be bringing in a lot of money, so it can be viewed as successful. Business schools should develop new case studies of the impact of patent infringement cases on technical progress and also of the impacts of the recent changes in patent laws and award calculations.

Internet Marketing Association (IMA)

The IMA is not a corporation per se but rather a professional association. It is included in this book for several reasons. One is that it is large and important, with more than 750,000 members. The other is that it illustrates that when technologies such as the internet and the World Wide Web become pervasive and important, people need to consider ethics and professional behavior. The third is that the internet and the World Wide Web have risen to become key marketing tools in the modern era. In fact, one of the reasons why newspapers are losing money is because much of the corporate money used for marketing campaigns has switched from newspaper ads to web marketing.

The IMA was started in 2000 in San Clemente, California, by Sinan Kanatsiz. Some funding was acquired from various sponsors such as Google, Microsoft, Facebook, YouTube, and quite a few more. Surprisingly, there are no fees or dues for members, which may be one reason why membership is so large.

The IMA features training, certification of internet marketing personnel, and a number of conferences and/or trade shows. It also issues annual awards called Internet Impact Awards. It provides conferences for clients such as Apple and also on its own behalf. Some of these conferences are large, with hundreds of participants.

The IMA is one of many professional associations that have surfaced to support computers, software, the internet, and the World Wide Web. Others in this space include the IEEE Computer Society, the Association of Computing Machinery (ACM), the Association of Information Processing Professionals (AIPP), the Society for Information Management (SIM), the Association for Women in Computing, the Society for Technical Communication (STC), and hundreds more in many countries.

Some of these groups are international, some national, and many, such as the Software Process Improvement Network (SPIN), are regional or support personnel in specific cities. Some are based on a single manufacturer or vendor, such as the IBM SHARE group that represents a majority of IBM computer and software customers. The IMA is included here as one example of a large class of social and professional organizations that have sprung up since computers and software became global corporate and business tools.

Meeting Zone

Meeting Zone is another company with a new niche that is entirely based on computers, software, and the World Wide Web. This company provides support for online meetings and webinars. This is a popular niche with many other players, including Adobe, Cisco, JoinMe, DumDum, and quite a few others. In fact, Meeting Zone itself offers Cisco WebEx support as well as Presenter and Glance.

This private company was formed in 2002 in Thame, England, by Steve Gandy and Tim Duffy. It supports both audio conferences and web conferences. The idea behind Meeting Zone is to have painless conferences with no intrusive downloads.

Meeting Zone expanded into the Scandinavian conference markets by acquiring Malmo in Norway and by collaborating with United Communications Sweden AB.

The market for video conferencing has been robust, and Meeting Zone has grown rapidly, having made a list of Britain's 100 fastest-growing companies in the Microsoft Sunday Times Tech Track. In 2011, several companies, including GMT Communications Partners and company management, acquired Meeting Zone for around £38.5 million.

Moody's Analytics

Moody's Analytics was founded in 2007 as a subsidiary of Moody's Corporation. It is a niche company that uses software to analyze a variety of financial and investment risks.

Note

Another interesting Moody's subsidiary from 2002 is the Moody's Foundation, which is a philanthropic organization that donates funds to assist and elevate mathematical and statistical education. It also sponsors various mathematical contests for high school students to use math to solve real-life problems.

The original parent company was founded in 1909 by John Moody, who invented the method of modern bond ratings. Of course, this was long before computers and software, and the calculations were done by hand. But the statistical and analytical problems were exactly what computers and software would later use to speed up the calculations. A U.S. financial crisis in 1907 showed a need for better data, and that motivated Moody to create his rating system and the U.S. government to create the Federal Reserve System.

Moody's Analytics has developed proprietary software for financial modeling, risk analysis, and other business-related topics. It also has a consulting group in the same areas. The Moody's Analytics subsidiary is a kind of umbrella organization that was used to combine a number of formerly independent companies, including, but not limited to, KMV, which has a software package for predicting credit defaults; Economy.com (economic modeling); Wall Street Analytics; Fermat International, the Institute of Risk Standards and Qualifications; CSI Global Education; and others.

The latter company, CSI Global Education, handles training and education in stocks and bonds and other financial securities. It also certifies professionals who handle and market such securities. This is a Canadian company and its courses are required for all Canadian stock and investment professionals.

Several of the other Moody's Analytics umbrella companies also provide training in various countries, but always in the fields of stocks, bonds, and financial instruments.

In the modern world, credit ratings are critical factors for companies and individuals alike. The mathematics and statistics for calculating these ratings are outside the scope of this book, but they have serious impacts on individual and corporate abilities to borrow or receive external funding.

In 2010, Moody's Analytics formed a partnership with Experian to produce a software package for allowing financial institutions to manage portfolios of consumer loans. Although computers and software are the key tools for credit ratings and risk analyses, they are not perfect by any means. There have been frequent criticisms of their accuracy, and some government investigations have begun.

There was intense criticism of three rating companies—Moody's, Standard and Poors, and Fitch's—due to their favorable ratings of financial companies that later became insolvent, such as Lehman Brothers, and also for risky mortgage-related packages that were implicated in the burst housing bubble.

There is no "cesium atom" or truly objective mathematical method for determining the accuracy of a credit rating, which is why several independent rating agencies are used and their results are compared.

The credit-rating financial software packages have also been known to contain bugs and defects, as do all other kinds of software applications. The credit-rating companies are nominally guardians of corporate and individual financial health, but the ancient phrase "Who will guard the guardians themselves?" would seem to apply.

Mozilla Foundation

The Mozilla Foundation has a very complicated history with many players and companies involved. Because Mozilla is an open-source organization, that is not surprising: many people are always involved. (The name "Mozilla" is amalgamated from the phrase "Mosaic killer" because the original browser was meant to displace Mosaic.)

The Mozilla Foundation was started in Mountain View, California, in July 2003 but has a longer history than that. Mitchel Baker was the founder. Mitch Kapor of Lotus provided some of the funds. Other funding came from a number of sources, including America Online (AOL), IBM, Sun, and Red Hat Software.

Mozilla was an internal name used within Netscape. The Mozilla organization was charged with creating a Mozilla Application suite with both a browser and an email client. Later, the browser became Firefox and the email package became Thunderbird. As discussed elsewhere, Netscape itself was acquired by AOL. Netscape and Microsoft competed in the browser wars during the previous decade, with Netscape losing market shares.

Note

While the Mozilla Firefox logo appears to show the front half of a red fox, the actual animal selected for the logo was a red panda. In fact, red pandas do resemble red foxes slightly but are a totally different species and are unrelated.

When AOL's revenues began to decline, it reduced emphasis on Netscape's products, and the Mozilla project within Netscape was shut down. When AOL and Netscape cut back the Mozilla project, the Mozilla Foundation was formed by a nucleus of former Netscape personnel plus others. There is also a separate Mozilla Corporation that is not tax exempt. The Mozilla Corporation produces the Firefox browsers. As can be seen, this is a very convoluted path. As a for-profit enterprise, the Mozilla Corporation can generate revenues and sell products. One of its main clients is Google, whose search engine is the default search engine on Firefox.

There are several Mozilla products, but the Firefox web browser and the Thunderbird email client are the best known. There are also SeaMonkey and Camino, a browser for Macintosh platforms.

Browser Competition

The topic of most significance here is that Microsoft often dominates industry segments. In the browser segment, Microsoft's Internet Explorer is still on top, but the market has several other strong players. The sequence for personal computers is Internet Explorer, Google Chrome, Firefox, Opera and, finally, Apple Safari. Other platforms such as tablets and smartphones have different patterns.

(Continued)

(Continued)

The browser segment is more competitive than, for example, office suites, where Microsoft is the major player by a large margin. (It is interesting that Intuit was able to compete successfully against Microsoft in the personal finance segment; indeed, Microsoft withdrew from personal finance.)

It is technically and socially interesting that an open-source application such as Firefox produced by a fairly small organization such as Mozilla is able to stay competitive in a major software business segment against well-funded, larger competitors such as Microsoft and Google.

Open Source Development Labs (OSDL)

The open-source movement in software seems to be unique among major industries. There are very few other industries where key products are available for no cost and where revenues derive from services such as training and consulting and sometimes maintenance and customer support.

OSDL was founded in 2000 in Beaverton, Oregon, and Yokohama, Japan. It was a sort of consortium aimed at improving and maximizing the usage of the Linux operating system. The six companies that provided the original funds were Computer Associates, IBM, NEC, Intel, Fujitsu, and Hitachi. Linux was of interest both in Japan and in the United States (as well as Finland, where it originated). Although the developer of Linux, Linus Torvalds, was not a founder, he did join the labs soon afterward.

Today, membership has grown to perhaps seventy-five organizations, and Linux is a well-respected and popular platform for embedded applications, servers, and even notebook computers. It also has become the operating system of choice for low-cost computers for emerging countries and for providing low-cost computers to schoolchildren.

In 2007, the Open Source Development Labs and the Free Standards Group combined to create the Linux Foundation.

Linux Emerges

Linux was derived from Unix and was developed by the Finnish software engineer Linus Torvalds. Torvalds was a student at the time he developed Linux. This is not the only important software topic that originated with a student. Facebook was also developed by students.

Unix was developed at Bell Labs by Dennis Ritchie and Ken Thomson in 1969. The power and utility of Unix led Richard Stallman in 1983 to consider the benefits of a free Unix system. This led him to create the GNU project and the GNU General Public License, which is the major license for open-source software, but not the only one. (The unusual name of "GNU" means more or less "GNU's not Unix.")

An interesting feature of the GNU license is something called a "copyleft" as opposed to a "copyright." Essentially, this means that users can pass along the code and deliverables to others and also modify them but do not charge for the result.

In 1991, when Torvalds developed the Linux kernel, it was not a full operating system. It also had its own custom license. Later, when it was released under the GNU license, other features were added and the product became known as GNU/Linux.

The name "Linux" had been rejected by Torvalds as being egotistical. A colleague working with him unilaterally started calling the software "Linux" and this became well known, so Torvalds eventually agreed. The earlier name was FreaX, which is not very aesthetic.

As many readers know, the logo or symbol for Linux is a penguin. The reason for this is not certain, but Torvalds was once bitten by a penguin while visiting a zoo in Canberra, Australia.

Several people and organizations other than Torvalds attempted to trademark the word "Linux." This led to some litigation and eventually Torvalds was awarded the trademark, which he donated to the Linux Trademark Institute, which is a subsidiary of the Linux Foundation.

Because the stated mission of the OSDL is to be the central body for Linux expertise and to expand its usage, this short discussion of Linux is relevant.

Open-source software and Linux in particular have established an interesting and important niche in the larger software industry. The widespread availability of source code under the GNU license and the ability of thousands of people to make improvements have led to many useful technical advances.

There has been opposition to the open-source movement from established companies such as Microsoft, but the open-source community has been successful in creating new business and achieving large numbers of satisfied customers.

PerfectMatch

PerfectMatch is one of a number of new companies in a very special niche. It uses computers and software to provide matchmaking services for men and women seeking partners. This book covers both the technical and social aspects of software, and matchmaking is definitely a social issue. Other players in this subindustry include EHarmony, Christian Mingles, and dozens of others. Some are national, while others are local.

PerfectMatch was founded in August 2003 in Kirkland, Washington, by Duane Dahl, Cindy Henry-Dahl, and Jason McVey. The company uses a questionnaire designed by a psychologist, Dr. Pepper Schwartz, together with predictive analytics and a large database of men and women who have specified a number of preferences.

A visit to the PerfectMatch website shows that some of the preferences that are used include being a pet owner, being a vegan, being a Democrat or Republican, and a host of other topics. Matchmaking is an ancient occupation with thousands of years of history. Many civilizations, including ancient Rome, India, Japan, and China, have used human matchmakers for centuries and still do in the modern era.

However, computers and software have added several new levels to matchmaking. Among these is a much larger set of potential matches due to the World Wide Web. The questionnaires used by various computer dating companies also seem to be fairly sophisticated in sorting out personal interests and background topics that may be relevant. This subindustry and PerfectMatch and its competitors show that computers and software are now permeating every aspect of human life, including how we meet and find our spouses or partners.

RPX Corporation

The RPX Corporation is a company with a novel and highly specialized niche. It uses predictive analytics to calculate the risks of U.S. patents, which is a very new niche indeed. (Because I have filed several patents myself, this company is of personal interest.)

As most readers already know, the computer, software, telecommunications, and other high-tech industries have filed thousands of patents. These industries are also subject to frequent patent litigation as competitors jockey for position. A new subindustry of "patent trolls" has surfaced, and the technical name for patent trolls is *nonpracticing entities* (NPEs).

The RPX Corporation was founded in 2008 in San Francisco, California, by John Barker and Geoffrey Amster. Their business model includes *defensive patent aggregation*, or acquiring patents that might be subject to litigation and committing never to litigate themselves about the use of these patents. This business model is an interesting contrast to the patent model of Intellectual Ventures, discussed earlier in this chapter, which does initiate patent litigation.

RPX has a number of clients in high-technology and high-risk business sectors. RPX also has a team of technical patent specialists who keep constant watch for patents that might be used to sue RPX clients. Then, if possible, RPX acquires these patents and hence prevents them from being used in patent infringement cases. Sometimes RPX acquires patents even after litigation has been filed. (These are fairly complex legal topics and I am not an attorney, so readers should seek advice from licensed attorneys about patent situations.)

Clients of RPX receive licenses to use the RPX patent portfolio by paying annual fees, which are not inexpensive. They start below $100,000 per year but can be more than $6 million per year based on the client's business and technology stack.

RPX has acquired more than 2,900 patents relevant to software, computers, electronics, telecommunications, and also to e-commerce and even computer games. These patents have been used to settle more than 20 infringement cases and have led to the dropping of more than 150 patent infringement charges.

The U.S. patent system is increasingly being used as a competitive weapon and as a source of significant revenues from patent litigation. The RPX business model is interesting because it is attempting to restore patents to their primary purpose of developing innovative products rather than being used to stop competition or to force companies to buy their way out of patent litigation.

SolveIT Software

SolveIT was founded in 2005 in Adelaide, South Australia. The four cofounders were Matthew Michalewicz, Zbigniew Michalewicz, Martin Schmidt, and Constantin Chiriac. These four were also coauthors as well as cofounders. Their joint book was *Adaptive Business Intelligence*, which was published in 2006 by Springer and received favorable reviews on Amazon and other book sites. The book discusses applying artificial intelligence to business problems.

SolveIT uses custom-designed software to apply predictive analytics and artificial intelligence to demand forecasting, scheduling, distribution, and supply-chain optimization. Because the company was located in one of Australia's wine regions, its early customers were from the wine industry, which is large in Australia.

However, in 2008, it was approached by the Rio Tinto Iron Ore Company and was asked to develop optimized solutions for mining operations. Seemingly, SolveIT was successful, because many other mining companies became clients and SolveIT established a mining unit to support its growing portfolio of mining clients. In 2011, SolveIT won an Australian award for e-logistics and supply-chain management. In 2012, SolveIT was acquired by a French company, Schneider Electric.

Computers and software, combined with artificial intelligence and predictive analytics, can solve a number of complex business and manufacturing problems, some of which had been resistant to prior solutions. SolveIT is not the only company using predictive analytics, but it is an example that this field is growing and becoming important to larger companies and larger industries.

Twitter

Twitter is interesting because it turned a novel way of communication called *microblogging* into one of the largest social networks in history. Twitter has become so popular among so many people that it almost seems like an addiction. The basic concept is that users can issue short messages of up to 140 characters called "tweets." These are broadcast to "followers."

Twitter was founded in 2006 in San Francisco, California, by Jack Derby. Twitter is based on the concept of the *short message service* (SMS) that was introduced into the cell phone domain in 1985 as part of the Global System for Mobile Systems Communications (GSM) standards. The limit was 160 characters. The first GSM/SMS message was sent on December 3, 1992. Soon, other networks adopted the same idea. After slow growth, text messaging became a huge subindustry with trillions of messages and billions of dollars in revenue.

Jack Derby was in a working discussion about GSM at a company called Odeo while an undergraduate at New York University. He proposed using SMS codes for communication. This idea had a working name of "Twittr" derived from the existing name "Flickr," both of which used five-character codes. The term "Twittr" was later expanded to "Twitter," which had an older and common meaning of short bird calls. This also led to calling individual messages "tweets" and to using a songbird as the Twitter logo.

At first, Twitter was used for internal communications within Odeo. In October 2006, a group of employees bought out Odeo and formed another company called Obvious Corporation. Among the assets acquired from Odeo was Twitter.com. Among the founders were Biz Stone, Jack Derby, Evan Williams, and others.

Twitter began to gain popularity as the result of a display at a conference in 2007. Two large plasma displays showed Twitter messages from various conference speakers communicating with each other.

After that successful conference, the rapid growth of Twitter and the phenomenon of millions of followers waiting for short messages from famous people deserve to be studied both at business schools and at medical schools that train clinical psychologists.

From a distance, it is hard to see why millions of short messages have such a strong appeal that some people spend hours per day reading and writing them. Twitter may have accidentally tapped into a fundamental factor of the human brain that demonstrates that most people prefer to absorb short messages of only a few words rather than full paragraphs or pages of text.

From looking at messages posted on another social network, LinkedIn, there may be some merit to limiting messages to 140 characters. Many LinkedIn posts are long, dreary paragraphs of unsupported opinions with nothing very useful in them. They often run on for hundreds of words. The larger LinkedIn post limit of 4,000 characters definitely leads to an excess of lengthy messages.

Twitter remains a private company with Jack Dorsey as Chairman. Revenues are not reported but are apparently large enough for the company to have more than 400 employees and to be in continuous growth mode. Twitter received two rounds of venture financing. Venture money usually means that either an IPO or an acquisition will eventually occur because the venture capitalists want a large return in a fairly short time period.

The Twitter network itself has become phenomenally large and popular, with more than 140 million users and more than 340 million tweets per day. Twitter did not stay with short text messages but added the ability to link photographs, and it also provides a news feed. Companies can also set up Twitter accounts and use them to communicate with customers.

Note

Jack Dorsey has also founded another interesting company called Square. The Square company allows credit card purchases via smartphones that use a small square card reader that plugs into a cell phone port.

Twitter has become an unusual social domain where the famous communicate with fans in a fairly benign and friendly social environment. It is one of the few places where ordinary people can read messages from celebrities and world figures like President Obama, Tiger Woods, and Jennifer Lopez on a daily basis.

In fact, it is partly due to the use of Twitter by A-list celebrities that makes it so popular to such a wide audience. Twitter gives ordinary citizens a glimpse into the daily lives of many of the most famous people in the world.

The fact that thousands of politicians, movie stars, and sports figures use Twitter is proof that computers and software have entered our daily lives and changed our methods of communication in new and unexpected ways.

YouTube

YouTube is an interesting company whose business is entirely based on new technologies. One technology is the World Wide Web and a second technology is that of digital images for photographs and videos. Of course, computers and software are needed as well. This company could not have existed more than 20 years ago.

This company was founded in 2005 in San Mateo, California, by Chad Hurley, Steve Chen, and Jawed Karim. All three had been employed at PayPal. Like Apple, YouTube was also founded in a garage in Silicon Valley.

The company started with "angel" funding, but in November 2005, it received about $3.5 million in venture funding from Sequoia Capital.

YouTube hit on what may be a basic human need for people to share images and videos of things that are important to them. People have kept scrapbooks and photo albums since the Civil War, but the advent of digital imaging in the 1980s (discussed in Chapter 7) made photography an instant phenomenon instead of a task requiring chemicals and lengthy development in darkrooms.

For whatever reason, YouTube exploded in popularity and a little more than a year after it started operation, it was uploading thousands of videos and pictures per day. It was soon ranked as number 5 in website popularity.

The demographics of YouTube usage is an interesting social commentary on the use of the World Wide Web in the modern era. For many reasons, young people are early adapters of new technologies. The majority of YouTube users are teenagers. Older people have habits and practices of long standing and are somewhat less energetic in moving to new techniques.

YouTube epitomized the legend of the rapid "rags-to-riches" ascents of Silicon Valley entrepreneurs. YouTube was started in 2005 and only a year later in 2006, it was acquired by Google for $1.65 billion. There have been very few industries in history that can create so much wealth in such a short time as the software industry.

YouTube not only grew rapidly but also soon caught national attention. *Time Magazine* featured YouTube as its "Person of the Year" in 2006 which, of course, attracted thousands of new clients.

In 2007, YouTube entered the political domain when, with the Cable News Network (CNN), it provided live footage of some of the presidential debates, with questions coming in through YouTube. This continues; YouTube also was part of the 2012 presidential debates and will apparently keep active in the political domain.

Although YouTube started as a host for amateur videos and pictures, it added professional films and videos in 2010 and also started a video rental service in competition with Amazon, Hulu, and other streaming video companies. Incidentally, streaming video is another modern technology that could not have existed 20 years ago.

The popularity of YouTube and its millions of members are factors in YouTube's advertising revenues. Many companies advertise via YouTube (and Facebook and Twitter) in order to reach vast numbers of potential new customers.

One critical issue affects YouTube and all other web-based video services. Streaming videos and images use enormous quantities of bandwidth. As more and more companies enter the streaming video and remote-image subindustry, it is possible to perhaps saturate the web and slow down overall performance.

In any case, YouTube seems to have hit on a psychological need to share personal images and information in a structured and reasonably safe environment. However, no personal information put on the web is truly safe or private.

Zillow

Zillow's special niche is providing real estate property values. Here, too, the niche depends on several recent technologies, including the World Wide Web, large databases, satellite and aerial digital images, and proprietary software applications that use proprietary algorithms. The company could not have existed 20 years ago because some of the technologies were not available. Zillow is a public company whose stock is traded on NASDAQ.

Zillow was started in 2005 in Seattle, Washington, by Rich Barton and Lloyd Fink. Both founders had been Microsoft executives and were technical entrepreneurs. Zillow was not the first to enter the real estate evaluation market, because Yahoo had a service called Yahoo Real Estate that started in 1998.

Real Estate Appraisals and Software

An older company, Vision Appraisal from 1975, has many contracts with municipal governments in a number of states to perform periodic property assessments. (Vision Appraisal has a contract with my home city for appraisals. Several years ago, it was necessary for me to appeal and correct several errors in my property appraisal, including an error in square footage and another error in elevation.)

Appraisals are frequently controversial and sometimes wrong. This topic is beyond the scope of this book, but suffice it to say that property taxes are based on formal appraisals often by commercial appraisal companies such as Vision Appraisal. If the appraisals are wrong, the taxes will be wrong. Real estate valuation is highly complex and also highly litigious.

There is also an Appraisal Standards Board and a nonprofit Appraisal Foundation, which are quasi-official groups that set standards for property appraisals against

(Continued)

(Continued)

which appraisal companies can be compared, in theory. There are also professional associations of appraisers, such as the American Society of Appraisers and the American Appraisers Association. Even so, real estate appraisals impact every home-owner and therefore will always be controversial and subject to complaints by disgruntled property owners.

Many appraisal companies use proprietary and secret algorithms, some of which are not even revealed to municipal tax authorities. What is probably needed is an expert system that would be a national standard method used by all appraisal companies and validated by neutral disinterested personnel such as university professors or nonprofit research groups.

Zillow generates its revenues by advertising on its website. In 2009, Zillow formed an interesting consortium by licensing its appraisal data to about 180 local newspapers around the United States. In 2011, Zillow and Yahoo Real Estate entered into a partnership that became the largest real estate ad venue in the United States.

Zillow has data on about 100 million U.S. homes and Yahoo had data on about 5 million U.S. homes. The combination of the two probably includes a majority of all U.S. homes. The data include both current values and historical past values. There are also images on the Zillow site, including aerial and satellite images.

The company was criticized when it changed its appraisal method in 2011 when it changed both current and historical valuations. Zillow claimed increased accuracy, but many users were not convinced. Zillow says that accuracy improved from matching actual sale prices from about 12% to better than 9%. Why historical data changes is not clear.

The site now has a number of products and services, including searching for mortgages, applications that work on smartphones, and a tool called *Zestimate* that can predict real estate sales prices. Zillow also produces local reports for about 130 metropolitan areas. Zillow also introduced a kind of Wiki service by allowing users to ask questions online of a community of appraisers and other users.

Zillow demonstrates the fact that computers and software now permeate every aspect of corporate and government activities. Property appraisals for tax purposes have been in use for more than 1,000 years. Prior to the computer era with large databases and the World Wide Web, appraisals could only be based on a small sample of very local properties.

In today's world, essentially every piece of real estate in the United States has data available online, so national, regional, state, municipal, and even neighborhood real estate data can be examined.

In theory, appraisals should be more accurate today than in the past, but the use of software containing proprietary and secret algorithms raises serious doubts about accuracy. Also, software applications have a distressing tendency to contain bugs and errors and no doubt this is true for appraisal software as it is for other kinds of software.

This decade witnessed a large number of niche companies filling in the gaps around more conventional database and corporate applications. Some of the new niches include predictive analytics, real estate appraisals, and even personal relationships.

Social networks began to go beyond normal everyday human contacts in terms of frequency. By the end of the decade, some young people had many more friends on social networks than in real life. More time was being spent tweeting and texting than talking to people face to face. Texting was becoming so common that it began to be a frequent source of automobile accidents, leading to new laws against cell phone and texting use by drivers.

Growth of Software from 2000 to 2010

The 2000s was an explosive decade in software growth, both among traditional forms of software and also for computer games and dozens of new niche applications that sprang up like mushrooms after a rain.

Table 9.2 shows the approximate number of U.S. software applications created during this decade.

Table 9.2   *U.S. Software Applications from 2000 to 2009*

Application Types	Applications	Percentage
Scientific	192,000	6.40%
Military and defense	450,000	15.00%
Civilian government	400,000	13.33%
Systems and middleware	360,000	12.00%
Embedded software	700,000	23.33%
Commercial	175,000	5.83%
Information technology (IT)	325,000	10.83%
U.S. outsource	78,000	2.60%
Offshore outsource	53,000	1.77%

(Continued)

Table 9.2   *(Continued)*

Application Types	Applications	Percentage
Web applications	250,000	8.34%
Games and entertainment	15,000	0.50%
Open source	2,000	0.07%
Total Applications	**3,000,000**	**100.00%**

Results for 1,000 Function Points Circa 2005

At the end of this decade, a new metric called *technical debt* was introduced by Ward Cunningham. Unfortunately, technical debt, cost per defect, and lines of code are not suitable for economic analyses due to uncertain definitions that have large variability from group to group.

Technical debt only covers about 13% of the true costs of quality, and it ignores canceled projects that are not delivered. Lines of code ignores requirements and design defects and also penalizes high-level languages. Cost per defect penalizes quality and achieves the lowest results for the buggiest software.

Function points for normalization combined with defect removal efficiency are the best for quality metrics. Work hours per function point and function points per staff month are the best productivity metrics. Benchmark data expressed using IFPUG function points outnumber other function point variations by about 10 to 1.

The same 1,000 function point application would look like this:

- Source code for 1,000 function points: 40,000 logical code statements

- Programming language: C # and MySQL

- Reuse percentage: 0% to 40%

- Methodology: Agile with Scrum

- Productivity: 9.50 function points per staff month

- Defect potentials: 3.50 defects per function point

- Defect removal efficiency (DRE): 92%

- Delivered defects: 0.28 defects per function point

- Ratio of development personnel to maintenance:
  - Development: 45%
  - Maintenance: 55%

The following are the background data for 2005:

- Average language level: 8.00
- Number of programming languages: 2,500
- Logical statements per function point: 40
- Average application size: 550 function points
- Average application size: 22,000 logical code statements

Summary

By the end of this decade, social networks such as Facebook and Twitter had become a new way of social interaction, with millions of subscribers and sometimes many hours per day devoted to cybercommunications; often, more time was spent online than in face-to-face communications.

Open-source applications such as Firefox and Linux began to have corporate significance and were added to thousands of corporate portfolios.

The dot-com bubble burst of 2000 and the Great Recession of 2008 changed the demographics of the software community and led to a number of downsizings among large companies and failures among small companies. They also led to an increase in offshore outsourcing to countries with lower labor rates such as China, India, and the Philippines. However, offshore inflation rates are higher than U.S. inflation rates.

Cloud computing and big data began to appear in articles and to a certain degree were in actual use. However, both would have more usage in the next decade.

Agile methods continued to expand in usage. However, in spite of Agile, failures and cancellations of major applications of greater than 10,000 function points remained troublesome. These large systems tended to use other methods such as waterfall due to the fact that Agile does not scale up as well as it might. Methods such as Rational Unified Process and Team Software Process proved to be successful for large systems but were somewhat cumbersome for small projects compared to Agile methods.

Chapter 10

2010 to 2019: Clouds, Crowds, Blogs, Big Data, and Predictive Analytics

This book was started in the middle of 2012 and finished in the spring of 2013. Therefore, only a little more than two years of actual history were available to discuss for this decade. Using trends from prior decades, I could make some predictions of things that might occur between 2013 and 2019. Of course, knowing the future can be difficult.

The early years of this decade witnessed a rapid growth of companies providing services for the *cloud* (applications and data stored remotely on the web but available for local use). There was also a remarkable increase in new companies that want to use *crowds* of possibly thousands of people to focus on common goals. The World Wide Web is a necessary enabling technology for crowd actions.

An interesting social phenomenon that is accelerating in the current decade is the widespread use of *blogs*, or collections of personal web articles that are published by individuals who have facts or opinions to share. Some blogs have become famous, are syndicated, and have millions of readers. Others are obscure and probably read only by personal friends and family members of the authors.

The emergence of *big data* has come about from hundreds of disparate databases that are analyzed together. The natural partners of big data are predictive analytics and intelligent agents. Predictive analytics use big data to examine large and complicated problems. Intelligent agents are extensions of search engines that include artificial intelligence to analyze findings and generate useful information based on dozens or hundreds of websites.

Agile development is expanding rapidly. While Agile is popular, there is a distinct lack of quantitative data that show real progress compared to other leading methods such as the team software process (TSP) and rational unified process (RUP). All three seem superior to the older waterfall and "cowboy" methods.

Predicting the Future

Predicting the future is always tricky and usually unreliable. But there are obvious trends based on current software levels of technology and the results of recent past decades.

The outcomes of the "patent wars" that are sweeping through the computer, cell phone, and software worlds are unknown. Amazon and Samsung are currently suing each other, and in fact almost every large high-technology company has one or more patent lawsuits in play.

There is also a new subindustry of "patent trolls" that acquire patents not so much for their intellectual worth but rather to use to sue or threaten to sue dozens of companies for patent violations.

The whole topic of software patents and patentability is fluid, and eventual Supreme Court decisions may change software patents in unknown ways.

Another critical prediction is that software security threats and government-sponsored "cyberwarfare" will continue to expand in frequency and seriousness of threats. Financial institutions, personal identities, and electric power grids are the most likely targets. Denial of service attacks are likely to increase also. Transportation is also at risk because hacking air-traffic control systems is probably not as difficult as it should be.

Interesting new hardware devices that operate by means of software are leading to some exciting future possibilities. Among the most interesting of these new devices is *3D printing*, which allows consumers to create plastic items; wearable computers such as Google Glass; and some potential new medical devices such as ocular implants, which could restore sight to the blind, similar in concept to cochlear implants that restore hearing to the deaf.

Of these new inventions, 3D printing technology is already in use for both industrial and medical purposes. For example, 3D printing can now be used to create a perfect replica of a tooth that can be implanted by a dentist to replace a missing tooth. Wearable computers in the form of glasses also exist, but these are not yet on the commercial market. Ocular implants are still in the experimental stage.

Professional Status for Software Engineering

Even after more than 60 years, software engineering is not yet a certified profession with licenses, board specialties, and malpractice monitoring, as occurs with the fields of medicine and law. While there have been some improvements in programming languages, requirements, design, and development methods, there is still a need for much more progress.

A number of state governments are beginning to cooperate and offer license examinations for software engineering. This is just beginning as the book enters production, so it is too soon to know how effective and beneficial these licenses will be.

So long as software applications are based on custom designs and hand-coding applications line by line, software cannot really be a true engineering field. Worse, it will remain one of the most labor-intensive occupations in human history.

Currently, software is built more or less like a Formula 1 race car or an America's Cup yacht. Skilled designers create custom designs that are then manually constructed by skilled programming craftsmen.

Consider the labor content of a Formula 1 car compared to an automobile such as a Ford or Lexus that is built on an assembly line using standard components and robotic devices. An ordinary car constructed on an assembly line from standard parts uses about 30 hours of direct labor. A hand-built Formula 1 car that may need precision machining and custom-made parts can take 3,000 hours of direct labor.

An application of 10,000 logical code statements that is hand-coded at a rate of about ten lines of code per hour will take about 1,000 hours. By contrast, the same application constructed from a set of 100 standard and certified reusable modules could be put together in about eight hours.

Today, a normal mix of software applications in the 500 function point size range developed using Agile and midlevel languages such as Java or C# would have an average total productivity rate of about 12 function points per staff month. This includes delivery, project management, and specialists such as technical writers and quality assurance.

Using the same kind of 500 function point sample with the same size skill mix but using 85% certified reusable materials, the predicted productivity rate would be closer to 110 function points per staff month, or 917% higher results using the Agile approach. Custom designs and hand-coding cannot possibly provide the economic gains that are possible with standard reusable designs and certified reusable code.

Quality and *technical debt* would also be improved using patterns and certified reusable components. Today, Agile projects average about 4.0 bugs per function point in requirements, design, code user manuals, and bad fixes. About 93% of these are removed prior to release, so the delivered defect rate is about 0.28 per function point. Technical debt, or fixing those delivered defects downstream, would cost roughly $150 per function point spread over the first 18 months of usage.

By contrast, an application constructed from proven design patterns and certified components would have a defect potential of only about 1.0 defect per function point (mainly in customized features). Defect removal efficiency would be about 99.4%. This leads to a delivered defect volume of only 0.006 defects per function point. Technical debt would be about $12.50 per function point for 18 months, or only about 8.33% of the technical debt noted with the Agile example.

Note

Waterfall projects similar to the 500 function point examples discussed above would have productivity rates of about 7.5 function points per staff month. Their defect potentials would be 5.0 bugs per function point, 85% defect removal efficiency, and 0.75 delivered defects per function point. Technical debt would be around $350 per function point, spread over 18 months. This is more than twice the Agile result and about 23 times the technical debt of design patterns and certified reusable components.

Of course, actually building the reusable materials is slow and fairly expensive. Average productivity for the initial construction of each component, assumed to be 25 function points, would only be about 4.5 function points per staff month. However, as usage of the certified components goes up, their economic value goes up. Needless to say, the reusable components would be subject to rigorous inspections, pretest static analysis, and a full suite of formal test stages performed by certified test personnel. The cumulative defect removal efficiency of the reusable components would be about 99.7%.

A fundamental question for the software engineering community that hopefully will be solved this decade is what are the enabling technologies to move software from laborious custom designs and hand-coding to reusable designs and certified reusable modules?

There are bold claims from various methodologies such as Agile that they make marked improvements in productivity and quality. But so long as software applications need custom design and hand-coding, they will be intrinsically inefficient no matter what methodology is used.

The following are some of the enabling technologies needed to move from manual construction and hand-coding of software to automated assembly of software:

- A full, scientific taxonomy of common features that occur in many software applications

- Effective methods of certifying reusable components that can guarantee with more than 99% certainty that they are free from overt defects and exploitable security flaws

- Methods of software architecture and design based on patterns derived from successful existing software applications (i.e., eliminate custom designs and use proven patterns)

- Standard interface methods for sending messages and data between modules

- Secure repositories of certified materials that can be extracted and reused either for a fee or via an open-source license

- Reusable ancillary materials such as test suites, user manuals, HELP screens, cost data, and histories of any bug reports against the reusable modules

Very few software applications created today are truly "new" in the sense that no one has ever built similar applications before. The vast majority of modern software involves either building newer replicas of legacy software or adding new features to legacy applications.

Probably less than 10% of contemporary software applications on a global basis are truly new in the sense that they are so novel that no similar applications have ever been built before. This means that patterns derived from the most successful historical applications can be encapsulated and used to design and build similar new applications.

Instead of the current process of conducting lengthy interviews with clients to ascertain requirements followed by creating custom architecture and design and then hand-coding, a possible future for software engineering might be as follows:

1. Engineers will meet with the client and scroll through libraries of standard design patterns based on the client's needs. The design patterns will be derived from successful applications that are already up and running. The designs will be sorted by industry, by application class, by application type, and by other relevant factors.

For example, there will probably be about 500 historical application "patterns" for each major industry such as banking, health care, insurance, telecommunications, pharmaceuticals, state governments, municipal governments, and probably more than 150 total industries. Assembling these patterns may require forensic analysis of samples of legacy applications.

2. Once the basic design is selected, engineers work out any special features that might require manual customization or new development. But probably these will be rare and if they occur will be less than 5% of the total application.

3. Because the costs and schedule benchmarks for the applications used as patterns are known, engineers can predict the costs and delivery time of the new application using a straightforward process. This would be very similar to buying a new automobile that has optional features. There are standard price lists for each feature.

4. Because the designs are accompanied by bills of material, the next step will be merely to select the standard reusable components that will be needed to complete the application. In fact, this step could be fully automated: every design will have a full parts list of standard modules needed.

5. Assuming that the application is going to be fully constructed from standard pieces, robots or some other form of automation will carry out the actual development of the application or connect the modules. Human developers might be needed to create the original modules for the first time, but once something reusable has been created, the development effort is trivial and can be fully automated.

6. Of course, it will be necessary to test the completed application once it is put together. But as the test cases and test suites are also reusable and included in the parts list, testing, too, could be carried out by robots or automated means. Samples of reusable data could be used to perform end-to-end testing of the application.

Human software engineers will still be needed to create truly unique applications and to design the reusable modules. This is the same kind of situation as seen in the circuit design world for building new computer chips and new integrated circuits. Each reusable software module is similar to a small integrated circuit.

There may also be a need for human software engineers and database specialists to assist in migrating legacy data to the new application. Legacy data migration is a complex and difficult task that today can take many months for large database applications.

The basic goal of software engineering should be to minimize costly and error-prone human tasks and replace them with automated tasks made possible by combinations of standard patterns and certified reusable components.

So long as software is custom designed and coded by hand, it will always be slow, expensive, risky, and subject to serious security vulnerabilities. Custom designs and hand-coding are intrinsically error prone, and no known methodology can do anything other than make comparatively small improvements.

To make really big improvements, software needs to begin to use proven architectures and design patterns, certified reusable code, and certified ancillary materials such as reusable test cases and reusable user documents. Reusable data samples are also needed.

The software engineering community should also move toward professional licenses and board certification. Although it is theoretically possible to achieve these goals by the end of this decade, it is more likely that they won't occur for perhaps another 25 years.

Near-term goals that might be accomplished by the end of the decade are more modest and can focus on improving a number of areas that are currently done poorly, such as quality control and change control.

Possible Software Engineering Improvements in the 2010s

Software productivity and quality will evolve slowly and sometimes in the fashion of a drunkard's walk, with progress and regressions both occurring more or less at the same time.

In order to make really major improvements, a number of chronic software engineering problems need to be solved:

- Productivity and quality measures are poorly done and usually inaccurate even today. Lines of code and cost per defect both violate the principles of standard economics. Function point metrics are the most accurate for economic studies, but they have been so slow and expensive that they have not achieved more than about a 10% penetration of software projects.

Hopefully, the emergence of high-speed, low-cost function points such as those in Software Risk Master (SRM) will make this metric a standard economic tool for software productivity and quality studies.

- Repositories of certified reusable components need to enter the mainstream. Custom design and custom code, even with Agile, are inefficient. Only construction from certified reusable components can achieve high levels of quality and productivity at the same time. Successful reuse needs several enabling technologies, one of which is a complete taxonomy of standard software features. Software reusability remains lower than it should be. Certification of reusable materials is almost totally absent, and using uncertified materials can be hazardous.

- Quality control remains only semicompetent today, with inspections and static analysis not being used as often as they should be. Software quality measures are a professional embarrassment. It is hard to imagine a physicist or chemist publishing data as flaky as the software literature. The industry has depended on testing, which is fairly low in defect removal efficiency. High quality comes from a synergistic combination of defect prevention, pretest defect removal such as inspections and static analysis, and formal testing using mathematically derived test cases.

- Change control is not well done. Applications grow at between 1% and 4% per calendar month during development and more than 7% per year after release. Agile applications grow at more than 10% per month. Many projects are not prepared for this rapid growth. Early predictions of requirements creep combined with formal change-control methods are needed for all major software projects.

- Project estimation is not well done and is semi-incompetent for many projects, as noted during depositions and discovery of projects in litigation. More than 95% of software projects with fewer than 1,000 function points still use manual estimating methods. Even above 10,000 function points, automated estimation is only used on about 25% of projects. Manual estimates become progressively optimistic above 250 function points and dangerously optimistic above 1,000 function points. Parametric estimation tools and predictive analytics hold accuracy up to more than 100,000 function points.

- Software security remains below the safe level. Cyberattacks, identity thefts, viruses, worms, botnets, hacking, and spyware are now major business and personal problems. Many companies and government agencies are working to improve security, but fundamental changes in computer and software architecture may be necessary.

- Software engineering needs to become a true profession with licensing and board-certified specialists. In this case, software should follow the same path as older professions such as medicine and law, where professional licenses are needed before being allowed to practice.

- In 2011, the International Function Point Users Group (IFPUG) issued guidelines for a new kind of metric for nonfunctional requirements. This metric is called *SNAP*, and as this book is being written, new data are starting to arrive, but the integration of SNAP with normal function point analysis is not complete.

- Early sizing and estimating before determining requirements are mandatory to allow time to make technology changes before moving in the wrong direction. High-speed function point predictions are also mandatory and fortunately both are available today.

- As the software industry ages, maintenance of legacy applications is now the dominant work of software engineers. In many companies, more than 65% of total budgets go to enhancing legacy applications and keeping them operational. Maintenance work is more complex than new development and needs much more research than it has received. Professional books on maintenance have less than a tenth of the frequency of books on new development. In today's world, there is a need for much better methods of renovating and repairing legacy applications, as well as much better methods for moving aging data onto new application platforms.

This decade is witnessing acceleration in the use of Agile with Scrum and also extreme programming. However, RUP and TSP are more widely used for major systems above 10,000 function points in size.

Interesting social trends started to appear in the last decade and are expanding rapidly in the early years of this decade. Now that the internet and World Wide Web reach millions of people, it is possible to assemble "crowds" that focus on common goals. The success of Wikipedia and open-source software illustrate that groups of independent workers can sometimes accomplish better-than-expected results. These same ideas are now beginning to deal with other social topics.

The use of personal diaries, or *web logs*, originated soon after the internet and the World Wide Web became operational. The early *usenet* services had some personal-opinion topics. However, in the first decade of the century, special tools became available to make it easier to create these logs. The term "web log" was condensed into the term *blog*, which has now entered the vernacular.

There are millions of blogs, and some have become popular enough to have large audiences. The web and various blogging tools are the enabling technologies that allow ordinary computer users to share opinions globally with very little technical difficulty.

Hybrid software methodologies are increasing that utilize the best features of various methods such as Agile, TSP, and RUP. The hybrids often have results that show synergy, or the combination being slightly better than the originals.

Other future trends will probably see an increase in virtualization and an increase in cloud-related applications and services. A nonprofit organization called Software Engineering Methods and Theory (SEMAT) is attempting a formal redesign of software engineering. By the end of the decade, some of their new concepts should begin to percolate through software engineering schools.

Companies Formed During the Early 2010s

In this chapter, only companies founded from 2010 to 2012 are discussed. For companies founded in 2013, there is not enough time to judge either their potential for success or the merits of their business plans. Table 10.1 shows many but not all of the companies founded from 2010 through 2012. As with earlier decades, the many small game companies that spring up constantly are not included.

Table 10.1   *Companies Formed from 2010 to 2012*

Companies	Year
Advania	2011
AngelPad	2010
AppAddictive	2011
Applied Communication Sciences	2011
Applogic	2010
Audimated	2010
Authr	2011

Table 10.1   *(Continued)*

Companies	Year
AVK	2012
Business 2 Community	2010
CharityKick	2012
Cloud Bees	2010
CloudVelocity	2010
Company 85	2010
Continuity	2011
CrowdCube	2011
Digital Clarity Group	2012
Euclideon	2010
Evry	2010
Fiverr	2010
Flattr	2010
Geekli.St	2011
GoFundMe	2010
Guide	2011
HiringThing	2012
Hortonworks	2011
ITT Excellis	2011
Mindshapes	2010
Namcook Analytics LLC	2012
Nest Labs	2010
NetsGroup	2010
Open Data Institute	2012
Peer Index	2010
Pneuron	2011
Raise 5	2012
Skill Bet	2012
Sky Word	2010
Streamworks International	2010
Thumb	2010

(Continued)

Table 10.1   *(Continued)*

Companies	Year
UBI Care	2011
Unified Inbox	2012
Vfiles	2012
Virtual Sharp Software	2010
Vungle	2012
Wahooly	2011
Wikistrat	2010
Yesware	2010

I now discuss recently formed companies that either have interesting business plans or are introducing new technologies and pioneering new business niches.

AngelPad

As shown throughout this book, the computer and software industries have had thousands of startup companies. Some of these fail quickly, but others, such as Amazon, Google, and YouTube, grow into large and successful corporations. Almost all of them needed some kind of seed money in order to get started when they were too small to attract professional venture capital groups.

AngelPad focuses on aiding startup companies that are too small and too new to attract regular venture funding but that show a promise of growth and future success. AngelPad was founded in 2010 in San Francisco, California, by Thomas Korte together with six former Google employees. The other founders were Richard Chen, David Scacco, Vibuh Mittal, Gokul Rajaram, Deep Nishar, and Keval Dasai.

AngelPad does not just write a startup a check and walk away. Candidate companies have to submit written business plans, which are reviewed. If the plans are accepted for funding, there are a number of companies grouped together as a *class*. In the initial class, ten startup companies are selected. Classes may have as many as 25 startup companies.

The companies in the same class meet and work together using office space provided by AngelPad. They are also mentored by AngelPad officers as needed. The class works together for a ten-week period. The idea is to share ideas and change startups from working in isolation in garages to sharing ideas and concepts with other entrepreneurs as well as with experienced technology workers from successful companies. The AngelPad startups each receive up to about $100,000.

AngelPad is not the only company that helps small startups. Another California company, Y Combinator, has a similar business plan. And there are several others. Cambridge, Massachusetts, is a hotbed of technology business startups and has an interesting business incubator. It will be interesting to see how many of the Angel-Pad startups succeed and later grow to become successful and possibly have IPOs.

Authr

Authr is a highly specialized but interesting niche company aimed at beginning authors. It is also a pioneer in the domain of *crowdfunding*, or obtaining many small financial contributions that together might be significant.

This company was founded in Los Angeles in 2011 by an author and entrepreneur named Eric Bownman. Authr.com is a website that allows authors to showcase book ideas before they are very far along. But the website goes beyond just presenting ideas. Authors can also request donations from other participants to help fund their writing. This is a novel concept, and its success is uncertain, but the idea is interesting. Crowdfunding is an expanding topic of interest in this decade, and several other similar companies are cited in this chapter.

With Authr, there is no charge to authors themselves. The authors who sign up get a book proposal tool, a cover design tool for e-books, and a book project page on the website where they can place text and information. Funds for Authr come in from ads. Authr has a novel business plan, and it will be interesting to see if it grows and expands, stays small, or fades away. In any case, crowdfunding is an emerging topic that is only made possible by the internet and World Wide Web.

CloudVelocity

This decade is witnessing the growth of many cloud-service and cloud-support companies. The fundamental idea of cloud computing is that remote servers, file storage, and applications can provide services to end users without filling up their disks or requiring installation of software packages.

For some companies such as Apple with its iCloud, data can be automatically synchronized across multiple devices, including iPhones, iPads, and Apple computers. Thus, a new addition to an address book shows up on every device. Another cloud-service example is the Google office applications that provide word processing and spreadsheets from the Google cloud. Of course, using the cloud depends on fairly high-speed connections with high bandwidth.

CloudVelocity was formed in December 2010 in Santa Clara, California, by Rajeev Chawla, Raman Chawla, Amand Iyengar, and Panagiotis Tsirigotas. The original name was Denali Systems, so this is yet another software startup that has gone through a name change.

The products from CloudVelocity are intended to allow Windows and Linux applications to run on public clouds with little or no change. The products are still in development and will come out later in 2013.

CloudVelocity is a private company that has already received more than $5 billion in venture funds. The principals of CloudVelocity all worked in other Silicon Valley technology companies, including Sun.

CrowdCube

CrowdCube was formed in 2011 in Exeter in the United Kingdom by Darren Westlake and Luke Lang. The company is an early pioneer in the new *crowdfunding* business model. In place of one or two angel investors or venture capital groups, crowdfunding opens up investments to dozens or even thousands of individuals whose investments are usually fairly small. This concept is new but has conventional bankers worried. A report from the Bank of England said that crowdsourcing, if successful, could make bank loans obsolete.

In order for crowdfunding to be effective or even legal, it is necessary to gain approval from various regulatory agencies. One of the reasons CrowdCube is cited here is because it has received regulatory approval from the U.K. Financial Services Authority. CrowdCube is the first U.K. crowdfunding organization to receive this certification.

This approval is quite recent, having been received in February 2013. Therefore, it is premature to know how successful the approach will be. CrowdCube has already attracted more than 28,000 investors and more than £5 million in investments. These are big numbers for such a new concept.

The crowdfunding model operates on an "all-or-nothing" basis. An entrepreneur specifies a target capital amount such as £50,000 and submits a business plan and relevant data via the CrowdCube website. If the business plan is exciting and people invest (as little as £10 can be invested), then the startup will receive the £50,000 or perhaps more in funds. If the total investments fall short of the goal, then the entrepreneur receives nothing and all funds are returned to the investors, minus a 5% administrative fee.

This all-or-nothing model is socially and technically interesting because it rewards effective business plans and eliminates ineffective plans. It also has the virtue of allowing investments to be made with comparatively low risks.

While crowdfunding will appeal to investors with marginal wealth, it also has an appeal to very wealthy and very experienced investors. The reason is that since many startup companies fail quickly, smaller investments in a larger variety of companies might optimize the chance for investing in a future Google or Facebook that will become a huge success.

As this book is being completed, crowdfunding is very new and is not yet available in every country. However, crowdfunding is using the power of the internet and the web to create an entirely new channel for investments that could not have existed 20 years ago. This is definitely a topic that will get close attention from the press, investors, and technical entrepreneurs.

Fiverr

Fiverr is another niche company that depends on the internet and the web to exist. There are thousands and perhaps millions of independent graphic artists, web designers, gardeners, cartoonists, and other arts and crafts providers. Fiverr provides a place to advertise services and also to receive payments for small jobs or tasks that cost as little as $5 or as much as $500.

Fiverr was founded in 2010 in New York by Micha Kaufman and Shai Wininger. There are also offices in Tel Aviv, Israel. Fiverr reports about 1.3 million services are offered, and many are offered for a flat fee of only $5.

Some of the services found on the Fiverr website are basically hobbies. For example, people offer to teach family recipes, restore old photographs, or create customized cartoons. Other services are more business oriented, such as document writing or editing.

The draw that Fiverr has for both vendors and potential clients is that it condenses into one accessible website hundreds of marketable skills, none of which are likely to be needed by more than about one person out of 50. But if a million or more potential clients visit the website, then enough transactions occur for some of the vendors to receive significant funds. In fact, about 15% of Fiverr vendors regard the service as a key source of income, which is surprising for such a young website.

The Fiverr business model is somewhat reminiscent of eBay, which turned virtual yard sales into a profitable web business. Fiverr hopes to turn small "gigs" into a profitable business. The idea is interesting. Fiverr has already been ranked in the top 20 websites in terms of monthly visits, which is quite a coup.

Fiverr is an example of a company that is providing what seems to be a useful service to thousands of independent craft and technical personnel. Not only does it give them access to a huge audience on the web, but it also handles the complexities of processing payments between clients and vendors.

Flattr

This is another new company with another interesting new niche that could not exist without the internet and the web. It is in the emerging business of crowdfunding and allows subscribers to donate funds to interesting websites.

This company was formed in March 2010 in Malmo, Sweden, by Peter Sunde and Linus Olsson. (Peter Sunde was also a founder of Pirate Bay, which uses the BitTorrent search engine. BitTorrent is reported to comprise about 35% of all web traffic.)

The company is a pioneer in the new domain of *microdonations*. These are small donations of $200 or less that are contributed over the web from computers or via a smartphone, often using PayPal or a web finance transaction method. (Surprisingly, microdonations have become so widespread that about 25% of the U.S. 2012 presidential campaign funds came from them. This was the first presidential election in history where microdonations were large enough to possibly impact the outcome.)

To use Flattr, a subscription is necessary. Users set up a Flattr account and contribute a fixed amount monthly, such as a few euros. Flattr itself takes 10% of these fees for the costs of maintaining the service. Once an account is established, users of Flattr can make contributions to various websites. The name "Flattr" is derived from the common word "flatter." The idea is to augment verbal encouragement of interesting and useful websites with small donations.

In December 2010, a tweet asserted that Flattr was being used to help fund the famous WikiLeaks site that distributes top-secret classified information to the dismay of the government and military officials. However, this is noted as a web assertion and is not a verified fact.

In order to receive Flattr donations, websites have to be prepared to accept them. Some blogging platforms such as WordPress and Blogger support Flattr. A special FireFox add-in is also available. Money is put in and taken out of Flattr accounts via PayPal or a number of credit card and financial companies that support the method, such as Bitcoin. Incidentally, the subindustry of electronic fund transfers of small amounts is becoming a major new social and financial topic of great importance during this decade.

Note

The Bitcoin method of funding small transactions was developed in 2009 and is rapidly becoming an accepted alternate currency for small web transactions. There is even a new Bitcoin currency symbol. The Bitcoin is both technically and socially important, being the first new global currency created since the euro. The Bitcoin currency is technically interesting because it uses cryptography to guard against the theft of Bitcoins.

Through Flattr, it is also possible to donate to offline organizations as well as websites. The enabling technology that allows this is *quick response*, or QR codes. These are the square black-and-white barcodes that are now widely found on consumer products. The QR codes can be scanned by smartphones and used for transferring Flattr donations, among other purposes.

The web is creating a number of new industries, and among these are what appear to be very important new niches dealing with electronic fund transfers of small amounts of currency and crowdfunding of both commercial and charitable organizations.

Geekli.St

The Geekli.St organization has become a significant social portal for software engineers in 170 countries. The Geekli.St website is part job site, part social network, and part publication about software achievements.

Geekli.St was founded in San Francisco, California, in 2011 by Christian Sands and Reuben Katz. The Geekli.St website grew to 10,000 users in about five weeks. It is a private company that has received external funding from angel investors.

A unique feature of the Geekli.St website is that it uses special "cards" that are structured to allow software engineers to illustrate and brag about their accomplishments. Examples of accomplishments might be developing new algorithms, building new kinds of websites, or anything else that is novel and of interest to a software engineering community. The cards are prominent on the Geekli.St website, and visitors or users can make comments about them.

Geekli.St is a good example of how the web is allowing people with common interests or who work in the same field to come together and share ideas or look for new jobs. There are more than 50,000 Geekli.St members, and the number is growing.

GoFundMe

GoFundMe is another new crowdfunding organization that is rapidly changing the nature of philanthropy. The company was formed in San Diego, California, in May 2010 by Brad Damphousee and Andrew Ballister; it is still a private company. The original name was CreateAFund, but like so many software startups, the name was changed. GoFundMe has become one of the largest U.S. crowdfunding sites and it also has some unique features and services.

GoFundMe supports ordinary charitable and nonprofit groups, but it also allows special fund-raising requests for private individuals and personal needs, such as needing money for a surgical procedure or needing money for buying new clothes after a major fire destroys a house. There is even a section for students who need funding to cover tuition costs. GoFundMe users can create their own linked sites that explain their needs and why they are asking for funds. Photographs and other information can be displayed. GoFundMe generates its own revenues by taking 5% of each donation to cover the logistical costs of keeping the site operational.

A few samples of interesting funds that were collected include getting almost $75,000 for three little girls diagnosed with the medical condition of mucopolysaccharidosis, which is a serious metabolic disorder. Another case was a request for $2,500 to send a terminal cancer patient on a short vacation, which raised almost $30,000. A third case was a request for $1,000 to support a wheelchair basketball program for children, which eventually raised about $27,000.

Crowdfunding is a recent innovation but one that is transforming charitable donations for the better by using the power of the web to provide information about worthy needs to potentially millions of web users throughout the world.

Namcook Analytics LLC

Namcook Analytics is one of the more recent companies cited in this book, having been incorporated in August 2012 in Delaware. Namcook does business in Narragansett, Rhode Island, and Hingham, Massachusetts. Namcook clients are globally based.

In the interest of disclosure, this company was cofounded by me and my business partner, Ted Maroney. I researched and filed several patents earlier in 2011 prior to formal incorporation. Namcook Analytics is a private corporation.

As the name implies, Namcook Analytics LLC is in the business sector of predictive analytics, with a special emphasis on predicting the results of software projects in terms of application sizing as well as predictions for risk, quality, schedule, staffing, cost, and maintenance.

Namcook patents are based on the use of pattern matching, which allows unusually early sizing and risk analysis. For example, the company's main predictive tool, Software Risk Master (SRM), can predict software project outcomes prior to full requirements, which is perhaps six months earlier than other methods of size prediction. The predictions are also rapid and average about 90 seconds per application regardless of its nominal size.

Pattern matching with SRM uses a proprietary questionnaire to gather information on new or planned software applications. The answers to the questions form a "pattern." This pattern is then used to extract results from the Namcook knowledge base of around 15,000 completed projects. The results of the historical projects with the same or similar patterns provide the base for the predictions of the new application.

The same questionnaire, augmented by data collection of project schedule, cost, staffing, and quality results for completed projects, is used to add new projects to the Namcook knowledge base.

Although pattern matching is a new method for software sizing and estimating, it is common in other industries. For example, the Zillow database of national real estate listings, discussed in the previous chapter, allows clients to look at the assessed values of homes similar to their own. This is useful in appealing possible errors in appraisals, which occur often. Users of Zillow utilize pattern matching to select comparable properties with similar size, age, layouts, construction, scenic views, and other topics that impact tax assessments.

Mathematical interpolation of projects without an exact match is a necessary feature. With 122 discrete elements in the Namcook SRM taxonomy, the permutations total to 214,200,000 possible patterns. Needless to say, more than half of these patterns have never occurred and will never occur. For the current software industry, the total number of patterns that occur with relatively high frequency is much smaller: about 20,000.

New patterns occur from time to time, as when new programming languages are used or when new methods are developed. (New programming languages appear almost monthly; new development methods occur at least once per year.) The SRM tool has a measurement mode that allows it to collect historical data and therefore absorb new technologies as they occur.

A unique feature is that measurements start with an SRM estimate. Clients can examine the estimate and accept or modify each activity. This makes the SRM tool a self-learning tool that can absorb new technical advances as they occur.

The fact that SRM measures individual activities allows very high precision measurements that, in theory, can top 1%. However, most corporate historical data "leak" and are incomplete, so interviews with team members may be needed to recover missing elements such as unpaid overtime, which seldom gets recorded.

SRM size predictions use function points defined by the IFPUG as the primary metric. However, the SRM tool is metric-neutral and in fact predicts software application size by using 15 different metrics, including SNAP nonfunctional metrics, COSMIC function points, story points, use-case points, logical source code metrics, and others. (COSMIC is a sort of strained acronym for "Common Software Measurement International Consortium." This is clearly an artificial arrangement of words.)

The idea behind early sizing and early estimating is that if potential problems can be identified early prior to determining requirements, then there is still time to deploy effective technologies before the project proceeds in a hazardous direction.

Many factors influence project outcomes. The variables that are used to show clients the outcomes of software projects include complexity of the problem set, data complexity, and code complexity; the methodology used for development; the experience of the development personnel; management experience; the programming language or combination of languages used; the level of the organization on the SEI capability maturity scale (CMMI); and several others. A total of 34 methods are supported, including Agile, iterative, waterfall, Prince2, Merise, RUP, TSP, and others. Hybrid methods are also supported.

It is useful to show clients side-by-side results of the same project with different technology stacks. For example, it is easy to show side-by-side results for a future project with one version demonstrating the Agile method and the C# programming language with 15% reuse, while a second version demonstrates the TSP method and the Objective-C programming language with 30% reuse.

The major cost drivers for software projects in approximate order are the following:

1. Finding and fixing bugs

2. Producing paper documents such as requirements and specifications

3. Developing code

4. Running meetings and other communications

5. Managing the project

6. Handling requirements creep

The SRM predictive analytics tool is aware of these historical software patterns and therefore predicts (and measures) software defects found in requirements, design, code, user documents, and bad fixes or secondary defects.

The SRM tool also predicts (and measures) the size and completeness of a variety of paper documents, including requirements, architecture, specifications, test plans, status reports, user manuals, and many more. Paperwork costs are a major factor in large-system development and especially so in defense software.

Requirements creep is a troubling phenomenon and averages perhaps 2% per calendar month. In extreme cases, software projects have doubled in size after requirements but before delivery. Therefore, dealing with requirements creep is a necessary feature for software predictive analytics and is a standard feature of the SRM tool.

Using Predictive Analytics

Predictive analytics, especially when used early prior to funding software applications, can eliminate or minimize the distressing tendency of software projects to run late, exceed their budgets, or be canceled without being completed.

Including clauses in predictive analytics can also improve the contracts used between clients and outsource vendors by asking the vendor to achieve more than 97% in software defect removal efficiency. Clauses for handling scope and requirements creep can also be demonstrated to both the client and vendor during contract discussions. Vendors could also be required to exceed industry productivity and quality levels, with some rewards for being better than average and possible penalties for dropping below average results. Because SRM can be used prior to requirements, it can also be used during contract negotiations. For that matter, SRM has a special feature for predicting the amount of venture funding needed for software startups.

Large groups of projects such as corporate portfolios to predict annual maintenance costs also benefit from predictive analytics. Large portfolios may contain more than 5,000 applications and total more than 10 million function points. The cumulative maintenance and enhancement of large portfolios absorb more than 65% of many corporate software budgets.

Predictive analytics are also useful in dealing with complex topics such as the costs and schedule of installing and deploying enterprise resource planning (ERP) tools such as SAP and Oracle. The installations and customizations of large ERP packages are complex and often run late and exceed planned budgets.

Long-range issues associated with global outsourcing can also be determined through predictive analytics. Because inflation rates are higher in both India and

(Continued)

(Continued)

China than in the United States, long-range costs may favor U.S. outsource partners or partners doing business in multiple countries.

Predictive analytics can also be used to predict the effort and costs of various process improvement initiatives, such as the costs of ascending the CMMI levels from 1 to 5. The costs of adoption and the productivity and quality gains from changing from waterfall development to Agile, RUP, TSP, or any other more recent methodology can easily be shown to clients. Having specific results available makes technology selection and deployment more effective.

The software industry has a bad track record for running late and delivering software with so many bugs or defects it does not work properly. Predictive analytics can help to reduce or eliminate these endemic problems.

Nest Labs

Nest Labs is creating an interesting niche by using embedded software combined with a form of artificial intelligence to optimize home heating and cooling via "smart" thermostats. The thermostats are connected to the web and only work in homes or offices with wireless connectivity. Because wireless homes are becoming common, the potential market for the Nest devices is growing rapidly.

However, products like the Nest thermostat are clearly aimed at affluent customers. Low-income families spend a much higher percentage of their disposable incomes on heating than do the wealthy, and they often do not have wireless support and probably could not afford the $249 for a Nest device.

This company was founded in Palo Alto, California, in 2010 by Tony Fadell and Matt Rogers. As energy costs increase, home heating and cooling are becoming major costs for low-income families and annoying costs for everybody else.

While programmable thermostats have been available for years, the Nest version includes some new features based on embedded software. The initial product was the Nest Learning Thermostat, which not only could be programmed but could also collect historical data and learn from and monitor the surrounding environment.

The physical thermostat devices use standard connections for most HVAC systems and can be installed either by local service personnel certified by Nest or by homeowners. The wireless feature of the Nest thermostats allows downloading of software releases as needed. The wireless capability also allows customers to make remote changes to the thermostat settings via smartphones. For example, if a user decides to take an unplanned weekend trip in winter, it is possible to lower the home temperature down to 50 degrees until shortly before the user's planned return home.

The Nest is one of an expanding set of *smart appliances* that use the internet for automatic upgrades. Others include modern television sets, Blu-ray disk players, and even some high-end microwaves and washing machines. Currently, the Nest thermostats are only sold in the United States and Canada. One reason for this is that the Nest uses U.S. zip codes to localize some of its seasonal features.

In 2012, Nest Labs was sued by Honeywell for patent infringements of seven patents dealing with the remote control of a thermostat, the circular shape of the wall unit, and other features. Nest Labs has stated that it will contest the validity of the patents and intends to see the case through a court trial. As this book is written, the results of the litigation are not known.

Nest Labs is one of a growing number of smart appliance manufacturers that are using software and the internet to provide services that were not formerly available, such as remote access and keeping historical data.

Peer Index

Peer Index is in a brand-new niche that is built on top of a slightly older niche. As social networks become common and compete with each other, both their owners and interested parties such as advertisers want to know which ones are most successful. Peer Index is one of several companies that measure social-network effectiveness.

Peer Index was formed in London, England, in February 2010 by Azeem Adhar, Ditlev Schwanenflugel, and Bill Emmott (the former editor of *The Economist*). The company has developed three complementary measures of website relevance: activity, audience, and authority. The social networks that are measured include Twitter, Facebook, LinkedIn, and Quora.

The activity metric deals with visits to a specific site. The authority metric tries to quantify the number of "likes" or favorable recommendations that a site accumulates. The audience metric tries to ascertain the demographics of site users when compared to the general population.

As social networks grow in numbers and popularity, derivative companies such as Alexa and Peer Index have sprung up to provide statistical evidence of effectiveness. This information is of some importance if the sites depend on advertisements for revenue. For example, a site used primarily by mature PhD physicists will probably not have as many ads, or the same kinds of ads, as a site visited mainly by teenage rock and roll fans. Peer Index attempts to provide these data.

Unified Inbox

Most computer users (including me) get information daily from dozens of websites. Unified Inbox attempts to streamline this process by providing a common focal point for common email and calendar sites and combining information into a unified inbox.

Unified Inbox was launched in 2012 on Waiheke Island, New Zealand, by Toby Ruckert and Markus Lehnert. The location of the company is clear proof that software is now a global commodity. About four years of research were spent prior to the formal launch. Some of the features are protected by a patent.

The basic idea is to consolidate input information from emails, Facebook, Twitter, Basecamp, Dropbox, Evernote, Google calendar, and others into a single stream. For corporate usage, individual input messages can be commented on and have notes affixed and are then routed to another user. The notes and additional information are persistent and are kept with the messages. For example, a bug report from a customer might be received by a help desk employee, reviewed, and then routed to a maintenance programmer with notes and text about customer comments.

The internet and the World Wide Web provide so much information from so many channels that "information overload" has become an endemic problem. Unified Inbox is one of a number of companies that are striving to simplify input information and make diverse sources connect to each other.

Yesware

Yesware is an interesting niche company that offers add-ons to email services. These additional features are aimed specifically at sales personnel, who have to collect substantial information about client contacts. Yesware was founded in 2010 in Boston, Massachusetts, by Matthew Bellows, Rajat Bargava, and Cashman Andrus. Bellows had been a salesman and was attempting to help other salespersons extract useful information from emails without the tedious reentry of data into customer resource management (CRM) systems.

Yesware is a private company that has received about $5 million in venture funding from Google Ventures and the Foundry Group. Usage grew rapidly from the day of launch to more than 100,000 users in about a year. Major companies such as Motorola have become clients.

Yesware is distributed as a free plugin for the Google Chrome and Firefox browsers. This plugin provides templates for various kinds of sales emails. It also shows when emails were opened and which embedded links were clicked. Email information can also be reformatted and routed to CRM packages.

Yesware uses a form of *freemium* business model (the term is a combination of the words "free" and "premium"). In this model, a basic application is provided to clients for free, but additional features are available on a premium-fee basis. Other applications using the freemium model include Dropbox, CCleaner, LinkedIn, WebEx, and several newspapers such as the *New York Times* and the *Providence Journal*. The freemium model is also a concept of the open-source community, where applications are free, but services such as training and consulting have charges.

The freemium model is deserving of business school case studies. It is made possible by the power of the web to reach enough clients so that respectable revenues might accrue from users of a basic free tool or service. The freemium model does not work for only a few clients but can also be effective for millions of clients. The internet and the web are the incubators of the freemium model.

The Yesware concept has gathered favorable comments in business journals such as *Forbes*, *TechCrunch*, and *CNN Money*. Yesware has received at least one award for being an effective sales tool.

As computers and software become universal business tools, there are thousands of new niches waiting to be exploited. Yesware is a good example of a special niche for sales personnel built on top of slightly older technologies such as email. Yesware depends on the internet and World Wide Web plus the existence of email clients. The company could not have been formed more than about 20 years ago due to the fact that the underlying technologies are all recent.

Predicting New Companies and Products from 2013 to 2019

One of the most interesting aspects of working in the software engineering field has been the numerous inventions of exciting new products, some of which are of life-changing importance. Some of these key inventions include medical devices such as cochlear implants, credit cards, GPS mapping, smartphones, social networks, and antilock brakes on automobiles.

Looking forward from today to the end of the decade, current momentum leads to the conclusion that cloud applications and crowd-based applications will become the mainstream. Big data and predictive analytics will expand in usefulness and begin to tackle real-world problems. But what else might happen?

The following sections consider some of the potential advances that might occur based in large part on technologies that exist today. Not every possible advance will be considered; this is only a sample to show what might be possible. Not every possible advance will really occur, but it is interesting to consider them. There may also be totally new inventions just over the horizon that can lead the industry in unexpected directions. In fact, new and unexpected inventions are what have made the computer and software engineering fields so exciting over the past 60 years.

Big Data

When computers and software started as business tools in the 1950s, their focus was on local and specific data needed by individual companies or government agencies. But with time, the World Wide Web has become the largest collection of data in human history.

Descriptions of every public and many private corporations, financial statements for every public company, sales statistics on millions of products, medical records for millions of patients, and buying preferences for billions of consumers all now float on the web. Useful information can be extracted from this universe of data.

However, extracting and assembling useful information needs a number of enabling technologies. Ordinary database products are not sufficient. Heterogeneous tools such as Hadoop are needed. Ordinary web browsing is not sufficient to find and extract all of the relevant information. New kinds of "intelligent agents" similar to Wolfram Alpha are needed to search and condense useful information from perhaps millions of websites.

The potential value of big data is high. It would be possible to analyze the business strategies of every company in every industry; it would be possible to evaluate the effectiveness of every possible therapy for critical conditions such as Lyme disease; it would be possible to compare every health-care program in the world for both medical results and cost-effectiveness; it would be possible to compare the performances of every state government and every municipal government. But new companies and powerful new tools will be needed to make big data as effective as theory suggests it might be.

Crowd Intelligence and Crowdfunding

The unexpected success of the Wikipedia encyclopedia, written by about 39 million authors, is one of the most surprising intellectual phenomena in human history. Until Wikipedia provided a proof of concept, it was never envisioned that large crowds working together could accomplish useful intellectual results.

The power of the web has also opened up new kinds of microinvestments where thousands of people put money into startup companies or new product ideas. The same idea has expanded to other fields such as funding political campaigns or making charitable and philanthropic donations via microdonations of small amounts. In fact, about 25% of the funds for the 2012 candidates in the U.S. presidential election were microdonations.

The power of the internet and the web actually could lead to a sort of "direct democracy" where critical urban, state, and national issues are placed before crowds who are asked to provide opinions and potential solutions to topics such as pension reforms and right-to-work laws. We can expect to see many new startups that will attempt to utilize crowdfunding or *crowd intelligence* to deal with an expanding array of issues.

Cybercrime and Cybersecurity

One prediction can be made with great certainty for the rest of this decade. Cybercrime will increase. Whether cybersecurity will be able to stay ahead of cybercrime is not as positive a prediction, but hopefully that will turn out to be true.

It is probably time for a fundamental evaluation of computer architecture and software constructs. The von Neumann architecture seems to have some intrinsic security flaws, and alternate architectures might eliminate them. Virtual memory is a key area of cybercrime exploitation. Permission mechanisms need a thorough reevaluation.

Comparing cybercrime to medical illness, firewalls are a bit like wearing latex gloves to prevent infection. Antivirus software packages are a bit like vaccines that attempt to keep harmful agents from becoming active by killing them. Search-and-destroy tools such as Malwarebytes are a bit like white blood cells that seek out harmful agents and destroy them.

However, as with real medical practice, none of the methods are 100% effective. Firewalls leak and are probably not more than 97% effective. Antivirus packages are only partially successful and probably don't block more than about 98% of known viruses. Search-and-destroy tools are probably not more than 95% successful. Assuming the percentages are realistic, the combined overall effectiveness of the three common cybersecurity methods is only a bit over 90%.

What is needed is fundamental research on methods of raising the immunity levels of both computers and software and making them intrinsically resistant to penetration and attacks.

It would also be useful, although technically challenging, to improve methods of backtracking attack vectors to their source. The structure of the internet and the web makes this almost impossible today. But that does not mean that it will be impossible forever.

Education

Within a period of perhaps ten years, the combination of cost-saving pressures and technology changes will probably make major differences in software learning methods. Online web-based information, e-books, and handheld devices will no doubt replace substantial volumes of paper-based materials.

In addition, virtual reality may introduce artificial classrooms and simulated universities where students and teachers interact through avatars rather than face-to-face in real school buildings.

The increasing sophistication of intelligent agents and expert systems will probably improve the ability to scan vast quantities of online information. The fact that companies such as Google and Microsoft are rapidly converting paper books and documents into online text will also change the access to information.

However, software has a long way to go before it achieves the ease of use and sophistication of the legal and medical professions in terms of organization of and access to vital information. For example, there is currently no software equivalent to the Lexis-Nexis legal reference company.

Over the next few years, changes in learning methods may undergo changes as profound as those introduced by the printing press and television. But the quality of software information is still poor compared to the quality of information in more mature fields such as medicine and law. The severe shortage of quantitative data on productivity, schedules, quality, and costs makes software appear to be more of a craft than a true profession.

As of 2013, the technologies exist to create a virtual reality software university that would resemble a real university, only with more sophisticated access to learning materials. The essential idea is to use concepts from virtual reality sites such as SecondLife but apply them to practical software education topics.

In order to do this, the process would start with licensing a virtual reality rendering engine from one of the sophisticated computer-game companies. But instead of using the engine to create virtual battlefields or forests, the engine would create a university campus complete with buildings and students. To be convincing, a virtual campus would probably need to be aesthetically pleasing and feature landscaping as well as campus buildings.

Potential students would be able to move their avatars through the campus and enter the buildings. For example, there would be buildings labeled Project Planning and Estimating, Project Governance, Project Requirements, Cybersecurity, Risk Analysis, and so forth.

Upon entering one of these virtual buildings, there would be a series of virtual classrooms and virtual offices for the instructors and professors. This model assumes that live experts will participate in the virtual university, so the offices would have the names of actual experts such as Dr. Barry Boehm, Dr. Victor Basili, Capers Jones, and others who entered into agreements to offer courses through the virtual university.

Of course, the instructional staff would not be present at all times, so office hours would be posted on the virtual offices. In addition, students would be able to leave messages and requests for the various professors and instructors.

The classrooms would appear to be actual classrooms similar to those at MIT, Harvard, Princeton, and other major universities. Several kinds of courses would be offered. One form of course would be presented in real time by the avatars of live instructors. (It is assumed that the avatars for the virtual university would be images of the actual instructors.) These live courses would be announced and could be scheduled. Some of these would be free, but others might be fee based.

There would also be recorded course materials that students could download and use at their convenience. The virtual classrooms would be more sophisticated than most real classrooms, in that all of them would be able to have multiple screens, feature animation and dynamic materials, and possibly even use 3D instructional materials.

Interaction between virtual students and virtual professors would be similar to real life, in that questions could be asked and answered. Some of the interactions might be even more sophisticated than normal human interactions, because the virtual university envisions working tools for topics such as planning, estimating, requirements, design, and of course, working compilers and interpreters for teaching various programming languages.

A very powerful capability of the virtual university would be a sophisticated curriculum planning engine. Potential students could identify their career choices or preferred occupations, and an intelligent curriculum engine would generate a full list of all courses needed to support their choices.

Not only would courses be identified, but also the current books and journals, professional associations, forms of certification and licensing that might be needed, and many other attributes for major occupations such as software engineering, project management, software quality assurance, database analyst, and perhaps 150 more knowledge-based occupation groups would be identified as well.

Every university needs a good library, and the library for the virtual university would be world-class. It would have features not offered in normal libraries. For example, suppose a student is interested in the topic of software testing. Not only would the library have abstracts of every published book and article on testing, but it would constantly be refreshed by means of intelligent agents that would scan the web for new materials.

Of course, for many topics, the number of books and reference items might be in the millions, so the library would also include tools for narrowing searches and for assigning relevance scores.

Because the virtual university might be accessed by students from several hundred countries, there would also be real-time translation services among all major natural languages. Thus, courses might be simultaneously available in English, Russian, French, Italian, German, Portuguese, Arabic, Spanish, Japanese, and essentially every human language.

Ideally, the translation services would encompass both text materials and perhaps even spoken discussions among students and faculty. A sophisticated virtual university would no doubt license language translation tools plus perhaps voice-to-text tools such as Dragon.

A virtual university would want to offer world-class facilities for those who might have physical limits. For example, to aid the deaf and hard of hearing, all spoken material could be simultaneously translated into printed text. All video and instructional films would automatically include closed captions or subtitles. This technology is available today. It would also be possible to offer simultaneous translations of spoken courses into sign language. However, translation of printed materials into sign language may not yet be fully available.

For the blind, all printed materials could be translated into audio files. This technology also exists today. It might even be possible to support simultaneous translation into Braille (because new 3D printers are now capable of printing in Braille), although that is perhaps outside the current possibilities.

For those in wheelchairs who prefer that their avatars also have wheelchairs, the classrooms and buildings of the virtual university would all be accessible to wheelchairs and also clearly identified verbally for the blind.

As with real universities, students would be able to interact with one another and would also be able to participate in special interest groups or Wiki sites on topics such as static analysis, inspections, requirements engineering, and dozens of others.

Because quantitative information is sadly lacking in real universities, the virtual university would have licenses from all major benchmark groups and would have working versions of a variety of planning and estimating tools, testing tools, and many others.

Unlike real universities, a virtual university would be operational 24 hours a day, 365 days per year. Of course, live instructors would take normal holidays and vacations, but the library and the recorded course materials would always be available.

Because topics of interest change fairly often, a virtual university could include a student center where students from many countries and many fields could interact with one another in order to exchange information and find out what techniques are being used successfully and which ones are difficult to master.

As with real universities, there would be many special interest groups or people who are all interested in the same topics. One service that the virtual university could provide would be access to local and national information from many countries such as the United States, China, Brazil, Japan, India, and many others. For example, each country might have its own bulletin board that could be used to announce courses and webinars that are located in the various cities of the home countries of the students.

Another service that the university might provide is a daily summary of webinars on selected topics such as testing, requirements engineering, and new tools and methods. Currently, there are so many webinars offered that it is not easy even to keep track of them.

In the student center, there could be a virtual bulletin board. Vendors of tools or services might place ads, and students with interests in special topics might start looking for "birds of a feather" groups.

The university might also use LinkedIn, Plaxo, Facebook, or another network service to send messages to students with special interests or with common interests who might want to communicate with each other.

Because students would not be on campus more than perhaps an hour or two per day, the university would also include links to various e-book sources such as Amazon, Barnes and Noble, and Google. Indeed, course curricula and selected texts would be capable of being downloaded and ordered as e-book packages for various courses such as testing, estimating, project management, and the like.

The fundamental idea for the university is to consolidate the huge but unorganized collections of knowledge about software topics into discrete learning packages that are aimed at specific and important topics such as quality control, estimating, planning, status reports, and dozens of others.

Each of the major professional associations such as the American Society of Quality (ASQ), IFPUG, the International Software Standards Group (ISBSG), the Project Management Institute (PMI), or the Software Engineering Institute (SEI) could have their own virtual buildings and offer both training and membership services.

The same concept would be available for major corporations such as IBM, Google, and Microsoft. They could design and commission corporate buildings on the virtual campus where training in their products could take place. In fact, some of the funding for the university would no doubt come from fees paid by corporations for these structures. Smaller corporations such as Computer Aid, Inc., and SmartBear might also want to have a presence on campus.

Another unique aspect of the university would be links to major conferences such as the Japanese Symposium on Software Testing (JaSST) or the IBM Innovate Conferences. The university could have several large conference halls where those who could not attend actual events in person would be able to participate in the major sessions and tutorials. Attendance policies for these virtual conferences would be set by the conference committees and would probably offer reductions on the fees for attending in person.

The university might also offer occasional guest speakers who are famous in the software world: Bill Gates of Microsoft, Sergey Brin of Google, Mark Zuckerberg of Facebook, and Larry Ellison of Oracle are examples. These software luminaries sometimes do speeches at real universities and conferences. But due to logistical limits, they seldom can address audiences of more than perhaps 5,000 people. With a virtual university, the same speakers might easily gather virtual audiences of 100,000 or even more.

The early versions of the university would probably offer short courses or webinars that lasted only an hour or less. However, it is technically possible to envision the university linking to real universities and offering standard curricula in virtual environments.

If the idea catches on, then eventually real universities such as Harvard, MIT, the University of Florida, or the University of Nalanda in India might participate and offer virtual courses either on their home campuses or through the facilities of the virtual university.

At some point, the facilities of the virtual university would be sufficient to administer examinations and offer professional certification in topics such as requirements engineering, function point analysis, testing, project management, and perhaps dozens of other technical disciplines where certification is available.

It is not impossible for the virtual university to eventually award actual degrees up to the Ph.D. level, however. That could only occur if the curricula and faculty were accredited. Actual degrees from the university might not be feasible for another 20 years or thereabouts due to the novelty of the concepts and the logistics of accreditation. The initial versions of the university would be aimed at professional training rather than undergraduate or academic training.

Security would have to be included as part of the design of the virtual campus. This is to keep hackers and viruses from damaging the course materials or disrupting the sessions by means of denial of service attacks. There is always a need for cybersecurity to discourage hacking, phishing, identity theft, and other endemic problems of the computer era.

Although it may be ten years or more before this kind of virtual university occurs, it is interesting that the essential technologies to build such a university all exist today.

Not only do the technologies exist but also the costs for constructing a virtual campus would probably be only in the range of $250,000, which is much less expensive than building real classrooms. Assuming that companies such as IBM, Microsoft, and Google, who already have course materials and instructors, wanted to do this, a virtual university could probably be up and running within ninety days of starting out.

It is not impossible that a virtual university could do for education what Facebook and Twitter have done for social networks: make learning so easy and enjoyable that attendance would reach into the millions.

Because of the lack of expenses for physical buildings and infrastructure, the virtual university would be much less expensive to operate than a real physical university. The main cost drivers would be instructional compensation, licenses for software, and network access fees.

A live one-day seminar that costs $895 per student might be profitable at $200 per student if offered through a virtual university. Student loads could be much higher in a virtual university than in normal live instruction.

For live professional training, the class sizes range from ten to perhaps 50 attendees. For virtual training via webinars and other online methods, class sizes could range from about 200 up to more than 1,500. Thus, lower costs per student are offset by higher numbers of students.

The concepts of the virtual university could also be used for other forms of education, such as medicine and law. (For medicine, it is obvious that real physicians would be needed for surgery and conditions involving examination of actual patients.)

It is even possible to apply the same ideas to primary and secondary education. Even today, it would be much cheaper to build a virtual school for the deaf than it is to build such schools in real life.

For primary and secondary education, there are already rather sophisticated e-learning tools on the market, such as IStation, Mindplay, Adobe, Riverdeep, Follett, and others, that use various dynamic and animated approaches to help hold the attention of students while imparting information. The same ideas can be applied to many other learning situations. There are also e-learning tools for faculty such as those by Virtual Education Software (VESi), which are congruent with the themes of this report.

Currently, it costs between about $75,000 and $100,000 per student per year to operate schools for the deaf and blind. If the virtual learning tools and methods discussed here were applied to teaching the deaf and blind, the annual costs would probably be in the range of $3,000 to $10,000 per student per year. The main barrier to applying the concepts from the virtual university to training the deaf and blind would probably be opposition from various educational unions and resistance from state assemblies and school boards.

The concepts of virtual learning are not as attractive for primary schools, as most parents depend on real schools to take care of children during the workday. But for secondary education and higher education, virtual training is much less expensive. There are no physical infrastructure costs. Licensing software is much cheaper than building physical classrooms that need heat, cooling, and maintenance. The ratio of students to teachers in a virtual classroom can easily grow to 35 to one or more. The cost savings potentials are significant.

It is possible to envision hybrid schools for the deaf and blind where virtual training would augment live instruction, and students would spend part of the time with live instructors and in regular classrooms.

A web search on "average college tuition" found a *CNN Money* analysis dated October 26, 2011, that showed that annual tuition costs for state and community colleges and universities were about $8,244 per year. Living expenses were about $13,203 per year, with total costs of $21,447 per year. Private university tuition averaged $28,500 per year with living costs of $13,724 per year for a total annual cost of $42,224 per year.

Assuming that the concepts of the virtual university were applied to normal undergraduate college education, the probable annual tuition costs might be only about $1,500 per year. There would be no physical infrastructure costs at all, combined with a much greater ratio of students to faculty than with real universities. Living expenses may or may not be lower with virtual training.

However, the real value of virtual training would only be partly based on cost reductions. It is theoretically possible, and research is needed to prove that the educational effectiveness of virtual education would equal and perhaps exceed that of normal classroom education.

For example, immersive training is easily accomplished by virtual methods, but it is expensive using live instruction. Sophisticated learning tools featuring animation and dynamic simulations are easy to accomplish with virtual methods, but they are seldom even attempted with live instruction. Continuing to study on weekends and during spare time is easy with virtual methods but very difficult with live instruction.

The bottom line is that technologies exist today to make significant technical advances in professional education. Some of the same technologies might be usefully applied to special education needs such as teaching the blind and deaf. Eventually, these technologies could extend to many forms of education covering many professions.

Intelligent Agents

In the context of this book, an *intelligent agent* is a software tool that scans the web for specific topics and citations. However, it would not just return web links and web pages. Instead, the intelligent agent would use artificial intelligence and neural networks to analyze and condense some of the information and return actual summary information.

To a certain degree, the new Wolfram Alpha search tool acts as an intelligent agent in exactly this fashion. The author found on the web an interesting example of a search using this tool. The question was, "What are the ingredients in McDonald's hamburgers?" Instead of just providing links to websites and relevant articles, the tool returned an actual list of ingredients, including meat products, salt, sugar, and oils together with information on calories, fat content, cholesterol, and other relevant topics.

It is hard to imagine a single intelligent agent being competent in all disciplines. What will probably occur between now and the end of the decade might be a series of individual intelligent agents that are highly optimized to seek out and report on specific topics.

Some of the kinds of topics where intelligent agents would be useful might be in experimental therapies for immune disorders, the comparative costs and revenue streams for open-source companies and products, the comparative strengths and weakness of health insurance programs in all countries, the relative learning curves and defect densities of common programming languages, and the effectiveness of air-traffic control systems in every country.

Given the huge and growing mass of data now available on the web, no single person can possibly stay current even in his or her own discipline. A good set of intelligent agents that constantly scans and summarizes important information would be a boon for scientists, college students, business and technical workers, civilian government personnel, and military planners.

Medical Devices

The impact of computers and software on medical practice has been profound. This is especially true for the many new kinds of small medical devices that can be surgically implanted, such as cochlear implants, which have restored hearing to thousands of profoundly deaf patients.

What we can perhaps expect before the end of the decade would be additional varieties of implantable devices. One new medical device already being researched would be an ocular implant to restore at least partial sight to the blind.

The same or a similar technology might also be effective in repairing spinal damage and perhaps restoring mobility for patients paralyzed because of spinal injuries.

As it happens, hearing aids are expensive devices and, due to successful lobbying, are not covered under normal health insurance programs or under Medicare. As a result, hearing aids, which cost perhaps $20 each to manufacture, sell for about $2,000 to $4,000 each.

The hearing aid manufacturers don't want insurance coverage because they fear prices would be driven down. The insurance companies don't want to cover the high costs of hearing aids because they know manufacturers want to keep prices high. (The government, which oversees Medicare, seems to be powerless and inept when it comes to balancing patient benefits against political contributions and persuasive lobbying.)

An interesting alternative solution is technically possible and, indeed, prototypes already exist. This new model of a hearing aid would put the main software for adjusting volume, pitch, and background noises into a smartphone. The device that goes into the patient's ear would need to be only a relatively simple receiver, amplifier, and speaker, probably constructed from standard components for a very low cost. In fact, such devices can be purchased today for entertainment purposes for $15 or less.

One of the potential side benefits of using a smartphone for a hearing aid might be to direct other kinds of signals such as music, emergency broadcasts, and possibly TV sound directly to the hearing aid via Bluetooth or some other form of short-range wireless transmission. Whether or not a similar technology would work with cochlear implants needs more research.

Another possible medical advance, although probably not seen during this decade, would be the development of submicron nano devices that would be inserted into patients. These could be remotely controlled or perhaps at some point made autonomous. Their purpose would be to act as phages and seek out troublesome conditions such as Lyme disease bacteria, antibiotic-resistant infectious agents and, possibly at some point, cancer cells.

These nano devices would probably be single-purpose devices that would operate until their targets were eradicated, and then the devices would be removed. Computers and software have already made large improvements in medical devices and diagnostic procedures, and even more exciting advances are technically possible.

Predictive Analytics

Predictive analytics, or using historical information to predict future trends, is much older than the computer era. In fact, informal weather predictions and crop-cycle predictions probably can be traced back more than a thousand years. Yet modern weather prediction based on a mathematical and statistical model is surprisingly recent.

Lewis F. Richardson was a mathematician and meteorologist who first formalized the mathematics of weather prediction. His work on "Weather Prediction by Numerical Process" was published in 1922, which is before the decades covered in this book, and also long before computers and software, although mechanical calculators were available. Although Richardson was troubled by inaccurate data reported by ground stations, his essential mathematics paved the way for modern weather predictions.

Richardson was also a pacifist, and he wrote other interesting books that used predictive analytics to analyze the outbreaks of wars. He studied more than 200 wars. He wrote two classic papers on the statistical origins of warfare: "Arms and Insecurity" in 1949 and "Statistics of Deadly Quarrels" in 1950.

Richardson noted that countries locked in an arms race became a linked oscillating system. He found that as annual costs for weapons and defense increased, at some point, the costs would be so high that they could not go higher. Whichever country reached the point of spending so much on weapons that it was damaging its civilian economy would attack first. The reason for this aggression is that the country knew its costs had reached a terminal limit, but it did not know whether or not a rival had reached a limit.

Richardson's analyses from 1949 and 1950 sound like they could be applied today to North Korea. North Korea has already reached a point where its spending on weapons has damaged its civilian economy, which has never been very strong. Probably one of the reasons North Korea is so aggressive is that it is at or near a maximum for weapons. That could easily lead to an ill-conceived attack on South Korea, whose economy is one of the strongest in Asia.

Predicting the orbits of the planets dates back to Johannes Keppler, who was born in 1571 and died in 1630. Keppler used the very precise observations of the astronomer Tycho Brahe as the basis of his calculations.

During World War II, the advent of operations research formalized some of the math used for predictive analytics and provided real-world benefits for the Allied forces in terms of optimizing logistics and dealing with complex military problems such as convoy sizes versus submarine attacks.

Computers and software sped up calculations and began to add new forms. For example, parametric software cost-estimating tools originated in the 1970s, and a number of them are discussed in this book.

Banks and financial institutions also use predictive analytics for dealing with the risks of various kinds of investments, including consumer loans. However, the financial crises of 2008 showed flaws in the algorithms, and several major disruptions of the stock market confirm the fact that predictive analytics are not perfect by any means.

More than a dozen predictive analytic companies are cited in this book in various decades, with the more recent decades showing a trend toward expansion of the topics being predicted. Now, predictive analytics are common for banks, insurance, hedge funds, and any business sector where large sums of money are subject to external risks.

As most readers who pay attention to national and state affairs know, the federal government and the political parties don't seem to have a clue as to the costs and benefits of new federal programs such as "Obamacare."

For example, Obamacare will increase patient loads by about 30% but will not increase the numbers of physicians, dentists, or nurses. It is a mathematical certainty that some new patients will not be accepted by physicians, that some specialists will be overbooked, and that elective procedures will have much longer waiting times. The higher costs for some medical procedures have already led to some hospitals to refuse to perform basic procedures such as obstetrics childbirth, because they lose money on every baby. Nobody in either party bothered to calculate such obvious phenomena.

As this book is written, an increasing number of interesting predictive analytic groups are providing increasingly sophisticated services and models to corporate clients. However, government agencies lag the civilian sector in use of predictive analytics by at least 10 years, with the exceptions of military planning and some of the security agencies. The normal civilian agencies are usually wrong and late regarding everything they predict.

Many state and municipal governments are rapidly heading toward bankruptcy under the ever-increasing debt loads due to overly luxurious pension systems (i.e., 3% to 6% cost of living adjustments and free lifetime medical care for retired employees and some relatives). It is simple math to predict that benefits such as these awarded to an increasing population of recipients who are living longer and retiring younger must lead to bankruptcy. There is no other destination.

The elected government is probably not qualified to solve these problems they created due to the fact that politicians pay more attention to lobbyists and special interests than to the actual good of the electorate. Appointed and salaried officials may know about the problems, and some might know solutions, but they lack the power to overrule bad judgments by elected officials.

Given the huge reach of the web, a neutral or benign nonprofit organization could apply predictive analytics to federal, state, and municipal laws and regulations before they are passed. The nonprofit by itself would have no legal standing, but it would use the power of the web to align millions of citizens to force elected leaders toward more rational behavior patterns, such as actually using predictive analytics prior to passing laws that will raise taxes and cause distress to a majority of voters and taxpayers.

It is too bad that such a nonprofit using predictive analytics was not able to tackle the periodic federal flaps on the budget ceiling, on sequester, on Obamacare, and on various entitlement programs. It is too bad that state nonprofits using predictive analytics were not available to tackle pension reforms, out-of-state college fees for illegal aliens, and welfare costs.

Predictive analytics at government levels are reminiscent of the Greek legend of Cassandra. She was given the gift of truthful prophesy combined with the curse of nobody ever believing her.

Wearable Computers

As many readers know, Google has been working on a prototype of a wearable computer called Google Glass. The device looks like an ordinary pair of glasses but contains an embedded computer with lenses that can display information.

This concept has been greeted with both favorable and unfavorable comments. The favorable comments are that the new device can provide useful information such as weather alerts, traffic problems, and emergency messages.

The unfavorable comments are that the views might occlude or interfere with ordinary or peripheral vision and hence cause automobile accidents. In fact, laws and regulations prohibiting Google Glasses from being worn under certain circumstances are already being promulgated. However, not enough empirical evidence is available to know whether the favorable or unfavorable views are the most realistic.

It is premature to judge the device because it is not yet commercially available, but the concept is of both technical and social interest. In thinking about the implications of Google Glasses, it is fairly obvious that computers are now small enough that they can easily be embedded in clothes or worn as glasses. The question is, what benefits might they provide over and above normal computers, pads, and smartphones?

There are many hypothetical features that may or may not be included in Google Glasses but are certainly technically possible. The first and most compelling feature would be the ability to have the glasses monitor the health condition of the person wearing them. Factors such as pulse rate, temperature, blood pressure, and other surface conditions could be monitored in a real-time fashion. With an accelerometer, the computer could also check for accidents such as falls or collisions. In case of a medical emergency, it could automatically summon assistance, which might not be possible if the wearer had a stroke or heart attack and was unconscious.

A second potential use might be improved night vision by light amplification. This is perhaps a bit tricky today but should be feasible by the end of the decade. A potential downside is that most forms of light amplification for night vision are somewhat bulky, but that is perhaps a solvable problem in the future.

A third potential use would be very valuable to those who are hard of hearing. This feature would show closed captions for movies and television shows that do not currently have captions. Also of value for hard-of-hearing users would be to include capabilities such as those provided by Dragon. Naturally speaking, or translating, spoken words into visible text would appear on the glasses.

This instant translation would allow a deaf person to understand verbal information in close to a real-time mode. In fact, computers are fast enough today, and will certainly be faster by the end of this decade, that real-time translation could easily occur. This idea might be opposed by the deaf community, but since it does not actually exist today, that is an unknown factor.

Yet another service for Google Glasses might be synchronization with hearing aids or cochlear implants so that important messages such as storm warnings or evacuation orders arriving via the web could be routed to hearing aids and cochlear implants as well as being displayed, assuming the glasses had Bluetooth or some other short-range connectivity.

Once spoken words are captured, it would also be possible to use an automatic natural language translation program. This would be very useful for international travelers. It is theoretically possible to have a kind of science-fiction capability in which, for example, a conversation between a Japanese speaker and an English speaker would be simultaneously translated into both languages. If both parties were wearing Google Glasses, they might be able to carry on what would be pretty close to a normal conversation. The Google translate application already does this, and coupling it with a verbal tool similar to Dragon would make global travel a great deal more convenient than it is today.

In fact, if the translated conversations could also be routed to hearing aids and cochlear implants, two deaf people who speak totally different languages might be able to converse fairly well.

Somewhat surprisingly, Google Glasses would also be of benefit to blind people if they could include sensors and artificial intelligence routines and could communicate with hearing aids or audible devices. For example, a blind person approaching an intersection could receive a verbal warning that the traffic light was red. It would also be possible that, by turning the head to the left and right, the glasses would provide additional warnings such as "high-speed auto approaching: danger."

Yet another feature for the blind would be the ability to scan text and convert it into spoken words. This might enable a blind person wearing Google Glasses to "read" ordinary books and e-books by merely aiming the glasses at them.

Google Glasses might also be of use to those with physical handicaps such as quadriplegics. If the glasses respond to voice commands, then those who can speak can use them to communicate. There are other future possibilities besides the ones discussed here, but these are all fairly important for those potential users with physical handicaps.

Projected Growth of Software from 2010 to 2019

By the end of this decade, cloud applications and software as a service (SaaS) should top 50% of all new software projects. However, maintenance and enhancements of legacy applications will top 65% of all software projects.

Table 10.2   *Projected U.S. Software Applications from 2010 to 2019*

Application Types	Applications	Percentage
Scientific	240,000	4.36%
Military and defense	900,000	16.36%
Civilian government	600,000	10.91%
Systems and middleware	720,000	13.09%
Embedded software	1,400,000	25.45%
Commercial	250,000	4.55%
Information technology (IT)	545,000	9.91%
U.S. outsource	156,000	2.84%
Offshore outsource	150,000	2.73%
Web applications	505,000	9.18%
Games and entertainment	30,000	0.55%
Open source	4,000	0.07%
Total Applications	**5,500,000**	**100.00%**

Smartphone and tablet applications will probably be more than 70% of all new personal software applications. Table 10.2 shows projected U.S. applications for the decade.

All types of software applications will grow in numbers, but currently web applications and smartphone applications appear to have the fastest growth rates.

Results for 1,000 Function Points Circa 2015

By the end of the decade, the same 1,000 function point project might look like this:

- Source code for 1,000 function points: 26,667 logical code statements

- Programming languages: Objective-C and Go

- Reuse percentage: 0% to 85%

- Methodology: Hybrid (TSP, RUP, Agile)

- Productivity: 12.00 function points per staff month
- Defect potentials: 2.50 defects per function point
- Defect removal efficiency (DRE): 96%
- Delivered defects: 0.10 defects per function point
- Ratio of development personnel to maintenance:
  - Development: 30%
  - Maintenance: 70%

The following are the projected background data for 2015:

- Average language level: 12.00
- Number of programming languages: 4,500
- Logical statements per function point: 26.67
- Average application size: 400 function points
- Average application size: 10,688 logical code statements

Software development in this decade experienced a rapid surge toward Agile development, but other methods such as RUP and TSP also produce good results.

Summary

In this decade, clouds and crowds account for the largest numbers of startup companies. Cloud computing will certainly continue to grow. Crowdfunding and crowd intelligence show promise, but it is hard to determine what issues they handle well and what issues they don't handle well.

Predictive analytics also has a large number of startups, some of which seem to be growing rapidly. This field is synergistic and congruent with big data and intelligent agents. In fact, the sum of the value of these three working together is far greater than if they are used independently.

Specialized social networks are beginning to appear, with musicians and authors being among the first of the specialties. For example, a recent Google search came up with 25 different social networks oriented toward musicians.

An interesting one for authors, named "Predators and Editors," warns against unscrupulous publishers and literary agents. It can be expected that many other kinds will follow.

While Agile has grown faster than other development methods (and water-fall has shrunk faster), hybrid methods are gaining in popularity. Because all of the major methods have some topics that are useful, it is a useful idea to try and select the best from each. Hybrid methodologies that utilize the best features of various methods such as Agile, TSP, and RUP often have results that show synergy, or the combination being slightly better than the originals.

Other future trends will probably see an increase in virtualization and an increase in cloud-related applications and services. SEMAT, a nonprofit organization, is attempting a formal redesign of software engineering. By the end of 2015, some of its new concepts should begin to percolate through software engineering schools.

Chapter 11

Modern Software Problems

Computers and software have brought many new capabilities to the modern world. But they have also brought many new kinds of problems, some of which never existed before in all of human history.

This postlude presents a short history of major software failures from the 1960s through the modern era. Each problem is explained, the lessons learned are discussed, and possible solutions for similar future problems are shown.

Analysis of Major Software Failures

This chapter revisits significant historical software failures. The idea is to analyze each failure and consider what lessons it taught and which forms of defect prevention or defect removal might have prevented the problems. Because the failures in this chapter are famous and information has been published about them, they are a useful set of historical data points for retrospective quality analysis.

The following are many forms of defect prevention and removal methods:

- Acceptance testing

- Automated code static analysis for common languages

- Automated text static analysis for requirements and design

- Beta testing with clients

- Code inspections

- Component testing

- Debugging tools

- Design inspections

- Function testing

- Mathematical test-case design based on design of experiments

- Pair programming

- Peer reviews

- Performance testing

- Proofs of correctness

- Quality function deployment (QFD)

- Regression testing

- Requirements inspections

- Requirements modeling

- Risk-based testing

- Security testing

- Subroutine testing

- Supply-chain testing

- System testing

- Unit testing

- Usability testing

It is an interesting phenomenon that all of the problems discussed in this chapter occurred even after several kinds of testing. A synergistic combination of pre-test inspections, pre-test static analysis, formal mathematical testing, and risk-based testing with certified test personnel could probably have eliminated almost all of the failures discussed here.

Note that the failures and problems discussed here are only the tip of the iceberg. There are thousands of similar problems, and they occur almost every day. Some forms of failure appear to be increasing in frequency and perhaps in severity. For example, automotive recalls due to software problems occur often for every major manufacturer. There are also recalls for many other kinds of equipment with computer controls.

1962: Failure of the Mariner 1 Navigation Software

The Mariner 1 probe for Venus went off course 293 seconds after liftoff. The apparent reason was that a superscript bar was missing in one line of code, which caused excessive deviations in control patterns.

Lessons learned: The primary lesson from this failure is that a single character in a single line of code can cause serious problems with software.

Problem avoidance: The problem might have been found via pair programming, code inspections, requirements modeling, or static analysis. Neither requirements modeling nor static analysis existed in 1962, but in today's world, either method would almost certainly have found such an obvious syntactical error.

Finding the problem via testing should have occurred but obviously did not. A test sequence that included control responses to inputs should have done the job.

1978: Hartford Coliseum Collapse

The Hartford Coliseum was designed using a computer-aided design (CAD) software package. The designer assumed only vertical stress on the support columns. When one column collapsed from the weight of snow, lateral forces were applied to surrounding columns that had not been designed to take lateral stress.

Lessons learned: The lesson from this failure is more about the human mind than about software per se. The assumption of pure vertical compression was faulty, and that was a human error.

Problem avoidance: This problem could have been found via inspections and probably by requirements modeling. The problem is unlikely to have been found via static analysis since it was a problem of logic and design and not of syntax. Because the problem was one of design, pair programming might not have worked. Ideally, having someone on the inspection or modeling team with experience in structures designed for heavy snow might have broadened the assumptions.

Finding the problem by testing should have occurred, but there is a caveat. If the same designer with the faulty assumption wrote the test cases, he or she would not have included tests for lateral stress. A certified professional tester might have found this, but perhaps not. Risk-based testing in today's world might have found the problem.

1983: Soviet Early Warning System

In 1983, the Soviet early warning system falsely identified five incoming missiles that were assumed to have been launched by the United States. Rules of engagement called for a reprisal launch of missiles against the United States, which could have led to World War III.

Fortunately, the Soviet duty officer was an intelligent person, and he reasoned that the United States would never attack with only five missiles, so he concluded it was a false alarm. Apparently, the early warning system was confused by sunlight reflected from clouds.

Lessons learned: The lesson learned from this problem is that complex problems with many facets are hard to embody in software without leaving something out. A second lesson is that bugs in major military applications can have vast unintended consequences that could possibly cause the deaths of millions.

Problem avoidance: This problem might have been found by inspections with experienced military personnel as part of the inspection team. The problem might also have been found by requirements modeling.

It is unlikely that static analysis would have found the problem because it was one of logic and not a problem of syntax. Pair programming probably would not have worked either because the problem originated in requirements and design.

Finding the problem via testing obviously did not occur, and it is uncertain if testing was the best solution. The problem seemed to be that there was insufficient attention paid to false positives.

1986: Therac 25 Radiation Poisoning

Between 1985 and 1987, a number of patients treated with the Therac 25 radiation therapy device received doses much higher than prescribed: some were 100 times larger.

There were two radiation levels with this machine: high power and low power. Older machines by the same company had hardware interlocks that prevented the high-power mode from being turned on by accident. In the Therac 25, the hardware interlocks had been removed and replaced by software interlocks, which failed to operate under some conditions.

Worse, apparently the operating console did not inform operators when high power was in use. There was an error message and the machine stopped, but it only said "malfunction" and did not state what the problem was. Operators could then push a button to continue administering the radiation.

Because of serious injury to patients, the Therac 25 problems were extensively studied by several government agencies. Readers who want a more complete discussion can do a Google search on "Therac 25" to get detailed analyses.

Lessons learned: The lessons learned from this problem are that medical devices that can kill or harm patients need state-of-the-art quality control. The Therac 25 apparently was inept in quality control, and government regulatory agencies did not properly oversee them.

Problem avoidance: The Therac 25 problems could probably have been found by any combination of inspections, static analysis, and risk-based testing. Later investigations by government agencies found laxness in all forms of quality control. Apparently, there were no formal inspections, no static analysis, no risk analysis, and far less rigorous testing than needed. Pair programming would not have worked because the problem spanned the physical operating console and inadequate training of personnel as well as software problems.

1987: Wall Street Crash

On Monday, October 19, 1987, the Dow Jones average dropped 508 points for the greatest 1-day loss in history.

The problems are somewhat murky, but apparently the long-running bull market had been shaken by various Securities and Exchange Commission (SEC) investigations and other reasons for loss of confidence. As live human investors began to sell stocks, programmed trading software that followed patterns began to generate so many sell orders that various stock-trading systems crashed and millions of shares were put up for sale, which deepened the panic.

Lessons learned: The key lessons from this problem are that, in today's world, software controls so many critical financial and government operations that bugs or errors can have vast consequences and cause problems almost instantly.

Problem avoidance: This problem might have been found through thoughtful inspections that included limits analysis. Requirements modeling might also have found the problem.

Static analysis probably would not have found the problem because it was a problem of logic and trends rather than a syntactic issue.

Testing might have found the problem but did not. Some of the modern forms of testing such as risk-based testing might have found this problem.

1990: AT&T Telephone Lines Shutdown

In 1990, a widespread shutdown of AT&T telephone lines lasted for about nine hours and caused major disruption of telephone traffic. Many airline reservations could not be made, and millions of calls, including some emergency calls, could not be connected.

What seemed to have happened is that one of AT&T's 114 switching centers had a minor mechanical problem (not software) and had shut down briefly. When this center came back up, it sent a message generated by software to all of the other centers, which caused all of them to shut down. Apparently, there was a bug in a single line of code that caused the shutdown.

Lessons learned: The lesson from this failure is that large interconnected systems governed by software are intrinsically risky and need elaborate buffers and error-correction protocols.

Problem avoidance: This error could have been caught by either code inspections or static analysis tools. The error appears to be one of syntax rather than one of logic. Requirements modeling would not have found the error, but it might have led to possibly more robust error-checking protocols. Pair programming is uncertain for this problem.

Why this problem was not found by testing, as it should have been, is an interesting question. Messages between switching centers is an obvious topic for testing. Risk-based testing with certified professional testers might have found the problem.

1991: Patriot Missile Target Error

In spite of many successes during the first Gulf War, in 1991, a Patriot missile did not stop an inbound Scud that landed in a U.S. base and killed 28 military personnel and injured 100.

The software error in the Patriot navigation and targeting routines apparently had a rounding error that threw off timing and caused the miss.

Lessons learned: The lesson learned from this problem is that every detail needs to be examined in mission-critical controls.

Problem avoidance: This problem would certainly have been found by code inspections. It might have been avoided by requirements modeling. Pair programming might have found this problem, too, unless the rounding error was introduced using borrowed or reusable code falsely assumed to be correct.

It is uncertain whether static analysis would have found this error because it was not an error of syntax and might have been missed.

Testing should also have found this error but did not. Modern risk-based testing might have identified the problem.

1993: Intel Pentium Chip Division Problem

In 1993, the new Intel Pentium chip was discovered after release to have a bug when dividing with floating point numbers. The error was small, only a fraction of a percent, and it did not actually impact very many users.

However, the error was located in about five million chips already installed and in daily use. Intel's first response was unwise: It wanted users to prove that they needed better accuracy than the chip provided in order to get a replacement. This caused a public relations flap of serious magnitude. Intel relented and provided new chips to anyone who asked for one, assuming the customer had purchased a computer with the erroneous chip.

Lessons learned: There are two lessons from this problem. One is obvious: Be sure that all mathematical operations work as they should prior to release.

The second lesson is that when a vendor makes an error, don't put the burden of proof on the consumer if you value your reputation and want to be considered an ethical company.

Problem avoidance: This problem would have been found by inspections. It is not likely to have been found by static analysis or requirements modeling. Pair programming probably would not have been used, nor would it have found the problem.

Why was the problem not found by testing? A possible reason is combinatorial complexity. A chip with as many circuits, transistors, and features as the Pentium might require close to an infinite number of test cases to find everything.

1993: Denver Airport Delays

As originally planned, the new Denver airport was supposed to have a state-of-the-art luggage-handling system that would be almost fully computerized and directed by software. What actually happened has become a classic story of a major software failure with huge costs and delays.

Overall, the software and hardware problems with the luggage system delayed the opening of the airport by about 16 months and cost about $560 million. This is one of the few software topics that became a feature article in *Scientific American*.

A cut-down version of the original luggage-handling design was finally operational and ran for about five years. However, the costs exceeded the value, and eventually it was replaced by a conventional luggage system.

The problems associated with the Denver airport luggage system are a litany of common problems found with large software applications:

- Optimistic cost and schedule estimates

- Underestimating bugs and defects

- No formal risk analysis

- Excessive and poorly handled requirements changes

- Inadequate quality control, lacking inspections and static analysis

- Poorly designed test cases

- Serious gaps in testing

- Progress reports that concealed major problems

- Failure to have any effective backup plans in place

- Failure to listen to expert advice

The Denver airport luggage system is one of the most widely studied software problems in history. In spite of numerous articles and retroactive reports, it is interesting that similar problems surfaced with luggage handling at Heathrow Terminal 5.

Lessons learned: The primary lessons learned from the airport fiasco are that optimistic estimates, poor quality control, and poor change control will inevitably lead to schedule delays, cost overruns, possible termination of the project, and almost certain litigation.

Problem avoidance: There were so many different forms of problems with the luggage system that no single method could have found them all. A synergistic combination of requirements modeling, pre-test requirements and design inspections, static analysis of text, static analysis of all code, formal testing based on formal test plans, and certified test personnel probably would have reduced the defects to tolerable levels. Pair programming in such a complex architecture that involved both hardware and software would have probably added confusion with little value.

1996: Ariane 5 Rocket Explosion

On its maiden flight in 1996, the Ariane 5 rocket and four onboard satellites being carried for deployment were destroyed at a cost of perhaps $500 million.

The apparent reason for the problem was an attempt to convert velocity data from a 64-bit format to a 16-bit format. There was not enough space and an overflow condition occurred, thus shutting down navigation. The flight lasted just over 36 seconds.

Lessons learned: The lesson from this problem is that all mathematical operations in navigation systems need to be verified before actually launching a vehicle.

Problem avoidance: This problem would certainly have been found by code inspections, perhaps in just a few minutes. It might also have been found by static analysis and also by requirements modeling or pair programming.

The problem was obviously not found by testing, as it should have been. In this case, there were probably poor assumptions on the part of whoever wrote the test scripts and test cases that overflow would not occur.

1998: Mars Climate Orbiter Crash

After successfully journeying for 286 days from Earth to Mars, the climate orbiter fired its rockets in order to shift within an orbit around Mars. The algorithms for these adjustments had been based on imperial units in pounds rather than in metric units in Newtons, as specified in the NASA requirements. This error caused the orbiter to drop about 100 kilometers lower than planned, so it encountered atmospheric problems that caused overheating and system shutdowns that led to the ship crashing onto the surface.

Lessons learned: The key lesson here is that requirements need to be checked and understood to be sure they find their way into the code.

Problem avoidance: If inspections were used, they would have found the problem almost instantly. Both requirements modeling and static analysis might also have found this problem. Pair programming might have, but if the error occurred upstream in design, then pair programming might not have found it.

The reason why this problem was not found by testing may be nothing more than carelessness. Attempting to transmit data from a subroutine using imperial units to another subroutine using metric units is about as obvious a problem as is likely to occur.

1999: Failure of the British Passport System

In 1999, the United Kingdom attempted to deploy a new automated passport system that had not been fully tested when it went operational. The staff using the new system had not been fully trained. Adding to the confusion was a new law that required all travelers under age 16 to have passports. This law caused a huge bubble in new passport applications at the same time that the new system was deployed.

Roughly half a million passports were delayed, sometimes for weeks. This threw off travel plans for many families. In addition, the U.K. passport agency faced millions of pounds of extra costs in the form of overtime and additional personnel, plus some liability payments to travelers whose passports were late.

Lessons learned: The obvious lesson from this problem is never, ever, attempt to go online with a major new system without fully training the staff and fully testing the system jointly with the older system to be sure the new system works. Also, when a new law is passed that adds a huge bubble of new clients, be sure you have the staffing and equipment to handle the situation.

Problem avoidance: The problems with the passport system appear to be a combination of performance issues with the software and logistical problems with the passport agency itself. Putting in a new system without training the personnel in how to use it is a major management error, not a technical problem.

Neither inspections nor static analysis nor requirements modeling would have found the logistical and staffing problems, although no doubt participants in the inspections would have warned management to be careful.

Performance and load testing should have found the performance problems with the new system, but apparently they were either not performed or not performed with realistic workloads.

2000: The Y2K Problem

The famous Y2K problem is a classic example of shortsightedness. When computer hardware was expensive and memory space limited, it seemed like a good idea to store dates in a two-digit format rather than a four-digit format. Thus, the year "1999" would be stored as "99." This compression of dates started in the 1950s and caused no problems for many years.

However, because dates are often sorted in ascending or descending order, a serious problem would occur at the turn of the century. Obviously, the year "2000" in a two-digit form of "00" is a lower mathematical value than "99."

Millions of software applications in every country used the two-digit date format and sometimes used it in new applications as late as 1995 when it was clearly obvious that time was running out.

Starting in about 1995, thousands of programmers began the labor-intensive work of converting two-digit dates into four-digit dates. Fortunately, the web and the internet were in full swing, because they allowed easy communication among Y2K personnel in sharing information and even sharing reusable code for affected applications. The fact that Y2K problems were not as severe as anticipated is due to the communications power of the web.

Y2K was not a pure programming problem. The two-digit date fields started as an explicit customer requirement, often in the face of warnings from software engineers that the dates would cause trouble.

Lessons learned: The lessons from this problem are not yet fully understood, even in 2013. For example in the year 2038, the Unix internal clock will expire, and this will trigger another set of mass updates. Fairly soon, digits will be added to telephone numbers. At some point, digits will be added to social security numbers. Field-length problems are endemic in software, and they always seem to escape notice until just before they actually happen.

Problem avoidance: The Y2K problem could have been found by almost any method, including inspections, static analysis, pair programming, and testing, except that two-digit dates were considered to be valid. For more than 30 years, the two-digit dates were not regarded as erroneous, so nobody wrote test cases to find them.

Starting in about 1995, this situation changed and not only did testing begin to look for short dates, but a number of specialized Y2K tools were built to ferret them out in legacy applications.

Although Y2K itself is now behind us, the problem of not having enough spaces for numeric information is one of the most common problems in the history of software.

2004: Shutdown of Los Angeles Airport (LAX) Air-Traffic Controls

On Tuesday, September 14, 2004, near 5 P.M., the air-traffic controllers at LAX lost voice contact with about 400 in-flight planes. Radar screens also stopped working. A total of about 800 flights were affected and had to be diverted. This was a very serious problem. A backup system failed about one minute after being activated. The system was out of service for around three-and-a-half hours.

The apparent cause of this problem was an internal counter that counts down from about four billion and then needs to be reset. The counter was used to send messages to system components at fixed intervals. Usually, it takes about fifty days to reach zero. Normally, the counter was reset after thirty days, but apparently that did not happen. The servers in use were from Microsoft. Apparently, a scheduled reset was missed by an employee who was not fully trained.

Lessons learned: The obvious lesson is that complex systems that require human intervention to keep running will eventually fail. Several kinds of automated resets could have been designed, or control could have been passed to backup servers with different reset intervals.

Problem avoidance: This was a combination of human error and a questionable design in the servers that required manual resets. QFD might have prevented the problem. Design inspections would certainly have found the problem. Neither pair programming nor static analysis would have identified this because of the mix of humans and software.

2005: Failure to Complete the FBI Trilogy Project

In or about 2000, the FBI started a major effort to improve case files and allow sharing of information. The project was called *Trilogy* and involved both hardware and software components. One of the purposes was to move data from dozens of fragmented file systems into a unified Oracle database. In 2005, the project was terminated with losses estimated at perhaps $170 million. The problems with this FBI system have been widely cited in the literature.

Although not specified, the probable size of the full Trilogy application would have been in the 100,000 function point size range. Failures and delays at this size level are endemic and approach 80%.

For big systems such as this, requirements creep runs about 2% per calendar month during design and coding, and the total development schedules run about five years. Total scope creep can approximate a 35% increase in required functions.

Defect potentials average close to 6.0 per function point combined with cumulative defect removal efficiency levels less than 85%. Make no mistake: These big systems are *very* risky and require state-of-the-art methods to have any chance of success.

Lessons learned: This system's failure is a textbook example of the problems of large monolithic software applications. They have rapidly changing requirements and they need careful architecture and design prior to coding. They also need a full suite of pre-test quality steps before testing even begins.

Problem avoidance: Big systems such as this need formal architecture and design phases combined with a full suite of pre-test inspections of requirements, design, and code. In fact, these systems need most of the methods listed at the start of this chapter: formal inspections, code and text static analysis, mathematical test-case design, and certified test personnel. Pair programming would be cumbersome on applications with 500 or so programmers because of the expense and the training needs. Inspections are a better choice. Proofs of correctness are probably not possible due to the need for thousands of proofs.

2005: Secret Sony Copy Protection Software

In 2005, Sony BMG secretly placed copy protection software on 52 music CDs. Customers who played those CDs on their computers had the protection software installed on their equipment without their knowledge or consent.

The copy protection software used a root kit, interfered with Windows, and created new security vulnerabilities on affected computers, which affected many customers. The copy protection also slowed down computers whether or not they were playing CDs.

When the problem was broadcast on the web, Sony BMG was sued by many indignant customers. Worse, it turned out that Sony had violated the GNU license in creating the copy protection scheme. At first, there was a denial of harm by Sony, but that was quickly proved to be wrong.

Sony's next response was to issue a pseudo-removal tool that made the problems worse and caused new problems. Here, too, the power of the web broadcast the failures of the first attempt and caused more embarrassment to Sony BMG.

Eventually in November 2005, Sony BMG issued a removal tool that seemed to work. The offending CDs with the copy protection were recalled and taken off the market, although some copies were found still available in stores weeks after the nominal recall.

Lessons learned: The lesson from this problem is that unless they are caught, some vendors think they can do anything they want to protect profits.

Problem avoidance: Because Sony deliberately and secretly put the flawed copy protection software into the hands of the public, it was outside of the scope of normal inspections, static analysis, requirements modeling, and every other quality control approach.

The second part of this issue is the fact that the Sony software was buggy and damaged host computers. This could have been found by formal design and code inspections. Neither static analysis nor pair programming would have found the upstream design issues.

What finally eliminated this problem was a combination of skilled software engineers finding out about the problem and using the web to broadcast this information to millions of others. Expertise on the part of sophisticated customers combined with the social pressure of the web caused Sony to withdraw the offending copy protection scheme.

It is interesting that this problem was finally picked up by the attorney generals of New York, Massachusetts, Texas, California, and some other states. The Federal Trade Commission (FTC) was also involved and filed a complaint.

Finally, as a result of class-action lawsuits, Sony paid damages to affected customers. This is not a good way for Sony to do business in a world with sophisticated clients who have instant access to the web.

2006: Airbus A380 Wiring Problem

The Airbus A380 is a giant passenger plane designed to compete with Boeing 747s on long-distance routes. The Airbus was delayed by more than a year due to software problems related to the onboard wiring harness.

Modern aircraft, including the A380, are highly computerized, and most controls and navigation are handled with software assistance. As a result, there are miles of electrical wires and thousands of connectors. The A380 has about 550 kilometers, or 330 miles, of onboard wiring.

The CAD design software for the A380 was a commercial package. The German and Spanish design teams used version 4 of the CAD package, while the British and French design teams used version 5. This caused configuration control problems.

Worse, the design team had the CAD package set up for copper wires, but aluminum wires were used in the wiring harness for the wings. The difference between aluminum and copper caused other problems because the diameter of the wires was not the same, nor was elasticity the same. It is harder to bend aluminum wires than copper wires.

Lessons learned: The primary lesson learned from this problem is that multiple design teams in multiple countries should all use the same versions of CAD packages and any other complex technical tools. A second lesson is that when you use software to model physical equipment such as wire diameters and elasticity, be sure to have the software exactly match the physical components.

Problem avoidance: The differences between copper and aluminum wiring could easily have been found by design and code inspections prior to final approval on the design. They might also have been found by requirements modeling. This is not a kind of problem where code static analysis might have found the problem, but perhaps a text static analysis tool could have identified it before serious harm was done. The damage was done by using the wrong settings on a CAD tool, so pair programming would not have found the issue.

The use of testing for this problem was not really in the mix because the problem manifested itself in physical problems noted during construction of the plane. Basically, the aluminum wires were too big for some holes and too stiff to bend around obstructions.

2010: McAfee Antivirus Bug Shuts Down Computers

In 2010, the well-known McAfee antivirus package had a new update. A bug in this update caused the McAfee software to identify part of the Windows XP operating system as a malicious file, which shut down thousands of computers that were running XP at the time.

This bug was front-page news in my home state of Rhode Island because it caused the suspension of surgical procedures in a number of Rhode Island hospitals. Schedules and contact information for physicians and nurses became unavailable when the computers stopped working.

Lessons learned: The lesson from this problem is to be sure that all releases of software are properly regression-tested prior to release.

Problem avoidance: The bug would certainly have been found by means of code inspections. It might have slipped through static analysis tools because it was a logical error rather than a syntactic error. Requirements modeling might have found the problem, but it was not used.

Clearly, testing should have found the problem but did not. The probable reason is informal test-case design rather than rigorous mathematically based test-case design.

2011: Failed Investment in Studio 38 in Rhode Island

In 2010, the Economic Development Commission (EDC) of the State of Rhode Island agreed to loan $75 million to the Studio 38 game company owned by former Red Sox pitcher Curt Schilling. In return, the company moved to Providence and began operations with about 250 employees.

As is common with software applications in the $75 million cost range, the main product of Studio 38 ran behind schedule. As is also common with startups, Studio 38 itself ran low on funds and fell behind in its payments to the state.

In the absence of fresh capital from film credits, external investors, the state, or other sources, the company missed payrolls, ran out of funds, laid off the entire staff, and then declared bankruptcy.

Looking at the history of what happened prior to the bankruptcy, there was no due diligence or risk analysis by the state prior to the loan. Once the loan was given, there was no effective governance. Both should have been done. It is easy to generate a risk analysis for software packages that cost about $75 million to develop. That is a very risky region with many failures.

Using industry defaults for projects with about 250 people and a development schedule of 42 months, they are almost always late and over budget. There were no contingency plans for this. A retrospective risk analysis that I created after the bankruptcy showed the following:

Risk of cancellation of the project	36.76%
Risk of negative return on investment	46.56%
Risk of schedule delays	49.01%
Risk of cost overruns	41.66%
Risk of unhappy customers	56.37%
Risk of litigation	17.15%
Average of all risks	41.25%
Financial risks	88.22%

These risks are so high that it was folly to invest more than $75 million without seeing a very detailed risk-abatement plan provided by Studio 38. Software startups of this size are among the most risky ventures of the modern era.

Lessons learned: The main lesson from the Studio 38 failure is that governments have no business trying to operate as venture capitalists in an industry where they have no experience or expertise.

Problem avoidance: Large software applications with teams of 250 people routinely run late by six to twelve months. These delays might have been reduced or minimized by better quality control up front, such as inspections and static analysis. Over and above normal delays, this project had no effective backup or contingency plans for how to get additional funds once the initial loan ran out.

Normal venture investments are preceded by a careful due diligence process that examines risks and benefits. Apparently, Rhode Island ignored due diligence and risks and was blinded by potential benefits.

2012: Knight Capital Stock-Trading Software Problems

On Wednesday, August 1, 2012, a software bug in the Knight Capital stock-trading software triggered a massive problem that involved 140 stocks fluctuating wildly. One of the additional problems was that the stock-trading software had no "off switch" and could not easily be shut down.

This is a cautionary tale about how software bugs can potentially damage national and global economies. The problem was almost immediately recognized as a software bug, but in an industry where millions of dollars of stocks change hands every minute, it took more than 30 minutes to stop programmed trading with the software. Apparently, the problem was in a new update installed on the day of the problem, clearly without adequate testing or validation.

Rogue trading software or major bugs in trading software has the theoretical potential of damaging the entire world's financial systems. Knight Capital's own stock declined by about 77% due to this software problem. There may also be future litigation from stock purchasers or companies who feel that they were damaged by the event. The SEC called for a meeting to examine the problem.

Lessons learned: The major lesson from the Knight Capital software bug is that financial software in the United States needs much stronger governance than it gets today. Financial applications should have, but do not have, the same kinds of certification that is required of medical applications by the FDA and avionics applications by the FAA. In these fields, bugs or errors can cause enormous and totally unpredictable damages. In the case of medical and avionics software, deaths can occur. In the case of financial software, national or even global malfunctions of the economy might occur.

Problem avoidance: In thinking about the Knight Capital software problems, formal inspections and requirements modeling are the two methods with the highest probability of finding the problems. Static analysis would probably have missed it since the issue was a logical omission rather than a syntactic problem. Pair programming might not have worked because the problem seems to have originated upstream in requirements and design.

Deeper analysis is needed to find out why testing did not identify the problem, but the obvious reasons are casual test-case design, lack of risk-based testing, and probably testing by amateurs instead of certified test personnel.

2012: Automotive Safety Recalls Due to Software

The original intent of this discussion was to show the specific software recalls for a single automobile line such as Toyota. However, the web has so many stories of software recalls involving so many automobiles that it is becoming an automotive industry scandal. Software now controls fuel injection, brakes, automobile engines, navigation packages, and other systems. Any or all of these software-controlled features can malfunction.

Within the past few years, numerous recalls for software bugs have occurred in automobiles by Cadillac, Ford, General Motors, Honda, Jaguar, Lexus, Nissan, Pontiac, Toyota, and others. Some of these involve the same components, but others are unique. Here are a few samples of very troubling automotive recalls:

- Buick recalled the LaCrosse in 2005 due to software controlling brakes. A separate recall for the same model was due to software handling climate control, which could affect visibility.

- Cadillac recalled the SRX in 2011 due to a software problem with air bags.

- Daimler recalled delivery trucks in 2011 due to a software problem that caused the outside turn and indicator lights to stop working after perhaps 10 minutes of operation.

- Ford recalled several 2011 truck models due to software problems with an integrated diagnostic system (IDS) module.

- Honda CR-Z hybrids were recalled in 2011 because the electric motor could reverse itself and turn in the opposite direction from the transmission.

- Jaguar recalled some of its diesel models made between 2006 and 2010 because a software bug prevented cruise control from being turned off. The engine had to be stopped to turn off the cruise control.

- Four-cylinder Accords were recalled in 2011 due to software problems controlling their automatic transmissions.

- Nissan recalled some of the electric Leaf models in 2010 due to software problems with air conditioning.

- Toyota Prius models between 2004 and 2005 were recalled due to a software problem that caused the gas engines to stall. The electric motor could be used to pull off the highway or go short distances. In states with "lemon laws," some owners were entitled to replacement vehicles.

- Toyota Priuses and some Lexus hybrids were recalled in 2010 due to a software problem that caused a delay between pressing the brake pedal and the brakes actually working.

  (Steve Wozniak, the Apple cofounder, owned a Prius and asserted that the dangerous acceleration problem was due to software rather than a mechanical problem. Toyota disputed the claim, but probably Steve Wozniak knows more about software than most people.)

- Volvo recalled a number of 2012 S60 sedans due to software problems with the fuel pumps.

Lessons learned: Automobiles are now sophisticated devices with a number of onboard computers and many systems either directly controlled by software or assisted by software. Therefore, automobile manufacturers should adopt a full suite of modern defect prevention and defect removal steps.

Problem avoidance: Because so many automotive features and controls are now affected by software, many software quality control methods are needed. These include QFD, pre-test requirements, design and code inspections, static analysis of text, and static analysis of code. Testing should be formal with mathematically designed test cases, and it should be performed by certified test personnel.

Over the past ten years, about ten million automobiles have been recalled due to software-related problems. One warranty company reported that about 27% of repairs are related to computer and software malfunctions. More analysis and better data across all automobile manufacturers are needed.

Summary

In the modern world, computers and software are the critical operating components of aircraft, medical devices, the stock market, banking, business, and government. Since software controls so many critical activities, it should be obvious that quality control is a key topic that needs to be fully understood, and companies need to use state-of-the-art methods.

But in the problems shown here and the thousands of similar problems that occur with other systems, quality control is often primitive and inept. The executives of the companies that produce bad software need to realize that quality problems are serious enough that litigation and damages can possibly cause bankruptcy, even for major corporations.

A simplistic reliance on testing and a failure to perform pre-test inspections or use static analysis is not an adequate response and does not lead to effective quality control. The industry needs to deploy a full suite of synergistic quality methods that include pre-test inspections; pre-test static analysis of text and code; and formal, mathematically based testing by certified test personnel. Anything less for mission-critical software applications can lead to the same kinds of problems discussed in this chapter.

Chapter 12

A Brief History of Cybercrime and Cyberwarfare

Because security problems are now endemic and in fact seem to be getting worse instead of better, this chapter includes a discussion of all known forms of software security problems through 2013, including, but not limited to, botnets, denial of service attacks, identify thefts, and far too many more.

Cybercrime is a "new" form of criminal activity that did not really exist prior to the development of the internet in the 1990s. There were older forms of hacking, such as using tones to gain access to long-distance telephone lines, but these did not actually steal valuable property.

In the modern world, criminals can steal financial data, drain funds from bank accounts, steal social security numbers and other forms of identity, shut down computers, and even cause physical damage to manufacturing equipment.

Cybercrime has moved from being committed by clever amateurs to being the focus of organized crime groups. Even worse, cyberwarfare has been integrated into the armed forces of every industrialized nation. All of the armed services now have cyberwarfare units that attempt to steal information and interfere with military equipment and command and control structures. The world is far more dangerous today than it was before computers and the internet existed.

A New Form of Crime

New technical devices are always targets for both amateur hackers and professional criminals. Many are also targets for national governments.

Long before computers, other kinds of technical devices were attacked. For example, in 1903, during a live demonstration of a supposedly secure wireless radio transmission developed by Marconi, a hacker interfered by sending his own Morse code message to the audience.

Later in the 1960s and '70s, telephone hackers found that various audio tones could be manipulated to gain access to telephone lines and make free calls. These hackers were called *phone phreakers* and they used a battery-powered *blue box* to aid in penetrating phone systems. Steve Wozniak, later to become famous as an Apple cofounder, built one of these blue boxes in 1972 while he was a student at Stanford.

After monitoring and tracing millions of calls, eventually AT&T brought charges against about 200 of these phone phreakers, who were convicted. These convictions put a damper on phone phreaking by amateurs because the consequences were severe and apprehension was probable.

Attacking computers and software was not feasible in the early days of the computer industry because each computer was physically isolated and only a select few programmers and engineers could access them. Later, when remote connections to computers via modems entered the picture, it was possible for hackers to gain access to computers and software from a safe distance.

Data communications between remote computers became possible in about 1968 due to the development of modems and multiplexors. This led to the ARPANET in 1969, which connected the University of California in Los Angeles to the Stanford Research Institute (SRI) in Menlo Park.

Internal computer networks began to appear in the mid-1970s. A technical set of standards that allowed internetwork communication paved the way for the internet. This standard was called the *transmission control protocol* (TCP) and the related *internet protocol* (IP). These were published under the abbreviation TCP/IP in 1974.

Other countries had also developed network capabilities, but many used different protocols. It was not until about 1989 that networks from Europe, Asia, South America, Africa, and the United States were able to share information. The global network later evolved into the modern internet. Networking, like personal computers, was to be a significant factor in cybercrime and cyberwarfare.

The Hacker Invasion

There are several points of historical interest that kicked off the arrival of the computer hacker.

In 1982, a group of hackers broke into 60 computer systems. *Newsweek* had a cover story about this and popularized the word "hacker." This attack led to the first congressional hearings on computer security and also to new laws against cybercrime.

In 1983, a University of Southern California graduate student named Fred Cohen first used the phrase "computer virus." This was the first scholarly paper on computer software attacks, and it would become an important milestone in later antivirus defenses. His paper was titled "Computer Virus: Theory and Experiment."

Note

As is often the case, science fiction predated real science. The concept of a computer virus was published in 1969 in a story by David Gerrold in *Galaxy Magazine*. And in 1984, the term *cyberspace* was introduced in William Gibson's science-fiction novel *Neuromancer*.

It is of sociological interest that hackers soon began to coalesce into organized groups that shared data and information. These groups started to appear in the early 1980s. In fact, hackers soon created a national magazine and began to hold conferences such as the famous Black Hat conference. This alarming social phenomenon led to a significant advance in virus and threat technologies, including polymorphic viruses, worms, botnets, and many others discussed later in this chapter.

As hacking became popular, several forms of hacking were defined by using hat colors to indicate different levels of ethics and criminality.

- A *white hat* hacker is one who hacks for benign purposes such as informing companies of security vulnerabilities. Many white hat hackers assist law enforcement groups.

- A *black hat* hacker is one who hacks for malicious purposes such as identity theft or disrupting computer and network operations. Many black hat hacks are criminal offenses in most countries, and law enforcement groups attempt to identify this class and arrest those who have committed serious criminal acts.

- A *gray hat* hacker is one who combines ethical and nonethical behavior. For example, a gray hat hacker might penetrate a security flaw in a corporate system. Instead of doing damage, the gray hat hacker might ask for money to tell the security officials of the company exactly what the security flaw is and how it can be fixed. This is not illegal but not ethical either.

- A *blue hat* hacker is usually an employee of a software or computer company who uses hacking skills to help test new software prior to release. This term is used within Microsoft, for example.

During the 1980s and '90s, hackers and cybercriminals seemed to be better organized and have access to more current data than those charged with defending networks from attack.

Note

In the late 1980s, I did an informal survey of books and journal articles on hacking and on defenses against hacking. The number of pages of hacking material outnumbered the number of pages of defensive materials by more than seven to one.

Preparing Defenses

As a result of widely reported attacks on computers and software, defensive antivirus programs began to enter the commercial market. There are many of these today, but Table 12.1 shows some of the earlier ones.

There are other antivirus and antimalware products besides the ones shown in the table. Readers are urged to seek out reviews of antivirus products and acquire one, then keep it updated with the latest threat information.

In 1988, the Defense Advanced Research Projects Agency (DARPA) created a cybercrime response unit. This unit is called the *Computer Emergency Readiness Team* (CERT), and it operates with the Software Engineering Institute (SEI) on the campus of Carnegie Mellon University in Pittsburgh, Pennsylvania. CERT carries out a number of research programs in cybersecurity.

Table 12.1   *Arrival of the Antivirus Subindustry*

Company	Year
AVAST	1996
AVG	1992
Avira	1988
BitDefender	2001
Kaspersky	1993
McAfee	1987
Microsoft AntiVirus	1993
Norton AntiVirus	1990
PANDA	1990
TrendMicro	1988
Webroot Spy Sweeper	2002

Early hacking and attacks during the 1980s were, for the most part, carried out by amateurs and often by teenage hackers. In the 1990s, hacking and cybercrime began to take a more serious turn.

The first cause of the increase in the sophistication of cybercrime is because the items that might be stolen greatly increased in value and quantity. By the end of the 1990s, huge corporate databases contained credit card data; social security numbers; banking information; real estate ownership data; criminal records; military records; voter names and addresses; medical records; and purchase information about autos, appliances, and thousands of other things.

Not only were valuable data stored on computers and in databases, but the defenses against theft of these data ranged from rudimentary to only fairly effective in the 1990s. As shown in Table 12.1, antivirus packages were fairly late arrivals. Another defense mechanism, also a late arrival, was that of computer firewalls to filter out attacks.

Digital Equipment Corporation (DEC) wrote the first technical paper on firewalls in 1988. Other work was done by Bell Labs circa 1990. Probably the first commercial firewall product was released in 1995 and was called Gauntlet.

In the late 1980s and early '90s, software defenders began to organize. For example, the well-known SANS Institute was founded in 1989 to provide security training and certification.

Other groups formed to study security in a variety of contexts. Many were associated with universities such as Stanford, MIT, the Imperial College in London, and most other large schools with computer science curricula.

Major computer companies such as IBM, Apple, and Hewlett-Packard formed internal corporate security research labs, as did large software companies such as Microsoft, Google, and Computer Associates.

There were also many government security groups within existing organizations such as the Secret Service, the FBI, the National Security Agency, the CIA, the Department of Defense, and the uniformed services. Later, Homeland Security would play a major role in cybersecurity.

The larger antivirus companies such as Symantec and Kaspersky and BitDefender found that they needed full-time research groups to keep current on threats, so this provided another form of cybercrime research.

In 2008, Congressmen James Langevin (a Democrat from Rhode Island) and Congressman Mike McCaul (a Republican from Texas) formed the Congressional Cyber Caucus. This group collects data on cybersecurity for both congressional use and public use.

Congress has thus far failed to pass enabling legislation on cybersecurity such as the bill put forth by Senator Joe Lieberman (an Independent from

Connecticut) and Senator Susan Collins (a Republican from Maine). This bill failed to pass on November 14, 2012, by a vote of 51 to 47. The name of the bill was the Lieberman Collins Cyber Security Bill.

This failure by Congress to take effective action on cybersecurity is yet another sign that Congress has become inept at dealing with cybercrime. With cybersecurity, congressional failure is often worse than ineffective: It is actually harmful to the U.S. infrastructure.

Although cooperation and coordination among these disparate groups were suboptimal, at least computer and software security was getting serious attention by competent research teams.

Increasing Seriousness of Cyberattacks

The existence of valuable commodities such as credit card numbers that could be sold or used naturally attracted criminals that had computer skills, which by the late 1990s was very common.

Compared to stealing physical objects such as money, stocks, jewelry, or electronics, the theft of computer records has some distinct advantages. First, the stolen materials have no physical presence and can be removed at almost the speed of light and relocated to any other computer in the world in any country.

Unlike the theft of physical objects, theft of data does not necessarily remove the stolen material; it only makes a copy. This makes tracking of stolen objects difficult because they usually are still in place, but a copy has been made.

Computer theft is also fairly hard to track, and even when specific computers are identified that took part in the theft, there is no easy way of knowing who actually used them to commit a crime.

Apprehending a clever and skilled hacking group is not impossible, but the rate of apprehension is probably well below the apprehension rate of armed robberies. Even so, monthly arrests for cybercrime currently top 500 per month in industrialized countries.

A second factor leading to an increase in computer crime is the attention paid to computers and the internet by political activists. The term *hactivism* was coined in 1996 by a member of a computer hacker's group. Political hacking often takes the form of denial of service attacks against offending companies or political organizations.

However, political hacking is also involved in the theft of secret and proprietary information. The political groups Anonymous and WikiLeaks, for example, are frequently cited in news stories about theft of government and military data. WikiLeaks became notorious for releasing classified emails and military information.

A third factor was the dissolution of the Soviet Union on December 26, 1991. The fragmentation and reduction of former Soviet security organizations would soon lead to an alarming increase on crime throughout the former 15 republics of the Soviet Union. In time, the Russian Mafia would become a feared international crime organization.

From the standpoint of computer crimes and hacking, a significant number of former KGB and state security officers were left without jobs, or at least without jobs that paid well. Some of these began to use their skills for hacking, and others became connected with organized criminal groups in Russia, Ukraine, and the other former Soviet bloc countries.

A fourth and perhaps the most important factor was the awareness by national governments of the importance of computers for national defense. A hundred years ago, wars took place on land, sea, and air. Starting in the 1960s, wars could occur on land, by sea, in air, and in space. Today, wars can occur on land; by sea; and in the air, space, and cyberspace.

All major industrial countries have large and growing cyberwarfare units that are staffed and operational: China, Cuba, France, Germany, India, Iran, Israel, Japan, North Korea, Pakistan, Russia, the United Kingdom, and the United States probably have, in total, more than half a million cybersoldiers and cyberofficers deployed, and these groups are growing faster than conventional armies, navies, and air forces.

Although these countries are not presently in armed conflicts with one another, attempted sabotage and theft of secret data probably occur on a daily basis. Cyberwarfare does not yet have effective treaties or any way of monitoring attacks that is 100% effective.

In recent congressional testimony, the Chief Security Officer of Oracle, Mary Ann Davidson, put forth the suggestion that the Monroe Doctrine should be modernized to include cyberattacks on computers in the Americas as hostile actions that the U.S. government would regard as belligerent.

In fact, truly successful attacks may not be recognized by the country receiving the attacks for months, if at all. This kind of warfare is new and plays by different rules from wars fought with conventional weapons.

When a country explodes an atomic bomb or launches a new missile or satellite, everybody knows about it the same day. When a country attacks computer systems in another country, a major part of the attack strategy is to keep the attack secret so that no one knows about it.

The antivirus company Symantec publishes lists that show where hacking attacks originate that have U.S. targets. The top, according to this list, are the following:

- United States

- China

- Brazil

- Germany

- India

- United Kingdom

- Russia

- Poland

- Italy

- Spain

Computer usage is now global, and computer crime is a phenomenon that requires global cooperation on the part of cyberdefenders.

Technically, cybercrime and cyberwarfare are about the same, but cybercrime is carried out by individuals or criminal groups, while cyberwarfare is carried out by military personnel, government organizations, and their civilian contractors under the command of senior officers or senior government officials. Both cyberattacks and cyberwarfare present increasingly serious threats to individuals, companies, governments, and military services.

A Growing Number of Victims

To show readers samples of how prominent cybercrime has become in the modern era, readers are referred to an interesting article by Taylor Amerding published on February 15, 2012, on the CSO Online website. The title is "The 15 Worst Data Security Breaches of the 21st Century." A few of his samples are discussed below, together with other noteworthy attacks:

- In March 2008, about 134 million credit card numbers were stolen from Heartland Payment Systems. The attack used a Software Query Language

(SQL) injection. A man named Albert Gonzalez was indicted along with two unnamed Russians. He was convicted and sentenced to 20 years in federal prison.

- In December 2006, hackers penetrated the network of TJX Companies (which owns the chain of Marshall stores). Data on about 94 million credit cards were stolen. At the time, the TJX internal network had no firewall. It is possible that the theft occurred from in-store kiosks used to apply for jobs.

- In March 2011, the email service company Epsilon was breached, and millions of email addresses and customer addresses were apparently stolen. Epsilon has more than 2,000 major companies as clients and handles perhaps 40 billion emails per year. The stolen information could be used for phishing attacks.

- In March 2011, a security company, RSA Security, was breached and had perhaps 40 million records stolen. This might have been done by a foreign government. When security companies like RSA are hacked, imagine how easy it is to hack less sophisticated companies.

- In May 2006, the Department of Veterans Administration was hacked and about 27 million records were stolen, including social security numbers, names, addresses, dates of birth, and other personal data. The data were not encrypted. This theft was triggered by the physical theft of an employee's notebook computer, which was stolen in a burglary. It is curious that the employee reported the theft to the police at once on May 3, but the Veterans Affairs Chief did not find out until May 16 and the FBI was not brought in until May 22. Eventually, most of the data were returned, but the hackers were not apprehended.

- On April 20, 2011, Sony was hacked and about 77 million PlayStation accounts were stolen. About 12 million unencrypted credit cards were part of the stolen data. Home addresses and email addresses were also stolen.

- In 2007, all internet service in the country of Estonia was shut down for two weeks. This included services to government sites, banks, newspapers, television, radio, hospitals, businesses, schools, and everything else. This attack was orchestrated from Russia and was apparently triggered by the removal of a statue of a Russian soldier from Tallinn on April 27, 2007. Sophisticated hackers sent out messages asking for help in a denial of service attack, complete with instructions. These messages stirred up hundreds of "script kiddies," or novice hackers. May 9, the anniversary celebrated in Russia as the end of the war against Germany, would be the date of the attack. The basic message for the world is that the internet is the fastest and most powerful tool for social action in human history.

- In July 2011, a South Korean company called ESTSoft was hacked and lost about 35 million records, which made up more than half of the total South Korean population. Apparently, this theft was by hackers in China because Chinese IP addresses were identified. The stolen data included names, addresses, phone numbers, user identifications for software, and passwords.

- In mid-2009, Google and other companies in California were hacked, apparently by the Chinese government. This attack exploited a weakness in Internet Explorer. The purpose of the attack was not clear but might possibly have been to identify Chinese subscribers who might oppose the government.

- In 2010, the VeriSign security company was hacked. It is bad news when a security company is penetrated. In this case, the news is even worse. VeriSign did not announce the theft or even notify anyone until 2011 when the Securities and Exchange Commission (SEC) mandated notification of security breaches. VeriSign has not yet disclosed what was stolen. Because VeriSign is the registry for .com and .net internet names, unknown theft of data is troubling. Part of the VeriSign business was acquired by Symantec in 2010, making it even more difficult to determine what was stolen.

- In August 2006, American Online (AOL) accidentally exposed records of 650,000 customers on one of its own websites. These data were intended for internal research purposes but were publicly posted by mistake. AOL removed the data after one day, but by then the news had spread all over the internet. The AOL Chief Technology Officer resigned due to this mishap.

- In June 2010, a new kind of attack occurred that was called the Stuxnet worm. Although Stuxnet was spread by Microsoft Windows, it targeted specialized Siemens industrial control computers. It happens that the Iranian government uses embargoed Siemens computers in its nuclear program for uranium enrichment. Although Stuxnet hit a number of computers in Europe, about 60% of the known attacks were in Iran. The creators of Stuxnet have not been identified but are probably countries at odds with Iran, which includes Israel and the United States, among others.

- In May 2012, another new kind of cyberattack hit the Middle East with Iran again being the main target. Syria, Lebanon, and the Sudan were also hit. This new attack was called *Flame*, and it is an alarming harbinger of attacks to come. Flame does not just go after a few things such as email addresses and personal information. Flame enters a computer as a Trojan horse and, once there, it seeks out and steals data, Skype conversations, photographs, and audio recordings. It also causes connected digital cameras to take pictures, which are also stolen, as are screenshots from running software. The stolen data are routed back to the source, which has not been identified. Given the sophistication of Flame, it is hypothesized that it could only have come from China, Israel, Russia, or the United States.

An alarming news article in the *Providence Journal* on December 1, 2012, stated that the former manager of the Social Security Office in Warwick, Rhode Island, was arrested and is being tried for identity theft. He tapped into social security files, possibly from his own office. He then used the data to create a stolen identity and a joint bank account. About $160,000 from the identity theft victim was siphoned into his account. This is an indictment and not a conviction, but even so, it paints an alarming picture.

Between federal, state, and municipal employees in various tax agencies and social agencies, almost a million government workers in the United States have access to everything needed to steal our identities and apply for credit cards or set up new bank accounts. It is clear that much stronger vetting of government employees is needed in the computer era. For that matter, internal monitoring and encryption of government files should be much stronger than it is.

An article discussing an unusual conflict was published by the INFOSEC Institute on March 21, 2012. According to the report, a member of the hacker group Anonymous was kidnapped in Mexico by a drug cartel called Las Zetas in October 2011. Anonymous published a threat on the web that it would begin to hack into the bank accounts of the cartel itself and of cartel leaders unless the victim was released. Anonymous also threatened to release cartel member names and also the names of police and government officials who cooperated with the cartel. Making these names public would not only lead to arrests but also provide clear targets for rival cartels.

The victim was released but had a note from the cartel saying that it would kill ten people for every name that Anonymous released. This dispute between cybercriminals and a drug cartel is an alarming indication that two of the largest forms of crime in the modern world may be nearing a conflict that could harm innocent civilians and cause collateral damages.

As can be seen from these examples of large-scale data thefts and hacking into major companies, software is both a critical asset and a critical liability to personal and corporate privacy.

The short list shown here of major attacks on corporations indicates that more than 200 million U.S. citizens have had some of their personal data stolen: credit cards, social security numbers, birth dates, email addresses, and so on. Many of these thefts are probably due to either organized criminal groups or hostile foreign governments. Make no mistake: Cybercrime and cyberwarfare are going to get worse before they get better.

To show the magnitude of cybercrime, a Google search on "arrests for cybercrime" in November 2012 found that in recent months, the Philippines had arrested 357 people; China had arrested more than 10,000 people; an FBI sting operation with a website that seemed to buy and sell stolen credit card and identity data arrested 26 people; another FBI arrest was for 12 people charged with stealing a million dollars from Citibank; Bangladesh arrested 12 people; Turkey is trying ten members of the RedHack group; and even Russia arrested eight people.

The important aspect of these arrests is that no matter in which country the arrests were made, the crimes themselves spanned the globe and many of the targets were U.S. companies and banks. Cybercrime is the first known criminal activity in history where the perpetrator and the victim can be 12,000 miles apart at the time the crime is committed.

Types of Cyberattacks

As cybercrime and cyberwarfare increase in frequency and severity, they are also morphing into an alarming number of different kinds of attacks. Almost every week, some new form of cyberattack is reported in newspapers and on technical websites. The following list shows the major forms of cyberattacks:

- Bluetooth hijacking
- Botnets
- Browser hijackers
- Computer voting fraud
- Cyberwarfare against civilian targets

- Data theft from corporations
- Data theft from unsecured networks
- Denial of service attacks
- Email address harvesting
- Electromagnetic pulses
- Identity thefts
- Keyboard trackers
- Macro viruses in Word and Excel documents
- Malware
- Pharming
- Phishing
- Root kits
- Skimming
- Smart-card hijacking
- Spam
- SQL injections
- Trojans
- Viruses
- Worms
- Zero-day security attacks

The following sections discuss these various security threats. These discussions are representative but not complete. Other forms of cyberthreats exist today, and new forms of cyberthreats seem to occur almost every month.

Bluetooth Hijacking

Bluetooth hijacking affects not only computers but also smartphones and tablets that have Bluetooth capabilities. This is a fairly short-range form of attack where the attacker and victim need to be within about ten feet of each other.

Once an attacker establishes a connection with a victim's device, it is possible to steal personal information, images and pictures, and perhaps banking information and other private data.

Botnets

The term "bot" is derived from the last half of the word "robot." In the context of cybercrime, a *bot* is a computer that has been seized and is under the control of a malicious software routine that arrived from the web or from an external source such as a disk or thumb drive. Botnets are illegal in the United States and most other countries. Government-sponsored botnets are another story.

The problem is bigger than just seizing one computer. The malicious software is self-propagating and can infect and seize dozens or even hundreds or thousands of individual computers. When these captive computers operate in concert, this is called a *botnet*.

The main use of a botnet is to direct concentrated attacks at websites or the computers of companies and government agencies with the idea that millions of incoming messages will swamp their defenses and either shut them down, slow them down, or prevent their normal work from taking place. This is called a *denial of service attack*.

The botnet can be controlled by a *bot herder* or *bot master*. The individual enslaved computers are sometimes called *zombie computers*. Although botnets are often used for denial of service attacks, they have other purposes. For example, they can be used to send out millions of spam messages or ads or anything else. Sometimes bot masters rent their bots to other individuals or cybercriminals who add different kinds of payloads.

Once infected, the individual bot computers may need to be repaired. Some forms of firewalls and network-based intrusion detection systems (NIDS) can stop bot attacks. Microsoft Windows is a popular target for botnet attacks. Some antivirus software packages can prevent them, but there is a constant race between attackers and defenders.

The origin of botnets is ambiguous, but they were found in 2004 and possibly before. Some of the more famous botnet attacks are named for the offending software: Conficker and Mariposa in 2008; Zeus in 2010; Bagle in 2004.

In total, there have probably been several hundred specific malicious bot software packages created, and the total number of computers impacted appears to be hundreds of millions.

As an example of the damages done by botnets, consider the Conficker attacks in 2008 and 2009:

- In January 2009, a French naval network was invaded and a number of aircraft were grounded for several days.

- Soon after, the British Ministry of Defense reported a Conficker attack that affected several ships and also grounded aircraft for several days.

- The British city of Sheffield reported a Conficker attack against hospitals and government installations that affected about 800 computers.

- The British city of Manchester reported a Conficker attack, possibly caused by the use of a thumb drive, on government computers in February 2009.

- In March 2009, computers used by the House of Commons in the British Parliament were affected by Conficker.

As can be seen from the significance of the victims, this was a very sophisticated attack with substantial self-defense mechanisms to prevent removal. The Conficker package was able to invade computer networks with serious professional firewalls and protection. Five variants of the Conficker botnet software package were identified and called Conficker A, B, C, D, and E. Later, other variants were found.

In February 2009, Microsoft formed an international working group with a dozen or more organizations to help prevent Conficker attacks and speed up the removal and cure for infected computers.

At least one of the variants was traced to Ukraine. The origins of other variants are either ambiguous or not yet published. Botnets pose a serious ongoing threat to home computers, corporate computers, government computers, and military computers.

It is apparent that much greater use of encryption for confidential government data is likely to occur in the future. This may also be true for proprietary corporate data such as client addresses, credit card numbers, and social security numbers.

Browser Hijacking

Browser hijackers are annoying and are semilegal malware packages that divert web browsers from their intended destinations and force them to alternate destinations. All of the well-known browsers, such as Bing, Chrome, Firefox, Internet

Explorer, and others, are affected. Some of the current browser hijackers include Abnow, CoolWebSearch, MySearch, search.conduit, and search-daily.

As with other forms of malware, browser hijackers attempt to make their package resistant to removal by antivirus and antispyware tools. If you have a computer that is infected by one or more browser hijackers, you need to do a search for effective solutions by contacting your antivirus or antispyware vendors.

The main purpose of browser hijackers is to divert web searches to alternate sites that have ads, pornography, or some other topic different from the one the user wanted. A common form of browser hijacking starts with some kind of message such as "WARNING YOUR COMPUTER IS INFECTED . . . ." If you click on this, your browser is diverted to a company that wants money to fix your computer, and it will not remove the browser hijacker unless paid.

Some browser hijackers rent their tools to others who supply their own destination websites. Sometimes browser hijackers are included in commercial software on disks or downloaded. The agreements that users have to check when installing such software may list specific spyware or browser hijackers.

Because some web advertising pays based on the number of hits that reach a specific website, a very common reason for browser hijacking is to artificially force hits to a specific website so that the advertiser has to pay higher fees.

Browser hijacking is not necessarily illegal. If it is used without the knowledge and consent of a computer user, it is probably illegal. If it is included in a license and the user agrees to it, then it is probably not illegal. Because most users don't read the full text of these licenses, vendors can stuff in alarming amounts of harmful clauses, including permission to download browser hijacking tools.

Browser hijacking often shows up in court. A common claim by people who are charged with downloading illegal pornography is that it was the result of browser hijacking. These cases are complex and difficult to prove one way or the other. However, the courts do not seem to accept this line of defense very often.

Computer Voting Fraud

For much of American history, votes were cast anonymously on pieces of paper and counted by hand by officials appointed by community election commissions. Close elections or possible errors could be recounted, also by hand. The whole process of counting was under scrutiny.

There were, of course, opportunities to change the paper ballot results illegally, such as by forging absentee ballots, by bribing voters, or by registering dead people. However, since all of these things left paper trails, investigation was possible.

Starting in about 1974, paper ballots were gradually phased out in favor of electronic ballots. Sometimes paper ballots with holes or special ink were used as the inputs, but the tabulations were done by computer. The paper documents provided backup paper trails if needed.

Later versions of computerized voting did away with paper inputs and used touchscreens or electronic pens for voting. When this happened, there was no longer an objective way to recount votes or correct errors.

Sometimes the software used to tabulate votes is treated as proprietary trade secrets by the voting machine manufacturers. In this case, the algorithms are not revealed to even the election committees in the communities using the machines.

Voting machines are not the only sources of possible election fraud. Every ten years, states are required to redistrict, and this is now handled by software. Quite often, the proposed new districts are overturned by judges or by complaints that they have bias for or against candidates, usually in favor of incumbents.

Instead of using free federal software, as did most states, Rhode Island paid about $600,000 for a custom redistricting package, apparently in order to gerrymander. The state had to redraw the districts several times due to visible biases, and it barely made the required submission date.

More recently in elections held in 2012, several candidates for the Rhode Island General Assembly were accused of inflating their popularity by using ghost respondents to visit their Facebook and Twitter accounts. In other words, either software or people were creating visits to Facebook and Twitter that never happened.

There are numerous published instances of voting machine errors, but whether these are unique or part of a more widespread pattern is difficult to ascertain because of the lack of any paper trail or backup counting methodology.

Software and voting machines are "validated" by state governments prior to acquiring the equipment. However, problems still occur even after validation, which shows that for voting machines, as with other kinds of software, testing has a fairly low level of defect removal efficiency.

The few sample errors from history listed below illustrate that electronic voting needs independent and objective quality analysis from neutral parties such as universities or bipartisan watchdog groups. The software itself should be subject to analysis by experts and also to the use of tools such as static analysis tools that might find errors that escaped the developers.

- In 1992 in Yamhill County, Oregon, computer votes for the district attorney had to be reversed. The computer software assumed the candidates were in alphabetical order, and it awarded the election to the wrong candidate.

- In 1993, published voting results in St. Petersburg, Florida, reported 1,492 votes cast in precinct 194, which had no registered voters for that election. As it happens, the election was decided by 1,495 votes.

- The journal *Governing* (Governing.com) reported that in Broward County, Florida, in 2004, voting machines by Electronic Systems and Software had a maximum limit of 32,000 votes, after which the machines began to count backward.

- In 2005, a hacker from Finland successfully penetrated voting machines in Leon County, Florida, just to prove that it was easy to do. He apparently did not try to modify results but only alerted officials to the fact that almost any hacker could do the same.

- In 2008, Ohio found that voting machines manufactured by Premier (reported in the *Washington Post* and *USA Today*) dropped votes when data from memory cards were transferred to the central tally point. At first, the problem was denied, then blamed on an antivirus package, and finally acknowledged to be a software error. The same machines were used in 34 states and the error apparently had persisted for ten years. Larger precincts were losing several hundred votes.

- In the 2010 elections, the Republican Party in North Carolina filed suit against the State Election Commission, charging that when voters attempted to select the Republican Party, the direct recording electronic voting machines overrode the choice and selected the Democratic Party.

The Common Cause website (www.commoncause.org) contains a master list of 70 verified voting machine problems in a number of states. Common Cause also reports that only five states (Minnesota, New Hampshire, Ohio, Vermont, and Wisconsin) had geared up to handle voting machine errors.

One case that deserves special scrutiny is the 2000 presidential election in Florida, which brought national attention to voting problems and is still controversial even today. The final recount awarded the election to George Bush by only 537 votes over Al Gore. A number of the irregularities involved software and computers.

Florida developed a "scrub list," or a list of voters to be removed or disfranchised because they were felons or for some other reason. Later analysis found this list to be biased against minorities because it removed about 1% of white voters and 3% of minority voters.

Worse, of the 96,000 disfranchised voters called felons, many turned out not to be felons at all and were incorrectly removed. Some were innocent citizens who had names similar to or identical to felons. About 3,000 were felons whose voting rights had been restored in other states and hence were eligible to vote in Florida.

This was a software-controlled activity and clearly deficient or incorrect in its results. Given that many of the disfranchised voters were Democrats, this arbitrary removal of registered voters probably changed the results of the national presidential race.

The Palm Beach County "butterfly" ballot had a physical problem that apparently switched more than 3,000 votes to Buchanan from either Bush or Gore. The Democrats were listed second in the left column, but punching the hole next to that listing was counted as a vote for Buchanan by the software tabulation program. This was more of a physical design error than a software error.

In Duval County, the presidential choices were spread over two pages, and the printed instructions on the ballots told voters to "vote on both pages." The results were thousands of overballots in which voters accidentally voted for both candidates instead of only their preferred candidate. Because of ambiguity of the ballot, some voters wrote the name of their candidate on the ballot, but if they voted twice (as instructed), their votes did not count. This was a human error due to poor design and editing of the ballots themselves.

Several thousand absentee ballots from serving U.S. military personnel and overseas travelers were thrown out because there were no visible postmarks. Because voters have no control over where and if postmarks are placed, this was an arbitrary rejection without good sense. Absentee ballots received by an election commission during a valid time window up to the day of the election should have been counted whether or not postmarks were visible. Stamping the arrival time and date should have been sufficient.

The television news services assumed that Florida polls closed at 7 PM. However, the western Florida panhandle was not in the Eastern time zone and closed at 8 PM EST. The major networks announced Gore as the winner of Florida at 7:48 PM. Later interviews in the Panhandle concluded that this error, which was probably a careless human error, caused about 15,000 voters to go home and not vote.

The Florida voting mess reached both the Florida Supreme Court and the U.S. Supreme Court. The final results, after a number of recounts, awarded the state's electoral college votes, and thereby the national election, to Bush.

This Florida mess was a cautionary tale that elections "by the people" might be evolving into future elections "by computer software that uses secret and unverified algorithms that cannot be validated by election officials and votes that cannot be recounted if they are wrong."

The bottom line is that computer voting is prone to errors, is fairly easy to hack, and can modify election results in unknown ways. The lack of paper or independent backups to validate voting accuracy makes these systems intrinsically unreliable.

The current "hot topic" in the area of voting is that of a requirement for voters to have some form of identification when they arrive at the voting precinct, such as a driver's license. But a voter ID is only one topic out of a chain of topics that need to be studied. Truly accurate voting needs to span the entire sequence of the voting process, which includes the following:

- Voter registration

- Logistics of absentee ballots

- Validation of state and municipal voting lists

- Voter identification when casting a ballot

- Removal of disfranchised voters

- Accuracy of electronic voting machines

- Backup and recount logistics in case of error

- Accuracy of precinct tabulations

- Accuracy of statewide tabulation of results

- Accuracy of national results

If each of these steps has a 1% probability of error, the full sequence of all steps might be off by 10%, which is more than enough to change election results. Currently, no one, including state officials and election boards, truly knows if our votes are being accurately counted and tabulated.

Cyberwarfare Against Civilian Targets

Readers may wonder why cyberwarfare should be a concern to civilians. The reason is that civilian targets are important to national economies and to defense preparation. They may also have less sophisticated defenses than military targets. In the United States, our telephone systems, our electric power generation and transmission systems, and our air and rail transportation systems are important components of military preparedness. They are also spotty in defenses against cyberattacks. Our financial systems are also a critical part of the national economy and are also spotty in defenses against cyberattacks. Recent web security reports indicate that U.S. banks and financial systems are prime targets for hacking by other national governments such as China, North Korea, and Iran.

Consider the impact of a successful cyberattack in winter on New England's electric power and communication systems that could shut these systems down for a two-week period. Without power, many stores would be closed and it would not be possible to purchase fuel and possibly food. Air and rail travel would be disrupted due to passengers not being able to make reservations, and there could also be possible airport and train station closures.

Within about a week, pipes would begin to freeze and burst in homes and office buildings. Without fuel, some automobiles and trucks would be abandoned wherever they stopped, which would interfere with road traffic. Snow plowing might stop. Food shortages would soon follow, possibly accompanied by thefts and riots. Within about two weeks, emergency generators would begin to fail at hospitals (unless they used natural gas). Thousands of patients might have to be relocated.

No doubt martial law would have to be declared, and emergency supplies would need to be brought in by military helicopters. Very likely, there would be deaths among the homeless and elderly who could not make it to emergency shelters. Billions of dollars of financial losses would accrue to businesses and individuals. These financial losses might lower tax and government incomes and possibly trigger some municipal bankruptcies.

The bottom line is that a long-term disruption of the U.S. infrastructure due to either cyberattacks or electromagnetic pulses (EMPs) could have wide-ranging consequences that could damage the economy for an extended period.

International cyberwarfare is already occurring. The Stuxnet worm attacks on manufacturing equipment were probably created by a national cyberattack unit. The newer Gauss virus attacks on banks and financial records were also probably created by a national government.

The Stuxnet worm attacked industrial control computers that are manufactured by Siemens. As it happens, these computers are used in Iran for a number of nuclear development programs. Based on the sophistication of Stuxnet, it was probably not done by amateurs. No country has claimed ownership. The *New York Times* reported the United States as the probable author, and other reports claimed it was Israel.

While about 60% of the Stuxnet attacks were in Iran, some were reported in Germany and other parts of Europe. These were asserted to be collateral damages from the Iranian attacks that somehow managed to reach other countries that were not targeted.

In August 2010, the U.S. government issued a public statement that it believed the Chinese government was gearing up for possible cyberattacks. Apparently, the People's Liberation Army of China was using civilian experts as well as military cyberwarfare specialists.

The Department of Homeland Security reported an increase in cyberattacks against U.S. industrial sites from nine in 2009 up to 198 in 2011. The targets included power plants, refineries, nuclear generators, and chemical plants.

In August 2012, the Saudi Aramco oil company was attacked by a worm or virus that affected most of its internal computers and workstations, although apparently not its refinery operations. As a precaution while eliminating the attacking malware, Saudi Aramco withdrew completely from internet access for several days. The specific virus or worm was not reported yet as this section was being written.

As it happens, Congressman Jim Langevin is an expert on cybersecurity and a member of the Congressional Cyber Security Caucus. He was highly critical of the failure of the Senate to pass the Cyber Security Act (S.3414), introduced by Senators Lieberman and Collins. As is becoming the congressional norm, the Republicans and Democrats could not agree even on a topic as urgent as cybersecurity.

Data Theft from Corporations

Verizon did a study of corporate data theft in 2011 and found about 855 incidents with thefts of perhaps 174 million corporate records. An interesting part of the study was that about 57% of the stolen data was taken by hacktivists who stole the data for political purposes rather than for resale to cybercriminals. Political groups such as Anonymous and Lulzsec also attack and deface corporate and government websites. The following are examples of corporate data theft:

- In 2009, three people were arrested for stealing about 130 million credit and debit card numbers for companies such as 7-Eleven and Hannaford Brothers. A card payment company, Heartland Payment Systems, was the target of the attack, which used a sophisticated SQL injection attack.

- In 2011, Norway's energy, gas, and defense companies were hit by ten apparently coordinated cyberattacks that swept disk drives for personal information and industrial secrets. An infected email was the host.

- Early in 2012, about 10 million customer accounts for Visa and MasterCard were compromised and probably stolen. Apparently, a third-party contractor, Global Payments, was the actual company targeted for the theft.

- In May 2012, the professional network LinkedIn reported data thefts of millions of passwords. Indeed, about 6.5 million LinkedIn passwords actually were displayed on a Russian website.

These samples demonstrate that corporate data theft will probably impact close to 25% of U.S. citizens within the next five years.

Data Theft from Unsecured Networks

I live in a fairly small town with a population of about 17,000. Within a mile of the office where I write are at least a dozen free wireless networks at local coffeeshops and restaurants.

In my neighborhood, all of the neighbors have private networks, which is common in today's world. Most home networks are secured, but some home networks are not. Recently, a friend with an unsecured network noticed a slowdown on his network and discovered that a teenage neighbor had signed onto the network and was downloading films and music.

Piggybacking on unsecured networks is fairly common and probably the least troubling kind of theft. However, it is not a victimless crime. The hijacked network fees will probably go up, based on the bandwidth and amount of material downloaded, so the true network owner will lose money.

Piggybacking is easy to do. If a network is unsecured and shows up on a computer list of available networks, it is only necessary to click "connect" and it can be used.

There are also commercial *sniffers* that will report the brands of local wireless routers within range. Once the brand is identified, the hacker can then download data from the manufacturer's website that gives the original password for the brand and model of router. With this information in hand, the hacker can then use the wireless network more or less at will.

Free public wireless hotspots are in daily use by hundreds of students from a nearby university, as well as by local citizens who happen to use computers, iPads, Kindles, and other wireless devices in the vicinity. Free wireless networks are a great convenience but are also fraught with danger of losing passwords, credit card numbers, and other forms of personal information.

How does this happen? One method is that skilled hackers can tap into the network and extract information from any or all users by using the router ID, as already described. A second method is that a hacker can construct a phony wireless hotspot with the same name as the ones used by coffeeshops or local restaurants.

When using public networks, be sure to specify "public network" when your computer asks about what kind of network it is. It is also best to do only casual browsing and avoid things like online purchases with credit cards or online banking. Of course, the most common use of a computer today is probably email or messaging, so there is a high probability of compromising the email addresses of both senders and recipients.

Denial of Service Attacks

Computers and servers are fast and can handle thousands of transactions per minute, but they all have a finite capacity that can be exceeded. This is why we sometimes have waits when we attempt to reach a website or perform a task.

The idea behind denial of service attacks is to saturate a computer or a server by sending millions of messages that require some form of processing and thereby exceed its capacities so that it no longer functions for its true and legitimate purposes.

In general, denial of service attacks are illegal in most countries, and they also violate the operating rules of essentially every internet host. Government-sponsored attacks are another matter.

Denial of service attacks require the coordination of a number of computers because a single computer or server is not fast enough to saturate a normal website or server farm. Therefore, botnets are a common adjunct to denial of service attacks. However, some groups or collections of cybercriminals can create denial of service attacks by means of voluntary cooperation. Some hacker groups have more than 100 members and if they cooperate, they can do significant harm.

There are many different forms of denial of service attacks. In fact, there are too many to discuss in this book. They range from relatively minor annoyances to severe attacks that can actually damage servers and computers.

In today's world of instant communication, it sometimes happens that a website has some new and exciting topic that causes millions of individuals to try and access it at about the same time. The impact on the site being accessed is the same as a denial of service attack, but it is not an attack but rather a spontaneous burst of users all trying to get to the same site at the same time.

This same situation can occur in reverse. An offensive internet posting may receive millions of indignant complaints at about the same time. As this is written, an actual offensive event, the publication of a video that mocked Mohammad and the Islam religion on YouTube, is absorbing millions of emails and computer cycles.

Electromagnetic Pulses (EMPs)

When an atomic bomb explodes at high altitudes above about 50 miles, an EMP is released that can shut down or damage unshielded electrical devices, including computers, cell phones, televisions, power transmission, automobile electronics, and many more.

The EMP was predicted by Enrico Fermi when atomic bombs were first being developed in 1941, so military electronics are now shielded in most cases. However, civilians are both unprepared and unprotected.

The first recorded civilian damages due to EMPs occurred in July 1962 when the United States detonated a 1.44-megaton atomic bomb about 250 miles above the Pacific. This test was called *Starfish Prime*.

Even though the Hawaiian Islands were about 900 miles away from the detonation (and this was a fairly small nuclear explosion), there were still civilian damages in the form of hundreds of streetlights shutting down, burglar alarms malfunctioning, and microwave transmissions being damaged.

EMPs are not the kind of threat that can be carried out by amateur hackers or even terrorist groups. They require a fairly powerful nuclear device that is launched by rocket to high altitudes. In other words, EMP threats are likely from national governments such as North Korea, Iran, and others who might be likely to attack the United States using sophisticated rockets and nuclear devices.

EMPs over areas with high population densities and major electronic usage could be devastating to a nation's economy, because many of the damaged devices might not be able to be repaired and would need replacement.

Imagine the impact on major urban areas such as New York or Los Angeles if they concurrently lost electric power, radios, telephones, televisions, and transportation systems, including automobiles, for a period that might last several months.

Other forms of explosions besides nuclear can produce an EMP but over shorter ranges. It is possible that "natural" EMP bursts can occur from major solar flares. In fact, on March 9, 1986, the sun ejected solar gas that hit the earth's atmosphere above Canada. About six million people lost electric power for around nine hours. To date, these natural EMP bursts have been less dangerous than nuclear EMP bursts.

Although long-range damages from EMPs require sophisticated rocket launches to altitudes of more than fifty miles, short-range EMP damages for a specific city or an area of perhaps ten miles in diameter might occur from a nuclear explosion at the upper limits of jet aircraft flight, such as 60,000 feet.

The bottom line is that an EMP is a serious threat that requires a national response by national military and civilian governments. Individuals, corporations, and local governments can do very little to protect themselves against EMP damages.

While EMP harm is discussed primarily as a threat against electronic devices rather than humans, a major EMP strike would kill a number of civilians. Those at risk would be hospital patients on life support, patients with embedded electronic medical devices such as pacemakers, and those who need relatively sophisticated medical treatments such as chemotherapy or radiation for tumors.

Deaf and hard of hearing citizens would also be affected because the EMP would no doubt destroy cochlear implants and hearing aids.

Email Address Harvesting

In today's world, email addresses are valuable commodities that are bought and sold on a daily basis. In many cases, these lists are available from reputable companies and often target either specific industries or specific kinds of jobs such as executives or technical officers. How are these valuable addresses obtained?

In 2003, laws were passed in Australia and the United States that prohibit some kinds of email harvesting, but there are still a number of legal ways available.

There are several ways of obtaining email addresses, and they vary in their ethics and legality. One way is to use a *harvesting bot* or *spider* that searches public sources of email addresses such as Usenet lists and internet forums. These email addresses are then collected and added to lists, sometimes collated by industry or type. This form of harvesting from public data is legal.

More unsavory forms of email harvesting include attacks on specific directories and websites. A clever way of gathering email addresses is to use lists of common names and then methodically try each name with a specific site. Suppose you have an email address that is something like CJones@privatemail.com. Once the server "privatemail" is identified, a harvesting tool would then send dummy emails to the site to see which email addresses are accepted.

For example, the harvesting tool might go through the alphabet and send email messages to "AJones," "BJones," "CJones," "DJones," and so on. If any are accepted, the valid addresses are added to a list and go to market. The same tool might have a list of hundreds of common names and try things like "Arthur," "Betty," "Charles," "David," "Emily," and so on to see how many work. This method now seems to be illegal.

A very common and legal method for harvesting email addresses is used daily by thousands of companies. The companies simply offer a free trial, a free service, or something else that might be useful and require that anyone who requests it must provide an email address.

Long before the arrival of computers, some companies such as magazines and consumer products would sell customer address lists. Address harvesting is merely a continuation of an idea that is hundreds of years old.

There are a number of countermeasures to reduce the incidence of email address harvesting.

Address munging, or changing the format of email addresses when they are displayed, is one measure. Thus, instead of Capers@privatemail.com the address would be "Capers at privatemail dot com." This can be overcome but adds costs to email harvesting.

CAPTCHA is a method that displays numbers or letters in a little box, often in graphic form. In order to complete a transaction, the user must key in the characters that are displayed. Harvesting bots are not able to translate this text or enter the keys. Thus, the CAPTCHA method minimizes the risk of email harvesting.

Spider traps are part of a website designed to attract email harvesters or spiders. The website includes a "honeypot" that is assumed by the spider to contain useful emails but in reality is a trap that blocks access.

There are other methods for harvesting emails, and this is a continuing problem for the modern world.

Identity Thefts

The crime of identity theft has become one of the most common crimes in the modern world. Data from the web indicate that about 4.8% of U.S. households will experience an identity theft. The absolute numbers are in the range of perhaps 15 million people per year in the United States alone. Surprisingly, identify theft also includes about three million dead people. Many identity theft victims are children. A disturbing fact about identity theft is that it often involves relatives or "friends" of the victims.

Identity theft is not a victimless crime because the stolen identities are often used to steal money from banks, make unauthorized use of credit cards, create phony credit cards, rent automobiles, travel by air, and do other kinds of serious harm to the victims. In a few cases, houses have been fraudulently sold by people who were not the true owners!

Worse, the credit ratings and sometimes the reputations of the victims are damaged by identity thieves, and recovery is not easy to achieve. Innocent people have even been arrested when an identity thief performs a crime such as armed robbery and the identity theft victim is wrongly blamed.

There are numerous ways of stealing identities. Some of these are listed below:

- Stealing mail such as bills from mailboxes
- Rummaging through dumpsters outside of office buildings
- Stealing wallets and purses
- Phishing or sending bogus emails that request personal information
- ATM skimming or using an illegal device that captures card data
- Hacking into the databases of retail stores and other businesses
- Stealing identity information from relatives or friends

Because identity theft is so common in today's world, there are, fortunately, resources available to aid in canceling credit cards and restoring credit ratings. These will vary from city to city and state to state, but in today's world, the police in major cities have trained investigators. Credit card companies can also provide support, as can banks. There are also commercial identity theft recovery companies, although not all of these are competent and effective.

Many government agencies can provide brochures and advice for those affected by identity theft. These include the Internal Revenue Service, the Social Security Administration, the Federal Trade Commission, and the FBI. Various military services have internal aid for members of the uniformed services.

A number of nonprofit organizations can assist in identity theft recovery either via the web or by phone. Examples include the Identity Theft Resource Center and CreditReport.

The credit-reporting companies of Equifax, Transunion, and Experian also have identity theft support services.

Identity theft is a continuing and growing problem and will probably stay that way for the indefinite future. Only the replacement of alphanumeric information with unique physical attributes such as retina prints or fingerprints is likely to bring about significant reductions in identity thefts. Encryption of personal data might also help, assuming that the encryption methods are secure.

Normally, identity thefts are of concern for individuals. However, the September 15, 2012, edition of the *Providence Journal* had an article about the identity theft of an entire LLC corporation, and a security company at that. The LLC had been registered in Florida. Someone sent in a corporate amendment form and a fee of $25 to the state. This amendment form, which was not checked or validated by state officials, provided a new owner for the corporation and a new business mailing address. The theft entitled the new "owner" to borrow money in the company's name because the State of Florida confirmed ownership by the hijacker!

To date, this may be a unique kind of identity theft without any other examples. Most state governments do not validate amendments to corporate documents when they are submitted. But this same kind of corporate identity theft could potentially take place in probably every state in the union.

Java Vulnerability Attacks

The Java programming language by Oracle is the most widely used programming language on the planet, because it is used in millions of hardware devices. Java is also used in major web browsers such as Chrome, Firefox, Internet Explorer, Opera, and Safari.

Unfortunately, Java has had a series of well-known and frequently exploited security vulnerabilities. Earlier in 2012, about 600,000 Macintosh computers were infected by the Flashback Trojan malware that entered via a Java flaw.

Web discussions of Java security flaws state that the very serious zero-day attacks seem to have originated from China. There are far too many articles and websites dealing with Java vulnerabilities to discuss. Readers are urged to do web searches using phrases such as "Java security flaws" to find out more information.

Note

A *zero-day* attack is one that occurs on the same day that a security flaw is first recognized and published. Zero-day attacks take place before software security personnel can build countermeasures.

Keyboard Trackers

A Google search on the phrase "keyboard trackers" will turn up more than half a dozen free or open-source tools that can be used to track keystrokes with or without the knowledge of the person using the keyboard. What would these be used for? Most of the web ads for these trackers use phrases such as "discreetly monitor all keyboard activity . . ." Who on earth needs to discreetly monitor someone else using a keyboard?

Some legitimate examples might be high-security government agencies or companies with proprietary information to ensure that nothing is sent out without permission. But the keystroke trackers themselves can dilute security.

If the keystroke tracker is secretly installed via a worm, Trojan, or virus, then it can be used to find passwords, bank accounts, social security numbers, or any other confidential information that happens to be typed with the infected keyboard.

There are quite a few different kinds of keyboard trackers—too many for this book to describe. Some are based on software and some are based on hardware. Various websites provide instructions for detecting and removing hardware and software keyboard trackers.

Considering the number of free and open-source keyboard trackers available, one might assume many legitimate uses. However, it is hard to envision a legitimate justification for tracking keystrokes other than as part of a criminal investigation or to protect highly secret information.

Without any statistical studies that report keystroke-tracking usage, the most common uses would seem to be something unethical and possibly illegal, such as seeking passwords, social security numbers, and other kinds of personal information from unsuspecting computer users.

Note

The term "malware" is a concatenation based on "malicious" in the sense of something harmful and the last half of "software." When combined, the term *malware* is a generic term that includes viruses, rootkits, worms, Trojans, spam, and other harmful software topics.

Macro Attacks in Word and Excel Documents

Microsoft Word and Microsoft Excel are two of the most widely used software applications in the world. Both of these have some advanced features that utilize macro instruction.

In the context of Word and Excel, macro instructions are small sequences of code created in Visual Basic for Applications (VBA) that can be used to simplify repetitive tasks or deal with ranges of information. There is a built-in macro recorder for storing these, and the macros go along with Word and Excel documents when they are emailed as attached files.

Unfortunately, hackers can use the Excel and Word macro recording feature to create harmful macros that can spread from computer to computer. Once inside a computer, the dangerous macro can replicate itself and also attack the computer files.

Pharming

The term "pharming" is based on "farming" and uses the same "ph" combination as "phishing." Pharming is a form of phishing that is aimed more at e-commerce and banking sites than at other kinds of users. One major issue with pharming is that it can affect routers, and once a router has invalid information, then anyone joining that network can be infected.

Because phishing and pharming are close to identical, there is some objection to the term "pharming." Of the two, phishing seems the oldest and was noted as far back as 1995.

Phishing

"Phishing" is an obvious play on the word "fishing" and has more or less the same meaning—cast an attractive bait and wait to see what bites. Phishing in several forms predates the computer era. Both surface mail and telephones have been used to solicit information from unsuspecting victims long before computers existed. Telegrams were also used in the days when they were a fast form of communication.

The most common forms of phishing today involve emails or instant messaging. In one very common form, the sender pretends to be an official of a foreign government (often Nigeria) who needs to transmit funds to an American bank. The email requests that the recipient send bank information so the money can be transferred, and the recipient will then be able to keep a portion as a reward. A more recent variation involves pretending to be a serving officer in Afghanistan or Iraq who has come across funds that can't easily be taken out of the country.

More recent and more subtle forms of phishing involve stolen email lists. Using a name known to the recipient from a stolen email list, the sender writes an email with a message like "I'm writing this with tears in my eyes . . ." The message then goes on to describe some kind of tragedy such as a mugging or stolen wallet that left the person with no money and no identification. There is a request to send funds to pay for a hotel, rental car, or something else.

Phishing attacks aimed at specific individuals using personal information such as their social networks or lists of friends from stolen email lists is called *spear phishing*.

An even more sophisticated form of phishing is called *whale phishing* because it is aimed at senior executives. This kind of phishing is preceded by very focused email thefts from a law firm or accounting firm known to be used by the intended victim. Sometimes a credit card firm or retail store is used. In any case, the idea is to present a convincing story that will cause the victim to provide personal information such as a bank account, social security number, or something else.

Perhaps the most sophisticated form of phishing appears to come from a bank used by the victim. However, if the victim clicks on the email to respond, he or she is diverted to a phony website that is designed to look like the real bank's website. Even worse, some phishing emails with web links direct the user to their own actual bank but secretly insert a pop-up screen that appears to be a request from the bank for personal information.

Phishing may have become an adjunct to cyberwarfare. There are reports on the web, not verified by me, that the Chinese government and military have been involved with attempts to target the Gmail accounts of U.S. government officials and military personnel. China denies this, of course. A study from 2006 showed a high frequency of phishing attacks originating from Russia from a group called the Russian Business Network, based on U.S. website accounts.

Early phishing was fairly common on the AOL system circa 1995. This was initially successful, but soon AOL and other internet hosts began to add text to their screens and messages that said "XXX will never ask for your password and billing information . . ." This phrase is now a part of almost every commercial internet service provider (ISP) and messaging service.

The nominal senders of phishing emails include the Internal Revenue Service, the FBI, many banks, the government of Nigeria, and many social networks. These, of course, are all hoaxes. In fact, users of social networks seem to be at greater risk from phishing than nonusers.

It is not uncommon to get a phishing email along the lines of "Contact this office of the IRS about an unclaimed tax refund." Anyone who clicks on the site is at risk of losing at least their email address and possibly worse if they supply data such as social security numbers or bank account information.

There is an organization called the Anti-Phishing Working Group that includes both industry and law enforcement organizations that work to prevent phishing. What we lack, though, is an effective way of tracking backward to the phishing site or exposing the site to law enforcement personnel without putting the nominal recipients at risk.

A useful feature of email services would be a "Suspected Phishing" command that would alert enforcement personnel and possibly track the message back to its origin point and do so without putting the target at additional risk.

Rootkits

The Unix operating system uses the word "root" to describe a privileged account that could make changes to the kernel. Linux uses the same concept. The word "kit" implies a collection of tools. When put together, a "rootkit" is a collection of stealth tools that can invade and change operating systems and software packages without detection by antivirus packages.

Rootkits are complex and difficult to eradicate. They attempt to acquire administrative rights to change operating systems and, if successful, they then burrow into the operating system and take control of its component parts.

Rootkits also have the ability to subvert tools such as antivirus software that attempt to find and root out viruses and other kinds of malware.

The Sony BMG copy protection scheme from 2005 is described elsewhere in this book; the company had secretly inserted a rootkit into music CDs. When the CDs were played on a computer, the rootkit installed a secret copy of software that limited access and prevented the CDs from being copied. But the rootkit also slowed performance and introduced security vulnerabilities into the infected computers.

Another rootkit had been used in 2004 in Greece to wiretap more than 100 mobile phones on the VodaPhone network in Greece. Alarmingly, most of the taps were on phones used by senior government officials. The taps were removed in 2005, but the identity of the perpetrators was not discovered.

This rootkit was novel in being apparently the first attempt to subvert an embedded device rather than a normal commercial operating system. The infected system was an Ericsson AXE telephone switching system.

Rootkits are serious threats because, if secretly installed, the operators of the rootkit can then open doors to many other kinds of malware.

Preventing rootkits from attacking, identifying them when they have attacked, and removing them from a computer are among the toughest kinds of computer and software protection in the modern world. Rootkit elimination is too vast a topic for this book, but it is a topic of increasing importance because rootkits can be used in cyberwarfare and can possibly subvert military computers as well as civilian computers.

Skimming

The presence of thousands of automated teller machines (ATMs) in public places has created a massive new kind of crime called *skimming*. Thieves are able to use either small hidden cameras or Bluetooth-enabled magnetic-strip readers to capture passwords, PIN numbers, and other information from debit and credit cards when they are used at ATMs.

There are also commercially available handheld card readers, including new models that plug into smartphones. Any of these could be used by unscrupulous retail clerks, waiters, or even gas station attendants to copy debit and credit card information.

According to an FBI report, magnetic credit card skimmers had been secretly installed in a number of gasoline pumps in Denver, Colorado. Given the number and distribution of such devices, this was probably the work of an organized group of cybercriminals and not the work of individual gas station employees.

Skimming and other kinds of unauthorized and illegal access to financial records are now a serious threat to global banking systems. This book only identifies such threats but is not large enough to discuss them in detail.

Readers are urged to use web searches to find out more. On the FBI website is the congressional testimony of Gordon Snow, the Assistant Director of the FBI Cyber Division. This testimony provides a very instructive summary of cybercrime. At the time of this testimony on September 11, 2011, the FBI was investigating more than 400 cyberattacks on financial institutions. These cases caused total financial losses of about $255 million.

The problem that both consumers and businesses face in the modern era is that financial data are comparatively easy to steal and are far safer targets for criminals than many other kinds of crime. Worse, computerized financial crimes attract a criminal element that is obviously fairly intelligent and also highly computer literate. Such criminals are hard to catch because they carry out their crimes inside their own homes or offices and not in public places.

It is unlikely that such crimes can be fully suppressed so long as identities use only alphanumeric information. Some forms of highly personal information such as facial recognition, retina patterns, fingerprints, or other unique attributes will probably be needed in the future. This will no doubt be opposed as a loss of civil liberties. However, citizens and companies need to balance the use of personal physical identity information against potential financial losses from cybercrimes.

If cybercrime continues to expand, which seems likely, at some point the world may need to create some form of unique biometric identification at birth and to assign unique identity information for each citizen. Perhaps retina prints or DNA tagging would be unique enough to prevent counterfeiting or the creation of duplicate identities.

Although "smart credit cards" with onboard chips that contain proprietary information are not yet used widely in the United States, they are starting to be used in Europe and abroad. It is fairly easy to extract information from these smart credit cards from a distance of five feet or more. This has led to the creation of stainless steel or metallic wallets that screen smart cards from remote detection.

It is an unfortunate fact of modern life that computer and software technologies are advancing so fast that unintended consequences of some new inventions are not discovered until criminals figure out how to use them to steal or make money.

Smart Card Hijacking

Smart cards were first patented in 1969 and their use is expanding rapidly, especially in Europe. Smart cards are plastic cards the size of older credit cards that have an embedded microchip with memory and sometimes a processor. Smart cards can contain personal information, financial information, passwords, and medical records.

Early smart cards required being inserted into a reading device. More recent smart cards can be scanned and read at a distance of a few inches. However, hackers can sometimes gain access to smart card data from a distance of a foot or more. Therefore, potential victims are at risk when standing in lines, when visiting crowded locations such as nightclubs, or when commuting on subways or buses that are full enough to require standing.

The technology used for smart cards is not restricted only to small plastic cards. Many countries now embed smart card microcircuits into passports. This brings up the problem that even government-owned passport readers may not be fully secure.

Hacking into passport readers and computers at major airports such as Heathrow or New York could be a very serious security threat. It is possible to envision a whole crew of terrorists entering a country if passport-reading devices are penetrated.

Note

An interesting white paper by a security analyst, Hagai Bar-El, entitled "Known Attacks Against Smart Cards," is at www.discretex.com.

As smart cards grow in popularity, various consumer defenses have entered the market. One of the most widely advertised is a wallet made of stainless steel threads, which blocks remote access to smart cards by shielding them.

A very common use for smart cards among the U.S. defense community is for accessing secure buildings and sometimes secure devices. An article by John Leyden on January 13, 2012, posted in *Security* states that the Chinese government has attempted to use the Sykipot Trojan to compromise and gain data from U.S. military smart cards.

Not only are smart cards and smart passports vulnerable to deliberate attacks, but they are also vulnerable to old-fashioned bugs or defects. In 2009, the *late millennium bug* affected the smart cards of about 30 million German citizens. A programming error caused the software in bank ATMs and credit card processors to stop working when the calendar changed from 2009 to 2010. German consumers could not use credit cards or withdraw funds from ATMs until the bug was repaired.

More than 70 million U.S. passports have been issued with smart card chips. More than 100 million credit cards in Europe are now smart cards. Because China uses smart cards for passports and credit, too, the global total of smart cards is probably passing one billion.

The bad news is that smart card usage seems to be expanding much faster than smart card defenses. This is a very serious future threat, with the greatest potential for harm aimed at affluent citizens with numerous credit cards who travel internationally.

Spam

It is unfortunate that the name of a commercial meat product has come to be used for an annoying kind of disinformation that can be rapidly distributed by email and instant messaging. In a computer context, the word "spam" refers to ads, emails, and pop-up screens that are sent to millions of computer users on a daily basis. (The term "spam" may have derived from a Monty Python sketch in which every dish in a restaurant contained the Spam meat product marketed by Hormel.)

Ordinary spam ads are legal in the United States under the CAN-SPAM Act of 2003 and are probably protected as a form of free speech under the Constitution. Spam that contains viruses or can cause harm to computers or consumers is not legal. The European Union, on the other hand, does have explicit laws against spam, although that is not the same as stopping it.

In every country, spam usually violates the terms of service of the ISP and can be blocked or deleted if detected. ISP owners can also attempt to collect damages from spam originators through lawsuits, although these are not easy cases to pursue. The damages are based on misappropriation of bandwidth and server resources, which have financial costs that can be quantified in court.

The fact that sending spam is now the largest user of internet resources has spawned two growing subindustries. The first is that of the spam creators who sell their services to clients who want to issue bulk ads. The second and smaller subindustry consists of the companies that design and market antispam tools for blocking spam from emails and instant message sources. The first industry of spam creation seems to be more profitable than the second industry of spam avoidance.

The actual technology of spam is complex and diverse and outside the scope of this book. There are more than a dozen variations for creating and sending spam messages.

The first known spam broadcast was perhaps an ad for DEC computers sent to 600 ARPANET users in 1978. In today's world, Microsoft's security unit reports that spam makes up about 97% of current email traffic. A remark by Steve Ballmer of Microsoft reported that Bill Gates, the Microsoft founder, is sent about four million emails per year, with the vast majority being spam.

Because spam apparently originated in the United States, it is interesting that it remains the number one country for spam origination. The European Union is number two and China is number three.

In today's world, email without effective spam blocking is almost unusable. (When I used older email servers that lacked effective spam blocking, about

200 spam messages arrived per day.) With modern email services, such as Gmail, that include spam blocking, only one or two spam messages seem to slip through.

Spam is no longer restricted to computers but is also present on tablets and smartphones. In fact, *robo calling*, or using software to make recorded calls to targeted lists of phone numbers, is a very annoying form of spam for landlines.

There is a technological race between spam originators and spam defenders. Hopefully, spam defenses will eventually become sophisticated enough to make spam disappear as a commercial undertaking. The spam-filtering approaches used on modern email services are fairly effective, but spam remains a major waste of human and computer resources.

SQL Injections

The SQL is a popular avenue for hackers. The idea is to create an SQL command that, if accepted, will perform some harmful act such as passing confidential data to the hacker. SQL injections are used against websites and databases.

SQL attacks are relatively easy to carry out but also easy to guard against by using normal, good coding practices that validate inputs including SQL statements. The SANS Institute provides a good paper by Stuart McDonald on avoiding SQL attacks. It can be found on the SANS Institute website, www.sans.org.

Trojans

The word "Trojan" harks back to the Trojan horse described in Homer's *Iliad*. The original Trojan horse was a giant statue of a horse given as a gift to the Trojans. Inside, a number of Greek soldiers were concealed. At night after the horse had been moved into the city of Troy, the hidden solders emerged and opened the city gates to the Greek army.

In today's computer era, the word "Trojan" means an attractive offering that conceals a hidden virus or some other nasty payload. A recent prominent Trojan virus called DNS Changer was front-page news in several papers, so it is worth considering.

In November 2011, the FBI identified a ring of cybercriminals that had released the DNS Changer virus. This virus infected about four million computers globally. Its purpose was to divert clicks on websites to other websites controlled by the cybercriminals. Apparently, the criminals charged fees for advertising and made about $14 million from pay-per-clicks until stopped.

In the United States, about half a million computers were infected. This virus had some unpleasant attributes besides browser hijacking. It also attacked antivirus software and kept it from being updated with virus definitions and tools that could stop the DNS Changer!

What happened after the arrests shows how significant some viruses can be. After the FBI seized the host computers that had issued the DNS Changer Trojan, it could not just shut them down because all of the infected computers would probably have stopped working. The FBI could only replace the rogue addresses with authentic addresses.

The FBI then got a court order that allowed it to keep the host computers running until July 9, 2012. The reason was to allow time for antivirus companies and the government to provide tools and methods for safely removing the DNS Changer without doing serious harm to half a million computers. If the host DNS Changer computers were merely stopped, then the infected computers would no longer be able to access the internet.

Tools were made available to check for infections in home and corporate computers, and then other tools were available to remove the Trojan. I used the DNS analysis tool on all computers used by my family, and fortunately none were infected. The URL of the inspection site was www.dns.ok.us. This site returned a green image for clean computers and a red image for infected computers. Users of infected computers were then routed to several repair tools.

A study of the DNS Changer Trojan on the web stated that about 12% of Fortune 500 companies and 4% of U.S. government computers were infected. No doubt an even higher percentage of private computers were infected.

The DNS Changer story is a cautionary tale that we should all take seriously. In the modern world, criminals have the technical ability to attack and seize even computers that have some protections such as firewalls and antivirus packages. The fact that a few clever cybercriminals could infect four million computers with a Trojan is not a good sign for the future when hostile governments might attempt something similar or worse.

Viruses

A natural virus is a small organism that has the ability to enter cells and divert RNA into making new copies of the invading virus. A computer virus is a piece of software that has the ability to invade computers and divert part of its functionality into making and distributing new copies of the virus and perhaps doing something harmful as well.

Viruses are harmful for the same reason that cancer is harmful: It metastasizes and infects and eventually shuts down host organisms. Computer viruses can do the same thing to operating systems and other kinds of software. The critical feature of a computer virus is that it can replicate itself and make other copies, which can then spread to other computers.

The concept of a computer virus showed up in science fiction before real computer viruses were developed. A story by David Gerrold in *Galaxy Magazine* in 1969 used the term "virus" in its modern sense. But there were no computer viruses in 1969. A few years later, a paper on self-replicating software packages was published in 1972 by Veith Risak, who built a working virus in assembly language that ran on a Siemens 4004 computer system.

The term "virus" as applied to a self-replicating piece of computer software was first used in a technical paper in 1984 by Fred Cohen of the University of Southern California. But apparently the term was coined by a colleague, Leonard Adelman. Neither seemed to know about the Gerrold science fiction story.

One of the first known computer viruses was created in the 1970s on ARPANET. It was called "the creeper," and it infected computers and displayed a message that said "I'm the creeper. Catch me if you can."

There are now thousands of individual viruses and many classes and types of viruses. This book is not the place to discuss viruses in detail. Readers need to take viral attacks seriously and be sure that their antivirus packagers are kept up to date.

There is a serious technological battle that is ongoing between virus creators and virus destroyers. Usually, the virus destroyers are able to win, but the more insidious kinds of viruses, such as polymorphic viruses and metamorphic viruses, are challenging to detect and eliminate.

It is technically possible to build viral-resistant computers, but doing so requires abandoning the von Neumann architecture. Viral-resistant software may also be possible, and here, too, there may be a need for fundamental changes in permissions and access rights.

Worms

Computer worms differ from computer viruses in one important way. Viruses spread by being attached to other kinds of software such as emails. Worms are freestanding packages that can travel and reproduce by themselves without requiring help from other kinds of software.

The actual term "worm" seemed to derive from a 1975 science fiction novel called *Shockwave Rider* by John Brunner. In that book, a self-replicating piece of software is unleashed on a global network, and it was called a worm by the main character.

The first worm to attract national attention was the famous Morris worm released in 1988 by Robert Morris. Although it did not have a payload and did not intentionally cause damage, apparently it infected and slowed about 10% of all computers attached to the internet. Morris was the first person tried and convicted under the Computer Fraud and Abuse Act of 1986.

Worms use the internet as their main mode of transit from one computer to another. Some worms were created merely to prove the concept and see how far they could travel. Even though no harm might have been intended, successful worms devour bandwidth and slow down networks. The Morris and MyDoom worms are examples of traveling worms without payloads.

Note

The 2004 MyDoom worm set the record as the fastest-spreading worm at the time. It attacked Microsoft Windows. To deceive recipients, it had a text phrase that read "Andy, I'm just doing my job, nothing personal, sorry."

More malicious kinds of worms include payloads that are designed to cause harm to computers, software, and networks. Some of these can introduce back doors into software that allow other kinds of malware to have access. Others can be used to create zombie computers that can take part in botnet denial of service attacks. Yet another payload encrypts computer files, with the idea that the file owners have to pay a fee to get their files back in usable form.

Not all worms were designed to do harm. A few were intended to be beneficial. One class of worm was designed by Microsoft to update the Windows operating systems in a benign and invisible way without user intervention. However, the results were not satisfactory because the changes were made without the owners' permission. Some of the changes required restarts of the computer at possibly awkward moments; this was more of an annoyance than a convenience.

Zero-Day Security Attacks

A zero-day security attack is an attack by malicious hackers that occurs on the very day that a new security flaw is identified and news about it is first released. As it happens, it is much easier and faster to develop an attack against a known security flaw than it is to develop an effective defense. Attacks can take place on the day the flaw is known, but it usually takes vendors from a week to a month to develop and release a fix or an effective countermeasure.

Some antivirus and antimalware packages include fairly sophisticated algorithms that attempt to seek out new threats that are not yet recorded in their databases of known threats. These techniques for stopping new kinds of attacks are not 100% effective, but they are better than nothing and may stop a significant number.

The Odds of Being Attacked

From reviewing a number of web reports on various kinds of cybercrime and data theft, it is interesting to speculate on the probability of being impacted by these events over the next three years. The results shown in Table 12.2 are speculative but are based on extrapolation from recent cyberattacks reported on the web.

The alarmingly high odds of personally experiencing cybercrime or cyberintrusions explain the rapid growth of three fairly new subindustries: insurance

Table 12.2 *Approximate Odds of Becoming a Cybervictim*

Form of Intrusion	Odds
Receive unwanted spam	100%
Receive an unwanted robo call	95%
Have your email address harvested	90%
Receive a phishing email	85%
Have a virus attempt to penetrate your computer	60%
Experience a browser hijacking	35%
Receive a spear phishing email	25%
Have credit/debit cards stolen	20%
Have your social security number stolen	18%
Experience personal identity theft	16%
Experience a zero-day security attack	15%
Have a smart card hijacked	14%
Experience a Java vulnerability attack	13%
Experience slowdowns from denial of service	12%
Have a Bluetooth device hijacked	12%
Have a credit card number used by thieves	10%
Experience an SQL injection	10%

Table 12.2   *(Continued)*

Form of Intrusion	Odds
Have a rootkit invade your equipment	10%
Lose data from an unsecured network	8%
Have viruses penetrate your computer	7%
Have your local voting machines hacked	6%
Have your municipal tax data stolen	5%
Have your credit or debit card skimmed	5%
Have your medical records stolen	3%
Have your federal tax data stolen	2%
Experience an EMP	1%
Average	26%

companies that protect against cybercrime; professional service companies and nonprofits that assist victims in recovery from cybercrime such as identity theft; and antivirus and antimalware companies that block or remove attacking viruses, Trojans, worms, and many other security threats.

Cyberattacks have also created a new professional occupation of Chief Security Officer (CSO) or sometimes Chief Information Security Officer (CISO). These positions began to appear in about 2000. Large companies have always had security departments, but these groups were mainly concerned with the physical security of buildings and with vetting new employees to ensure they did not have criminal records.

The new CSO position and computer security organizations handle computers, software, purchased software, and corporate databases. Most large companies today have full-time computer security staffs, and they also have a number of key personnel standing by as emergency responders in the event of a cyberattack or a denial of service attack. Constant vigilance is the key to good cybersecurity.

Defending computers and software against viruses, worms, and other threats is not a task for amateurs. Training and certification of computer and software security personnel is mandatory to be effective, and continuous education updates are also needed. We are dealing with threats that morph and evolve continuously. Some of these threats are created by the brightest minds within hostile governments. Computer and software defenses are not something to pass along to untrained generalists.

Computers and software have brought many benefits. But they have also brought new kinds of crime and new threats to individuals, corporations, governments, and military organizations.

Improving Defenses Against Cyberattacks

Countries are often involved in "arms races" with other countries. A very important arms race is taking place more or less out of sight. This is the race between cyberattackers and cyberdefenders and between the United States and possible future enemies such as Iran and North Korea.

Unlike conventional arms races, which are between national governments, the cyber arms race is between organized criminal groups and government cybercrime defense units at local through national levels.

To date, conventional defenses against cyberattacks have included firewalls to block intrusions, antivirus packages to prevent and remove intrusions, and additional tools to block spam and annoyances that are not dangerous.

Because many security vulnerabilities are due to poor programming practices, a number of research groups have started to publish lists of common coding problems. The list by the SANS Institute and MITRE is a useful example. The first list in 2009 had 25 common problems, but newer versions have added more.

Examples of some of the coding problems from the original SANS list that cause security flaws include the following:

- Buffer overflows

- Cross-site scripting

- SQL injections

- Operating system command injections

- Uploading hazardous file types

- Improper controls for file names

- Integer overflow or wraparound

- Downloading reusable code without validation

- Failure to authenticate critical features

- Encrypting data using algorithms that have been hacked

Readers are recommended to go to the SANS website and read the latest version.

A number of static analysis tools have started to include or beef up checks for security flaws in common languages such as Java, C, C##, SQL, and the like. Some older languages such as ADA, COBOL, and FORTRAN are also covered by static analysis. However, out of the current total of 2,500 known programming languages, only about 25 are covered by all of the static analysis tools put together.

A few samples of static analysis tools with security checks include CAST Software, CheckMarx, Code Armor, Code Sonar, Coverity, Findbugs, HP Fortify, IBM App Scan analyzer, Intel static analysis, Klocwork, Parasoft, VeraCode, and XTRAN.

There are many more static analysis tools. In fact, that market seems to be getting crowded, and the vendors need some new tricks to differentiate themselves. It would probably be a smart business move for the larger static analysis tools to expand by offering text readability tools, text static analysis, inspection support, mathematical test-case design, test and static analysis coverage tools, cyclomatic complexity tools, and a suite of other tools and methods proven to benefit quality and security.

In 2009, the National Institute of Standards and Technology (NIST) ran a large study on static analysis tools called SAMATE, which stands for Software Assurance Metrics and Tools Evaluation. The results can be seen on the web at http://samate.nist.gov/. More than 100 tools were evaluated of various kinds, including static analysis tools.

Static analysis tools with security features are a new and useful weapon for security defenders. These are rule-based applications that can easily be updated as new threats occur. A vanilla static analysis tool right out of the box might find 90% of known security flaws for common languages.

Of course, effectiveness against new zero-day problems can't be evaluated until after the fact. If your software is in a language such as BLISS, CHILL, CORAL, or MUMPS that is not supported by static analysis, then manual inspections would be needed.

A number of nonprofit organizations, federal agencies, and also state and local police departments now have information about cybercrime and resources to help companies and individuals recover from cyberattacks.

Incidentally, the approximate average cost to recover from a personal identity theft attack tops $10,000 in lost time, legal fees, and logistics for creating various notarized and certified documents needed to restore creditworthiness, remove possible criminal charges filed erroneously, and restore personal integrity with law enforcement groups.

A combination of federal agencies, including the Department of Justice and the FBI, publishes annual reports on cybercrime in the United States. As of the end of 2012, only 2011 data are available. The group is called the Internet Crime Complaint Center and the annual report is the Internet Crime Report.

In 2011, there were more than 400,000 cybercrime complaints, which was an increase of 3.4% compared to 2010. Personal identity theft complaints were coming at a rate of more than 26,000 per calendar month. The states with the highest incidence of identity thefts included California, Florida, Texas, New York, and Ohio. The average amount of money stolen before credit cards and accounts could be canceled was $4,187 per victim.

Raising Our Immunity to Cyberattacks

The similarities between the field of security and the field of medicine provide an interesting metaphor. The correlations are not identical, but thinking in medical terms is useful for software and computer security specialists.

Firewalls are a bit like rubber globes or surgical masks: They stop the passage of harmful vectors such as viruses or worms. However, as with real gloves and real masks, the firewalls might leak. Currently, they seem about 90% to 95% effective against known threats, but they are of lower effectiveness against zero-day threats.

Static analysis tools are a bit like vaccines, and they also raise immunity levels. Static analysis tools can identify weaknesses in source code and eliminate them before applications are released.

Antivirus programs are a bit like antibiotics and vaccines. They can stop many harmful vectors and can kill most of the vectors that manage to penetrate to a computer or software package.

However, tests of antivirus packages published on the web and in computer journals indicate an effectiveness of between 83% and about 99% for stopping known vectors before they gain access and perhaps 85% for removing known vectors that have established themselves in a computer. Here, too, effectiveness is reduced for zero-day vectors that are so new that antivirus vendors have not examined them and hence depend on heuristics or hypothetical models of unknown threats.

Organizations that help in recovering from cyberattacks are a bit like nursing homes or rehabilitation homes. They help injured companies and individuals to recover stolen identities and to restore damaged credit ratings.

In today's world, all major banks and many large consumer chains have full-time security offices for dealing with stolen credit cards and identify theft.

So do larger police stations, state police, the FBI, Homeland Security, the Secret Service, and other government groups. These can be helpful, but by the time their help is needed, something has already been stolen or damaged.

The bottom line is that while defensive methods such as firewalls and antivirus programs are pretty good, they are not perfect.

What are the prospects of raising the immunity levels of computers and software packages so that they cannot easily be attacked by viruses or worms? Although a lot of attention is being paid to security by thousands of organizations, coordination and cooperation could probably be better than it is.

From a distance, it seems useful to design a computer and software security engine for corporate and government use and also for sophisticated private computer users with valuable data such as patents and new intellectual property. This engine is probably too expensive to work as a retail product, but access to its features would be available by license.

The computer security engine would be linked to every national security agency in friendly countries and also to corporate and private security groups. The engine would perform real-time monitoring on a global basis for new zero-day threats as soon as they occur in any time zone. This monitoring would use intelligent agents.

The artificial intelligence (AI) kernel in the computer security engine would also notify major vendors of firewalls and antivirus packages in order to alert them to the threat, and it would, of course, send messages to all government security offices as well. The AI would also analyze known facts about the threat and classify its method of action against any similar threats detected on a global basis.

As responses and defensive measures become available, the AI feature would analyze their effectiveness. The AI would calculate how many networks and computers had been infected.

As effective countermeasures become available, users of infected computers and networks would be notified using an uninfected channel such as radio, telephone, or a special shortwave band (which would be needed since internet connections may be compromised).

Subscribers to this computer security engine would be able to register their own computers by make, model, operating system, and other factors. When subscribers turn on their computers, they would receive a start-up screen that informed them of current threats that might affect their equipment, including zero-day threats from other time zones. If proven solutions are available, they could be downloaded at once. These might even have been downloaded as soon as the subscriber's computer powered up.

In case a subscriber's computer or software had already been hacked and was under hostile control, the AI engine would direct the most effective removal method to the computer.

Subscribers could also notify the security engine of the credit cards, banks, and stores at which they are likely to shop. The subscribers would receive real-time notices of any attacks or data thefts from the major banks and service providers used by those companies.

It would be possible but perhaps unsafe to also perform real-time global monitoring of client names and identities in case a new identity is being created illegally. Ideally, the computer security engine would have connections to major banks and businesses so that any suspicious account activity could be reported to the subscriber in real time.

The computer security engine would also have a constantly updated list of the security contacts at every bank or store, as well as the contact numbers for the cybercrime units of local and state police, the FBI, and other government agencies.

Some of these features are available today, but they are fragmented. Antivirus vendors try to keep tabs on zero-day threats. Banks and major stores keep tabs on suspicious credit card transactions. However, nobody keeps real-time tabs on human identities, and the faster duplicate identities can be recognized, the easier it is to stop damages.

Because many security breaches are due to the theft of notebook computers and tablets or smartphones, the physical security of portable devices also needs to be considered. It would not be difficult to include GPS tracking in every notebook and tablet, because they are already in cell phones. With GPS tracking, stolen computers could easily be found.

It would not be difficult to include an electromagnet inside the cases of computer hard drives. If the computer is reported as stolen, a signal would trigger the electromagnet and degauss the hard drive to erase all data. This would need a separate battery because thieves would no doubt remove the main battery.

Other kinds of physical security for portable computers and tablets include switching from passwords to biometric data such as retina prints.

Data encryption should be offered as a standard feature on all computers. Every saved file such as a spreadsheet or a Quicken bank statement could be saved in an encrypted form instead of plain text. Encryption should also be at least an optional feature on thumb drives because they are easily stolen and easily read by any computer.

It would also be possible to have the built-in cameras on portable computers take a picture of whoever opens the case each time it is opened. These pictures could be sent to the computer security engine cloud site. This feature might be set up to activate when a computer is reported as stolen.

This would probably be a secret feature used only on computers assigned to FBI agents and others who might have very high security information on their computers. This feature could be activated by notifying the computer security engine that a notebook computer has been stolen. The activation message might go over the internet or perhaps through a special radio connection if the computer is used for really high-value classified information.

These pictures could be transmitted to security sites that have facial recognition software that would perhaps identify criminals or known terrorists, assuming they tried to use a stolen high-security notebook. In any case, a digital photo from a computer with its GPS location and a timestamp would probably provide sufficient evidence to prove theft.

Another current weakness is the von Neumann architecture itself. Current computers—both personal and mainframe—are intrinsically vulnerable since data and instructions are treated the same. At least one highly secure alternate hardware architecture was patented by a group of retired IBM engineers. This was the ALTOPS patent number 5,742,823 issued by the Patent Office on April 21, 1998, to Nathen Edwards.

The long-range prognosis for raising computer and software immunity levels is theoretically very good, but a lot of work is needed.

The following sections cover a sample of possible approaches for immunizing software, computers, passwords, and data from external threats by black hat hackers who attempt to steal information or cause harm.

Access Controls

The topic of access controls is large and complex. It deals with how people, software, messages from other systems, and data enter a computer or a software application. Once allowed in, what features can they use and what features are prohibited?

Users of ordinary personal computers and notebooks know that a class of user called an *administrator* is the only person authorized to make changes to many features of the computer and its operating systems. This is intended to strengthen security. However, access control is somewhat porous in the modern world of multitier applications and global internet connections.

It would be helpful for a combination of computer hardware manufacturers, software companies, security companies, and database companies to create protocols for access at all levels of software, hardware, and data.

As of 2013, access controls are part of a defense strategy, but they need formal analysis of how to improve the safety of access by software packages and external internet messaging.

Authentication Controls

Authentication and access are two parts of a complex problem. Access deals with what features might be used. Authentication deals with how a person, a computer, or a piece of software knows that a message or a delivery is truly what it claims to be.

A few months ago, an email arrived that identified itself as an email from a personal friend, so it was opened. The message itself immediately looked like a fraud, which it was. The message started by saying "I'm writing this email with tears in my eyes." It then went on to say that there had been a robbery while traveling abroad in London; wallet and credit cards stolen; no help from the embassy; hotel was evicting them; please send money; and so forth.

This is a common scam that occurs when email addresses are stolen and used by a third party to phish for money or other valuable commodities. But it can also occur more subtly via a "man-in-the-middle" attack. In this case, my friend and I might really be sending emails to each other, but someone is intercepting them and changing them in perhaps subtle ways.

In the future, it might be possible to use biometric information such as retina prints or voiceprints. Trusted friends and colleagues would have catalogs of authenticated biometric information. A biometric "tag" might be affixed to email messages sent between trusted friends and colleagues to ensure that the message is really from the true sender and not from an identity thief or a man in the middle. Of course, biometric tags might themselves be stolen, so they would need encryption and probably timestamps.

Authentication is a complex issue, and it needs coordinated research. Some combination of certificates, biometric tags, and a real-time database of stolen email addresses and identities is needed.

In the future, biometric information might also be embedded in smart cards so that they can be used by only the person with the same unique voiceprint or retina print as the person to whom the cards were issued.

EMP Protection

Unfortunately, transistors and integrated circuits are susceptible to serious damages from an EMP. They may be physically damaged and will never operate again. To date, civilians are largely unaware of the EMP threat, and computer manufacturers ignore it.

A relatively simple and inexpensive device called a *Faraday box* is capable of shielding small electronic devices such as cell phones, tablets, and notebook computers from EMPs. A Faraday box is a metal container made of steel, copper, aluminum, or some other metal that conducts electricity. It can be made from either sheet metal or screens, but it must be a continuous and fully closed container.

Objects placed inside a Faraday box should be safe from an EMP if the box is closed. A caveat is that whatever is inside can't touch the metal of the box, so it would need to be wrapped in plastic or some other nonconductive material. Another caveat is that whatever is inside the Faraday box should be turned off. No electric cords should be exposed or plugged in.

As it happens, computers with magnesium or aluminum cases may have some EMP protection from the cases themselves. Checking EMP resistance in a lab would be needed to quantify their effectiveness.

Assuming metal cases do provide EMP resistance, it would be inexpensive to include some kind of metal mesh, probably aluminum, embedded in the Kevlar or plastic commonly used for notebook computer cases. Tablets and smartphones with open screens and no clamshell lids would need separate metal cases or at least metal screen covers.

Unfortunately for consumers and homeowners, a major EMP attack would probably leave them without working automobiles if they have embedded computers and without television sets, wireless networks, computers, and "smart" electric appliances. Old-fashioned appliances without computer chips might survive. Old automobiles without modern electronics might also survive.

Modern equipment may be destroyed beyond repair. A normal affluent family could easily lose almost $500,000 in ruined equipment that will never work again.

Encryption

Encryption, or concealing plain text by means of symbolic substitutions or transposition, is much older than the computer era. An excellent book called *The Code Breakers* by David Kahn gives the entire history of codes, codebreaking, cyphers, and other forms of hiding information. This book starts with the Sumerians and continues through the date of publication in 1996.

For some reason, China did not excel in codes and encryption, but India did. An early sutra on the life of Buddha from perhaps 300 AD mentions that Buddha as a child amazed one of his childhood teachers by explaining 64 kinds of writing, including several that appear to be cryptographic.

An even older Hindu Indian document from perhaps 200 BC is the famous *Kama Sutra*. One section lists 64 skills that women should learn, and skill number 45 in this list is writing in code.

Encryption with a computer in today's world is not difficult, and many encryption software applications are available, including some that are free and from open-source providers. A fairly early form of encryption using software was an application called Pretty Good Privacy by Phil Zimmerman in 1991.

Encryption should be more widely used and offered as a standard feature. Computer experts can easily include encryption packages in their personal computers, but novice computer users probably don't even know about encryption packages.

Some of the things that should be kept in encrypted form for safety include:

- Email address books

- Password catalogs, if stored in a computer

- Quicken and financial files

- Credit card information, if stored in a computer

- Text documents with secret or proprietary information

- Spreadsheets with secret or proprietary information

- Database records with secret or proprietary information

In addition, office products such as word processing, spreadsheets, and databases should include an encryption selection when using the "save as" command. It would not be hard to save an office file as an encrypted document.

Estimating Cyberattack Recovery Costs

Cyberattacks are now so common that it is possible to predict the approximate costs for stopping attacks, assessing and repairing damages, notifying clients of any missing data, and beefing up security so that the same kinds of attacks can't happen again.

My Software Risk Master (SRM) tool began to estimate cyberattack recovery costs starting in 2012, and no doubt other commercial parametric estimating tools will soon include similar estimates. SRM also predicts the probable number of latent security flaws in deployed applications.

Latent security-flaw predictions are based on a combination of factors that include programming languages, development methodologies, use of pre-test inspections and static analysis, team experience, and the nature of the application itself. CMMI levels are a minor factor as well. (The initials CMMI stand for "capability maturity model integrated," which is a software practice evaluation method developed by the SEI and now widely used.)

Insurance Against Cybertheft and Cyberattack Damages

In the 1990s, insurance companies began to receive new kinds of claims from corporate clients about damages from hacking and data theft. The existing policies from that decade did not have any explicit language for these losses, so some companies paid the claims and some did not.

By about 2000, the insurance industry recognized that these claims were increasing rapidly, and it began to offer new forms of cybertheft and cyberattack policies. These did not sell as well as expected because the costs of the damages varied widely, and there were not effective algorithms for underwriters to use.

According to a study presented at a Cyber Liabilities insurance conference in April 2012, about 72% of U.S. companies do not currently have any cyber liability insurance in place. The authors of the study were Peter Foster, David Molitano, and Brad Gow from various insurance companies.

Of the 28% that do have insurance, about half have small policies that probably won't cover more than a fraction of the total costs for a major attack.

The Cyber Security Agency of the European Union, the European Network and Security Agency, published a similar report that cited fairly low cyberattack insurances throughout the European Union.

To date, cyberattack insurance costs vary widely and range from between about $15,000 per million of coverage to $35,000 per million of coverage. This is perhaps why many companies self-insure for cyberattacks.

Personal cyberattack insurance does not seem to be currently available, or at least it does not show up in web searches for "personal cyberattack insurance."

Secure Programming Languages

Because many security flaws are due to poor programming practices, it is theoretically possible to develop hack-resistant languages that would help in preventing cybercrime. Several languages such as E and Joule are cited as being secure.

The SEI started a programming language security initiative as part of the CERT program. There are security standards and guidelines available for a number of languages.

However, more and better data about language vulnerabilities are needed. The computer security engine discussed earlier in this chapter would have a feature that analyzed all reported attacks, including zero-day attacks, and generated statistics of attack frequencies by programming language. In addition, the computer security engine would try to identify the specific vulnerabilities that the attack utilized and generate potential countermeasures.

Some companies such as CAST Software also perform studies of both bugs and security flaws associated with various programming languages such as COBOL, Java, SQL, C and C dialects, and the like.

The software industry has at least 2,500 known programming languages, and new languages are being announced at rates in excess of two per month. It is not easy to stay current on the security features of programming languages without using intelligent agents to gather data in real time followed by statistical and forensic analyses of successful and unsuccessful attempts at hacking the languages.

It is also clear that hack-resistant languages need to stay away from computer hardware and computer BIOS files. A synergistic combination of hack-resistant hardware combined with hack-resistant software and hack-resistant languages, plus a suite of strong firewalls and antivirus packages, all seem to be congruent in eliminating one of the major threats of the 21st century.

The Increasing Frequency and Costs of Cyberattacks in the United States

In the autumn of 2012, Hewlett-Packard was wrapping up a security survey of 56 companies. Data from this survey were published in an article by Matthew Schwartz in *Information Week* on October 8, 2012, and republished in the Information Week Security online newsletter on November 28, 2012.

According to these data, the average damage from a cyberattack against the 56 survey respondents was about $8.9 million. This was an increase of 6% from 2010 and 38% from 2009.

Alarmingly, these 56 companies were receiving about 102 attacks per week. This is up from 72 weekly attacks in 2010 and 50 weekly attacks in 2009.

Cleanup and recovery after an attack takes an average of about 24 business days and costs an average of $591,000. This is an increase of 42% from the 2011 cost of $416,000 for recovery. The increase is probably due to the increase in attack sophistication.

In August 2012, General Keith Alexander, the Director of the National Security Agency and head of the U.S. Cyber command, gave a public speech at the American Enterprise Institute in Washington, D.C. He commented that cyberattacks and recovery are costing the United States about $250 billion per year. The figure seems to be escalating.

The bottom line about cybercrime and cyberwarfare in today's world is alarming:

- Cybercrime is one of the most widespread forms of crime in human history.

- Cybercrime is the most global kind of crime in human history.

- Cybercrime is the longest-range form of crime in human history.

- Cybercrime has harmed more companies than all other white-collar crimes.

- Cybercrime may soon have more human victims than any other crime.

- Cybercrime is increasing in frequency faster than any other kind of crime.

- Cyberwarfare aims at civilian targets as well as military targets.

- Cyberwarfare military groups are expanding faster than any other military group.

Hopefully, a concentrated and coordinated defense against various kinds of cyberattacks and cybercrime can reverse these recent alarming trends.

It is theoretically possible to raise the immunity of computers and software to penetration by harmful viruses, Trojans, and worms. Both hardware and software resistance needs to improve by perhaps an order of magnitude compared to today's standards.

It is technically possible to increase the effectiveness of current defensive measures such as firewalls and antivirus software. Firewalls should block at least 99% of known threats and 90% of zero-day threats. Antivirus packages should knock out and remove at least 99% of viruses and worms that penetrate the firewalls.

To reverse the number and seriousness of cyberattacks, it will be necessary for corporations, universities, and government agencies such as Homeland Security and the FBI to collaborate on both fundamental research and also on deployment of proven technologies.

As computers and software continue their exponential growth rates and permeate every aspect of business and government, better cybersecurity is a major concern for every government, company, and citizen.

Summary

Computer and software have brought enormous benefits to individuals, companies, and government agencies. They have also created hundreds of major new companies and wealth beyond what anyone anticipated prior to the 1970s.

But computer and software failures of medical devices and embedded devices have taken lives and caused injuries. Identity theft has wiped out savings and bank accounts for thousands of victims.

The good uses of computer and software are in sharp contrast to the harmful uses by cybercriminals and cybersoldiers.

Every individual, company, and government agency needs to stay at full alert and constantly upgrade their security measures in the modern world.

Annotated Bibliography and References

Most of the research for this book was done using web sources rather than books. Therefore, it seems best to include an annotated bibliography rather than a standard set of references. There were also a number of published books used, but websites outnumbered actual books by more than 100 to one. For example, I visited websites for about 200 corporations and about 25 nonprofit organizations and professional associations.

Many of the books cited in this bibliography are "classics" that have influenced several decades of software engineering process. For example, Fred Brooks's *The Mythical Man-Month* and Jerry Weinberg's *Psychology of Computer Programming* remain popular today, even though they were first published in the 1970s. In fact, Brooks's book even had a 25-year special republication with new materials.

Book Sources

Like every major industry, the computer and software industries have attracted authors who are interested in historical and social topics as well as in the actual technologies of the industry. There are many good books that have historical slants. Some are pure history, while others mix historical topics with technical issues. Software engineering also has much to learn from older professions such as medicine and law.

Boehm, Barry. *Software Engineering Economics*. Prentice Hall, Englewood Cliffs, NJ, 1981.

This book is among the best-selling software books of all time, deservedly so. Dr. Barry Boehm was a pioneer in tackling the complex issues associated with the architecture, design, and cost predictions for major software projects. This was a pioneering book that showed many of the factors that influence the results of software projects, and it helped to turn software estimation into an effective discipline with accurate parametric tools.

Brooks, Fred. *The Mythical Man-Month*. Addison-Wesley, Reading, MA, 1974, rev. 1995.

Dr. Fred Brooks was in charge of the IBM S/360 operating system. This was the largest IBM software package of the decade and the first to encounter the problems of cost and schedule overruns, which have become endemic. This book is a classic of software engineering and is filled with sharp insights and pithy observations, such as adding people to a late project makes it later.

Campbell-Kelly, Martin. *A History of the Software Industry: From Airline Reservations to Sonic the Hedgehog*. MIT Press, Cambridge, MA, 2004.

This interesting book came out in 2004 and does a good job of discussing the companies and trends from the 1950s forward to 2004. The book also shows sales volumes and revenues for selected kinds of software spanning several decades. It was a useful reference source for this book to ensure that the focuses of each decade were congruent between the two.

DeMarco, Tom, and Lister, Tim. *Peopleware*. Dorset House Press, 1999.

Tom DeMarco is a famous consultant, public speaker, and author on a variety of important software topics. Tim Lister is a colleague of Tom's and a partner in the Atlantic Systems Guild. The book selected for this annotated bibliography was chosen because it, along with Jerry Weinberg's *Psychology of Computer Programming*, deals with the fundamental issue that software applications are designed and developed by human beings.

Weinberg's book dealt with programmers as individuals. DeMarco and Lister's book expands the view to groups and also to the physical environments provided for the groups. For example, *Peopleware* was the first book to address the issues of office space and privacy. This book, along with many others by Tom DeMarco, has been influential across several decades.

Gack, Gary. *Managing the Black Hole—The Executive's Guide to Project Risk*. The Business Expert Publisher, Thomson, GA, 2010.

The current book states several times in several chapters that large software projects are subject to unexpected delays, cost overruns, and outright failure. This interesting book by Gary Gack is congruent with the statements in this book, and it provides additional evidence. It also provides some suggested solutions for avoiding these endemic problems, including use of formal inspections and better quality control.

Gilb, Tom, and Graham, Dorothy. *Software Inspections*. Addison-Wesley, Reading, MA, 1993.

Formal inspections of requirements, design, code, and other deliverables were invented at the IBM Kingston development labs in the 1970s. Two well-known pioneers of inspections were Michael Fagan and Ronald Radice.

Tom Gilb and Dorothy Graham, as well as several other authors, studied the inspection methodology and wrote books about it. This book was chosen for this bibliography for international reasons, because it is popular in Europe. (Tom lives in Norway.)

For more than four decades, formal inspections have been the top-ranked method of removing defects in terms of defect removal efficiency. Inspections average about 85% of removal efficiency, or more than twice the average efficiency of most forms of testing. This book is a solid introduction to a topic that every software engineer, and in fact every reader of this book, should know about.

Glass, R. L. *Software Runaways: Lessons Learned from Massive Software Project Failures*. Prentice Hall, Englewood Cliffs, NJ, 1998.

As major software projects began to top 10,000 function points and one million source code statements in the 1970s, they began to experience severe problems with cost and schedule overruns and outright cancellation due to negative returns on investment. These problems remain chronic and endemic problems of software engineering even today. This useful book by Bob Glass examines a number of famous failures and explains what went wrong.

For example, the failure of the Denver airport luggage-handling system is a microcosm of large-system mistakes, including optimistic estimates; poor architecture and design; arbitrary schedules; poor change control; poor quality control; and very poor and even deceitful status tracking.

Humphrey, Watts. *Managing the Software Process*. Addison-Wesley, Reading, MA, 1989.

This is yet another software engineering classic by a famous software engineering expert. Watts Humphrey had a long and successful career at IBM. He was IBM's Director of Software and introduced many important process improvements.

Watts then moved to the Software Engineering Institute (SEI), where he pioneered the famous capability maturity model. Watts also developed the team software process (TSP), which is one of the strong quality methods used successfully on large and complex applications.

Overall, Watts had a multidecade impact, starting with IBM in the 1960s and continuing through the SEI era of the 1980s and up through the 2000 era. Watts is the author of many more books, but this one was selected because it has been influential for more than two decades.

Isaacson, Walter. *Steve Jobs*. Simon and Schuster, New York, 2011.

In addition to being an excellent biography of one of the great pioneers of computing and software, this book is a fascinating account of the emergence of the computer and software industry to global importance. It is an excellent source of historical information about the rise of the Silicon Valley region from the 1970s through the 2000s.

All of the big names of software (Bill Gates, Larry Ellison, and Ken Groves) are included, as are some of their actual conversations with Steve Jobs. This book is strongly recommended for anyone who is interested in software and computing history and also interested in the fascinating history of Silicon Valley. In fact, the entire software industry is reflected in the book.

The main focus is on Steve Jobs and his companies, including Apple, NeXT, and Pixar. However, Steve interacted with dozens of other companies and hundreds of software luminaries. He also had interesting relationships with politicians; movie stars; musicians such as Joan Baez and Bob Dylan; and the California Buddhist community, including the Zen monk Kobun Chino, who performed Steve's wedding service. Jobs comes across as brilliant but decidedly eccentric and also not a very kind person to some of his employees and friends.

This book was a useful source of background information for the chapters on the 1970s through 2000s.

Jones, Capers. *Assessment and Control of Software Risks*. Prentice Hall, Englewood Cliffs, NJ, 1994.

This older book is included in part because it was an attempt at a cross-disciplinary experiment between medicine and software. The format of the book was an exact replica of the medical book *Control of Communicable Diseases in Man*, published by the U.S. Public Health Service.

As it happens, medical practice has many lessons for us in software engineering, including diagnostic techniques, immunization against problems, and also control of communicable problems. The format of the medical book was a good model for a book on software risks, and the sections on epidemiology, identification, diagnosis, and treatment are relevant to both fields. Of course, software projects do not have truly communicable diseases such as smallpox so that they require isolation. However, many of the problems that occur with software projects are clearly "contagious" because they occur with hundreds of other projects.

Medical practice provides many other valuable lessons for software such as licenses and board certification and malpractice monitoring. Readers are referred to the later entry in this bibliography for Paul Starr's book on the social transformation of American medicine.

Jones, Capers. *Estimating Software Costs*, 2nd edition. McGraw-Hill, New York, 2007.

This older book discusses the methods and techniques used by parametric software estimation tools, an industry that began in the 1970s. A total of five parametric estimation companies are discussed in the current book, since this is a significant subindustry of software project management.

The book provides examples and some algorithms for predicting the quality, cost, schedule, effort, and staffing for software development and software maintenance projects. It also shows how estimates need to be adjusted for various methods, programming languages, and team experience levels.

The book is included here because it has a summary treatment of the history of the software estimating subindustry. Software estimates have been made easier by the development of function point metrics. These simplify estimates for requirements, design, and other noncoding tasks. Collectively, the effort for producing paper documents is sometimes much more than for code itself. Some military software projects have spent more than twice as much on paper as on code.

Jones, Capers. *Applied Software Measurement*, 3rd edition. McGraw-Hill, New York, 2008.

This book includes some historical data on productivity and quality levels between the 1960s and the 2000s. The book also includes information on how quality and productivity rates differ among the various types of software, such as embedded applications, systems software, commercial software, internal information systems, web applications, domestic and offshore outsource groups, and many others.

Jones, Capers. *Software Engineering Best Practices*. McGraw-Hill, New York, 2010.

This book includes data and descriptions of a number of development methods and practices, and it also discusses where past experiences may lead to in terms of future software engineering. In one chapter, it makes a big leap and considers what software might be like in 2049.

Software engineering is much more than just coding, so the book covers requirements, architecture, design, coding, inspections, static analysis, change control, integration, configuration control, maintenance, enhancements, planning, estimating, status tracking, and many other software engineering topics and software project management topics.

Jones, Capers, and Bonsignour, Olivier. *The Economics of Software Quality*. Addison-Wesley, Reading, MA, 2011.

As the current book points out, software quality has been a chronic weakness of the software industry since it started to grow in the 1950s. This book discusses the economics of quality and shows the effectiveness of defect prevention, pre-test static analysis, pre-test inspections, and 25 kinds of test methods. Poor quality remains an endemic problem in 2013.

Kuhn, Thomas. *The Structure of Scientific Revolutions.* University of Chicago Press, Chicago, IL, 1996.

There is no question that computers and software are both scientific revolutions and also social revolutions in the way they have impacted human commerce, communications, and also medicine and warfare. Kuhn's book is a classic, but it is not about software at all. It is a fascinating analysis of many older scientific revolutions and their impact on human consciousness.

An interesting phenomenon about many new scientific revolutions is that the technologies were originally resisted. Only when evidence became overwhelming is there a fairly abrupt adoption. Some of the scientific topics resisted at first include vaccinations, Copernican theory, continental drift, and even quantum theory.

The same kind of resistance to new ideas also shows up in mechanical inventions. For example, Samuel Colt's revolver and John Ericsson's invention of screw propellers for ships were not only rejected, but both inventors also went bankrupt. Ericsson even spent time in debtors' prison.

In the case of Colt, the unexpected acquisition of 100 revolvers by the Texas Rangers began to turn things around. In the case of Ericsson, he later became famous when he built the *Monitor* for the Union navy during the Civil War.

It is a matter of both technical and social importance that the rejections of both inventions were not based on due diligence or even full consideration of their merits. The psychologist Leon Festinger proved that humans have a kind of "cognitive dissonance" that leads to strong rejection of new ideas when first encountered if the new ideas are in opposition to existing ideas. Kuhn's book on scientific revolutions deals with the same concepts in a historical setting.

Love, Tom. *Object Lessons.* SIGS Books, New York, 1993.

Tom Love is one of the codevelopers of the Objective-C programming language (together with Brad Cox). As readers of the current book know, Objective-C was selected by Steve Jobs as the primary language for both Apple and NeXT software projects.

Tom Love's book is a good introduction and history of the object-oriented paradigm, which is now a major asset of software engineering. The book also includes a fascinating discussion of an early example of the damages that can be caused by late and unwise requirements changes.

In 1628, the new Swedish ship-of-the-line *Vasa* was launched and then capsized and sank after traveling less than a mile. Apparently, as construction was nearing completion, King Gustavus Adolphus ordered an extra gun deck on top of the existing gun deck against the advice of his naval architect and the builder.

The new gun deck plus the heavy bronze cannon it carried caused the ship to become top-heavy. As soon as the breeze freshened, the *Vasa* keeled over and sank, with the loss of many lives. Although a ship is not software, the *Vasa* provides a strong lesson that ill-considered and late requirements changes can cause unanticipated consequences.

The ship was recovered and is now located at a permanent museum in Stockholm, Sweden. This museum has nothing to do with software, but it does provide interesting historical facts about late requirements changes.

I have visited the museum while working in Stockholm. The *Vasa* is a beautiful ship and well crafted, except for being top-heavy. It was intended to be the state of the art at a time when Sweden was a major military power in northern Europe.

McConnell, Steve. *Code Complete: A Practical Guide for Software Construction*, 2nd edition. Microsoft Press, Redmond, WA, 2004.

This book first came out in 1993 and was soon very popular among the software engineering community. This is a technical book aimed at practicing software engineers who actually code applications. It has remained popular (hence a second edition) and continues to provide practical information even in the current decade. It remains one of the top-selling books in the software engineering sector.

Pressman, Roger. *Software Engineering—A Practitioner's Approach*, 6th edition. McGraw-Hill, New York, 2005.

This book is an enduring classic by a top professor of software engineering. Roger Pressman is a good writer, and this excellent book covers software engineering from beginning to end, including requirements, architecture, design, coding, testing, and even the managerial tasks of planning and estimating. This book stays current, as can be seen by its number of editions.

This is a large book filled with interesting information. It is not the only book on software engineering, but it was chosen for this bibliography because of its continuing relevance and its good writing.

Royce, Walker E. *Software Project Management—A Unified Approach*. Addison-Wesley, Reading, MA, 1998.

This book dates from 1998 but is still modern enough to be useful. It has the virtue of looking at and considering a number of older software project management methods before presenting the method recommended by the author.

Walker Royce is an IBM vice president and the chief economist of IBM Rational. He has many years of experience behind him, so the book is based on empirical evidence. The reference is included in the current book because failures in software project management lead to more lawsuits and canceled software projects than technical failures by the software engineering community.

Walker was also a pioneer at Rational in the development of the rational unified process (RUP), although many colleagues at Rational also made major contributions.

Starr, Paul. *The Social Transformation of American Medicine*. Basic Books, New York, 1984.

This is not a software book but rather a history of the emergence of U.S. medical practice from a minor craft to a major profession. The book won the Pulitzer Prize for nonfiction in 1984. There are excellent lessons for the software community in how the American Medical Association (AMA) was able to improve medical education, initiate licensing and board certification, and weed out quackery.

Only 150 years ago, medical practices and medical education were worse than software today. Many medical schools were for-profit institutions and did not demand college degrees or even high school completion. Over half of U.S. physicians never went to college. Medical degrees were two-year programs and did not include internships or residency programs. Worse, students never even entered hospitals because the hospitals had their own private medical staffs. There was no malpractice monitoring. Harmful products such as arsenic and opium could be freely prescribed. There was no Food and Drug Administration at that time. Paul Starr's book should be read by every person interested in software process improvement or in improving software engineering college programs.

Weinberg, Gerald M. *The Psychology of Computer Programming*. Van Nostrand Reinhold, New York, 1971.

Weinberg's classic book came out in 1971 as software was rapidly expanding and on its way to becoming a major industry with millions of practitioners. (Weinberg and I were colleagues at IBM during the same decades, as were Fred Brooks and Watts Humphrey.) Jerry's classic book was the first to examine the tasks associated with software development from a psychological standpoint.

Yourdon, Edward. *Decline and Fall of the American Programmer*. Prentice Hall, Englewood Cliffs, NJ, 1993.

Ed Yourdon is a well-known author, public speaker, and software management consultant. He also does expert witness work in software litigation. (Ed Yourdon and I have been expert witnesses in several cases, once on opposite sides and once on the same side.) Among Ed's books relevant to software engineering are *Death*

March, *Rise and Resurrection of the American Programmer*, *CIOs (per Web) at Work*, and quite a few more.

This book was selected because it was published when offshore outsourcing to India, China, Russia, and other countries with low labor costs were generating alarm among the U.S. software engineering community. The theme of this book is that U.S. software could be world class and highly competitive if we used effective methods, including effective quality control. The lessons in this book remain valid even today.

The title of Ed's book is, of course, a derivative of Gibbon's famous history book, *The Decline and Fall of the Roman Empire*.

Web Sources

Computers and software rank among the newest of industrial technologies. Yet their social and economic values have led to a very significant number of museums and historical websites. This is due partly to the wealth created by computers and software and partly to the donations and contributions of major companies such as IBM, Microsoft, Oracle, Apple, and others for preserving the early knowledge of the computing and software industries. Readers with an interest in computing history are urged to visit as many of the museums as possible. The websites of the museums also provided data for this book, including several timelines of computer evolution.

Boston Computer Museum

This museum opened in 1979 and operated as an independent museum until 1999, when it merged with the Museum of Science in Boston. The Boston Computer Museum also started an affiliate in California in 1996, which evolved into the current Computer History Museum in Mountain View, California. (I founded a software company in Cambridge, Massachusetts, in 1984. While living in Massachusetts, I made many visits to the Boston Computer Museum with colleagues, friends, and relatives.)

In the 1970s, Cambridge, Massachusetts, was a major competitor to the Silicon Valley region of California as a hotbed of computer and software research, thanks in part to MIT and other Massachusetts universities.

The museum received some materials from the Digital Equipment Corporation (DEC) Museum, which had been started in 1979 by Gordon Bell and Gwen Bell. In 1982, the museum became a nonprofit corporation and soon opened a facility on the Boston waterfront.

Between the materials on display at the Boston Science Museum and the Computer History Museum in Mountain View, California, the bulk of the Boston Computer Museum's exhibits are still available. However, the demise of the actual Boston museum and its reemergence in Silicon Valley shows how computing and software technologies shifted from east to west between the 1970s and 1990s.

Computer History Museum; www.computerhistory.org

This museum is now located in a large and impressive building in Mountain View, California, in the heart of Silicon Valley. The museum started as an offshoot of the Boston Computer Museum but soon outgrew its parent. Eventually, the Computer History Museum absorbed many of the displays from the Boston Computer Museum when it ceased to operate in 1999.

The computer museum has a rich collection of computing devices and also large collections of reference materials. The museum features a useful computer timeline from prehistory through the modern era. In addition to being a museum, there are also courses and interactive materials. Some information is broader than just computers, such as a history of Silicon Valley before it became a technical hotbed. (I lived in Silicon Valley in the 1960s and '70s and saw its transformation from fruit orchards to high-technology companies.)

The Computer History Museum also has a subsection dealing with the history of computer software, as discussed later in this bibliography.

Computer Science Lab; www.computersciencelab.com

This is a website that offers software training materials. However, it is cited in this book because it also has a beautiful monograph titled "An Illustrated History of Computers," with very good pictures ranging from stone counting boards and early abacus versions through modern computers. Many of the pictures are in color. The specific website for the illustrated history is www.computersciencelabe.com/ComputerHistory/History.htm.

These interesting photographs provide a quick sweep of human attempts to speed up calculations from the medieval era through modern times. The early mechanical calculators are of great historical interest.

Computerspielemuseum; www.computerspielemuseum.de

This interesting museum is located in Berlin, Germany. One of its unique aspects is a very wide-ranging set of displays dealing with computer games. Computer gaming has become a major subindustry of both hardware and software. In some areas such as computer graphics, the game industry is actually ahead of other software fields.

In fact, the massively interactive games where thousands of players use avatars to move about virtual worlds would have great value in other fields such as education, virtual conferences, military planning, and even business planning. With actual travel becoming more expensive and less convenient and enjoyable, it can be predicted that immersive hyperrealistic simulated environments will move out of the game world and into other forms of activity where groups or crowds need to communicate.

Congressional Cyber Security Caucus; www.cybercaucus.langevin.house.us

The Congressional Cyber Security Caucus is a rare example of bilateral cooperation between Democrats and Republicans. The caucus has also developed into one of the major sources of data on cybercrime and cyberwarfare. Readers interested in cybersecurity are strongly recommended to subscribe to the weekly online bulletin.

The bulletin of the caucus is one of the best sources of security data available from the web. Because congressional sources are more sophisticated than those available to most civilians, this is a top resource for security topics.

Dr. Dobb's; www.drdobbs.com

This journal originated in California in the 1970s with the curious name of *Dr. Dobb's Journal of Tiny BASIC Calisthenics and Orthodontia*. This attempt at a humorous name was soon abandoned. Over time, Dr. Dobb's evolved into a significant journal aimed specifically at coding programmers and software engineers. The journal also looks at programming tools and programming environments, including syntax checkers, debuggers, and other ancillary tools.

Dr. Dobb's also issues annual awards for innovative products, called Jolt awards. For readers interested in the technical aspects of software engineering and the effectiveness of various programming languages and toolsets, Dr. Dobb's is a valuable resource.

In recent years, Dr. Dobb's evolved from a published paper journal to a web journal with an associated repository of articles and monographs. (I had several of the older paper editions, which appeared to be printed on newspaper stock paper rather than on finished paper.)

History Timelines; www.history-timelines.org.uk

This website has numerous timelines dealing with diverse topics. However, the computer history timeline on this site is very extensive and also includes enabling inventions such as transistors, circuitboards, and disk drives. The noncomputing timelines cover wars, national histories, and biographical timelines of famous people such as George Washington.

These timelines are useful in showing the context of computers and software in terms of what was happening in the world during specific eras. Often, technical timelines are closely intertwined with social timelines. For example, World

War II clearly accelerated the need for faster calculations for ballistics, decryption, and other military purposes.

Hoover's Business Guides; www.hoovers.com

For readers interested in some of the specific companies cited in this book, the collection of corporate data contained in the Hoover's Guides is recommended. Hoover's materials cover not only individual companies but also more than 900 industry segments. The Hoover's data also include historical trends over time. The Hoover's Guides were used as background information in this book as a resource for showing the context of software use by industry and company over time.

IBM Corporate Archives; www.ibm.com/ibm/history

IBM is the only company cited in this book that has lasted more than 100 years. As a result, the IBM archives present a long and varied history of IBM inventions and business changes. The IBM archives were used in several chapters of this book, starting with the chapter on the 1930s when IBM as well as other companies were in the grip of the Great Depression. Indeed, if Thomas J. Watson, the founder of IBM, had not been ready to help the federal government handle Social Security processing when the law was passed in 1935, IBM might not have survived or grown into the major corporation that it is today.

It is difficult to imagine the computer industry without IBM, but the Depression from 1929 through 1935 was a close call for IBM. It is of social interest that IBM did not have layoffs during the Depression and had even improved employee benefits, as cited in the 1930s chapter of this book.

Other companies have useful corporate histories, but not many companies have been around as long as IBM or developed so many inventions and innovations that became part of the computer and software industries.

IBM Math Timeline; www.mindsofmath.com

In the 1960s, IBM produced a fascinating wall chart on the history of mathematics. In commemoration of the centennial of Ray Eames, the chart has been turned into an interactive application for iPads. Hopefully, the same application will be ported to other platforms. For those interested in the close ties among mathematics, computing devices, and later software packages such as Mathematica, this timeline provides a fascinating picture. The new interactive version is a good example of what touchscreens are good for.

IEEE Computer Society; www.computer.org

In one form or another, the IEEE Computer Society dates back to 1946. It took its current name and structure in 1971 when it was created as a nonprofit group from several older organizations. The IEEE Computer Society publishes a number of leading refereed journals, hosts a number of international conferences, and also has several subgroups that are interested in computing and software history. This is a very large and multifaceted group that has been part of the computer and software industry sectors since they began.

Information Technology Metrics and Productivity Institute (ITMPI); www. itmpi.org

This organization is a wholly owned subsidiary of Computer Aid, Inc. ITMPI has offered seminars, webinars, and technical papers for more than 10 years. Its website has grown to become a very rich repository of technical articles and monographs on software risks, software productivity, software quality, and many other relevant topics.

The ITMPI director and the CAI president have not built the organization just as a sales tool. They have sought out leading authors and software thinkers and, in total, more than 50 top software engineering researchers have contributed materials. Some papers deal with historical topics.

ITMPI also offers a variety of courses via the web, some of which are certified by the Project Management Institute (PMI). There is a strong focus in the ITMPI data and reports on project management issues, as well as on standard software engineering issues such as quality control.

ITMPI is not a pure programming resource, such as Dr. Dobb's, but rather a resource covering a wide bandwidth of software engineering and software project management issues using a variety of authors and experts. The combination of published documents and recorded webinars is a useful resource for readers interested in modern and successful methods and practices.

The ITMPI source materials increase rapidly in size and probably grow by more than a dozen papers and monographs per month. ITMPI is a commercial organization and not an academic organization, so both the authors and the clients tend to be interested in business applications rather than in more esoteric software engineering topics.

International Function Point Users Group (IFPUG); www.ifpug.org

Function point metrics were developed at IBM in White Plains by Alan Albrecht and colleagues in the 1970s. IBM placed function points in the public domain in 1978. Soon after, a nonprofit group of function point users was started in Canada and then moved to the United States.

IFPUG has grown to become the largest software metrics association in history, with affiliates in about 30 countries. All of the data in all of my books use function points for normalization. Function point metrics are the only current metrics that satisfy standard economic criteria for measuring software productivity. The older lines of code metric does not meet economic criteria and, in fact, I consider lines of code to be professional malpractice for software economic analysis.

Very few readers of this book need to know how to count function points. This is the same as saying very few readers need to know how to calculate octane ratings for fuel. With octane, drivers just need to know what kind of fuel to put in their cars.

For function point metrics, every reader should know that productivity rates above 15 function points per staff month are good; below 5 function points per staff month are bad. Readers should also know that defect potentials of more than 5 defects per function point are bad; defect potentials below 2.5 defects per function point are good. While on the topic of quality, defect removal efficiency (DRE) rates above 98% are good; below 85% is very bad, but unfortunately 85% is close to the U.S. average.

International Software Benchmark Standards Group (ISBSG); www. isbsg.org

This interesting nonprofit group was founded in 1997 and discussed in the chapter dealing with the 1990s. ISBSG collects benchmarks of software productivity and quality. Their data come from many companies in many industries and many countries. It is a good source for checking productivity and quality information. The ISBSG data also include data on many software development methods, such as Agile, waterfall, and RUP, and on many different programming languages. Although its data only go back to 1997, one of the forms of data offered by ISBSG is changes in results over time.

IT History Society; www.ithistory.org

This nonprofit organization has goals similar to this book (i.e., to collect data on software companies and software technical advances). It currently has a database with information on about 4,500 software-related companies. Hardware companies are included, too. There is also an honor roll of people viewed by IT History Society officers as having made a contribution.

This is an active and growing site, and readers of this book will find large volumes of similar information. Overall, this is a good resource for historians and those interested in software engineering topics. Membership includes both individuals and also corporate sponsors. The IT History Society will even fund occasional historical projects, which is unusual, but welcome, for a museum.

Melbourne Computer Museum; www.museumvictoria.com.au

The Melbourne Museum has more than computers, but the computer section is home to the famous CSIARC computer. This was the first computer built in Australia and one of the first in the world. The name is derived from Commonwealth Scientific and Industrial Research Organization Automatic Computer.

The National Museum of Computing; www.tnmoc.org

This British computer museum is located adjacent to the famous Bletchley Park, where the World War II codebreakers were housed, as discussed earlier in the 1940s chapter of this book. The National Museum of Computing has a rich collection of historical devices and also interactive materials and a library. A Colossus computer is one of the displays.

Rhode Island Computer Museum; www.ricomputermuseum.org

This is an unusual museum with a volunteer staff. It started in 1996 with collections of British automobiles and then switched to computers. It is a true nonprofit organization organized under 501c(3) Internal Revenue Service code. It was formally incorporated in 1999. Among the collection can be found Cray computers, DEC PDP computers, and a variety of smaller computers. The collection is international, with British as well as U.S. computers. Some computer game consoles are also included. It is socially interesting that private computer enthusiasts would come together to create such an interesting and useful museum.

Software Industry Special Interest Group; www.softwarehistory.org

This is a subset of materials in the Computer History Museum, described earlier in the bibliography. This is a special interest group (SIG) devoted to the history of software and software pioneers. The content of its website includes recorded oral histories of famous software gurus; descriptions of a number of software companies; and collections of essays and monographs on software topics of interest.

Perhaps the most intriguing are the oral recordings. Among those who provided recordings are Dan Bricklin, John Cullinane, Robert Frankston, Grace Hopper, and perhaps 50 more researchers, industry leaders, and inventors. There are also monographs, technical papers, and histories of interesting meetings among various pioneer organizations. This is a rich collection of software engineering memorabilia.

Wikipedia; www.wikipedia.com

As discussed in several places in this book, Wikipedia has become the largest encyclopedia in the world. It was often used as a reference for this book. Among the uses of Wikipedia for this book were lists of companies incorporated in any given calendar year. Also useful were numerous histories and short descriptions of thousands of companies. Not all of the Wikipedia descriptions are accurate, and some may be closer to marketing material than objective discussion. Even so, Wikipedia is a useful general reference for many topics, including the history of software and the history of the computer business.

Index

FREE
Online Edition

THE
TECHNICAL AND
SOCIAL HISTORY OF
SOFTWARE ENGINEERING

CAPERS JONES

Safari
Books Online

Your purchase of **The Technical and Social History of Software Eng**
to a free online edition for 45 days through the **Safari Books Online**
Nearly every Addison-Wesley Professional book is available online throu
Online, along with thousands of books and videos from publishers suc
Cram, IBM Press, O'Reilly Media, Prentice Hall, Que, Sams, and VMwar

Safari Books Online is a digital library providing searchable, on-dema
of technology, digital media, and professional development books and vi
publishers. With one monthly or yearly subscription price, you get unlim
tools and information on topics including mobile app and software devel
on using your favorite gadgets, networking, project management, graphi
more.

Activate your FREE Online Edition
informit.com/safarifree

STEP 1: Enter the coupon code: GIYAYYG.

STEP 2: New Safari users, complete the brief registration form.
Safari subscribers, just log in.

If you have difficulty registering on Safari or accessing the online edition,
please e-mail customer-service@safaribooksonline.com

Addison Wesley · Adobe Press · ALPHA · Cisco Press · FT Press · IBM Press · Microsoft Press · New Riders · O'REILLY

Peachpit Press · PRENTICE HALL · que · Redbooks · SAMS · SAS Publishing · vmware PRESS · WILEY · wrox